THE *I CHING* ON MAN AND SOCIETY

An Exploration into its Theoretical Implications in Social Sciences

Chang-Soo Chung

University Press of America
Lanham • New York • Oxford

Copyright © 2000 by
University Press of America,® Inc.
4720 Boston Way
Lanham, Maryland 20706

12 Hid's Copse Rd.
Cumnor Hill, Oxford OX2 9JJ

All rights reserved
Printed in the United States of America
British Library Cataloging in Publication Information Available

Library of Congress Cataloging-in-Publication Data

Chung, Chang-Soo
The I Ching on man and society : an exploration into its
theoretical implications in social sciences / Chang-Soo Chang.
p. cm.
Includes bibliographical references and index.
1. I ching 2. Social sciences—Philosophy. Title.
H61.15.C44 2000 300'.1—dc21   00-057750 CIP

ISBN 0-7618-1798-0 (cloth: alk. ppr.)
ISBN 0-7618-1799-9 (pbk: alk. ppr.)

∞™ The paper used in this publication meets the minimum
requirements of American National Standard for Information
Sciences—Permanence of Paper for Printed Library Materials,
ANSI Z39.48—1984

For my wife Young-Ja
and our three children
Yu-Sun, Eunice Hee-Sun, and Peter Hyun-Chin

Contents

List of Tables and Figures		xi
Preface		xiii
Acknowledgments		xix
Chapter 1	Introduction	1
Chapter 2	**Structural Components of the Hexagram**: **Representation of Situations**	17
	1) The Positional Attributes of the Lines in the Hierarchical Structure of the Hexagram	18
	2) The Situational Variation of the Lines in the Hierarchical Structure of the Hexagram: Yin and Yang Lines	34

Chapter 3	**Patterns of Relationships among the Structural Components of the Hexagram**	39
	1) Situational Patterns of the Dyadic Relationship	43
	2) Situational Patterns of the Triadic Relationship (Trigrams)	47
	3) The Ruler of the Hexagram	61
Chapter 4	**Hexagrams: Representations of Various Types of Social Situations**	63
	1) The Two Primary Hexagrams: the Two Most Ideally Integrated Situations	74
	The hexagram *Qian* (Pure Yang)	75
	The hexagram *Kun* (Pure Yin)	80
	Summary of Theoretical and Empirical Propositions	86
	2) Six Yang-Centered Hexagrams : Yang-Centered Modes of Integration	87
	The hexagram *Fu* (Return)	89
	The hexagram *Shi* (The Army)	97
	The hexagram *Qian* (Modesty)	101
	The hexagram *Yu* (Contentment)	106
	The hexagram *Bi* (Closeness)	110
	The hexagram *Bo* (Peeling)	114
	Summary of Theoretical and Empirical Propositions	120
	3) Six Yin-Centered Hexagrams: Yin-Centered Modes of Integration	122
	The hexagram *Gou* (Encounter)	123
	The hexagram *Tongren* (Fellowship)	128
	The hexagram *Lü* (Treading)	133
	The hexagram *Xiaoxu* (Lesser Domestication)	138
	The hexagram *Dayou* (Great Holding)	142
	The hexagram *Kuai* (Resolution)	145

Summary of Theoretical and Empirical Propositions	148
4) Other Types of Integrated Situations	150
The hexagram *Tai* (Peace)	151
The hexagram *Sui* (Following)	156
The hexagram *Lin* (Overseeing)	159
The hexagram *Heng* (Perseverance, Stability)	162
The hexagram *Jin* (Advance)	167
The hexagram *Zhongfu* (Inner Trust)	171
Summary of Theoretical and Empirical Propositions	175
5) Situations Characterized by Internal Conflicts or Disunity	176
The hexagram *Song* (Contention)	177
The hexagram *Pi* (Obstruction)	181
The hexagram *Mingyi* (Suppression of the Light)	186
The hexagram *Kui* (Contrariety)	190
The hexagram *Gen* (Restraint, Keeping Still)	195
The hexagram *Feng* (Abundance)	198
Summary of Theoretical and Empirical Propositions	201
6) Situations in Which Order Is Esestablished or Reestablished for a Newly Emerging State or a Society that Has Undergone Disintegration	203
The hexagram *Zhun* (Birth Throes)	204
The hexagram *Xie* (Release)	208
The hexagram *Ding* (The Cauldron)	210
The hexagram *Huan* (Dispersion)	215
The hexagram *Jie* (Control)	219
Summary of Theoretical and Empirical Propositions	222

7) Situations in Which Movements to Bring About Changes in Existing Order Take Place	223
The hexagram *Gu* (Ills to Be Cured)	224
The hexagram *Ge* (Radical Change)	228
The hexagram *Zhen* (Quake)	232
The hexagram *Sun* (Compliance)	236
Summary of Theoretical and Empirical Propositions	240
8) Character Situations: Situations that Are Composed of Types of People with Certain kinds of Behavioral or attitudinal Orientation	242
The hexagram *Bi* (Elegance)	243
The hexagram *Wuwang* (No Errancy)	246
The hexagram *Sheng* (Climbing)	249
The hexagram *Kun* (Impasse)	253
The hexagram *Dui* (Joy)	257
Summary of Theoretical and Empirical Propositions	260
9) Situations Signifying Patterns of Reciprocal Relationships Centering at Specific Tasks	261
The hexagram *Meng* (Juvenile Ignorance)	263
The hexagram *Shihe* (Bite Through)	265
The hexagram *Yi* (Nourishment)	269
The hexagram *Xian* (Reciprocity, Influence)	274
The hexagram *Yi* (Increase)	278
Summary of Theoretical and Empirical Propositions	283
10) Hexagrams Representing Social and Political Institutions	284
The hexagram *Jiaren* (The Family)	285
The hexagram *Sun* (Diminution)	289
The hexagram *Jian* (Gradual Advance)	292
The hexagram *Jing* (Well)	297

The hexagram *Guimei* (Marrying Maid)	299
Summary of Theoretical and Empirical Propositions	303

11) Hexagrams Representing Patterns of Power Relations — 304

The hexagram *Daxu* (Great Domestication, The Taming Power of the Great)	305
The hexagram *Dazhuang* (Great Strength)	309
The hexagram *Cui* (Gathering)	313
Summary of Theoretical and Empirical Propositions	317

12) Hexagrams Representing Organizations with Ill-Balanced Structure — 319

The hexagram *Daguo* (Major Superiority, Preponderance of the Great)	319
The hexagram *Xiaoguo* (Minor Superiority; Preponderance of the Small)	325
Summary of Theoretical and Empirical Propositions	329

13) Hexagrams Representing Military Situations — 329

The hexagram *Xu* (Waiting)	330
The hexagram *Dun* (Withdrawal)	334
The hexagram *Weiji* (Ferrying Incomplete)	338
The hexagram *Jiji* (Ferrying Complete)	341
Summary of Theoretical and Empirical Propositions	344

14) Hexagram Representing Specific Political and Social Occasions — 344

The Hexagram *Xikan* (The Constant Sink Hole)	345
The Hexagram *Guan* (Viewing)	350
The Gexagram *Li* (Cohesion)	354

	The Hexagram *Jian* (Adversity)	356
	The Hexagram *Lü* (The Wanderer)	358
	Summary of Theoretical and Empirical Propositions	362
Chapter 5	**Conclusion: Theoretical Implications of the *I Ching* in Modern Social Sciences**	363
	1) The *I Ching* as a Field Theory	363
	2) The *I Ching* as a Field theory on the Constitution of the Social World	373
	3) Theoretical Implications and Relevance of the *I Ching* for Some Issues in Modern Social Sciences	382
	4) Issues and Problems	395
Notes		399
Bibliography		425
Index		431

List of Tables and Figures

List of Tables

1.	Trigrams and Their Situational Attributes	59 - 60
2.	64 Hexagrams (1/4 - 4/4)	64 - 67

List of Figures

1. The Structural Components of the Hexagram	27
2. The Dual Dimensions of the Hexagram	33
3. A Graphic Representation of the Contemporaneity of a Hexagram	369

Preface

Many years ago a professor whose major field was Confucian philosophy told me that the *I Ching* informs us of universal principles governing such a wide range of cosmic and human realities that any attempt to interpret its meanings within a specifically defined frame of reference would either bring distortion to its true nature or do injustice to its profundity. The opinion expressed by this professor reflects a more or less typical belief that has been held long and widely by Asian *I Ching* scholars: the *I Ching* offers a vast reservoir of wisdom and knowledge covering almost every phenomenon under heaven. The tendency to think that the knowledge offered by the *I Ching* has such broad applicabilities, first of all, should have to do with the nature of the book. The original text overall was written in highly ambiguous symbolism which allows no easy clear-cut understanding, and therefore has yielded many different interpretations. Most *I Ching* scholars seem to have taken this ambiguity rather as a sign of highly general knowledge and wisdom than of defective knowledge having no clearly definable substance. This will explain why there has been a tendency among scholars to remain non-committed to any specific and clear interpretation: an attempt to narrow on or side with a specific interpretation would undermine the traditionally held belief in the *I Ching* as containing a system of profound knowledge covering a wide range of natural and human realities. But, trained in an area of modern social sciences and having observed well enough that any knowledge is a human product having only a limited validity or utility, I have been skeptical of such a claim for the "boundless" profundity of the *I Ching*.

However, once we refuse to grant this mysterious classic a privileged status as containing a system of omnibus knowledge relating to many different levels of realities, we now have to face a situation in which all the interpretations which the *I Ching* has yielded so far simply do not cohere into a systematically organized body of knowledge. In my view, the reason for which the *I Ching* still remains largely a mysterious book unapproachable by the rational mind could be attributed to the situation which I described above. Any person who wants to achieve a rational understanding of the *I Ching* will find himself perplexed as he goes through a series of earlier commentaries on the text and more recent interpretations on them as well, obviously because they on the whole would appear to lack not only thematic clarity but also logical coherence. As a matter of fact, this was a situation I actually experienced myself when I first read the text and related commentaries twenty some years ago. After the first reading of the book the impression that struck me was that I was being thrown into a maze of disjointed information that seemed hardly likely to add up to a systematically integrated body of knowledge. It did not seem to be a book which a social scientist like myself would like to search for what may be regarded as rational knowledge.

Nonetheless, there was something very interesting that held my attention on this ancient classic. I detected an important theme that underlies considerably large segments of the original text of the *I Ching* and of various commentaries written in later periods. It appeared to me that the perspective and the conceptual devices with which the *I Ching* depicts the essential conditions of the social world were of significance in modern social sciences and their main ideas could be translated without much difficulty into sociological terminology. To identify from the text materials and their variable interpretations underlying sociological themes — which I find to be the most distinct and important element in the Chinese intellectual tradition centering on the *I Ching* — may be compared to extracting a factor by a mathematical procedure known as *factor analysis*. Factor analysis in terms of its essential function may be characterized as a technique to delineate underlying hypothetical dimensions in the light of which an observed pattern of correlations among a set of numerical values can be explained meaningfully. To put a little differently, the analysis is used as a means to explore theoretical concepts that can account for an observed pattern of correlations among a set of numerical values measuring specific properties of things or individuals. By comparing the nature of the analysis carried out in this study to that of factor analysis, I want to bring into focus the following that seems to me to have a great deal of importance in elucidating the basic aim of this study.

As might have been suggested above, my aim in this book is not to create my own version of an interpretation of the *I Ching*. Of course, this book can be characterized quite appropriately as a *sociological interpretation*, a rather unique characterization for an exposition of the *I Ching*. The term "sociological," if it refers to the *I Ching*, may sound even exotic to scholars whose major field is Chinese philosophy. Then let me explain in a bit more detail what I actually have done in this study. The original text of the *I Ching* was written in such highly ambiguous symbolism that, through the long Chinese intellectual history, many prominent figures in Chinese philosophy were drawn into the challenging task of expounding upon what should be the real significance of the ancient classic and wrote volumes upon volumes of expository notes to facilitate a clearer and meaningful understanding of it. Unfortunately, however, the resulting situation has been problematic as I pointed out already. All the interpretations that have been rendered so far simply do not cohere into a systematically organized knowledge. Or, we may say, there is so much an excess of divergent or even colliding explanations that readers may still have to rely very much on their own judgment, uncertain at best, to infer what kind of specific entities or events the *I Ching* really concerns. The primary procedure in my own solution for this problematic situation is to establish an overall perspective with which I can bring together as many pieces of available information as possible under the purview of a thematically integrated body of knowledge. It is in this sense that I compare the nature of the analysis done in this study to that of factor analysis; I will attempt to separate out, from the whole mixture of knowledge cluttered with unrelated or conflicting themes, only those elements that converge into a unified theme. This would result in a version of the interpretation in which the *I Ching* is viewed as dealing with far more narrowly and sharply focused topics than having been interpreted generally in the main tradition of *I Ching* scholarship.

This approach, as we will see in this book, has produced the kind of interpretation of the *I Ching* whose distinctive features are characterized chiefly as sociological and political. I tend to believe that my trained capacity as a sociologist would facilitate deriving the interpretation presented in this study in which sociological and political ideas stand out prominently. No doubt, I should have been more receptive to the sociological and political ideas than to pay attention to other aspects in which scholars in other disciplines would be more interested. No one would be free of a selective cognition of this sort. However, one of the main purposes of my study was to explore the unique mode of the Chinese thought of itself as expressed in the *I Ching*, or, to put it more properly, as expressed through the specific manners in which the symbolism of the *I Ching* has been interpreted by the main tradition in Chinese philosophy. It was not by any means my intention to cloak my own ideas under the garment of the *I Ching*. Instead of projecting my own interpretation onto the *I Ching*, my role in this study may be viewed as a mediating one with which I simply take maximum advantage of my trained capacity as a sociologist in looking into its underlying ideas which, even considered by themselves, may best be characterized as sociological and political. I certainly tried to make the most out of a happy coincidence that my position as a sociologist could be well utilized for studying the *I Ching*. However, to emphasize again, this book is about the *I Ching*, or, to put it more properly, is to explore the unique mode of Chinese thought expressed through the manners in which the *I Ching* has been interpreted, rather than to create and promote my own conception of it.

Considering the important role that the *I Ching* has played long in the East-Asian cultural region, my attempt to expound upon this ancient classic seems to be a meaningful task in itself. More significantly yet, this study has a distinct feature in that it has approached the *I Ching* aiming at a system of knowledge which can square with today's academic standard in terms of both clarity in meaning and logical coherence. Nonetheless, other than the prospect that the *I Ching* could be understood as involving rational knowledge that deserves serious consideration even today, there was an additional reason for which I was drawn into this particular project. The way in which the *I Ching* depicts the essential features of social and human situations is closely analogous to that of Kurt Lewin's field theory in psychology. The unique perspective of the *I Ching* as such drew a keen interest from me; it struck me as having important implications with respect to some critical issues in modern social sciences. It was this promising potential judged as worth exploring even today, besides my long-held aspiration to attain a rational understanding of the *I Ching* in itself, that motivated me strongly to hold on to this study. In view of the present state of modern social sciences which, in my view, is suffering from a poverty of new and bold theoretical ideas, it seemed all the more worthwhile to search for whatever potentials the *I Ching* might have in this respect. In this study I therefore tried to explore theoretical implications that the unique way in which the *I Ching* depicts the essential features of the social world may well have with respect to such important issues in social sciences as the nature of relationship between individuals and society and the chronic discord between functionalism and conflict theory. And, I will argue that the *I Ching* involves interesting theoretical ideas that may be judged as feasible even today. Of course, my argument as such may be received differently depending upon viewpoints to which individual scholars are committed respectively. Regardless of what one may think of actual or potential merits of my position taken in this study, I nevertheless am sure of one important contribution to be made by a study such as this one; it will take us on an excursion through a system of thought whose novel ideas are diametrically different from our usual modes of thought and therefore provide interesting subject matter for scholarly discussions.

This study has relied as its main source of reference on an English translation of the *I Ching* rendered by Robert Lynn, Professor of Chinese Thoughts and Literature at the University of Toronto. Lynn's version, entitled *The Classic of Changes: A New Translation of the I Ching as Interpreted By Wang Bi*, is, as far as I know, the most thoroughly documented English translation among the many different versions published in recent decades. I express heart-felt thanks to Professor Lynn for allowing me to cite his valuable work. After the completion of the first draft of this book, I could not help but brood over how well or badly my English writing would be received by competent English writers; this was the first book I had written in English and I was not quite sure of how accurately and well my ideas would have been transplanted into English words and sentences. So my words of thanks have to go to Joyce Lann Kim who is now a graduate student at Harvard University. She, by proofreading and, whenever necessary, editing the manuscript, rendered me a great deal of help when I really needed it. I also should thank Terry Nelson whose office I visited so freely whenever I had questions about proper usage in English. The research that produced this book was supported by a Sung Kyun Research Grant; I am grateful for its timely support rendered to me right at the time I was most upbeat about embarking on this research project.

Before submitting a proposal to publish this book to the University Press of America, I made contact with 7 or 8 university presses in the U.S. A typical response from them was that they were not interested in my book proposal for some reason they did not communicate exactly, but their decisions as such, they added, had nothing to do with the scholarly value of my work. After a search, I found UPA, a publisher who upholds the principle that the scholarly value of a study should be the primary consideration in academic publishing. In the social sciences and humanities, no one is ever quite sure beforehand of how favorably his study will be received by fellow scholars and publishers. So it was truly encouraging to me that UPA, well known for its commitment to scholarship, agreed to publish my work. I would like to express a deeply felt gratitude to the staff at UPA, especially Dr. Robert West, the editorial director.

Acknowledgments

This book, by its nature, contains fairly large volumes of materials reprinted from the following sources:

1. *The Classic of Changes: A New Translation of the I Ching as Interpreted by Wang Bi*, translated by Richard John Lynn © 1994 Columbia University Press. Reprinted with the permission of the publisher.
2. *The I Ching or Book of Change.* The Richard Wilhelm Translation rendered into English by Carry F. Barnes. Copyright © 1967 and renewed 1977 by Princeton University Press. Reprinted by permission of Princeton University Press.
3. *The Tao of Organization*, Cheng Yi, translated by Thomas Cleary, © 1988. Reprinted by arrangement with Shambhala Publications, Inc., Boston, www.shambhala.com.

A translation of the *I Ching* involves much more than just translating the Chinese text into another language and requires a great deal of research into, and critical assessment of, various ways in which meanings underlying the peculiar symbolism of the *I Ching* have been understood in the native traditions of *I Ching* scholarship. The books listed above, therefore, by themselves represent scholarly achievements of considerable significance. I truly feel honored in sharing the intellectual achievements of the authors and thank each of the books' publishers for granting me the permission to reprint the needed rematerials.

There are other related works that may not oblige me the formal permission to utilize them in my study. Nevertheless, readers will find that they also have made significant contributions in various points in writing this treatise. They include: James Legge's *The I Ching: The Book of Changes* (trans. with an introduction and exegetical notes), New York: Dover Publications, 1963; Ki-Dong Lee's *Lectures on the I-Ching,* 2 vols. (in Korean) (trans. with a general treatise on the *I Ching* and exegetical notes), Seoul: Sung Kyun Kwan University Press, 1997; In-Whan Kim's *The I Ching* (in Korean) (trans. with Translator's foreword and exegetical notes), Seoul: Nanam, 1997. So I sincerely thank the authors of the above works for their valuable ideas without which I might have experienced a lot more difficult time in finding easier paths out of the symbolic mazes of the *I Ching*.

Chapter 1

Introduction

The purpose of this book is two-fold in nature. First, it aims at an exploration of a thought system contained in the *I Ching* (the Book of Changes) that, as I will argue, is mainly sociological and political. Secondly, utilizing what I will obtain from the task above, I will carry my analysis a step further to extract and examine theoretical assumptions, hypotheses, or paradigmatic perspectives that have relevance to some issues in modern sociology. At this point, however, to most readers who are either entirely unfamiliar with the *I Ching* itself or have only a vague image of it as a cryptic divination manual of ancient China the purpose of this book stated as above may not mean much. So I am obliged to start with a brief introduction of the *I Ching* — a book that has played highly significant roles in Chinese culture by occupying the minds of native scholars for more than two thousand years.

A proper place to become acquainted with this peculiar book is to expound upon the meaning of the title, *I Ching*. I will begin with the first word, *I*, and explain the meaning of it because it is this word that best sums up what this old Chinese classic is all about. According to "an early apocryphone to the *I Ching*," "The name *I* has three meanings. These are the easy, the changing, and the constant" (Wilhelm, 1960:15). Based on a traditional view from which the above interpretation is derived, Wilhelm explains that "the easy" emphasizes that "the book starts from what everyone sees and can immediately grasp" (p.16). That is, the *I Ching* provides a simple method to derive symbolic images that will help people grasp the changing phenomena in the world.

The other two meanings of *I*, "the changing" and "the constant," are more self-explanatory. The terms reflect a recognition that everything is in a state of change, yet even throughout this change, there is a certain unchanged order or framework within which the changes take place. This mode of thinking, in its inception, might have been associated with, thus invariably attested by, the seasonal change of natural phenomena in which there is an unchanging order underlying the endless process of change. *Ching,* the second word of the book's title, is translated simply as "classic" or "book." Therefore, the *I Ching,* translated as the Book of Changes (or the Classic of Changes), can be characterized as a book dealing with changing phenomena in the world from the perspective implied by the word *I* as above.

Considering the nature of the book, however, there are two things that make modern scholars hesitant to delve into the *I Ching* to dig out knowledge that has current relevance in social sciences. First of all, the *I Ching* is an old book, one of the oldest books in the world. The text consists of several layers of graphic symbols, brief cryptic statements attached to graphic symbols, commentaries added in later periods to provide more detailed interpretations and explanations for those symbols and attached statements. The age of each layer of the text has been a matter of dispute among sinologists. A popular view backed by a long, native tradition of China puts forward a doubtful claim that the oldest part of the text, three-line figures (trigrams) made of unbroken and broken lines (—— and — —), was devised by Fu Hsi, the legendary cultural hero of China known as the inventor of the fishnet, around the 34th century B.C. (Gao, 1995:17-18; Legge, 1963:5; Wilhelm, 1967:lvii). Most scholars agree that the main portion of the text, as distinguished from the appended ten Commentaries, was completed about 3,000 years ago in the last decade of the 12th Century B.C. The appended Commentaries, called the *Ten Wings*, are believed to have been compiled much later than the *I Ching* proper, i.e., the main body of the text. However, even when considered in its entirety, the antiquity of the book extends back to some time between 340 ~ 350 B.C. (Legge, 1963:1-8; Lynn, 1994:2-3; Wilhelm, 1960:1-12). The antiquity of a text such as this may raise doubts regarding the applicability of knowledge drawn from the *I Ching* on modern social sciences.

Another source of doubt regarding the importance of the *I Ching* in modern social sciences lies in its historical usage in Asian societies. The main function of the *I Ching*, when it evolved from the tortoise oracle[1], was divination. It has been used until today to look ahead into what kind of "fortune" or "misfortune" a person can expect from an upcoming situation, thing, or event, that is of urgent concern. The oracle messages regarding future affairs are given, as the traditional method of obtaining divination prescribes to follow (Lynn, 1994:19-22), through a random manipulation of yarrow stalks or, to use a simpler method, by casting coins. If the function of the *I Ching* described as above is brought into relief, the *I Ching* could be regarded as a divination manual. Again, question may arise; from a fortuneteller's manual, can we expect to obtain rational knowledge which relates to the concerns and issues of modern social sciences?

It is obvious, therefore, that the *I Ching* has an aspect in which mysticism plays a large role. And, as pointed out above, its actual authorship is undetermined. What we are left with is that its origin traces back to some remotely distant, obscure periods in the ancient Chinese civilization in which people were known to have had a peculiar tendency to play with mystic ideas and hidden meanings. Thus, the *I Ching* is an old book borne with questionable origin and utility.

Nevertheless, if we look at the roles the *I Ching* actually played in China and neighboring countries like Korea, few will fail to notice that the *I Ching* had not been simply a divination manual or an object of bibliographers' scholarly curiosity. For quite a long time, the *I Ching* has been playing highly significant and profound roles in the Chinese intellectual scene. As a matter of fact, the *I Ching* was elevated to a status that may compare to that of the Bible in Western societies, under which many different ways of thinking and many religious practices have developed. In this respect, the *I Ching* was not simply a cultural product. Rather, it was a highly productive cultural resource or tool-kit that produced rich and multifarious subcultures. I call it a "cultural resource" or "tool-kit" rather than a "cultural product" to emphasize the following aspect. If we are to objectively assess the knowledge the *I Ching* actually contains, it would be difficult to say that it conveys definite ideas about whatever it intends to describe or explain. It only provides a set of graphic symbols and brief enigmatic statements attached to those symbols.[2] For those who consult with the *I Ching* for divination, these symbols and statements are supposed to carry messages for future affairs. Despite the peculiar nature of this book as such a fortuneteller's tool, an interesting phenomenon happened in China. The *I Ching* continued to overwhelm the minds of leading Chinese intellectuals throughout history. These intellectuals received it as one of the most authentic sources of knowledge with almost unbelievable unanimity in spite of the book's cryptic nature. The prestige of the *I Ching* was raised to such a level that both

Confucianism and Taoism, the two major ideological doctrines of China, equally acknowledged it as a vast treasure house of true knowledge and wisdom. Wilhelm (1960:viii) observes that the *I Ching* occupied a position that "could be compared in other cultures to the place of sacred scriptures inspired by divine revelation." Numerous commentaries on it were written one after another and the line-up of individuals who wrote them ranges over the entire history of Chinese philosophy from Confucius himself to such important figures in succeeding generations as Wang Bi (226-249), Cheng Yi (1033-1107), and Zhu Xi (1130-1200) (Lynn, 1994:5-18). Even to scientists as well as a variety of pseudo-scientists in China, the *I Ching* was not only a source of inspiration, but also a theoretical manual believed to be powerful enough to explain almost every physical phenomenon under heaven (Needham, 1954:329-333). Of course, the influences of the *I Ching* were not limited to circles of the learned. The *I Ching* was and still is a primary source by which various schools of divination based their authority and their claims for potency. Thus, the *I Ching* had many different meanings and usages for many different individuals depending upon what kind of personal concerns, background, or learning a person might have. Figuratively speaking, the *I Ching* provided the tool or the materials from which people built many different things in ways that suited their needs and prior conceptions. It was a rich reservoir of cultural symbols from which people were able to draw out or build up suitable schemes to describe or explain the nature and conditions of whatever things or events attracted their attention.

What aspect of the *I Ching* made itself capable of keeping one of the great civilizations in the world like China under its influence throughout its long existence? Needham (1954:304) attempts to answer this question by stating:

> These symbols were supposed to mirror in some way all the processes of Nature, and Chinese medieval scientists were therefore continually tempted to rely on pseudo-explanations of natural phenomena obtained by simply referring the latter to the particular symbol to which they might be supposed to 'pertain.' Since each one of the symbols came, in the course of centuries, to have an abstract signification, such a reference was naturally alluring, and saved all necessity for further thought. It resembled to some extent the astrological pseudo-explanations of medieval Europe, but the abstractness of the symbolism gave it a deceptive profundity .... the sixty-four symbols in the system provided a set of abstract conceptions capable of subsuming a large number of the events and processes which any investigation is bound to find in the phenomena of the natural world.

Needham suggests that a primary reason for the overwhelming reception conferred upon the *I Ching* lies in "the abstract symbolism" that "gave it a deceptive profundity." And, he continues, it was due to such an unquestioned authority of the *I Ching* that the development of scientific ideas in China lagged behind that of Europe. The view that the predominance of the *I Ching* over the intellectual lives of China had posed a hindrance rather than a help to the development of true science may be plausible, although I have little knowledge to assess its actual validity. Whatever factor or factors might have been operating in the background, however, one thing seems clear. The people in ancient China saw too much and thus tried to squeeze out too much from this old book. It was a tool-kit that was overused far beyond the point where it could produce an actual advancement in knowledge or technology.

Why then do we have to bother ourselves with a study to deal with a book that contains such symbolism that seems empty in real substance and whose meanings were stretched out in so many directions? To answer this question, and in an effort to outline the significance that this treatise has on social sciences, I would like to point out two things. One concerns the dominant tradition in the scholarship on the *I Ching*. The 64 graphic symbols called *gua* (hexagrams) that make up the core element of the *I Ching* have a uniform structure in which "six (broken or unbroken lines are) . . . . arranged one atop the other in vertical sequence" (Lynn, 1994:1), as shown in an example presented in endnote (2) of this chapter. Of these, the *Ta Chuan* (the Great Treatise), one of the Commentaries appended to the *I Ching*, explains:

> The holy sages were able to survey all the confused diversities under heaven. They observed forms and phenomena, and made representations of things and their attributes. They were called the images. (Translation as rendered by Wilhelm, 1967:304)

The 64 graphic symbols are supposed to convey the essential features of the "forms" and "attributes" of all the diverse phenomena in the world.[3] So, "they are called the Images (*xiang*)." It is probably in view of this assertion that Wilhelm (1967:xli,lvii,300) sometimes uses the word "archetype" to convey a meaning roughly equivalent to what is indicated by the hexagrams. Let us stop here and suppose that those graphic symbols, or hexagrams, were put to use more often than not with the narrower and specific intention to indicate the essential features of the forms or attributes of *human collectives*, rather than quite indiscriminately *everything* in the world. We now seem to have more reason to be interested in this book that has been revered as one of the premier classics in China. Before I continue, let me emphasize that the *I Ching* in fact had been viewed and interpreted in this manner throughout generations by the mainstream intellectuals in China. That is, to most Chinese scholars in the intellectual tradition of China, it contained a repertoire of knowledge about the conditions of their social reality and the moral teachings believed to be pertinent under those social conditions. Related specifically to major concerns of modern sociology is what has been interpreted to be the core idea of the *I Ching* — a view that the critical conditions of society are determined by activities of individuals who occupy different positions that will bear unequal life chances upon their occupants. Therefore, the way that the *I Ching* had been interpreted under this dominant tradition clearly involves a line of ideas that can be properly called "social" or "political" in nature.

The second reason for which the *I Ching* should be viewed as a proper subject for a study in social sciences is related to a position that Needham takes with respect to why the book was able to exercise such a powerful influence over the minds of Chinese intellectuals. The position that he takes regarding this issue is offered as an answer to a question that he raises as follows:

> It (the *I Ching*) tempted those who were interested in Nature to rest in explanations which were no explanations at all. The book of Changes was a system for *pigeon-holing novelty* and then doing nothing more about it. Its universal system of symbolism constituted a stupendous *filling-system*. It led to a stylisation of concepts almost analogous to the stylisations which have in some ages occurred in art forms, and which finally prevented painters from looking at Nature at all . . . . There is a question here which refuses to be dismissed, namely, *why* did the universal symbolism of the *I Ching*, to which Europe can offer nothing parallel, grow up, and *why* did it show such extraordinary longevity and preference? (1954:336-337)

Needham then offers the following answer:

> Was the compelling power which it had in Chinese civilisation due to the fact that it was a view of the world basically congruent with the bureaucratic social order? . . . . The point to be made is that the system of the Book of Changes might be regarded as in a sense the heavenly counterpart of bureaucracy upon earth, the reflection upon the world of Nature of the particular social order of the human civilisation which produced it . . . . Perhaps the entire system of correlative organismic

thinking was in one sense the mirror image of Chinese bureaucratic society. Not only the tremendous filling-system of the *I Ching*, but also the symbolic correlations in the stratified matrix world might so be described. Both human society and the picture of Nature involved a system of coordinates, a tabulation-framework, a stratified matrix in which everything had its position, connected by the 'proper channels' with everything else. (1954:337-338)

In the above passage, Needham holds in effect that the correlative organismic perspective towards Nature had its root in a mode of thought that had been formed after the model of the hierarchically organized bureaucratic society of China. In other words, the mode of thought that the people in ancient China had developed while observing the forms and attributes of their own society also applied to other realms of knowledge. As a result, it was consequently elevated to the status of a "universal filling-system" where one could find a fitting frame of reference for almost every social or natural phenomenon in the world. This thesis that an understanding of the sociopolitical realities in the ancient Chinese society provided, or evolved into, a universal philosophical foundation has important implications for this study. There is one thing we can safely assure the *I Ching* has to offer: if the *I Ching* in fact contains an aspect of knowledge that deserves serious consideration by modern scholars, we should find it in the ideas that are "social" or "political" in nature. Needham's thesis renders a supporting argument on this account. That is, our search for the proper meanings of the *I Ching* must be done in the "organismic" conception that reflects the social and political realities of Chinese bureaucratic society.

Of course, the *I Ching* is not like a theory book in modern sociology or political science. Even to knowledgeable readers in Chinese classic works, this book does not allow an easy and straightforward understanding. This is why the understanding of the *I Ching* posed a major philosophical enterprise to succeeding generations of scholars in China. Commentary after commentary was written by major figures in Chinese philosophy. By furnishing an exegesis on the sign-symbols and cryptic statements of the book, some wanted simply to help readers understand the knowledge and wisdom that the *I Ching* is supposed to impart while others had a more ambitious intention to put forward one's own ideas by leaning on the authority of the *I Ching*. In the process, the meanings of the graphic symbols and related statements of the *I Ching* were understood differently depending upon how commentators conceived the significance, or the potential utility, of the book. As a matter of fact, commentaries seem to have some major as well as minor differences in their interpretations of the various parts of the text. But, asking which interpretations are the most faithful to the "original" meaning of it, or possibly the most valid one, is not a relevant question here as far as the aim of this thesis is concerned. Considering the book is filled with enigmatic symbols and words, it would be an unavoidable fact that many different interpretations were borne with the changing trends in thought and ideological interests throughout the long history of China. At any rate, authoritative commentaries served as a medium to help ordinary readers wade through the opaque world of the *I Ching*. It was mostly through interpreted accounts of such commentaries, rather than the *I Ching* itself, that most people looked into the nature and attributes of their social and political world and found themselves situated with defined possibilities and limitations.

Now the question dealt with in this study has to be re-addressed in a somewhat different way. What sort of knowledge or wisdom had those commentators relied upon as authoritative sources by intellectuals in the main stream of the Chinese scholarship found in the *I Ching*? Put another way, what did the sociopolitical world found to be depicted in the *I Ching* by the dominant intellectual tradition in China look like? What were the "forms and attributes" of the sociopolitical situations presented by the *I Ching*? Does the picture of social reality described by the *I Ching* contain thoughts worth serious examination today in that they carry ideas relevant to the pending concerns of modern social sciences? These questions summarize the main concerns of this book which serves to explicate the social and political ideas of the *I Ching* as they had been interpreted by the dominant tradition of *I Ching* scholarship in China and, at the same time, to explore the possible implications that these ideas can have for modern social sciences.

I already touched briefly on the dominant intellectual tradition of China. But, more specifically, what is the most distinctive characteristic of the orientation of this tradition toward the *I Ching*, and who represents this tradition? This tradition is often called the School of Righteousness and Reason (Kim, 1996:69-77) and includes a wide variety of sub-schools under its umbrella. Nevertheless, they share a common outlook in the way that they approach the *I Ching* — a belief that the most profound and desirable function of the *I Ching* is assisting individuals with moral lessons and behavioral maxims so individuals may avoid errors in managing worldly affairs. If this were all that the *I Ching* offered, however, it would not be different from any other ordinary book teaching morality. Yet, to individuals who followed this tradition, the moral lessons and behavioral maxims they drew from the

I Ching were offered in line with a set of symbols and statements describing the situations to which those lessons and behavioral maxims could apply as relevant. What gives the *I Ching* a particularly unique characteristic is its depiction of the situational context represented by the 64 graphic symbols and related statements appended to each symbolic component. This situational context constitutes what Needham (1954:338) describes as "symbolic correlations in the stratified matrix." I will discuss this later in detail. Anyway, there seems to be no doubt that, as far as scholars in the main stream of Chinese intellectual tradition were concerned, the situations they read from the *I Ching* were certain sorts of social and political situations that posed the most pressing reality over their lives.

The main text that I will study for this treatise, *The Classic of Changes: A New Translation of the I Ching as Interpreted by Wang Bi* (translated by Richard John Lynn, 1994), is a product based on materials drawn from sources that gave birth to and therefore embody the characteristic orientation of the above mentioned tradition. As indicated by the title, Lynn's translated version of the *I Ching* includes Wang Bi's commentaries upon which he relies for the most part. Of the position that Wang Bi's interpretation of the *I Ching* occupies in the native tradition of *I Ching* scholarship, Lynn (1994:7) explains:

> Wang Bi may be said to have written the first philosophical commentary upon the *Changes* — that is, apart from those sections of the classic that are themselves commentaries. His approach synthesizes Confucian, Legalist and Daoist views, with Confucian views predominant. His version of the *Changes* was extremely influential and became the orthodox interpretation during the course of the pre-Tang and Tang eras (fourth through tenth centuries A.D.) and was finally canonized in Kong Yingda's *Zhouyi zhengyi*. Although the commentaries of the later Neo-Confucians largely eclipsed Wang's interpretation, much of what he had to say was incorporated into what eventually became the official Neo-Confucian orthodox view of the Changes, and what they rejected also helped to shape that view. A comparison of Wang's commentary with those of Cheng Yi and Zhu Xi reveals how carefully Cheng and Zhu must have read Wang's remarks and how his arguments tended to shape theirs, whether they agreed with him or not (the disagreements largely result from their rejection of what they perceived to be elements of Legalism and Daoism in Wang' thought). The synthetic Neo-Confucian version of the *Changes* that emerged after the thirteenth century would have been very different if there had been no Wang Bi commentary first.

The above passage by Lynn clearly suggests that Wang Bi was

responsible for the initiation of the dominant tradition into the interpretation of the *I Ching*. Of course, as Lynn (1994:7-8) also points out, even within the dominant tradition "there is no single *Classic of Changes* but rather as many versions of it as there are different commentaries on it." But, it seems clear that Wang Bi revolutionized the way of seeing the *I Ching*, and the guidelines and perspectives that he set up to clarify the puzzling symbols and sayings of the *I Ching* paved the way for the Confucian orthodox views of later generations. Thus, considering the main purpose of this study is analyzing the social and political ideas contained in the *I Ching*, as understood by the dominant intellectual tradition of China, the version of the *I Ching* translated by Lynn along with Wang Bi's commentary provided the appropriate material. The choice of the text for this study was made with these considerations in mind.

In addition to Lynn's text, other translated versions of the text and commentaries appended to them will also be utilized from time to time as occasions may call for it as necessary. In particular, there are two translated versions of the text on which I rely frequently for this treatise, even if far less frequently than Lynn's text: they are Legge's (1963) and Wilhelm's (1967) texts rendered in English.

But, before I proceed with the task proposed for this study, it would be helpful to provide a more detailed description of the *I Ching*. Although pieces of information were briefly stated in the course of previous discussion, many readers may still wonder what kind of specific materials we are going to deal with in this inquiry. The translated version of the *I Ching* rendered by Lynn includes several layers of materials, each of which dates from widely varying ages. Of these materials, the following ones constitute the main body of the text: 1) the graphic symbols called hexagrams (*gua*), each of which is made up of six unbroken or broken lines arranged one atop the other in vertical sequence; 2) names of the hexagrams (*guaming*); 3) hexagram statements (*tuan*, judgments) that state briefly the meaning of each hexagram as a whole, and 4) line statements (*yaoci*) that explains each line individually. Each of the above elements is followed by commentaries that were written much later than the main body of the text. The nature of the connection between the original usage and meanings of the older portions of the text and those as interpreted by the later commentaries, however, is not clear (Lynn, 1994:4). The ten chapters of commentary, thus called the *Ten Wings*, have been treated traditionally as an integral part of the *I Ching* text. The unquestioned authority that the *I Ching* exercised over Chinese intellectuals might have been derived from a long held view among Chinese bibliographers that the ten chapters of commentaries, or at least a part of them, were written by Confucius himself (Lynn, 1994:2-3). Regardless of who wrote them, scholars raise little doubt that the perspective, or interpretive scheme, applied for compiling the commentaries is of Confucian leaning. Thus, we may say that these commentaries shed light on the mystic world of the *I Ching* mainly from a Confucian standpoint. Yet, to "shed light" may not be the best fitting expression because those commentaries themselves are full of poetically narrated, symbolic verses that are still open to many different interpretations about what the various components of the *I Ching* actually signify. It therefore seems natural that there would be further needs for yet another commentary to clarify the old Commentaries themselves. Wang Bi's commentary is one of such later commentaries that were written to satisfy the need for clearer explanations on the knowledge or lessons that the *I Ching,* together with the above mentioned *Ten Commentaries*, is supposed to convey. Lynn's translation, therefore, introduces two layers of commentaries, the old Commentaries and Wang Bi's commentaries with cross-references from other major commentaries of still later periods, all presented together in sequence of the former being immediately followed by the latter.

The basic format of the materials arranged in Lynn's translation of the *I Ching* are as follows. The text opens with Wang Bi's "*General Remarks on the Changes of the Zhou* [*Zhouyi Lueli*]." As the title itself suggests, this is a general treatise with which Wang Bi explains his overall perspective on how the nature of the *I Ching* as a whole and its various components should be viewed and interpreted accordingly. Introduced next to this treatise are a series of commentaries from the old *Ten Commentaries*, and Wang Bi's sub-commentaries are appended to each related portion of the above materials. The rest of the whole text is divided into 64 sections, each of which deals with an individual hexagram. At the top of each section a graphic figure (called a hexagram), made up of six lines arranged from the bottom line to the top one in vertical sequence, is presented with its name. Hexagrams differ from one another in their overall make-ups of broken or unbroken lines located at one of the six positions in the hierarchically arranged six-line complex. If we assume, only if tentatively here, that hexagrams were devised to represent the organizational structure of certain sociopolitical situations, it is the unique combination of broken or unbroken lines that determines the meaning of an individual hexagram, and therefore the title name given to it indicates the specific characteristic of a situation as a whole. Next, a brief statement(s) called a hexagram statement (*tuan,* judgment) follows. This describes in a bit more details the overall meaning or diagnosis of a situation symbolized by a hexagram. This portion of the text carries short statements written in a few highly abstract and symbolic words that also demand a stretch of the imagination. It would be for this reason that a number of commentaries including Wang Bi's sub-commentaries on the older Commentaries were written with intention to clarify what were supposedly meant by the hexagram statements. In Lynn's text, each hexagram statement is followed by a related older Commentary and Wang Bi's sub-commentaries are also appended respectively to each of them.

Closely related to the hexagram statements and the commentaries on them are the *Commentary on the Images* (*Xiangzhuan*). It is another commentary that, coupled with the *Commentary on the Judgments* (hexagram statements), explains the meanings of each hexagram as an integrated entity. In content, there seems to be little significant difference between the two materials, the *Commentary on the Judgments* and the *Commentary on the Images*. They were written in the same vein that reflects the Confucian spirit (Lynn, 1994:4), and, where they differ, simply give further bits of information that are complementary to one another. Lynn (1994:2) points out that of the *Ten Wings*, only these two Commentaries seem to date from the same period ("the Sixth or Fifth century B.C."), and "appear to have been the direct product of Confucius' school, if not the works of Confucius himself."

Along with the materials I have mentioned thus far, there are still other materials that will be given special importance regarding the aims of this study. They are the line statements (*yaoci*) and the related commentaries. Line statements are statements attached to each of the six individual lines making up a hexagram. As we can easily guess from the fact that a hexagram statement explains what a hexagram indicates as a whole, a line statement explains what an individual line means under the situational context of the hexagram to which the individual line belongs. Of these Lynn (1994:2) explains:

> The line statements have a sequential or associational organization based on the general topic given in the Judgment; each states a specific, differentiated instance or variation of the topic, which in complete line statements (many statements seem to be fragments) is followed by a charge or injunction that one should take some action or refrain from it and a final determination ("misfortune," or "good fortune," etc.).

Specific examples will be given when we discuss hexagrams and individual lines in detail. At this point, it will be enough to simply point out that six lines, unbroken or broken, as a unit constitute a hexagram. Each hexagram has a specific make-up to distinguish it from other hexagrams in the sequential arrangement of its constituent lines, and each of the line statements tells what the meaning of its position is in its specific location under the specific situation that a hexagram represents as a whole. We can compare this to a functional entity. A whole and its constituent parts mutually determine each other and the role or meaning of the parts is determined by the overall context whose meaning likewise depends upon the organization of the parts as a unit in relation to one another. The same may be said of the relationship between a hexagram and its constituent lines. Thus, the line statements offer information on the specific situations individual constituent elements (represented by individual lines) respectively face under the context of the total situation that a specific hexagram signifies. Let us assume that an individual line symbolizes a person or a stratum of individuals that is under a specific sociopolitical situation represented by a hexagram to which the line belongs. The line statement attached to that line then explains the specific situation the person or stratum of individuals who occupy the line position will face under the sociopolitical situation represented by the corresponding hexagram.

As was the case for hexagram statements, line statements also consist of terse, abstract, and symbolic verses. Therefore, like hexagram statements, earlier commentaries and later commentaries on the earlier ones were added to the line statements.

Thus we have in our hands many layers of materials that date from many different ages. Personally, I doubt whether there will be available an integrated, overall frame of reference with which consistent and systematic interpretations can be made across. For example, suppose that a second line in a hexagram is interpreted as representing a specific situation that a person or group of individuals face under an overall situational context of that hexagram. This interpretation then should have a systematic and coherent relationship with other interpretations in other text accounts and commentaries regarding the second lines of all the other hexagrams. Or, if a particular line is interpreted in a certain way in relation to the hexagram to which it belongs, this interpretation will set a limit on the possible range of interpretations on all the lines located at the same position in their respective hexagrams. This is because we should not commit logical inconsistencies by applying *ad hoc* rules that vary from one hexagram to another. A systematic body of knowledge requires logical consistency. Of course, we must not overlook the fact that the various parts of the *I Ching* and related commentaries show a certain measure of inner consistency. But, as far as I see it, it would be much closer to the truth to say that many commentaries provide what seem more like *ad hoc* interpretations. That is, there seems to be no single, integrated frame of reference applied consistently throughout the entirety of the materials. We will examine this in detail as our discussion progresses. At this point, let me simply point out that the *I Ching* and related commentaries are better viewed not as containing a single, integrated theory but rather a set of small or large theories on the sociopolitical reality of old bureaucratic China. These theories, rather implicitly contained in the original text materials and related commentaries, seem to have been formulated in piecemeal fashion through individual scholars' efforts to achieve a rational understanding out of the mysterious symbols and statements of the old text. In this process, commentators had to work on many different levels such as hexagram names, hexagram statements, commentaries on the Images, line statements, and, most importantly, the most general level at which all 64 hexagrams and all other related materials are to be interpreted as a systematically integrated whole. The outcome was what we see now — the failure to come up with a coherent line of logic, a conceptual framework, with which all the old text materials of the *I Ching* and appended commentaries are put together as a logically integrated body of knowledge. Without such an overall conceptual framework to organize the elements of the *I Ching*, the text materials and appended commentaries could not help but be interpreted case-by-case and in an *ad hoc* fashion. This suggests that conceptual frameworks from the perspective of which the commentaries were written on the hexagrams and lines diverged from one another. For instance, a frame of reference that is applied to the interpretation of a certain hexagram or line may not be consistent with what is applied to the interpretation of another hexagram or line. Consequently, we can identify a number of theories or perspectives from the *I Ching* or from its commentaries that often lack any clear logical links with one another. As far as I see it, this is the case with the *I Ching*. Although there are aspects in which the *I Ching* can be viewed as containing a thought system having some inner consistency, it is also true that it has unresolved complexities that have defied every effort by generations of scholars who strove for a coherent and clear understanding of the symbolic figures and cryptic statements of the *I Ching*.

This study starts with a recognition of this limitation of the *I Ching*. It does not convey a coherent system of ideas about the sociopolitical reality of the old Chinese society run by the bureaucratic apparatus organized of ruling elites. All it offers is sets of partial ideas, "partial" in the sense that they as a whole evidently fall short of forming a coherently organized body of knowledge. Nevertheless, as I am going to show this to be the case throughout this treatise, many of those partial ideas still offer quite unique and interesting viewpoints that may have some current relevance to issues in modern social sciences.

There is an additional limitation. The *I Ching* was not written in logically coherent and lucid discourse. It only gives a series of symbolic images and very brief descriptions, often expressed in metaphor, about various types of hierarchically structured situations under which individuals find themselves with varying possibilities, opportunities or limitations. Accordingly, the conceptual schemes by which the *I Ching* takes cognizance of the sociopolitical reality of bureaucratically organized Chinese Empire may be said to consist mostly of sketchy ideas lacking enough specificity and clarity. Yet, a development of detailed ideas always starts with a rough outlining of them, an essential stage in the process of developing knowledge, and we sometimes will have happy occasions, if only too rarely, to come across rudimentary ideas having promising potentials at its formative stage. Would this be also the case with the *I Ching*? To put another way, do I believe that our encounter with the ideas of the *I Ching* will turn out to be such a happy occasion? At this point, let me just say that it is one of the purposes of this study to conduct an analysis of the *I Ching* by which I, hopefully, lay bare ideas that are worthy of serious consideration.

Of course, considering the nature of the archaic materials of which the *I Ching* is composed, immersing ourselves in them may still be viewed as a venture that promises little. At this point, however, let me offer some words of justification by saying that sociology and other social sciences today seem to be undergoing a stage of stagnation, are running out of creative ideas and, therefore, are in need of being supplied with new and bold ideas. It could be said that routine research activities performed on existing paradigms in modern social sciences are at a point of what Kuhn (1970:66-76) describes as crisis. The practitioners in our profession nowadays seem to have less confidence in their fields than they once had. If this diagnosis is right, developing or searching for new ideas should be a much-needed endeavor in the social sciences. At this point, given that my attempt to search for new ideas begins with an uncertain venture into the mysterious world of the *I Ching*, I admit, we have every reason to question whether such a project will have a promising outcome. Yet, if generations of Chinese intellectuals had been enamored by the ideas of the *I Ching*, such ideas nevertheless should be equipped with some remarkable qualities so as to have kept the eyes of the people focused for such a long period of history. In this book, I will give these ideas a chance for a presentation.

Now, before I set out for the exploration of the *I Ching*, a brief explanation of the structure of this book is in order. Overall, all the discussions in this book focus on two major topics, the analyses of the hexagrams and the implications and relevance that the ideas of the *I Ching* have for modern social sciences. Of these, the detailed analysis on each of the 64 hexagrams appears in the forth chapter titled "Hexagrams: Representations of Various Types of Social Situations." It may raise some curiosity and interest among those who are knowledgeable in the *I Ching* that I do not follow the sequential ordering of the hexagrams as customarily presented in the text and instead have adopted a very unusual classification scheme with which hexagrams are put together in kinds as we will see in that section. The scheme employed has no precedent and therefore needs some caution in using for other purposes than this particular study. As far as the aims of this book are concerned, it serves a useful function in two respects. One is that the ways in which the hexagrams are classified reflect the nature of this study which aims at understanding the *I Ching* from the perspectives of modern social sciences. The other is that by grouping hexagrams into similar kinds the book looks more organized and becomes easier to read. The second and the third chapters deal with the components of the hexagram such as yin and yang lines, the positions of the lines, trigrams, and so on. These chapters prepare readers with basic information needed before they go into the fourth section where the main topic of the book, the hexagrams, is discussed. Thus, the two sections may well be regarded as introductory sub-sections to the fourth, the main body of the book. There are two places where I discuss the implications and relevance that the ideas of the *I Ching* might have in modern social sciences. One place is at the end of each sub-section of the fourth chapter. Here theoretical and empirical propositions having some relevance to current concerns of modern social sciences are derived from the interpretations of each hexagram and its line statements and presented in summary. The theoretical significance that the *I Ching* as a system of knowledge has overall and how its core ideas can relate to important issues in modern social sciences are discussed in the conclusion. It will be in this last section that the potential merits of the *I Ching* are examined and assessed mainly in terms of its applicabilities to modern social sciences.

Chapter 2

Structural Components of the Hexagram: Representation of Situations

A hexagram is a graphic symbol made up of six lines, each of which occupies one of the six locations arranged one on top of the other in hierarchical sequence. For example, the Hexagram *Li* (Cohesion) has a graphic composition made up of six lines, two broken and four unbroken lines, which take their positions respectively at one of the six locations in the hierarchically arranged six-line complex as follows:

As we can see from the above example, the unique structure of a hexagram is determined by a combination of two factors: the position of each unbroken line or broken line and the dichotomic variation of the lines at each positional location in the structure of the hexagram. Their level or their respective positions in the hierarchically ordered structure differentiate the lines from one another. It is customary that the lines are read from bottom to top. Thus, starting from the bottom line moving upward, the lines are respectively called the first (or beginning) line (*yao*), the second, the third, the fourth, the fifth, and the top (or ending) one (Kwak, 1990:242; Gao, 1995:303; Lynn, 1994:1). The situational variation of the lines is expressed either as unbroken (———, yang) or broken (— —, yin) lines. Thus combined, for example, the hexagram *Li* is said to consist of First Yang, Second Yin, Third Yang, Fourth Yang, Fifth Yin, and Top Yang.[1] Thus, to understand what the hexagram as a whole and each of its constituent lines respectively signifies, we must know what sort of attributes the hierarchical arrangement of the six locations and the two-way variation of the lines, either yang or yin lines, are posited to symbolize.

1) The Positional Attributes of the Lines in the Hierarchical Structure of the Hexagram

According to Wang Bi's commentary, "positions are places ranked as either superior or inferior, abodes suitable for the capabilities with which one is endowed.... Positions are either noble or humble...." (Lynn, 1994:33). Therefore, the respective locations of the positions arranged in hierarchical order signify the ranks of the positions in a social organization constituted of human individuals. This perspective is the basis for the more narrowly defined specific meanings of the six positions as representing official positions or statuses in the stratification system of Chinese society. For example, the bottom position is interpreted as corresponding to that of "common people," the second "lower officials," the third "heads of the regional administration" or "higher ranking officials," the fourth "ministers at the royal court," the fifth "the reigning Emperor," and the last one "ex-emperor in retirement" or "sage."[2] (Kim, 1992:29; Gao, 1996:303; Lee, 1997[I]:43-46; Shchutskii, 1980:8; Wilhelm, 1967:360). Nevertheless, the common tradition in the *I Ching* scholarship, including that attributable to Wang Bi, would be reluctant to exactly pin down what is meant by the respective positions of the hexagram as specifically defined ones as indicated above and this reluctance is understandable. Those who believe in a universal validity of the *I Ching* tend to have little doubt that the 64 hexagrams of the *I Ching* have much broader applicability and cover a wider range of entities or realities than any narrowly limited aspect or category of human situations.[3] Thus, the specific interpretation given above would be considered only as one of many such possible applications. Therefore, although the hierarchical arrangement of the positions of the hexagram was often interpreted as a schematic representation of the hierarchical social formation of the Chinese Empire, such an interpretation would be viewed only as one possible application among a much broader range of human situations to which the hexagram is believed to be generally applicable.

Here we must ask, do a wide variety of human collectives share certain essential characteristics so that their basic structures can be equally described with the same general schematic representation? The opinion described above seems to suggest an affirmative reply to this question. That is, as far as the dominant tradition in the *I Ching* scholarship views it, the hexagram involves a highly general schema applicable to varying kinds or levels of human collective situations.

Such a position then may simply imply a truism as follows: when adopting a six-point ordinal scale as a classification scheme, any hierarchical order could fit into the stratification system with a ranking order ranging from the first bottom level to the sixth top one. In other words, given a suitable scheme to assign ranks as "either superior or inferior" or "either noble or humble" relative to each other, we can easily sketch out a stratification system for any social grouping in such a way that it can fit the hierarchical formation of a hexagram. What seems obvious, however, is that an assignment of simple rank values to social positions would be meaningless unless the ranked positions were also given some substantive meanings as more substantively defined nominal categories.

As a matter of fact, the six positions of the hexagram have been interpreted as carrying more specific, substantive meanings than expressing merely some quantitative variation in prestige or power measured in terms of "noble or humble" or "superior or inferior." Of the specific meanings that the respective positions have as relative to one another, Wang Bi (Lynn, 1994:33-34) explains:

> If we exclude the first and top places when we discuss the status of positions, then the third place and the fifth place each occupy the upper most position in their respective trigrams, so how indeed could we fail to call them yang positions? And since the second place and fourth place each occupy the lowest position in their respective trigrams, how indeed could we fail to call them yin positions? The first position and the top position are the beginning and the ending of an entire hexagram and respectively represent what precedes and what follows a given situation. Therefore since neither of these positions has a constant status and since situations have no regular representation in either place, these positions are not to be designated as either yin or yang. Whereas there is a fixed order for noble and humble positions, there are no regular masters for the ending and the beginning positions.

I will explain what is meant by "yin" or "yang" positions mentioned in the above and the meaning of a "trigram" as a sub-unit of a hexagram when we discuss the situational variation of lines. But, before we get down to Wang Bi's remarks on the positions of the hexagram, I will establish a comparable conceptual frame of reference with which sociologists or political scientists of today are more familiar. To do so, let us give a quick glance at a passage quoted from Dahrendorf (1969:212):

> Whenever men live together and lay foundations of forms of social organization, there are positions whose occupants have powers of command in certain context and over certain positions, and there are other positions whose occupants are subjected to such commands. The distinction between "up" and "down" — or as the English say, "Them" and "Us" — is one of the fundamental experiences of most men in society.

And, again,

> Every position in an imperatively coordinated group can be recognized as belonging to one who dominates or one who is dominated. Sometimes, in view of the bureaucratic large-scale organization of modern states — under the influence of the state — this assumption may at first glance seem problematic. However, a sharper analysis leaves no doubt that here also the split into the dominating and dominated is valid, even though in reality a considerable measure of differentiation is discernible among those in the dominating group. (p.219)

Now, by putting aside for a while the bottom and the top lines which Wang Bi describes as having no "constant status," we are left with the four middle positions. Wang Bi groups these four positions into two higher-order units each of which contains two positions as sub-components. The four middle positions should be understood as a symbolic representation of a stratification structure that is made up of an upper and lower unit, each of which is further divided into two sub-components, upper and lower positions. It is along this line of interpretation that Wilhelm (1967:357) characterizes the relationship between the upper and lower units. One is above, dominant, in front, and contains the other within while the other is below, subordinate, behind, and contained within the dominant. As we can easily see, the terms "noble or humble" and "superior or inferior" as Wang Bi uses them and Wilhelm's notions of the relationship between the upper and lower units carry meanings that are not much different from what is

Structural Components of the Hexagram 21

suggested by such terms as "up and down" or "dominating and dominated" as appeared in Dahrendorf's statements. The idea that these words and statements are to emphasize in essence regarding the basic structure of society or any organized social entity seems straightforward: "(wherever) men live together and lay foundations of forms of social organization," (Dahrendorf, 1969:212) the positions that men occupy are divided into two basic units, that of domination and of subordination. The only difference between the positional attribute of the hexagram lines and Dahrendorf's statements is that the upper and the lower units in the hexagram contain a smaller replica of themselves, i.e., the upper and the lower units divide further into upper and lower components (positions).

A sufficient explication on the meaning of the four middle positions in the context of a hexagram will not be complete until all the positions of the hexagram and the situational variation of lines are brought to clarification. As our discussion progresses, therefore, a further elaboration will be done on the meanings of the four middle positions.

We are now ready to address the top and the bottom positions which have been put aside until now. Why these two positions are separated from the four middle positions can be explained by a characterization of them rendered by Wang Bi. In the passage quoted on the previous page, Wang Bi explains, "neither of these positions has a constant status and since situations have no regular representation in either place, these positions are not to be designated as either yin or yang. Whereas there is a fixed order for noble and humble positions, there are no regular masters for the ending and the beginning positions." What Wang Bi emphasizes is simply that the positions do not directly belong to a formal, hierarchical rank order system of social organization. Let us recall the interpretation of the hexagram as a schematic representation of the hierarchically organized social formation of the Chinese Empire. In this specific application, the bottom position is interpreted as corresponding to that of "common people," the second "lower officials," the third "heads of the regional administration" or "higher ranking officials," and so on. What then is a common factor underlying the two positions, the top and the bottom positions? Wang Bi suggests the answer can be found in that "neither of these positions has a constant status and . . . . situations have no regular representation in either place." Therefore, both positions share the common characteristic that they represent "off-line" positions entrusted with no formal function in the Chinese Empire, both outside the line of the formal hierarchical order. These positions lie outside the main stage of a situation whose chief characteristics are determined mainly by the centrally located core elements, i.e., the principal actors represented by the middle four positions of a hexagram.

This interpretation also finds a suitable illustration in the case that the hexagram applies to the family situation. Here the top and the bottom places are said to represent the positions of "grandparents" and "youngest child," respectively (Choi, 1992:23; Lee, 1997:43-46; also see endnote [2] of this chapter). The analogy can be seen where the "ex-emperor in retirement or sage" and the "common people" are analogous to the "grandparents" and the "youngest child." "Grandparents" play no "constant" or "regular" role in the management of family affairs once they have passed the headship of their family to their grown children. "The youngest child" supposedly is a family member who is not yet allowed to participate in the management of family affairs due to his youth or immaturity. Thus, both positions are considered to correspond to those seated outside of the main action field of principal actors acting or interacting under a situational context represented by a hexagram.

A crucial difference between the top and the bottom positions may be noted, however. While the top position represents that of a person (or persons) passing out of a situation due to old age or retirement, the bottom position is called the beginning line because it represents someone waiting to advance into the main stage of an action field. In a social organization, there is always someone who carries out actions mostly on orders from above, and therefore under ordinary situations,[4] is not yet in a position to exercise any significant influence over other positions. In contrast to this bottom or beginning position, the top position is called the ending line. It symbolizes a position of someone who once had reached the apex of authority and presently, under a given situation, is "out of office" and thus vested with no formal power. This position is placed on the top, the most exalted position of honor, yet stays out of the main action field where the activities of people incumbent in formal offices are staged. Thus, Wang Bi comments upon this position, "although noble, he lacks a position" (Lynn, 1994:33).[5]

Now, let us sum up and elaborate upon what we have discussed so far with respect to the hierarchical ordering of the six positions in the hexagram. First, the four middle positions of the hexagram are grouped into two units, the upper and lower, by pairing up the adjacent two positions each into a unit. It is thereby said, in line with Wang Bi's interpretation (Lynn, 1994:34), that "the fifth place and the third place each occupy the upper-most position" in their respective units. And, this leaves "the fourth place and the second place each [occupying] the lowest position" in their respective units. Then, the question arises, what do the corresponding positions in the two different units have in common and how do they differ from each other? Aside the obvious distinction and similarity between them as being located at the "uppermost" places or "lowest" places respectively in their "upper" and "lower" unit, how else can we characterize more specifically the relationship between the two positions?

To address this question, I will begin with the relationship between the fifth and third positions. Of these two positions, there is a brief explanation in the *Commentary on the Appended Phrases* [Xici zhuan], *Part One* (one of the *Ten Commentaries*): "The third and the fifth lines involve the same kind of merit but differ as to position" (Lynn, 1994:92). Wang Bi clarifies this statement with the following commentary: "Their yang merit is identical . . . . (but between them) there is the difference between nobility and servility" (Lynn, 1994:92). (A more detailed explanation of "yang" will be provided later. For the time being, let us assume simply that the term is used to indicate a "leadership" function that a position holder performs for a hierarchically organized social group.) The words "nobility" and "servility" are more self-explanatory. A person in a position of nobility controls others below him and makes them work upon his orders. On the other hand, one in a position of servility takes orders from those above him and is engaged in works upon their orders. Following from this, Wang Bi's statement quoted above can be interpreted to mean that the fifth and the third positions have an identical function in their leadership position, but they differ in their "nobility" and "servility." The former holds the leadership position in the "governing" or "regulating" unit and the latter performs the leadership function for the "operative" unit working under the control of the former.[6] It is in this context that the fifth place, under ordinary situations, is often called the "ruler" of an entire hexagram (Lynn, 1994:92).

This interpretation matches quite well with the illustration of the respective positions of the hexagram and their application in specific cases. In the case where the hexagram is seen to be a symbolic representation of the Chinese Empire where bureaucratically organized political institutions played the key role, the fifth place is viewed as representing the position of emperor, the supreme ruler of the Empire. The third place corresponds to the leadership position of the regional administration or a higher-ranking official. Thus, the combination of Wang Bi's view of the respective significance of the fifth and the third positions and the application of the hexagram to the structure of the Chinese Empire provides a good match. The positions of "emperor" and "the head of the local administration" converge well with Wang Bi's view that "they (the fifth and the third positions) have an identical function in their leadership position . . . . (but) they are different in that while the former holds the leadership position in the 'governing' or 'regulating' unit, the latter performs the leadership function for the "operative" unit working under the control of the former." The same line of reasoning applies equally well to occasions when the hexagram is used to describe family situations. As we have seen, the hierarchical make-up of the family structure is characterized as consisting of two generation-units, the parents and the children's generation. Hence, the fifth position is considered as representing the head figure of the parent generation and the third position is that of the second generation. Those who are familiar with Asian culture know that Asian societies used to have, and still have, strict norms for enforcing a status distinction between the sexes and between the young and the old. Thus, the father acts as the head of a family and is venerated for his position as such, and the oldest son is treated as person who stands out as the leader among children.

The meanings attributed to the fourth and the second positions are a little more complicated than the two "yang" positions discussed above. Wang Bi comments on these two lower positions by stating "since the second place and the fourth place each occupy the lowest position in their respective trigrams, how indeed could we fail to call them yin positions?" And, it was already pointed out that yang involves an idea associated with a leadership function. The dualism between yang and yin results in yin conveying an idea that is opposite yet complementary to what is characterized as yang.[7] "Yin positions," then, obviously refer to the subordinate status of positions being placed under the leadership represented respectively by the fifth and the third positions. Of course, the relationship between these two lower positions is viewed as analogous to that between the fifth and the third positions. In other words, the same statement, "(they) involve the same kind of merit, but differ as to position," applies equally in describing the relationship between the two lower positions (Lynn, 1994:33). Nevertheless, in the case of the fourth and the second positions, "the same kind of merit" in content carries the opposite meaning, that both of them are equally in the "yin" (subordinate) position. So, it should be read that they (the fourth and the second positions) have an identical function in their *subordinate* position, but they are different in that while the former holds the subordinate position in the "governing" or "regulating" unit and the latter represents that which belongs to the "operative" unit working under the control of the former.

However, as I have already pointed out, the positional meanings of the fourth and the second positions are a little more complicated than the two "yang" (leadership) positions above them. Notice that the first, beginning position is immediately below the second position. Where the hexagram is interpreted as a symbolic representation of the stratification system of the Chinese Empire, the first position symbolizes the "common people." The people represented by a first position should not play any "constant" or "regular" roles in the formal hierarchy and, therefore, their influence should not be taken into account "under ordinary situations." Nevertheless, as governed subjects, they are subject to the authority of those above them. This, according to the *I Ching*, makes the second position that of "honor" — a position empowered to exercise authority due to its responsibility for administrative works dealing with those at the lowest position. Thus, Wang Bi (Lynn, 1994:91-92) comments upon this position, "Second lines occupy positions of harmony and centrality. Thus for the most part they involve honor . . . . Second lines are able to be 'without blame' by being soft or yielding and being centrally placed." The comment "for the most part they involve honor" means that the *I Ching*, for the most part, gives favorable judgments for those who occupy the second position. In other words, occupants of this position are judged to enjoy a certain degree of prestige, advantages, or a state of well-being under ordinary situations. The latter part of the comment, "second lines are able to be 'without blame' by being soft or yielding and being centrally placed," is a behavioral maxim that, if followed, is supposedly beneficial for those who occupy this position. It gives the advice that since they are in between the governed subjects and those watching over them from above, it would be beneficial for them to maintain a moderate and balanced posture while being obedient to their superiors. Of course, the specific condition of a particular actor (or actors) in this second position must be understood in terms of the total context of the situation represented by the entire hexagram structure.

With respect to the fourth position, Wang Bi, commenting upon a related account written in one of the old Commentaries, offers his own comment as follows: "That fourth lines often involve fear is because they are near the rulers. In terms of its Dao, the soft or yielding has to provide aid and assistance" (Lynn, 1994:92). At least in Asian societies, the head of an organization such as the emperor or the father was revered as a patriarchal ruler who wielded power demanding careful deference to his authority. Deference then is of greater importance for those who "are immediately next to the rulers" (Lynn, 1994:92). The fourth position corresponds to those who, like ministers of the royal court or mother, attend closely on the "ruler" represented by the fifth position. Traditionally, the function of their position is not leadership. Since it is in a "yin (soft and yielding)" position, its primary function, as far as the *I Ching* views it as a matter of principle ("Dao"), lies in providing "aid and assistance" for the ruler. Thus, it is said, "they often involve fear." In following, the messages of the *I Ching* given to the occupants of this position are often filled with cautious warnings about their insecure or uncomfortable situations.

We are now ready to take up an additional and more comprehensive perspective of the structural components of a situation represented by the graphic symbol of a hexagram. A simple and obvious fact we should take note of is that whereas the position holders of the first line are not given any "formal" roles to exercise power within a given social organization, their existence is the main reason why the roles performed by those at the second and the third positions are instituted. In other words, the reason people who are in charge of administration or leadership exist is obviously because there are people who are to be governed. This makes the lower three positions of the hexagram bound into a functionally interrelated unit whose constituent members are divided into those with governing functions and those who are subject to the governing functions exercised by the former. Obviously, the governed subjects are represented by the first position while the second and the third positions stand for the ones with governing functions. To recapitulate, remember that the *I Ching* views the third position as a "yang (leadership)" position whereas the second one is viewed as a position involving "honor" and also being "centrally placed." As explained earlier, the fifth and the fourth positions put together form the higher echelon of incumbent governing elites. This then makes the third and the second positions the governing elites of the lower echelon. And finally, the first and lowest position, considering its relationship with the second and the third positions, is viewed to form a functionally interrelated unit with the second and the third positions. As a matter of fact, the three positions located in the lower half of the hexagram have been interpreted as representing the regional or periphery structure of the political community of traditional Chinese society. The conventional interpretation that views each of the three positions to represent respectively "common people," "low ranking officials," and "head of the regional administration" gives a clear illustration of this perspective. Meanwhile, the top three lines, i.e., the positions indicating respectively those of "ministers at the royal court," "reigning emperor" and "ex-emperor in retirement" or "sage," are interpreted to constitute the upper echelon of governing elites located at the core of the power structure.

A three-line complex made up of three broken or unbroken lines is called a "trigram (*shuo gua*)." The *I Ching* views a political community or a social organization as consisting of two primary units, (1) the core group of governing elites located at the center and (2) the periphery group under the rule of the former. Since these two basic units are composed of three positions each, these two trigrams make up a hexagram. Details on the significance of trigrams in the context of the hexagram will be discussed later. For now, it is sufficient to point out that a pair of trigrams arranged one atop the other is a reflection of a social organization. Now, let us sum up what we have discussed so far about the meanings of the six positions in the hexagram. First, look at <Figure 1>.

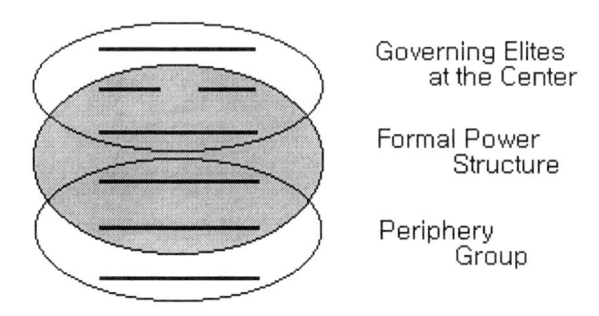

<Figure 1> The Structural Components of the Hexagram

<Figure 1> presents a miniature image of the social world as conceived by the *I Ching*. Notice that the space surrounding a hexagram is divided into several sub-areas. There are two kinds of sub-areas, shaded and unshaded, and three circles divide the six positions into three units. Of course, the shaded, unshaded and encircled areas overlap one another. This double and triple overlapping structure is indicative of the complexity of a conceptual framework used to analyze the structure of a socially organized entity. The two positions, the top

and the bottom, are located in the unshaded area and lie outside the formal power structure or out of the formal line of authority. Nevertheless, these two positions are distinguished from each other by the fact that the top position belongs to the "noble" elite group at the center of power and the bottom one is of governed subjects who are subjected to the authority of those above, but have no one below themselves in the hierarchical system. The four middle positions that lie in the shaded area compose the formal power structure manned by incumbent officials including the top ruler at the fifth position. These constitute the governing organization that rules over the subjects represented by the bottom position. However, as I mentioned above, the four middle positions are divided into two different units, one at the center and other at the periphery. And, further, the two positions in each unit are differentiated in their functions and rankings.

What merits would this kind of a complex conceptualization have when viewing the essential nature of the social reality that existed in China? How can it be compared to modern perspectives in sociology towards the stratification system of human society? A fuller exploration of these questions and more will have to wait until all the meanings associated with the hexagrams and its component elements are brought to clarification. At this point, however, let me just point out the following. In Asian societies where the influence of Confucian ideology has loomed large, amongst the five basic human relations,[8] the relationship between the ruler and the ruled and between the father and the son had been regarded as having the most fundamental significance. And, given this perspective, it is understandable that intellectuals in ancient China, especially Confucian philosophers, believed the operation and management of their society would depend mainly upon the states of relations between the ruler and the ruled subjects and between father and son. Accordingly, the schematic representation of the sociopolitical world as figured by the *I Ching* should have made ample sense to generations of intellectuals in China, an image of the world as people of the Chinese civilization thought it to be. When applied to the social system of their country, the hexagram carried a miniature image of the Empire where sovereign, ranking officials served the bureaucratically organized government and common people were subservient to those above them. When the hexagram applied to the family system, it provided a miniature image of the typical family where grandparents, father, mother, and their children made up a familial hierarchical order. Lynn (1944:8) quite aptly summarizes the basic perspectives of the *I Ching* into three points:

1. Human society is by nature hierarchical.
2. The state is the family writ large, and the family is the state in miniature.
3. Both state and family are by nature patriarchies.

The beliefs and values put forward by the above statements reflect not only the existing order of the society experienced actually as such by the native people of ancient China, but also what they thought it ought to be. It would be in this context that the *I Ching* provided a comprehensive and convincing conceptual frame of reference with which intellectuals of China were able to gauge the life situations of their own society. In sum, the image of the social world presented by the *I Ching* fit well with what the native people believed to be actuality and also with what they believed should exist.

Although the *I Ching* is not free of its culturally conditioned typical prejudices and values, formulating a graphic representation of the stratification system of bureaucratic Chinese society and its hierarchical relationship is not an easy feat or a meaningless task, even to the eyes of sociologists today. However, the remarkably unique aspect of the *I Ching* that draws our attention does not lie merely in this kind of a schematic representation of the stratification system of old China. A rather important and interesting feature of the *I Ching*, as I see it, can be found in the representations of "varying situations" in the stratification system by the hexagrams. According to the *I Ching*, individuals meet with unequal life chances depending upon positions they occupy in the hierarchy. Such an "inequality" is included in the formal definition of "class structure" or "stratification system." Wang Bi's comments that "positions are either noble or humble" or that 'nobility' or 'servility' involve the same kind of connotation. Yet, the concept of "varying situations" adds another important dimension to this purely formal aspect of the stratification system that until now has relied upon positional attributes. The power potential of position holders is determined not only by the formal authority entrusted to one's position but also by situation-specific factors operating under a given situation. For instance, a position holder's power potential in relation to others will increase or diminish depending upon the different conditions associated with situationally varying factors or his actual performance in that position. Thus, this kind of situational variation will not only offer different opportunities or limitations upon the activity of people in the same position but will also bring about different outcomes from an identical action. Now, we will begin examining this aspect of the *I Ching*, the role of the hexagram as the schematic representation of the varying situations of a society.

But, before I move on to the next section, there is one issue that requires further clarification with respect to what the six positions of the hexagram signify. Following the interpretation thus far, each position of the hexagram represents a social position. Thus, taken together, the hexagram symbolizes a social organization composed of unequally ranked positions related to one another in a chain of domination and subordination. But, at the same time, the six lines in the hexagram are also often interpreted as a series of temporal stages in the development of a situation or an event. According to this view, each of the six lines of the hexagram indicates a state of a thing or of an individual at one of the stages that must be passed through the course of an event from its inception to the final phase. This "temporal" interpretation has been accepted as being as authentic as the "positional" interpretation by many scholars (Gao, 1995:303; Lee, 1997:43-46; Shchutskii, 1989:219-220; Wilhelm, 1960:45). To further elaborate, let us take a look at an excerpt from Wang Bi's commentary where he states the "hexagram unites a concept as it progresses from its beginning to its end point" (Lynn, 1994:90). Interestingly, a positional interpretation is given in the very same section (see Wang Bi' commentaries on the 9th section, *Commentary on the Appended Phrases, Part Two*, Lynn, 1994:90-92) where this temporal one is presented, yet no explanation is offered for this obvious inconsistency.

One plausible explanation is provided by Helmut Wilhelm, one of the authoritative figures of *I Ching* scholarship in the West. Of the dualistic usage of the hexagram and the motive underlying such mixture of the temporal and spatial dimensions, he offers the following explanation:

> Here, then, change is seen in a temporal schema which not only is unilinear but also incorporates a rigid hierarchical scale . . . . The projection of change into "unchangeable" finds expression here in spatial images of the relation between above and below. Thus the conception rests on the mixture of two categories, time and space. An attempt is made to understand the temporal in spatial terms. Thinking influenced by hierarchical feeling superimposes one dimension of space on that of time. The origin of this fallacy is easy to grasp: the logic of an order easily established in space leads to the wish for an analogous mastery of time that is much more difficult to order — and it was thought that this could be accomplished through borrowing from spatial modes of thought. (1957:213)

The first thing that we note from the above passage is a view of the world in which the order of things is conceptualized primarily in terms of "spatial images of the relation between above and below." "The logic of an order" of this kind, hierarchical in nature and rooted in the belief that things exist as ordered entities, had been deeply rooted in Chinese modes of thought. Let us call this a "hierarchical conception of order." This is both a normative conception and an ontological belief about existing reality concerning what is real but also what ought to be so. This kind of conception regarding the essential nature of the social order underlies the conventional perspective with which the significance of the *I Ching* is accounted for. Wilhelm suggests that this conception of a hierarchical order influenced the conception of time and the temporal development of an event also came to be viewed as having a "rigid hierarchical scale." Accordingly, an event will be viewed as starting from a beginning point, moving up to higher stages of development step by step, then finally coming to completion by reaching its end point. This is like mapping out a hierarchically ordered sequence of an event starting from a beginning stage, through intermediate stages, to its end, and resulting in a scheme that resembles an organized chart. A motive behind this transition of thought from the spatial dimension to the temporal one has been outlined by Wilhelm. He says "The logic of an order easily established in space leads to the wish for an analogous mastery of time that is much more difficult to order — and it was thought that this could be accomplished through borrowing from spatial modes of thought." This seems to provide an adequate account of how the positions of the hexagram had come to acquire the dualistic dimensions of the meanings. Nevertheless, should this be called a "fallacy" as Wilhelm characterizes it to be?

If one's reasoning is guided by sound logic, how can a hexagram express a structural composition of social positions coexisting at a certain point of time and, at the same time, temporal stages of an event progressing along the time dimension? There is also another plausible explanation where such an overlapping or a confusion of the spatial and temporal dimensions is not necessarily conceived as logically inconsistent or fallacious. This author believes this kind of duality should not necessarily be considered a fallacy. Analyzed from a certain sociological perspective, there seems to be a rather simple, yet interesting idea operating in the background of such convergence of the two different dimensions, temporal and spatial. The idea is that if position holders are getting older or are making advances in their career, they do so by moving along a life course or career pattern that develops by stages along a hierarchically ordered line of social positions. The hexagram that represents the hierarchically organized formation of social positions can then be transformed, or unfolded, into a representation of a ladder of temporal stages that individuals are expected to pass through in their family life cycle or career path.

Let us take a closer look at this dualistic usage of the hexagram from a different angle. First, for instance, suppose that we are to construct the life course of a typical person in some meaningful way. Since every person has a unique life experience that differs from other individuals, this task can be compared with constructing an ideal type, or typical pattern, of the life cycle for typical individuals in a given society. One possible way to construct an ideal type of this sort is to plot a series of occupations or social positions that an individual is expected to go through during his life or career span. The resulting scheme would look like a flow chart of occupations or social positions marked with a temporally ordered chain of transition stages. Thus, if we assume a certain ideal type of social organization or individual whose position is advancing along a defined channel of mobility, it is easy to see that each position in hierarchical order corresponds to a stage of transition evolving on a temporal dimension. This allows us to unfold the organizational structure represented by a hexagram onto a time dimension as illustrated in <Figure 2> (see p.33).

<Figure 2> suggests that a position of a hexagram can be interpreted both ways. As you can see from <Figure 2>, the third position of the vertically arranged hexagram *Li* is located in the third place of the horizontally arranged hexagram *Li*. This alteration of form is a representation of the view that a position can be interpreted as a structural component of a social organization and also as a stage of transition in an individual's life cycle or career mobility. <Figure 2> illustrates the epistemological possibility that a situation can be plotted simultaneously on one or both of the dual dimensions, cross-sectional and longitudinal. Thus, while the third position of the vertically arranged hexagram *Li* represents a position holder's situation in the overall context of the organization to which he belongs, it also represents a particular stage or cycle in his or her entire life-cycle.

The explanation presented above regarding the dual meanings of hexagram's positions was created and drafted by this author. However, since there are no other sources of documentation on my explanation, it has not had the opportunity to be proven accurate even though there are no alternative versions or interpretations.

Structural Components of the Hexagram 33

```
        ▲
        │
        │             ── ──
        │             ─────
        │─── ─── ───  ── ──  ─── ─── ───
        │             ─────
        │             ── ──
        │
        │
Temporal                                        ──────▶
dimension                              Spatial
                                       dimension
```

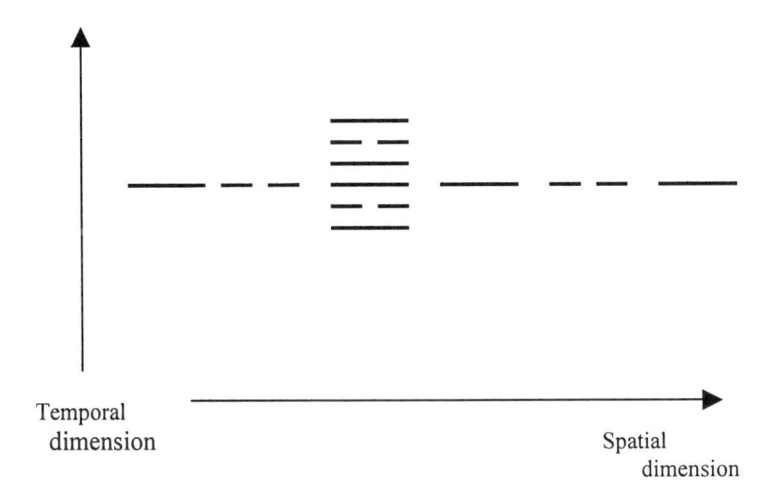

<Figure 2> The Dual Dimensions of the Hexagram

Before I conclude this section, there is still one issue that I must address due to its importance to the meanings represented by the positions of the hexagram. A careful examination of Wilhelm's view on the positions of the hexagram reveals that that he inclines more towards the interpretation of the hexagram's positions that favors the "changes along the time dimension" perspective over the "unchangeable structure on the spatial dimension" perspective. For Wihelm, "the different lines represent progress in the situations" (1960:45).[9] In contrast, there are times in Wang Bi's commentary that tend to lean towards the alternative opinion, towards the view that the positions represent structural components of hierarchically organized human groupings. Thus, T'ang Yung-T'ung (1947:144) sums up Wang Bi's position on this issue by stating "In Wang's interpretation of the I Ching stress is laid upon the 'situation' 時 and the 'position' 位." A clearer and more detailed account on these two terms is offered in a footnote supplemented by Tung (1947:144) himself:

> In the I Ching these terms have a technical meaning, namely, shih 時 the prospects of a certain person whose future is depicted in one of the hexagrams, wei 位 the position of the single "player" depicted in one of the lines (as "the ruler," "the teacher," "the subject," "a member of a family," etc.). With Wang Pi *shih* means the general, favorable or

unfavorable, cosmic situation ("the heavenly market-situation") and *wei* the position somebody occupies in this situation (A ruler may be endangered where a subject is not, etc.).

The position stated in the above passage clearly is at odds with Wilhlem's. However, equally obvious is that both Wang's commentary and Wilhelm's explanation on the positions of the hexagram do include seemingly inconsistent accounts, thus allowing room for dual interpretations. I am more inclined towards the spatial-positional interpretation for two reasons. One reason is that, as a sociologist trained in Western sociological views, the spatial-positional interpretation carries more relevance to theoretical issues in modern sociology than the temporal interpretation. However, the question of the spatial-positional interpretation's particular relevance to issues in modern sociology will be dealt with in later sections. Secondly, as I already pointed out, once the spatial-positional interpretation is given, it can be easily transformed into the temporal one, thus making the latter logically compatible with the former.

2) The Situational Variation of the Lines in the Hierarchical Structure of the Hexagram: Yin and Yang Lines

As general terms, the concepts of yin and yang refer to a wide variety of opposite yet mutually complementing qualities. The case most often cited as exemplifying the cosmic principle of the polarity between yin and yang is the sex distinction between male and female. The two sexes are opposing and complementary traits that by their nature are in need of each other. Darkness and brightness are another pair of polar concepts that have been compared with yin and yang. Wilhelm (1960:30, also Wilhelm, 1967:*lvi*) suggests that the original idea of yin and yang duality may have been derived from these contrasting or alternating phenomena in the natural world. According to his explanation, the Chinese character for yin originally had the meaning of "cloud, thus meant 'overshadowing,' 'the dark'." "The character for yang shows a yak-tail, or pennant fluttering in the sun. Thus, something 'gleaming in the light,' something bright, was meant." Since a remote point in history, however, the duality of yin and yang has developed into a highly abstract concept of broader generality so as to refer to a range of contrasting properties and things also in human phenomena. Bodde (1957:34) presents a summarized list of qualities and things associated with each of the yin and the yang concepts as follows:

Yang principle: brightness, heat, dryness, hardness, activity, masculinity, Heaven, sun, south, above, roundness, odd numbers.

Yin principle: darkness, cold, wetness, softness, quiescence, femininity, Earth, moon, north, below, squareness, even numbers.

The dual notions of yin and yang have been elevated to such a general level and incorporated into the Chinese cosmological thinking so that they have become "the two primary principles, or forces, of the universe, eternally interacting with each other, yet at the same time eternally opposed" (Bodde, 1957:34; cf. Wilhelm, 1967:297).

Of course, the signs of yin and yang (— — and ———) employed to represent the situational variations of the hexagram should have their roots in the same thought system explained above, thus conveying meanings well established in that thought system. In this particular application of the yin-yang dualism, however, we do not take into consideration all the possible meanings of the concepts but a narrower range of meanings that have specific relevance to what the lines of the hexagram indicate. Let us recall that a hexagram consists of six hierarchically arranged yang or yin lines. There is a brief statement related to this in the *Commentary on the Appended Phrases, Part Two* (one of the old Commentaries on the *I Ching*), which explains, "the lines reproduce how things act" (Lynn, 1994:76). We can then replace "things" with "individuals" or "groups of individuals" with little alteration in meaning and result in a statement that explains "the lines reproduce how individuals act." The full implication of this short statement cannot be known or explained sufficiently until all the hexagrams have been subject to clarification in detail. But, at this time I can explain that the polar concepts of yin and yang are used by the *I Ching* to denote the contrasting modes of behavior or influence potentials of individuals who occupy any of the six positions of the hexagram. In essence, it conveys the simple idea that a social organization may have constant formal properties, as seen in the hierarchical arrangement of social positions and the division of functions along those positions, yet still be presented with various constraints or opportunities depending on how the "individuals (who occupy the positions) act." Obviously, the dual concepts of yin and yang work as a binomial classification scheme where the different ways individuals act are classified into one type or the other. But, what sort of specific variations in "how the individuals act" does the *I Ching* intend to describe with the yin and the yang concepts? What does the symbolism expressed with broken or unbroken lines signify with respects to the various situations of a society? A complete answer to this question will have to wait until all the hexagrams have been fully examined. For now, however, let me tentatively adopt a "quick" definition that will provide a rough idea of what the yin and yang lines in the hexagram purports to signify.

I will briefly explain the "firm" and the "yielding" lines — terms chosen by Wilhelm (1967) to translate the yin and yang lines. One is said to be "firm" if he is in a position or has potential or action orientation to exercise influence over others rather than responding passively to influence exerted from others. In this sense, the word "firm" seems to have a meaning equivalent to the terms "active," "initiating," "leading," and "influencing." On the other hand, its opposite "yielding" means "yielding to that which is firm," thus can be used interchangeably with the terms "passive," "conforming," "led," and "influenced." In the *I Ching*, the relative characteristics of actors under a given situation are described mainly in terms of whether the individuals occupying their respective positions are firm or yielding in interacting with one another. Therefore, one of the crucial factors determining the respective situations or fates of individuals is the difference in influence potential that individuals are able to exercise in relation to one another.

We now come to the question of what is the essential nature of the relationship between individuals who are characterized as either firm or yielding? One aspect already presented by the above accounts suggests that influence flows from individuals whose conditions or potentials are indicated by firm lines down to those who are characterized by yielding lines. In terms of influence potential, therefore, in addition to the "formal (*de jure*)" inequality associated with the positions of the hexagram, a "practical (*de facto*)" inequality between individuals or groups of individuals holding the positions is indicated by firm and yielding lines. This practical inequality refers to that of an informal dimension which varies from one situation to another concerning who has upper hands over whom in applying one's will.

The relationship between the firm and yielding ones should not be thought of as in contradiction or conflict, as some social scientists in the West may quickly assume, but rather as in an opposite yet complementary relationship with each other. Bodde gives a concise account about the nature of the relationship between the two contrasting characteristics of yin and yang:

Chinese philosophy is filled with dualisms in which, however, their two component elements are usually regarded as complementary and mutually necessary rather than hostile and incompatible. A common feature of Chinese dualisms, furthermore, is that one of their two elements should be held in higher regard than the other. Here . . . . therefore we have an expression of the [prevalent Chinese] concept of harmony based upon hierarchical difference. (1953:54, quoted in Bodde, 1957:35)

However, there is one thing that we have to be careful about when we apply a general statement regarding the nature of yin and yang to the *I Ching*. As pointed out at the beginning of this chapter, the meaning that a line has in a hexagram, i.e., a specific situation of an individual or group of individuals that a line in a hexagram signifies, will be interpreted on the basis of two factors. One is the position at which the line is located. The other is whether the line is expressed as either a yang or yin line. Therefore, when assessing the meaning of a line, we must take into account the two variables at the same time. In the previous section, we examined the types of social realities the different positions of the hexagram symbolize. Then, what difference will the expression of a line as either yin or yang have on an individual in that line position? An answer to this question can be given immediately and without hesitation. Whether one finds himself in a state of yang or yin makes a crucial difference in his situation and it is this fact that makes the *I Ching* unique as a system of knowledge. A hexagram is made of six precisely arranged lines, and if any component of that situation, represented by a line of a hexagram, changes, then the overall structural composition of the lines change into a different hexagram. That is, if a change occurs in the situation of an individual with respect to his influence potential in relation to others, the overall patterns of relationship among all actors involved in a given situation is also altered. When this occurs, we will say that a change in social situation has taken place in the social organization represented by a given hexagram. In the *I Ching,* this change will be noted by the transformation of a hexagram into another one.

There is another important consequence for individual position holders when their influence potentials change as noted by changes in the lines. The *I Ching* itself offers comments on this transformation of hexagrams:

Good fortune, misfortune, regret, and remorse are all generated from the way the lines moves . . . . The lines reproduce how particular things act, and the images provide likenesses of particular things. As the lines and images move within the hexagrams, so do good fortune and misfortune appear outside them. [This refers to the failure and success that one experiences in matters.][10](Lynn, 1994:76).

A rather simple truth is stated by the above passage — changes in the influence potentials of individuals bring about related changes in the fates, "fortunes or misfortunes," of the individuals involved. However, a simple elementalism that might be inferred from the dualistic thought associated with the contrasting characteristics of yin and yang properties is not suggested here. To illustrate, since yang is "held in higher regard than the other (yin)," individuals in a state of yang may be thought to hold a leading, thus more influential position over those in yin state. Nevertheless, we must be cautious to note that the lines, symbols indicative of situations of individuals, are interpreted in the overall context of an entire hexagram and not apart from the whole. The overall pattern of relationships is formed through the lines of an entire hexagram as an organized unit. To understand the meanings of the individual lines of a hexagram therefore requires an understanding of the hexagram in its entirety. In my opinion, one of the most remarkable aspects of the *I Ching* is this holistic-relational perspective towards the organized nature of human reality. In the next section, we will examine variable patterns of relationships formed between or among people as they are represented by the lines of the hexagram.

Chapter 3

Patterns of Relationships among the Structural Components of the Hexagram

A social situation is represented by a hexagram. As such, a hexagram symbolizes a situation created by involved actors with given tendencies for action interacting with one another. In the *I Ching*, the characteristic situation represented by each of the 64 hexagrams is epitomized in the name given to that hexagram. For example, the hexagram *Bi* (☵☷) (translated as *Closeness* by Lynn, 1994:184; as *Holding Together* or *Union* by Wilhelm, 1967:35) gets its name because it represents a strong integration among all involved actors under the unitary leadership of a ruling monarch or a position holder at the helm of a given social organization (Cf. Lee, 1997:147-155). Under this situation, the state of relationships among members of the social organization is not the same as a functionally integrated situation explained by social theorists with a functionalistic orientation. Rather, the situation of *Bi* represents a situation with the monopoly of political influence being highly concentrated upon the ruling figure. Thus, this is a situation where a strong integration is maintained but only due to the power holder's superior ability to compel or induce loyalty from all the other actors involved in that situation. The detailed analyses on individual hexagrams are reserved for later sections, at which point we will see how individual hexagrams with unique line compositions represent specific social situations.

Once again, the example presented above emphasizes the point made in the preceding section — the meaning of a situation represented by a given hexagram is related to the particular composition of the lines of that hexagram. In the case of the hexagram *Bi* (☷☵), the only yang (or firm) line is present at the fifth position (the position of the ruler for the entire hexagram), and the remaining lines are all yin (yielding). It conveys the image of "holding together," a type of integration centered around a strong leadership of the principal ruling figure located at the fifth position. Thus, as illustrated by this example, the overall meaning of the situation represented by the hexagram *Bi* is understood in reference to the specific configuration of all its constituent lines considered as a whole.

It is important, however, to keep in mind that a hexagram is made up of multiple interlocking layers of component units that give rise to doubly and triply overlapping relationships among its constituent members. This implies that the relationships among members of a social organization can be analyzed into several sub-sets of relationships. If you recall from the previous chapter, the second and third positions together form a sub-unit of a hexagram, and thereby a dyadic relationship would be formed between these two position holders in a given social organization. For illustration, let us separate this unit from the hexagram and examine possible patterns of relationship between these two positions. Since there are only two possibilities, yin or yang, for each position, all the possible variations are expressed as follows:

The same is true of the fourth and fifth positions also. The four possible combinations of the lines above indicate the four possible situational variations of patterns of relationship between two individuals or groups of individuals who occupy higher and lower (or dominant and subordinate) positions respectively. The type of relationship formed between the dyadic parties depends on the influence potential each interacting partner can exercise in relation to the other. This leads us to analyze the differences in inter-personal or inter-group situations and the relationship between the two parties in unequal positions as signified by each of the four possible variations of the two-line complexes. How are the four different patterns of relationships distinguished from one another? This question also applies to the more complex cases of triadic relations represented by the trigrams.

Now, when taking into consideration relationships within sub-units, we become involved with a rather complex issue. In the case of the hexagram *Bi*, the dominant position of the sole yang line is located at the fifth place presiding over all other yin lines. This implies that under this particular, highly integrated situation we do not have to take into account any sub-group formation within the appropriate social organization. But, there are other hexagrams in which sub-groups form, and we therefore have to take into consideration the dyadic or triadic sub-set relationships to gain an understanding of characteristic features of the entire hexagram.

The case requires an additional consideration. Depending upon whether a hexagram is viewed as composed of a pair of three-line composites (trigrams) or of more finely divided units involving dyadic relations, the situation represented by the hexagram may be subject to different interpretations. How then do we analyze any given hexagram in terms of the characteristic formation of its component units? How do we determine the most appropriate way to interpret the situation represented by a hexagram? For now, let me simply say the analysis of a given hexagram depends upon the situationally determined, overall condition of the hexagram itself. From a sociological perspective, this reluctance to lay down any unitary principle for analyzing the component units of a hexagram is based on a simple, yet seemingly convincing idea: the prevailing condition of a social organization as a whole will determine what kinds of sub-groups or sub-sets of relations are formed within that social organization, and, for the same reason, the existence of sub-groups or sub-sets of relations formed within the social organization will reflect the characteristic condition of the social formation that exist at that point of time. To put it simply, there is no fixed and permanent principle with which the formation of social groupings can be determined and thereby identified. It is dependent on the overall condition of a given social organization that changes from situation to situation.

Nevertheless, to understand a social situation represented by a hexagram as a whole requires us to somehow examine the specific patterns of dyadic or triadic relations found among the individual lines of that hexagram. By this we are now presented with the dilemma of determining with which unit of analysis we should begin. The nature of the difficulty here is one of circular logic — to understand the whole, its parts have to be understood; yet, to understand the parts, the whole has to be understood. This kind of dilemma is similarly encountered when readers attempt to understand the meaning of sentences written in a foreign language. Faced with the problem of understanding a sentence either by examining the sentence as a whole or word by word, the strategy usually adopted by learners of foreign language is simply to acquaint themselves with the meanings of single words. Although eventually one realizes that it is not sufficient to learn meanings of words apart from the actual operations of those words in the sentences in which they are used, it does some effective service in the process of learning a new language. So, we will start likewise with some general principles to interpret the situational variations formed within the partial context of dyadic and triadic relations, rather than a hexagram as a whole.

But, before we proceed, to establish a comparable frame of reference, I would like to bring up a perspective from Western sociology that is an interesting counterpart to the topic we are about to approach. The task of interpreting the dyadic and triadic relations in view of all the possible combinations of yin and yang is closely analogous to a topic which Simmel (1950) dealt with in his so-called "formal" sociology. His formal sociology is best known and significant in its attempt to establish a unique domain of sociological studies by developing an extensive typology on all possible "forms" of "dyad" and "triad" relations among individuals or groups of individuals (Wolf, 1950). Particularly interesting is Simmel's analysis of various forms of dyad or triad relations among individuals in terms of their influence potentials. This is obvious if we scan through the major terms that appear most frequently in his analysis of so-called social "forms." They include such terms as "superordination," "subordination," "domination," "downward gradation," "upward gradation," and so on,[1] which we have become familiar with through the previous discussions. Thus, we detect some definite similarity between Simmel's interest in the patterns of social relationships and the ways in which social situations are depicted in the *I Ching*.[2] To be more specific, I would like to bring out two aspects in which similarities between them show up quite clearly. The most obvious aspect is that the social formation in the *I Ching* as represented by the hexagram is viewed analyzable into sub-sets of relations involving dyadic and triadic relations. Thus, to both the *I Ching* and Simmel, the dyadic and triadic relationships are the most elementary units of interactions among individuals or groups of individuals in a social relationship. The second aspect is that the essential patterns and nature of the dyadic and triadic relationships are characterized mostly in terms of influence potentials that the actors involved exercise in relation to one another. Differentials in power potentials, as we have seen, are expressed in terms of yin and yang lines (firm and yielding lines), each having to do with subordination and domination, respectively. It may be said, therefore, that Simmel's formal sociology is, in the aspects explained in the foregoing, rested upon the same orientations as those found in the *I Ching*.

We are now ready to address the question of how the *I Ching* characterize patterns of dyadic or triadic relations between or among individuals in interactive situations. As our discussion progresses, we may find that some explanations on certain components of the hexagram do not match well with explanations on other components. This problem seems to arise because the various text materials and commentaries written on the components of the hexagram differ in time origin and authorship. As pointed out in the introduction, it is a well-recognized fact among *I Ching* scholars that there is no single frame of reference with which a logically consistent interpretation can be made across all the text materials. In the following discussion, if important inconsistencies are found they will be drawn to our attention. However, at the same time, I will exercise some discretion so that when conflicting interpretations or ambiguities arise, I will move along a track that is sound and rational by today's standards of social sciences.

1) Situational Patterns of the Dyadic Relationship

In the *I Ching*, the four possible variations in patterns of dyadic relations are represented with a set of graphic symbols as shown previously: ― ―, ― ― ―, ― ―, ―――. This typology applies equally to each of the two possible pairs of the dyadic relations in the hexagram, between the fourth and fifth positions and between the second and third positions. If the formally defined hierarchy of positions is taken into account, the upper position is called the "yang" (leading) position and the lower one is "yin" (being led). In the tradition of the *I Ching*, if a situation occurs so that these two lines "hold together" to form an "interdependent" dyadic relation, the line at the upper place is said to "ride" on that at the lower place. And, the line at the lower position is referred to as "carrying" the upper position (Gao, 1995:312; Lynn, 1994:29, 41; Wilhelm, 1950:362)[3]. These two terms, "riding" and "carrying," are used to indicate that a mutually interdependent dyadic relationship is in formation between the two parties represented by the respective lines. However, these terms also imply that under certain situations no such dyadic relation would be formed. In the *I Ching*, every possible pattern of the relationship between the two lines can be expressed through yin-yang variations as follows:

— — : The yang line above, the yin line below. Thus, the one who exercises *de facto* leadership, as normally expected for the leadership position in a formal hierarchy, is "riding" on the occupant of a subordinate position who yields to the authority from above him. The *I Ching* generally renders a favorable judgment to this kind of relationship, this being related to the "hierarchical conception of order." As stated earlier, this concept was part of a specific world view held by the people of the old Chinese civilization and is typically expressed in Confucius's doctrine known as the *Rectification of Names* (Legge, 1971: 263-264). This doctrine refers to a Confucian moral maxim emphasizing that one's actual behavior must comply with normative expectations laid down for the social position assigned to him. The spirit of the normative expectations is to promote a desirable social order by inducing individuals to maintain their proper standings in line with the hierarchically organized order of society. This principle is well exemplified in the advice Confucius gave to a feudal lord (the *Duke Ching*) who inquired about the elements of a good government: "there is government, when the prince is prince, and the minister is minister; when the father is father, and the son is son" (Legge, 1971:256). Thus, the type of relationship expressed here reflects a proper or "harmonious" order, viewed as such from the Confucian moral principle (Lee, 1997:46). For this reason, it is said that each position in this type of relationship is "appropriately occupied,"[4] and, therefore, this situation in general is judged to be a "favorable situation" (Gao, 1995: 302-319).

— — : The yin line above, the yang line below. This is the opposite of the situation above, so it is said that the positions are "not appropriately occupied" (Gao, 1995:302-319): a yielding individual is in the leadership position and the one who takes the lead in action is in the lower, subordinate position. Thus, viewed from the hierarchical conception of order, this type of relationship is seen as "abnormal" or "incongruous." The actual roles of the dyadic partners are not in agreement with what is expected from their formal positions and, therefore, rather "unfavorable" judgments are often rendered on the position holders in this situation (Gao, 1995: 304). Interestingly, this type of situation is not seriously taken into consideration by Western sociology. It can be said that Western sociology generally views potentials for power or influence as a "structurally determined" property, something only formally vested in the positions of a social organization.[5] Consequently, a formal power structure tends to be equated with the distribution of real power potentials to the appropriate members of the group in question. As far as the *I Ching* views it, however, the coincidence or, to use Wang Bi's expression, "congruity" between the formally invested power and one's actual potential to exercise the formal power vested to his position is not guaranteed at all times, rather it varies according to the situation. Recall that the *I Ching* means the Book of Changes. One's power potential undergoes changes, expanding or contracting as situations change.

───── : The two yang lines are at both the high and low positions. Since both are actively seeking to engage leading role, there would be little possibility to form a dyadic relation that can be characterized as "carrying or riding." In other words, no harmoniously interdependent relationship is formed between these two position holders. However, according to Lee's explanation (1997:46), since activism and rivalry on the parts of the involved actors are implied in this situation, this type of dyadic relations may produce positive effects when the overall condition of a social organization is geared toward dynamic development. However, what will happen if the involved actors are not "held together" under this situation? Wang Bi comments on this by saying *"resonance* provides an image of shared purpose" (Lynn, 1994:29). Resonance refers to the tendency to seek a union or fellowship with someone who is not directly related but has a shared purpose. Thus, in case of any situation represented by a hexagram, a resonant relationship may be formed between actors who occupy positions located apart from each other. For example, a position holder at the second position may form a resonant relationship with one in the fifth position. There is a simple and plausible reason for the tendency to form a resonant relationship. If one has some difficulty in carrying out a harmonious relationship with others closely related to him, he will seek for a union with someone else who is distant, yet ready to respond to his needs. This suggests that resonant relationships, if the nature and motivation involved are considered, could be formed between actors whose needs or purposes are complementary to each other. As a matter of fact, in the *I Ching*, "as a rule, firm lines correspond (resonate) with yielding lines only, and vice versa" (Wilhelm, 1967:361; cf. Gao, 1995:342-356)[6]. This principle simply suggests that a resonant relationship would be formed between actors with different yet complementary purposes or needs. Therefore, if this type of dyadic relationship (▬▬) appears in a hexagram, to repeat, each of the two yang lines will look for a resonant partner among lines that are distant but responsive to its needs.

▬ ▬ ▬ ▬: The two yin lines are in both upper and lower positions. This is the opposite of the situation presented above, which means that there is no one who takes the lead. A typical characteristic of this relationship is offered by a characterization rendered in the hexagram *Kun* (a hexagram constituted of all yin lines), "the Dao (fundamental principle) of *Kun* consists of compliance" (Lynn, 1994:144). No one would come forward to initiate action, so "compliance" describes their receptivity towards anyone who comes forward forcefully to take the lead. But, since there is no leading element within them, the expected outcome of this type of situation is the same as the situation expressed with the two yang lines. That is, there is little chance of forming a dyadic relation that can be characterized as "carrying or riding." And, depending upon the condition of a hexagram as a whole, this situation may give rise to a formation of "resonating" relationships between position holders who are distantly located in separate sub-units.

The above accounts on the patterns of dyadic relationship between a pair of lines can be applied where the relationship between two lines have to be understood only in context of the two. But a hexagram consists of six lines and the relationship between any pair of two lines will not be formed only in the context of the two. Therefore, the above typology should not be regarded as a general scheme with which the characteristic of any possible dyadic relationship between two lines is interpreted. As far as the *I Ching* is concerned, this is because the relationship between or among individual lines should be assessed, as I have emphasized, not only in terms of the lines themselves but in the total context of a given hexagram. In this holistic-relational perspective, a specific situation should be regarded as inseparably correlated with the conditions of the overall situation, and, accordingly, there will be always more than just two parties involved even where two parties interact with each other. Of course, this holistic perspective does not deny the workings of the yin-yang principle underlying the formation of interpersonal (or inter-group) relationships. Rather, it is firmly based on that principle. After all, individuals or groups form relations by attracting or repelling one another according to how they orient their actions to one another. The giving (yang) and receiving (yin) of influence is regarded as the most fundamental principle that gives rise to the types of social relations. Although social relations take place in the complex hierarchical structure as depicted by the hexagram, the basic principle of variation in human relations are in essence derived from the yin-yang (influencing and being influenced) duality in action orientations. Then, let me finish this section with a passage quoted from Simmel. It provides an interesting perspective compared to that of the *I Ching*. Although it reflects a concern quite similar to what we have discussed so far, it also displays a somewhat similar as well as different outlook towards some basic principles underlying the formation of human relationships.

> The contrasting element complements us; the similar element strengthens us. Contrast excites and stimulates; similarity reassures. Both, though by very different means, give us the feeling that our particular existence is legitimate. But where we feel that the one is appropriate in regard to a particular phenomenon, the other repels us. Contrast then appears hostile, while similarity bores us. Contrast presents us with too high a challenge; similarity, with too low a task. (Simmel, 1950:217-218)

2) Situational Patterns of the Triadic Relationship (Trigrams)

A trigram is a three-line complex made up of three yin or yang lines arranged one over the other in hierarchical sequence. As we can see, since there are three positions and two variations of a line, either yin or yang, for each of the positions, the possible combinations of the lines results in eight unique trigrams in all. And, the total number of unique combinations of two trigrams for every possible individual hexagram can be obtained by a simple calculation, "8 x 8 = 64."

Understanding the situational meanings of a hexagram, the meanings of its sub-units represented by the two trigrams comprising the hexagram and their combined effects must be taken into consideration. In fact, it has been an established practice in the tradition of *I Ching* scholarship that a hexagram is viewed to consist of two constituent trigrams, and, therefore, that the meanings suggested by the two trigrams are taken respectively and jointly into consideration to make a judgment about the situational meanings of both the hexagram and its individual lines. For example, the *Commentary on the Images* of the hexagram *Xiaoxu* (Lesser Domestication) states: "Wind moves through the Heaven: this constitutes the Image of *Xiaoxu*. In the same way, the noble man cultivates his civil virtues. (Here one finds that he cannot yet exercise his power, and this is why one here can do nothing more than 'cultivate his civil virtue)" (Lynn, 1994:192).[7] "Wind" and "Heaven" refer to symbolic images that the *I Ching* uses to characterize each of the two constituent trigrams of the hexagram *Xiaoxu*, respectively. Shortly, I will explain the specific ideas associated with such symbolic images in regards to each of the eight trigrams. But, before we set out to discuss the trigrams in detail, let me bring up some preliminary issues that must be dealt with first so that I do not hastily lead unprepared readers into the mazes of mysterious and seemingly irrelevant symbolism associated with the topic at hand.

First of all, it is not unreasonable to view a social organization as being divided into two sub-groups, the ruling elite group at the center and the operative group in the periphery. It also does not seem unreasonable to maintain that a characteristic situation of a social organization can be understood in terms of the pattern in which its sub-groups relate to each other. And further, it can also be assumed that the possible modes of relationships between the two sub-groups would vary depending upon the type of action orientation that each of them as a group displays towards the other. Now, suppose that the trigrams are a set of symbolic devises that represent typical modes of the action orientation of each sub-group. Then, the meaning of a situation represented by a hexagram can be interpreted in the light of the combined effects of the action orientation of the two sub-groups indicated respectively by the two trigrams. But, we encounter one problem with this kind of an interpretive scheme due to the peculiar nature of the text accounts given to the trigrams. Let us examine this problem first.

If a hexagram is believed to consist of two three-line complexes, or trigrams, it follows that a pair of triadic relations is in formation within any social organization. Then, any typical characteristic represented by a trigram refers to the certain attributes that the patterns of relationships of the three interacting parties exhibit at a group level. To put it simply, a trigram, being a component of a hexagram and therefore like the hexagram, refers to human collectivity, featuring a set of attributes that interacting individuals display as a group. Continuing our interpretation of a hexagram as a hierarchically ordered, bureaucratic social organization, it is obvious that the trigrams also refer to a set of certain characteristic modes of relationships among individuals holding unequal statuses. Keeping in mind what I have said thus far, let us quickly examine the following passage taken from one of the old Commentaries devoted entirely to explaining the trigrams:

> *Kan* (☵ , Sink Hole) is water, is the drains and ditches, is that which lies low, is the now-straightening and now-bending, and is the bow [and] the wheel. In respect to men, it is the increasingly anxious, the sick at heart, the ones with earaches. It is the trigram of blood, of the color red. In respect to horses, it is those with beautiful backs, those that put their whole hearts into it, those that keep their heads low, those with thin hooves, and those that shamble along. In respect to carriages, it is those that often have calamities [i.e., breakdowns/accidents]. It is penetration, is the moon, and is the stealthy thief. In respect to trees, it is those that are strong with dense centers. (Lynn, 1994:124)

Supposedly the listed things and properties must share a common characteristic to be included under the same category of the single trigram, *Kan*. But, where do we find properties associated with human relationships? Knowing that trigrams are partial components of the hexagrams, how do we reconcile the discrepancy between what we know about the hexagrams so far and the wide variety of natural objects and properties presented in the above list? Is there any place to find a possible path to bridge the broken logical linkage between them?

Gao (1995:229-238) offers a possible explanation for the above questions. According to Gao, the things and properties that the trigrams are said to represent are for the most part natural phenomena. In contrast to this, a substantial portion of the text materials and commentaries on the 64 hexagrams are directly related to human affairs involving social relations, ethics, family organization, political institution, and so on. Such a difference, Gao traces back to a change in people's fundamental living conditions that took place between the two periods when the 8 trigrams and the 64 hexagrams were produced, respectively. During the period when the trigrams were invented, objects and events in the natural environment were the most important factors that influenced people's lives. Due to this historical background, the trigrams were originally associated with eight objects and events in nature — Heaven, Earth, thunder, wind, water, fire, mountain and lake. Other subsidiary meanings related to such things as horses, man's personality, carriages, etc. also accompany the eight primary imageries. These might have been brought up in a process to expand the use of the original symbolism by relating them to a much broader range of phenomena. At any rate, Gao maintains, the eight objects and events of nature symbolized by the eight trigrams would have been the most important reality for the pre-historic people whose living depended largely upon the conditions of the natural environment.

I Ching scholars generally agree with the view that the 64 hexagrams were derived by superimposing one trigram upon the other (Gao, 1995:56; Legge, 1963:13; Lynn, 1994:4; Wilhelm, 1967:li). As pointed out above, however, the hexagrams came to reflect the conditions of a newly emerging civilization that was radically different from that of the simplistic nomadic society in which the trigrams were born. Political institutions had emerged, and with it came standing armies, bureaucratic organizations, and social ranks of a wide variety. The conditions of the sociopolitical system with which individuals were involved now had become a dominant reality that brought differential opportunities into their lives. According to Gao, this radical transformation of society explains the seemingly unbridgeable gap between the trigrams and the hexagrams regarding the kinds of objects and events to which they refer.

So, how do we address this problem? One reasonable solution seems to be that we discard the trigrams as a unit of analysis and just move on directly to the analysis of the hexagrams because it is only in the latter that we find what we can be call sociological and political ideas. Perhaps, this strategy was adopted by Wang Bi to deal with this problem. A careful reading of his general treatise on the *I Ching*, *General Remarks on the Changes of the Zhou*, reveals that while relatively frequent remarks are made on dyadic relationships between two lines, remarks on trigrams are rare and also rather brief in passing. My impression is that Wang Bi might have wanted to avoid an unnecessary inconsistency or unjustifiable logical juggling that might have occurred by trying to have the meanings of the trigrams fitted into those of the hexagrams which were developed in quite different social and cultural environments. Nevertheless, he still leaves open another possibility with respect to the formation of triadic relations (as represented by trigrams) by saying, "In *Lü* [Treading, Hexagram 10, ☰☱], Third Yin is the ruler of the trigram *Dui* [Lake, Joy] and so in resonance with the trigram *Qian* [Heaven, Pure Yang]. The formation of the entire hexagram depends on this line" (Lynn, 1994:35). In Wang's comment, the trigram *Qian* refers to a three-line composite made up of three yang lines located at the upper three positions. Thus, Wang Bi's comment suggests by implication that the position holder represented by the third yin line is in a "resonant" relation with the ruling elite group at the power center, i.e., with the group involving a triadic relationship which displays a certain typical characteristic symbolized by the trigram *Qian*. What becomes obvious is that the trigrams, if interpreted in this sense, seem to have nothing to do with such symbols as Heaven, horses, and other natural objects. As a matter of fact, Wang Bi, commenting upon a principle related to interpreting these kinds of seemingly irrelevant symbols, says:

> Images (i.e., trigrams and hexagrams)[8] are the means to express ideas. Words [i.e., the texts] are the means to explain the images. To yield ideas completely, there is nothing better than the images, and to yield up the meaning of the images, there is nothing better than words. The words are generated by the images, thus one can ponder the words and so observe what the ideas are. The ideas are yielded up completely by the images, and the images are made explicit by the words. Thus, since the words are the means to explain the images, once one gets the images, he forgets the words, and, since, the images are to allow us to concentrate on the ideas, once one gets the ideas, he forgets the images. (Lynn, 1994:31)

Wang Bi's main point is that the hexagrams, trigrams and related statements in the texts of the *I Ching* are merely symbolic means to convey certain ideas. Then, at least in Wang Bi's view, what are the main ideas represented by the trigrams? Regarding the actual meanings associated with symbolic imageries of the *I Ching*, Wang Bi has this to say:

> This is why anything that corresponds analogously to an idea can serve as its image, and any concept that fits an idea can serve as corroboration of its nature. If the concept involved really has to do with dynamism, why must it only be presented in terms of the horse? And if the analogy used really has to do with compliance, why must it only be presented in terms of the cow? (Lynn, 1994:32).

Wang Bi's intention is expressed clearly in the above passage. He will accept those "images" and "words" as meaningful only as long as they are interpreted as expressing notions that are related to certain qualities or states of human actions or social relationships. But, what ideas are actually conveyed by the trigrams with regard to the possible types or characteristics of the triadic relationships in human groups? Although Wang Bi's position on the "ideas" is very instructive in dealing with the ideas represented by the trigrams, there seems to exist no systematic and detailed account in this regard either in his commentary or in any other's commentary. However, in my opinion, there seems to be an obvious and plausible connection between the line structure of each of the trigrams and some of the abstract attributes of the trigrams or "ideas" conveyed by them as suggested by the *I Ching*. And, it is at this point that we can start to expound upon the sociological meanings of the trigrams.

1) ☰ (*Qian*) : "*Qian* [Pure Yang] means strength and dynamism" (Lynn, 1994:122). Yang lines occupy all the three positions. Thus, all the position holders in their respective places are active and dynamic and are exercising initiatives in actions towards one another. Thus suggested is a balance of influence potentials among the individuals forming the triadic relationships. This is a situation under which all the involved parties are influencing and being influenced by one another. There is a dynamic yet balanced development of events due to mutually stimulating and, at the same time, mutually constraining energies that the involved actors exercise upon one another. Therefore, the main situational characteristic represented by this trigram is dynamic harmony and progress. This type of situation may be compared with what Parsons (1964:491-492) calls as "moving equilibrium." In the *I Ching*, this situation is considered an ideal situation, thus called "the prince and the father" among situations. The activism that is generated by a triadic group under this situation is so dynamic and progressive that the *I Ching* relates this situation to images of various horses that symbolize dynamic progression (Wilhelm, 1967:275).

2) ☷ (*Kun*) : "*Kun* [Pure Yin] means submissiveness and pliancy" (Lynn, 1994:122). Yin lines occupy all the three positions. Since there is no yang line in this trigram, this represents a triadic group in a static state with no leading element to initiate dynamic

Patterns of Relations among the Structural Components 53

activity. Thus, while the trigram *Qian* signifies a triadic group that undergoes a dynamic development through an exchange of mutual influences among the actors involved, this trigram *Kun* expresses the state of a group that is ready to submit to influences from outside if such a source exists. Otherwise, being in a state of "static harmony," little change will take place in things or events under this situation. With no leading element to initiate action, a group characterized by this hexagram will simply go through a cycle of reproducing its pre-established order and continually operating around a fixed form of order. Ironically, we may elicit from this situation an impression that is often held of traditional Asian society — "harmonious," but "static" or "quiescent." Whether this characterization is a true representation of the historical reality of Asian societies is of course not the question here. However, the idea of "static harmony" seems to express well the situational characteristic of the triadic group represented by this trigram *Kun*. It is important to note that this trigram is a symbolic example of the moral virtue of Pure Yin, the virtue of conformity to what one ought to conform. Figuratively speaking, the state symbolized by the trigram *Kun* can be compared to the way things and events on Earth yields to Heaven, the law giver; all the manifestations of things and events on Earth follow what is dictated by the law of Nature. For this reason, the *I Ching* characterizes this trigram with various symbolic imageries bringing up ideas of "submission" to authority or "receptivity" to influences imposed from without:

> *Kun* [Pure Yin] is Earth, is mother, is cloth, is a cooking pot, is frugality, is impartiality, is a cow with calf, is a great cart, is the markings on things, is the multitude of things themselves, and is the handle of things. In respect to soils, it is the kind that is black. (Lynn, 1994:123).

3) ☳ (*Zhen*) : "*Zhen* [Quake] means energizing" (Lynn, 1994:122). In this trigram, the only active element is found in the lowest place. The seasonal image of this trigram is spring, the time when living things on the ground grow vigorously with moisture brought by thunderstorms. ("Thunder" is one of the images symbolizing this trigram.) Notice that, at least in the context of this trigram, the graphic image of the two yin lines seems to

portray rain-falling (in fact, wetness is one of many properties identified with yin, Bodde, 1957:34) while the bottom line then symbolizes the ground that is sprinkled with rain. Thus, this trigram represents a situation in which the position holders in the two upper positions are totally devoted to the nourishment of the one in the lowest position. Aided by those above and free from overpowering authorities, the one who is located at the lowest position is identified as the central figure who is charged with an "energizing" strength for growth. As Wilhelm (1960:41) explains about this trigram, it carries an image of "the strong and rapidly growing son, on whom, as first born, the mother's care and the father's concern are expended."

4) ☴ (*Sun*) : "*Sun* [*compliance*] means accommodation" (Lynn, 1994:122). This trigram is the opposite of the above trigram *Zhen*. It has two yang lines above and a yin line in the lowest position. As the single yin line at the bottom indicates, this trigram is primarily characterized by the "hard labor" performed by the lowest position holder who complies with the guidance of the two strong leaders from above. Thus, the main characteristic of this trigram, compliance and accommodation, is defined in terms of the weighty pressure and rigid control imposed by the ones at the higher positions over the lower one. One interesting thing about this trigram is seen in that the symbolic images attributed to this trigram are clearly associated with the idea of diligent work and profit-seeking behavior. Let us read the following excerpt taken out of the *Explaining the Trigrams*, a commentary exclusively devoted to the trigrams:

> The Gentle ("Compliance" in Lynn's translation) is . . . . the guideline, work . . . . Among men it means the gray-haired; it means those with broad foreheads; it means those with much white in their eyes; it means those close to gain, so that in the market they get threefold value. (Wilhem, 1967:277)[9]

In the above passage, ideas suggested by the words "gray-haired," "broad foreheads" and "those with much white in their eyes' do not seem clear at all. Although some scholars (Lee, 1997:430-431; Wilhelm, 1967:277) come up with some explanations on these, I see no consistent logic or reasonable viewpoint underlying their explanations. However, if we follow Wang Bi's advice and, therefore, seek out possible "ideas" conveyed by such symbolic images, we can make some informative guesses on this rather perplexing symbolism. My interpretation is rather simple: if the lowest position is represented as one who is engaged in hard work under the guidance of strong leaders and who also accumulates wealth owing to his hard labor, the position holders in the two upper positions could be characterized as authoritative figures who rule over the lowest position with stark discipline. Then, the symbolic expressions "gray-haired," "broad foreheads," and "much white in their eyes" can be interpreted as Lee (1997:431) suggests, symbolizing the densely formed yang (i.e., leadership) elements in the upper part of any organic or social entity.

5) ☵ (*Kan*) : "*Kan* [Water] means pitfall" (Lynn, 1994:123). A sole yang line is located in the middle position between two yin lines in the top and the bottom positions, respectively. The *I Ching* characterizes this trigram with the various symbolic images we already cited (p.49). Curiously enough, most of these symbols seem to have been derived from its pictorial image. The yang line indicates movement between unmoving things, represented by the two yin lines — an image of flowing water. Also, "Penetration is suggested by the penetrating line in the middle wedged in between the two weak (yin) lines" (Wilhelm, 1967:278). This also carries the image of something hidden inside — like "blood," "the drains and ditches," "that which lies low," "the sick at heart," "the ones with earaches" and "thief." Also associated with the pictorial image of the trigram is the image of a horse that has a wild courage and a strong backbone but weak legs and a low head that, therefore, stumbles. Thus suggested in this trigram is something in a "pitfall" or an "abysmal" situation (Wilhelm, 1967:277). With respect to patterns of triadic relationships, however, this trigram seems to offer no clue suggesting any ideas that can be related to collective human situations. Supposedly, the one in the middle-ranked position is actually in a position to exercise power while the two other position holders at the top and bottom positions are yielding to the source of influence. To the eyes of the Chinese, it might have been believed that a concentration of influence potential on a middle-ranked position holder located inside a group is an undesirable or rather dangerous situation. Then, why does a similar interpretation not apply to the trigram Zhen (☳) that also has only one yang line at a subordinate

position? It may be explained that the youngest or one at the lowest position under normal situations would not pose a threat to anyone, and especially to the one in the ruling position. However, a person who is immediately next to the ruler and shares a certain measure of authority due to his intermediate position could be an unpredictable factor that it might push his superior into a pitfall if given such an opportunity. And, this trigram could be interpreted to represent such a situation. This reminds us very much of a Machiavellian world-view. As a matter of fact, as we will see ourselves in a series of following discussions, the *I Ching* is full of advice and warnings to those who were supposedly living in the same world as that which Machiavelli should have thought of himself to live in.[10]

6) ☲ (*Li*) : "*Li* (cohesion) means attachment" (Lynn, 1994:123). This is the opposite of the trigram *Kan*. There is a yin line at the center and two yang lines at the top and the bottom positions. This trigram's symbolic meaning of fire seems to be derived from the yin-yang structure this trigram has. The two yang lines symbolizing brightness envelop the middle yin line, a symbol of matter. This results in the characteristic of "dependence on the matter consumed" (Wilhelm, 1960:43). Other symbols such as "turtle," "crab," "snail" and so on represented by this trigram are obviously associated with its pictorial image, something soft (yin) inside covered by the hard shells (yang) outside. These symbolic images should have been extended by association to other related attributes such as "heat," "dryness," "helmet," etc. However, as was the case in the trigram *Kan*, the accounts of the *I Ching* on this particular trigram offer little clue for any characteristic related to collective human situations. Perhaps the only clue is found in the name of the trigram, *Li* (Union), which is said to mean "attachment." It represents a situation in which the two position holders at the top and bottom positions are attached to the one in the middle position. In other words, it represents a triadic group where two parties exercising strong influences are integrated around a position holder in the intermediate position who acts yieldingly to accommodate influences from both above and below. The central role for the integration is played by the second yin line symbolizing an actor with accommodating behavior, a familiar situation to our everyday experience. If a person behaves flexibly enough to play an intermediary role between individuals pressing forward with

Patterns of Relations among the Structural Components 57

strong wills, the group would be integrated around the one with accommodating behavior. But, notice that such a person must occupy the middle, intermediary position in a social organization as represented by the trigram *Li*, a structural condition for this type of integration to be achieved.

7) ☶ (*Gen*) : "*Gen* (Restraint) means cessation" (Lynn, 1994:123). There is a yang line at the top and two yin lines at the middle and the bottom positions. Many of the symbolic images associated with this trigram are related to its pictorial image of a gate. Thus, the *I Ching* says, "*Gen* [Restraint] . . . . is the footpath, is the small stone, is the gate tower . . . . is the gatekeeper, and the palace guard . . . . is the dog . . . ." (Lynn, 1994:124). Other objects such as "tree fruit" and "vine fruit " seem to be derived from the spatial pattern in which its yang and yin lines are arranged: the yin elements that have ceased in movement are located at the bottom and middle places, and the only yang element is still active at the top place. This transmits the idea of a fruit tree bearing fruits in the fall season. "Rat" and "trees . . . . the kind that is sturdy and much gnarled" also seem to be based on the same kind of reasoning — the image of an old tree with signs of death on its trunk. Like some of the other trigrams, the text accounts on this trigram include no symbolic image that can be directly related to any characteristic property in social relationships. Nevertheless, we can draw out more or less meaningful interpretations associated with the symbols attached to this trigram. As we can see, the top line is the leader, both *de facto* and *de jure*. In the triadic group represented by this trigram, all the power is in his hands, thus "Restraint" is the name given to this trigram: "Restraint" communicates the idea of submissive elements under the domination of strong leadership. Viewed from this perspective, the symbolic images of a "gate," the "gatekeeper" and the "dog" acquire a definite meaning as something watching over those who pass through the gate. The symbol "fingers" could be understood as an object that serves to point out definite directions or "serve(s) to hold fast" (Wilhelm, 1967:278-279). An interesting fact is that the *I Ching* describes this situation as indicating "cessation" or inactiveness: no vitality or energy for growth is observed in this situation, and an obvious outcome of this stagnation would be "corruption," an idea also embodied by such symbols as a "rat" that gnaws an established

order secretly from some hidden places.

8) ☱ (*Dui*) : *Dui* [Joy] means to delight (Lynn, 1994:123). A yin line is at the top position, and two yang lines at the middle and bottom positions. This trigram is the opposite of the trigram *Ken*. Wilhelm (1967:279) explains that a number of symbolic images associated with this trigram also have to do with its pictorial image, something open at its upper part. Thus, the following accounts are rendered by the *I Ching* regarding the symbolism in this trigram: "*Dui* [Joy] is . . . . shamaness, is the mouth and tongue" (Lynn, 1994:123). "Shamaness" is related to the "mouth and tongue" in the sense that she is "a woman who speaks" (Wilhelm, 1967:279). Other symbolic images such as "the deterioration [of plant life], and the breaking off of what has been attached" can be explained in a rather different context. Where the trigrams are interpreted as being associated with the geographical directions the trigram *Dui* symbolizes the West that is "connected with the idea of autumn," the season of deteriorating plant life (Wilhelm, 1967:279). However, considering all the symbolic images associated with this trigram, the reasoning behind its name "*Dui* (Joy)" is not clear. At best, I can offer that the name of this trigram is related to its line formation, a yin line at the top and the two yang lines at the middle and bottom position. In contrast to the previous trigram *Ken,* characterized by the restraining power of the top over the subordinate positions, a weak leader who is yielding to the subordinate ones with strong influence potentials characterizes this trigram. Thus, "the sheep," according to Wilhelm (1967:279), an "outwardly weak and inwardly stubborn animal" which "is suggested by the form of the trigram," seems to convey the characteristic condition of the triadic relationship represented by this trigram: two stubborn subordinates under a weak leader. Why then is this trigram called *Dui* or Joy? This may be associated with the fact that this trigram represents a type of situation that is enjoyable at least to those who are in subordinate positions with the ability to exercise freedom in their actions under a weak leader. An interpretation such as this seems to make more sense in view that this interpretation can also be derived from, and thus is consistent with, the interpretation given to the previous trigram *Ken*. As we will remember, "the trigram *Ken* (Restraint) means cessation" (Lynn, 1994:124). *Ken* is called "Restraint" because the strong leader is exercising a restraining power over the two weak subordinates. *Ken*'s situation is

interpreted as having no vital energy for growth and thus "means cessation." Here, in *Ken*, an idea of oppression, rigid control and resulting stagnation is implied. Meanwhile, given the reversed structure in its line formation, the trigram *Dui* exhibits a situational characteristic directly opposite to that of the trigram *Ken*. There are two strong components in the two lower positions that may be described as "free-floating" because there is no strong leader restraining them. These are elements that Wilhelm refers to as "stubborn" as a sheep. Lee (1997:435) suggests that the situation represented by this trigram is a pursuit of pleasure going beyond the boundary of established norms as indicated by another symbol attributed to this trigram, "concubine." Thus, this trigram *Dui* implies situations of unrestrained freedom and pleasure seeking to the point of anomie.

Having finished a brief review of the accounts of the texts and the commentaries related specifically to the trigrams, I would like to sum up the above discussions on the trigrams into two points as follows. First, many of the symbolic images associated with each of the eight trigrams seem to be derived from their pictorial images or other archaic symbolism in the old Chinese civilization, and therefore do not seem to bear any utility or relevance whatsoever for our purpose here. Secondly, a somewhat systematic and meaningful perspective on the varying patterns of triadic social relationships could be identified from those ideas condensed in the names and the meanings of the trigrams (for example, "*Ken* (Restraint) means cessation"). In other words, considering that the trigrams represent patterned types of triadic relationship, what catches our eye is the undeniably meaningful linkage between the formation of the lines of each trigram and the characterization of it as regards the nature of a triadic relationship represented by the trigram. An analysis on this aspect of the trigrams is presented in <Table 1>.

<Table 1> Trigrams and Their Situational Attributes

Line Structure	Name	Meaning (Situational Characteristic of the Triad)
1) ☰	*Qian* (Pure Yang)	Strength and Dynamism (moving equilibrium)

2) ☷ *Kun* (Pure Yin)   Submissiveness and Pliancy (static equilibrium)

3) ☳ *Zhen* (Quake)   Energizing (growth at the bottom)

4) ☴ *Sun* (Compliance)   Accommodation (conformity at the bottom)

5) ☵ *Kan* (Water)   Pitfall (power rested inside)

6) ☲ *Li* (Closeness)   Attachment (integration centered around the middle)

7) ☶ *Gen* (Restraint)   Cessation (*de jure* and *de facto* leader at the top)

8) ☱ *Dui* (Joy)   Delight (joy and pleasure at the middle and bottom)

    The meanings of the trigrams as described thus far bear a good measure of importance because they are an important element of our foundation for interpreting the situations represented by the hexagrams. However, we must be careful when applying the meanings of the trigrams directly to the interpretation of the hexagrams. As already pointed out above, the meanings of the trigrams are only *one* of the basic elements with which the situational meanings of a hexagram are interpreted. If we try to derive the situational meanings of the hexagrams solely from the constituent trigrams, the meanings of the hexagrams may be, so to speak, "underdetermined." After all, a trigram is only a part of a whole hexagram, and a hexagram has a unique structure and meaning that is distinguished from that of the trigram. Thus, once two trigrams are combined to make a hexagram, the hexagram acquires many additional properties that the trigrams do not have as partial units. The hexagram as a whole involves more complex meanings than is implied by its parts.

    Depending upon where a specific trigram is located in a hexagram, either the upper or the lower place, the same trigram refers to rather different social positions. And, for the same reason, each of the lines of the trigram connects rather differently with every other line within a

Patterns of Relations among the Structural Components 61

hexagram. Moreover, in some occasions, due to a situationally specific condition of a social formation, triadic relationships may not be formed at all, as we saw from the example of the hexagram *Bi*. For these cases, it is not necessary to take into consideration the situational characteristics of the triadic relationships (the meanings of the trigrams). Of course, by pointing out the limited utility of the trigrams, I do not imply that we can move directly to the analysis of the situational meanings of the hexagrams without stepping upon the trigrams. First of all, it is a generally agreed fact among *I Ching* scholars that the trigrams gave rise to the hexagrams. Thus, although there seems to be a big logical gap between the meanings signified by the trigrams and the hexagrams, there still is an undeniable connection between them. The ideas of the trigrams nevertheless survived in the hexagrams, but only in ways somewhat discordant with the conditions of the new era that gave rise to the more complex mode of thinking reflected in the hexagrams. When we deal with the situational representations of the individual hexagrams in the coming section, we will have a chance to look at this problem more closely.

3) The Ruler of a Hexagram

Under what kind of structural conditions can we do away with the trigrams in the interpretation of a hexagram? Or, to put it differently, if there are situations in which no triadic groups are formed within a social organization, what is the characteristic of such situations? This question carries important weight because its answer provides an important guideline to analyze the structural components of a hexagram. The rulership of a hexagram offers a clue in answering this question. The ruler of a hexagram refers to the position holder who plays the key role under a given social situation. Of the occupant of this position, Wang Bi says:

> The rare is what the many value; the one that is unique is the one the multitudes make their chief. If one hexagram has five positive lines and one negative, then we have the negative line be the master. If it is a matter of five negative lines and one positive line, then we have the positive line be the master. Now, what the negative seeks after is the positive, and what the positive seeks after is the negative. If the positive is represented by a single line, how could the five negative lines all together ever fail to return to it! And if the negative is represented by a single line, how could the five positive lines all together ever fail to follow it! Thus although a negative line may be humble, its becoming

the master of a hexagram is due to the fact that it occupies the smallest number of positions. And then there are some hexagrams for which one may set aside the hexagram lines and take up instead the two constituent trigrams, for here the substance of the hexagrams involved does not evolve from individual lines. (Lynn, 1994:26)

First, let us look at the last line of this rather long passage quoted above. It describes the specific condition for the formation of triadic relationships within a social organization. Thus, Wang Bi here maintains that there are some hexagrams whose main characteristics are determined by the two trigrams making up the hexagrams. The other point Wang Bi makes is that the presence of the master (or ruler) line for a hexagram indicates that the entire social entity represented by the hexagram is integrated around that specific line. With this latter point, Wang Bi also proposes a specific condition for the presence of the ruling element in a social organization: if everybody is vying for domination except for a single element who is yielding to the influences exerted upon him, the single one who is yielding will play the key role over all the others under the situation; if one is exercising a strong influence over all others who are submissive to the influence, the single strong one will assume the *de facto* leadership role. In both cases, we find strongly integrated situations centered around the one with the most unique characteristic. This is the hypothesis that Wang Bi applies when he analyzes the situations represented by the hexagrams, and to this author, it seems to be a very interesting hypothesis indeed. It is commonsensical to most of us to assume that a social organization is integrated around a strong leadership. Let us call this a yang type of integration. However, there is the possibility that a negative (yin) type of integration centered around the most submissive position also exists. For example, a yielding and understanding mother can play the central role for a family in which strong-willed male figures have difficulties adjusting to one another. But, here again, an actual validity or practical utility of such a perspective does not concern us. Right now, what concerns us is how the hexagrams, with their specific line formations, represent patterned types of social situations; what are the important characteristics and aspects with which those situations differ from one another? We will deal with these subjects in the next section.

Chapter 4

Hexagrams: Representations of Various Types of Social Situations

The main concern of this chapter is focused on the hexagram, the unique typological device with which the *I Ching* depicts variously possible types of social situations. The situations represented by the hexagrams have been believed to have important meanings because they bring about different life chances to individuals or groups of individuals placed under those situations. As explained thus far, the typology is built on two crucial variables, social positions and types of action orientation. And, as far as this author is concerned, there is no mysterious meaning involved with these two variables. The only thing that will make the classification scheme of the *I Ching* look unapproachably complex is that it involves, say, a 2 x 2 x 2 x 2 x 2 x 2 cross-classification table made up of the six levels of social positions and the two types of action orientation, which results in a total number of 64 cells, i.e., the 64 hexagrams (see <Table 2, 1/4 – 4/4>, p.64-67).

Considering the mathematical characteristic of the hexagrams that can be transformed into the binary numeral system,[1] there is no question that the 64 patterned types of social situations were not obtained by inductive reasoning, i.e., by generalizing observed facts. If there was some logical reasoning involved in the development of the hexagrams, it would have been purely deductive reasoning, probably as follows. Assuming that the essential features of social situations are determined by the types of action orientation of acting individuals (yin

<Table 2> 64 Hexagrams

(1/4)

social positions	yin-yang variation (action orientation or power potential)								
top	▬	▬	▬	▬	▬	▬	▬	▬	▬ ▬
Fifth	▬	▬	▬	▬	▬	▬	▬	▬	▬
fourth	▬	▬	▬	▬	▬	▬ ▬	▬ ▬	▬ ▬	▬ ▬
third	▬	▬	▬	▬ ▬	▬ ▬	▬	▬	▬	▬
second	▬	▬ ▬	▬ ▬	▬	▬	▬	▬	▬ ▬	▬ ▬
bottom	▬	▬	▬ ▬	▬	▬ ▬	▬	▬ ▬	▬	▬ ▬
hexagram name	Qian	Gou	Tong-ren	Dun	Lü	Song	Wu-wang	Pi	Xiao-xu	Sun	Jia-ren	Jian	Zhong-fu	Huan	Yi	Guan

(2/4)

social positions	yin-yang variation (action orientation or power potential)										
top											
fifth											
fourth											
third											
second											
bottom											
hexagram name	Dayou	Ding	Li	Lü	Kui	Weiji	Shihe	Jin	Daxu	Gu	Bi	Gen	Sun	Meng	Yi	Bo

(3/4)

social positions	yin-yang variation (action orientation or power potential)											
top	▬▬	▬▬	▬▬	▬▬	▬▬	▬ ▬	▬ ▬	▬ ▬	▬ ▬	▬ ▬	▬ ▬	▬ ▬
fifth	▬▬	▬▬	▬▬	▬▬	▬▬	▬▬	▬ ▬	▬ ▬	▬▬	▬ ▬	▬ ▬	▬ ▬
fourth	▬▬	▬▬	▬▬	▬▬	▬ ▬	▬▬	▬▬	▬ ▬	▬ ▬	▬▬	▬ ▬	▬ ▬
third	▬▬	▬▬	▬ ▬	▬▬	▬▬	▬ ▬	▬▬	▬▬	▬ ▬	▬ ▬	▬▬	▬ ▬
second	▬▬	▬ ▬	▬▬	▬ ▬	▬▬	▬▬	▬ ▬	▬▬	▬▬	▬▬	▬ ▬	▬ ▬
bottom	▬▬	▬▬	▬▬	▬ ▬	▬ ▬	▬ ▬	▬▬	▬▬	▬▬	▬▬	▬▬	▬ ▬
hexagram name	Kuai	Daguo	Ge	Xian	Dui	Kun	Sui	Cui	Xu	Jing	Jiji	Jian	Jie	Xikan	Zhun	Bi

social positions	yin-yang variation (action orientation or power potential)										
top											
fifth											
fourth											
third											
second											
bottom											
hexagram name	Da-zuang	Feng	Feng	Xiao-guo	Gui-mei	Xie	Zhen	Yu	Tai	Sheng	Ming-yi	Qian	Lin	Shi	Fu	Kun

or yang) who respectively occupy unequal positions (6 positions), we obtain a determinate number of possible types of social situations (64) each of which, being constituted of a unique combination of the two variables, is thought to have some unique characteristics. Suppose that on the basis of the above reasoning we have in our hands the 64 hexagrams — all the configurations of social situations that, given the two crucial variables, are thought to be logically possible. Now, the next task would be to write down appropriate interpretive accounts for each of the unique types of situational configurations, hexagrams, created through a purely deductive method by the cross-classification of the two base concepts. The essence of the job at hand is to construct the most plausible meanings of the hexagrams and of the individual lines one by one from the specific arrangement of six yin or yang lines in each hexagram. This would require us to reflect on possible patterns of social relations that are expected from a plurality of actors with given characteristics as represented by each specific hexagram. In the process of such reflection, one may have to take into account all possible patterns of relationships among the components of the situation as explained in the previous chapter. At any rate, once the reflection is done, we then can name the hexagrams to denote their situational meanings as a whole, add some general statements to explain the given situation, and, further, write even more detailed statements about specific situations that would be confronted by each of the position holders. As a matter of fact, traditionally it had been believed that King Wen and his son, the Duke of Zhou, actually carried out such intellectual endeavors and wrote the text of the *I Ching* (Legge, 1963:6; Lynn, 1994:2; Wilhelm, 1967:*liii*). Legge (1963:10) reconstructs what supposedly happened in history as follows:

> The subject-matter of the Text may be briefly represented as consisting of sixty-four short essays, enigmatically and symbolically expressed, on important themes, mostly of a moral, social, and political character, and based on the same number of lineal figures, each made up of six lines, some of which are whole and the others divided . . . . The Text says nothing about their origin and formation. There they are. King Wan takes them up, one after another, in the order that suits himself, determined, evidently, by the contrast in the lines of each successive pair of hexagrams, and gives their significance, as a whole, with some indication, perhaps, of the action to be taken in the circumstances which he supposes them to symbolise, and whether that action will be lucky or unlucky, Then the duke of Kau, beginning with the first or bottom line, expresses, by means of a symbolical or emblematical

illustration, the significance of each line, with a similar indication of the good or bad fortune of action taken in connection with it. The king's interpretation of the whole hexagram will be found to be in harmony with the combined significance of the six lines as interpreted by his son.

The outcome of their efforts was a sort of a dictionary on the 64 possible social situations with which concerned individuals could make diagnosis on the conditions of their life at a certain specific moment in time. But, actually how good a dictionary is it? Were they really successful in establishing a good and sound logical connection between what could be implied by the structure of the lines of the hexagrams and the written accounts added to explain them? What about logical relationships among the hexagram names, hexagram statements and line statements? Were conceptual frames of reference underlying the explanatory accounts consistent throughout the hexagrams? I am raising these questions to draw attention to difficulties that the authors of the *I Ching* would have encountered while engaging in this kind of an intellectual enterprise. But, logical inference alone would not be adequate to complete this task. After all, the meaning attributed to each hexagram or each line of a hexagram had to bear some relevance and significance to a real life situation.

At any rate, the final outcome, the *I Ching*, is here in our hands. In view of all the questions and issues that could be raised, how can we evaluate the merits of the *I Ching*? This question can only be answered after a thorough examination is made of all the individual hexagrams with reference to all related text materials and commentaries. The *I Ching*, regarding its dubious origin and the various ways in which it had been put to use, is expected to have many limitations. And, as far as I see, one of the most serious limitations of the *I Ching* is that it does not offer a logically well-integrated body of knowledge. This limitation can be attributed to the simple fact that the typology presented by the *I Ching* involves 64 conceptual categories and is too complex to be reduced to a logically coherent system of knowledge. Thus, as we will see, while there are types of social and political situations (hexagrams) in which the underlying perspectives and ideas are sensible even to the eyes of those who are suspicious about the credibility of the *I Ching*, there are still others of which we, in view of our ordinary stocks of knowledge or usual modes of thinking, cannot help but find unconvincing. In this study, the former will be given preferential treatment to aid in my search of sound knowledge that relates to the concerns of modern social sciences.

Having said all this, we can now move into the somewhat rough terrain of the *I Ching* with the understanding that it will not be exempt from irrelevant ideas, perspectives or defective reasoning. However, I would like to make some additional points so that the readers do not start with a misunderstood notion about the nature of the problems that the *I Ching* was said to have. Usually, where relatively simple and empirical types are involved, a simple logical operation will be sufficient to construct a typology. For example, if the sex of a human is either male or female and each person is assumed to have a horn or no horn, logic leads us to the conclusion that there will be four types of people; males with a horn or no horn and females with a horn or no horn. The definite advantage of this style of typology building is derived from what is commonly expected from any validly executed deductive reasoning. If the premises are true, the types derived from the given premises cannot be "fictitious" in the sense that they in fact will exist in the real world. Thus, from the above example, if there exist the two sexes among people and these people have either a horn or no horn, there will be no doubt about the actual existence of the four types of people classified as such.

But, not so simple as this are typology-buildings in social sciences where abstract concepts of higher levels are involved. Then, first, let me illustrate difficult problems associated with more complex typology-buildings with an example that seems as complex as that of the *I Ching*. In modern social sciences, the most complex classification scheme I have ever encountered is Parsons' classification scheme on the patterned types of value-orientations built upon his five pattern variables. Each of the pattern variables includes two alternative choices and the total number of the unique value orientations resulting from the cross-classifications of the five variables and the two choice levels (2 x 2 x 2 x 2 x 2) comes to 32 items (Parsons and Shils, 1951:247-275). A classification system with the size and complexity of this one would likely find no comparable counterpart in social sciences. Thus, this may be considered a remarkable feat in the theory-building efforts of sociology. However, the logical operation through which the meanings of the 32 different types of value orientations were generated is simple. If one's action is geared to "universalism (as against particularism)," "affectivity (as against neutrality)," "specificity (as against diffuseness)" or "self-orientation (as against collectivity-orientation)," the type of value orientation for his action in this particular case is characterized as the "valuation of specific emotional gratifications in specific types of situations or with specific types of ascriptively designated persons" (Parsons & Shils, 1951:261). Thus, the described value orientation is nothing more than a logical construct made simply by summing up the five basic value concepts into a sentence. But, what is the significance of Parsons' classification of value-orientations? Why hasn't Parsons' classification scheme to map out types of value orientations in men's social actions attracted the attention of fellow social scientists? I can think of two reasons for this. One is that typology building itself does not generate "theories." Homans (1967:19; 1969), in a similar context, points out a limitation of this type of knowledge. He argues that a typology or a conceptual framework by itself does not constitute theoretical knowledge through which we can explain the existence of objects or events of our concern. The other reason, more important in the context of our ongoing discussion, is that meaningful second-order concepts cannot be constructed simply by cross-tabulating a number of basic concepts however significant the meaning of each basic concept. It would be almost inevitable that the automatic execution of cross-tabulating concepts will create conceptual categories with artificially contrived and thus empirically dubious meanings. For example, what insight into man's value orientations can we have by introducing such contrasting concepts as "valuation of specific affective expression toward particular (ascriptively designated) persons" and "valuation of general affective action in relation to ascriptively designated particular persons or groups" (Parsons and Shils, 1951:262)? What is the difference between "specific affective expression" and "general affective action" toward "ascriptively designated persons"? If poorly constructed, the logic can create quite awkward ideas that are hard to understand even with a help of sharply disciplined logic.

Now, keeping in mind the problems embedded in the Parsonian classification scheme, let us turn to the 64 patterned types of social situations represented by the hexagrams. The problems associated with Parsons' scheme suggest a strong possibility that the *I Ching,* which involves a much more complex typological scheme, also may suffer from the same problem. But for now, let us suffice pointing out a crucial difference between the ordinary typological scheme as exemplified by Parsons and the 64 patterned types of social situations presented by the *I Ching.* First of all, the typology of the *I Ching* is not of ordinary kind: it does not stop at simply being a typological scheme but also addresses other kinds of knowledge including what may be called *theories,* large and small. The complex nature of the *I Ching* and its system (or systems) of knowledge as such can be explained summarily as follows. A graphic representation of a social situation, i.e., a hexagram, alone does not provide sufficient information about the unique features of the relationships among constituent members of a social organization represented by that hexagram. In other words, a logical analysis of the characteristic of an overall situation represented by a hexagram would remain incomplete or "underdetermined" if we were provided only with two primary concepts, the social positions of involved actors and the types of their action orientations. Since a hexagram represents the collective situation of an organized group, what we really need is considerations on *aggregation* or *relation* effects, i.e., considerations on certain characteristic conditions of a group that emerge where a plurality of individuals with given characteristics interact with one another as a collective unit. Thus, all the interpretive accounts given to each of the 64 hexagrams, including hexagram names, hexagram statements, line statements and related commentaries, are related to the "composite" effects of a social formation consisting of a plurality of individuals interacting with defined characteristics. To put it differently, the written accounts appended to the hexagrams seem to be the products of intensely thought-through reflections upon possible patterns of relationships that can be expected to take place whenever an aggregation of individuals holding different social ranks interact with determined tendencies in action orientation. Knowing that there are certain kinds of people at certain positions would not give us knowledge of what may be called the group (or aggregation) effects, i.e., knowledge of the characteristic patterns in which the people are related to one another in the total context of a collective unit. To take a simple example, how are the two trigrams *Zhen* (⚎, Quake) and *Kan* (⚏, Water) interpreted in view of their respective line structures? Looking at the situational meanings attributed to these two trigrams (see the previous chapter), one may wonder how to grasp the significance of the relationships supposedly represented by each trigram? Even provided with the knowledge of the ranking order of the line positions and the types of action orientation indicated by the yin-yang lines, a logical inference alone would lead us nowhere. But if logic alone does not get us the meanings of the two trigrams as attributed by the *I Ching*, where did they come from?

As we know already, there are four yin or yang lines at the middle positions of the eight trigrams. Yet, the characteristic meaning or significance of the same yang or yin line differs in each trigram. This is because the meaning of a line must be interpreted in reference to the specific composition of the trigram to which the line belongs. Thus, in this sense, every line requires a unique interpretation that will be applied to that line only. And, this implies further that since the meaning of a line can be understood only with reference to a specific property unique to its trigram or hexagram, determining the meaning of a line first requires an understanding of the meaning of the hexagram itself. This, of course, returns us back to the question of the overall meaning of the hexagrams. Here I will venture to say that the author(s) of the *I Ching*, prior to writing the book, should have had a great deal of knowledge about various patterns of social relationships and types of social situations at more general level. And, given the many possible interpretations which could be imagined from any given trigram or hexagram, the author(s) had chosen one that could be thought as making the best possible sense in the light of their prior knowledge of social reality. This knowledge is not stated explicitly but lies rather implicitly behind the narrated accounts of the *I Ching*, yet still can be read into with tangible clarity. At any rate, if we collect them and make a list, we have an inventory of many interesting propositions on such important social phenomena as social integration, conflict, and other significant aspects of social relationships. As I pointed out, they do not constitute a well-integrated system of knowledge. Thus, the *I Ching* has limitations as an old book of wisdom whose author(s) probably had no intention or necessity to produce a systematically organized body of knowledge. Due to this limitation, we will deal mainly with many "partial" ideas that seem to have little systematic linkages among themselves. Nevertheless, some of those partial ideas contain quite interesting concepts or theoretical perspectives worthwhile enough for us to give careful scrutiny to their potential merits in relation to issues in modern social sciences.

Now, we will move on to an analysis of the core element of the *I Ching*, the hexagrams. But, before we proceed, there still remains one important matter that requires a specific mention. As I pointed out already in the introduction, knowledgeable readers will notice that the arrangement of the hexagrams in this book does not follow the sequential order in which the 64 hexagrams are presented customarily in the text. In the following section where each hexagram is discussed, the hexagrams are grouped into different categories (14 in all) on the basis of certain similarities in the characteristic features of situations they represent. In assessing the rationale underlying this classification scheme, it will be helpful to note first that an interpretation of what kind of a specific situation a hexagram symbolizes is basically propositional. In other words, the way in which the meanings of individual hexagrams are grasped will depend largely on the perspective of an individual interpreter from which the *I Ching* is understood as containing knowledge or wisdom pertaining to human situations of specific kinds. Accordingly, any attempt to classify the hexagrams on the basis of the kinds of situations that the hexagrams are thought to represent will be done within the purview of one's specific perspective on the essential natures of knowledge and wisdom that we expect to derive from the *I Ching* overall and each of the individual hexagrams in more detailed aspects. The basic perspective that I have taken up in bringing to light the significance of the *I Ching* is clearly indicated by the subtitle of this thesis *An exploration into its theoretical implications in social sciences*. And, obviously the classification scheme that I have adopted for this particular study could not have been developed without applying a perspective from which the hexagrams are viewed as depicting the essential features of ancient Chinese society in such manners as to have some important theoretical implications in modern social sciences. For this reason, to classify the hexagrams in kinds as we see in the following discussion makes evident the basic orientation of this thesis aiming at a social scientific study.

Besides the aim of this study to address itself as a *sociopolitical* version of the interpretation of the *I Ching*, there is an additional and important consideration with which the classification scheme employed is regarded to have specific importance for the study. As far this author is concerned, if our investigation of the *I Ching* is to be guided by such norms of rational knowledge as clarity in meaning and logical coherence, the first requirement we will have to comply with is that we make evident the perspective with which the *I Ching* is interpreted. Only then, the merit of one's interpretation can be evaluated in the light of the soundness of the proposed perspective itself and how clear, meaningful and coherent understandings the perspective actually yield from the ancient classic. In view of this consideration, the employed classification scheme of the hexagrams will make evident my commitment to a specific point of view by which the *I Ching* is interpreted, and thereby expose this study to critical evaluations as regards the soundness or merit of its specific interpretations rendered to each hexagram.

1) The Two Primary Hexagrams: The Two Most Ideally Integrated Situations

Traditionally, the two hexagrams, *Qian* (☰) and *Kun*

(☰ ☷), have been considered to represent the most ideal situations, the best possible ones among all the 64 situations. Both consist solely of yang or yin lines at the six positions of each hexagram, for which many positive characteristics are attributed. First, let us look at the hexagram *Qian*.

The hexagram *Qian* (☰ , Pure Yang)

The *I Ching* and later commentators describe the conditions or characteristics of the situation represented by this hexagram with such various terms as "strength and dynamism," "change and transformation," "fitness and constancy" and "the great harmony" (Lynn, 1994:129-130). What is meant by these terms is that every position holder of a social organization under this particular situation is engaging in dynamic activities in his respective position. Therefore, a great deal of "change and transformation" is taking place as the outcome of the creative activism so characteristic of all the position holders' action orientations in this particular situation. In addition, the *I Ching* also emphasizes the presence of harmonious cooperation among the involved actors who are "functioning according the moment involved" (Lynn, 1994:129). All of them are acting "fittingly and with constancy." That is, they all act in fulfillment of normative expectations imposed upon them under the situation. It may be appropriate to use sociological terminology here by saying that there would be little dissension or conflict among any of the actors involved in this specific situation. Thus, the situation as a whole is summarily characterized as that of a "great harmony." This situation of *Qian* almost reminds us of a utopian situation. Some of us at this point may recall that the "integration theory of society" proposed by Parsons has been criticized for its utopian conception about the essential nature of social order (Dahrendorf, 1958; Lockwood, 1956; Mills, 1959:25-49). Although the situation of *Qian* in some aspects is not unlike what is called a "moving equilibrium"[1] by Parsons (1951:36n), all the expressions used to characterize the hexagram *Qian* seem to make the situation sound even more idealistic than the latter. However, there is one important issue to pay attention to with respect to a frequently heard criticism toward Parsons' so-called "utopian" conception of social order. If Parsons' theory is to be criticized, it should not be for his proposal for an idea of a utopian situation per se. Rather, the real issue with his equilibrium model of society should lie with his intention aiming at *generalization*.

In other words, his theory seems to be couched upon a seemingly problematic idea that the society *in general* tends to be in a state of harmonious integration. Therefore, compared with the functionalist conception of social order as proposed by Parsons, the *I Ching* offers quite a contrasting perspective. The hexagram *Qian* represents an ideal situation, one of the best possible ones indeed, but it occurs only as one of many possible situations; a social organization cannot be integrated in such an ideal way all the time.

Therefore, in accordance with the ideal state represented by the hexagram, the *I Ching* likens most position holders in this hexagram to the dragon, the mythological animal in Oriental societies that symbolizes a heroic leader or person with an extraordinary ability who acts as a creative force to bring great things to realization. Thus, for example, the line statement added to the first yang line reads, "A submerged dragon does not act" (Lynn, 1994:132). The term "submerged dragon" usually applies to a person who possesses great potential but requires self-restraint perhaps because he has no official position or "is not yet perfected" (Lynn, 1994:132). Accordingly, the advice stated, "do not act," is given to the one who occupies this position. Yet, is it really true that one's action will yield no remarkable achievement unless he is in an official position so that he can make use of a certain amount of power associated with that position? The advice given to the one at the first, lowest position certainly seems to reflect such a belief. That is, it warns that a "submerged dragon" having a limited capacity to accrue in his lowest position should refrain from taking action because there would be little prospect for his effort to yield a gainful outcome under this particular situation. This is certainly interesting advice to give to anyone who stands at the lowest position in a social organization, although its actual validity or efficacy may leave room for doubt.

Meanwhile, the second yang line is characterized as "a dragon in the fields" (Lynn, 1994:133), a dragon who appears on the main field of action where activities of actors occupying positions with more or less important weight are staged. Of all the active lines in the hexagram, the *I Ching* marks this particularly as the workhorse of a social organization under the specific situation represented by the hexagram *Qian*. About the crucial role that the position holder plays in this particular situation, Wang Bi comments, "although this is not the position for a sovereign, it involves the virtue of a true sovereign" (Lynn, 1994:133). In other words, in this time of dynamic change and development, the one who is at this second, i.e., centrally placed position in the lower trigram plays a central role to carry out the tasks required by the situation. Thus, the advice, "it is fitting to see the great man" (Lynn, 1994:133), is given to the one who occupies this crucially important position. "To see the great man (*daren*)" is an expression that appears fairly frequently among the line statements of the *I Ching*. Of this statement, Wang Bi explains, "when one who has a sovereign's virtue occupies a position in the lower trigrams, it is an occasion for him to draw on the resources of others" (Lynn, 1994:133). Thus, "to see the great man" simply means that one has to seek aid or advice from others who can extend helping hands with needed resources.

With respect to the third yang line, Wang Bi's following commentary stresses a delicate balance of posture that has to be struck out by the person who occupies the position:

> Here one occupies the very top of the lower trigram and is located just below the upper trigram, situated in a nonmean position and treading on the dangerous territory of the double strong.[2] Above, he is not in Heaven, so cannot use that to make his exalted position secure, and below he is not in the fields [Earth] so cannot use that to make his dwelling place safe. If one were to cultivate exclusively here the Dao of the subordinate, the virtue needed to occupy a superior position would waste away, but if one were to cultivate exclusively the Dao of the superior, the propriety needed to fill a lower position would wither . . . .
> If occupying a high position one were free of arrogance, in filling a low position were free of distress, and were to take care appropriate to the moment, he would not fall out with the incipient force of things and, although in danger and beset with trouble, would suffer no blame. (Lynn, 1994:134)

The main point that Wang Bi tries to make in the above commentary is that the position holder at the third position has both strong superiors above and equally strong subordinates below. Since he is being thrust between vigorously active superiors and subordinates and has to play the double roles of both a subordinate and a superior, he may experience what can be called role incompatibilities. What he needs under this situation, therefore, is to strike out a delicate balance of posture between the incompatible role expectations that incur by exercising, to use Wang Bi's own terms, both the "*Dao* of the superior" and the "*Dao* of the subordinate." Keeping in mind Wang Bi's explanation above, let us now look at the line statements of the *I Ching* given to this position; "The noble man makes earnest efforts throughout the day, and with evening he still takes care; though in danger, he will suffer no blame" (Lynn, 1994:134). The statements quoted above impart an image of a middle-positioned leader who is actively engaging in the works assigned to him, yet in a position to "take care" of problems associated with his "insecure" position with the mixed roles. But, why is he given the diagnosis that "he will suffer no blame" "though in danger"? For this question, simply notice that the hexagram *Qian* represents a well-balanced and integrated situation where every position holder is sharing a potential to exercise a certain measure of power toward another. This is a situation in which a *great harmony* prevails. Thus, the one at the third position also "will suffer no blame."

Even under the situation of this great harmony, however, the *I Ching* seems to suggest that not every one fairs equally as well as others. To see how this is the case, look at the specific situation that the one at the fourth position is in. The one at the fourth position represents an individual (or individuals) who has reached a point only a step apart from the fifth, highest position. But, as Wang Bi points outs in his commentary, "this (i.e., the fifth position) is not something his leap can reach." Thus, the line statement on this position reads, "hesitating to leap, it still stays in the depths, so suffers no blame" (Lynn, 1994:136). The above statement, narrated with poetic brevity, has to be supplemented with some explanation. Because a strong leader is present at the position of the formal leadership, i.e., at the fifth position, the one at the fourth position has no choice but to stay in his own lower position although he may have some intention to leap over to that position. However, no unfortunate incident will happen to him. It is exactly in this situational context that Wang Bi's following advice makes perfect sense; "He concentrates on preserving his commitment to the public good, for advancement here does not lie with private ambitions" (Lynn, 1994:136).

When everyone is actively engaged in cooperative works to the utmost of his creative potential, the *I Ching* likens the leader of this group, operating with such a vigorous energy and harmonious consensus, to "a flying dragon in the sky" (Lynn, 1994:137) — a symbolic image of an active leader who is engaged in a grand enterprise with a full mobilization of creative energy. Thus, the *I Ching* says of this one at the fifth position, "when a flying dragon is in the sky, it is fitting to see the great man." It was explained already that "to see the great man" is a phrase that describes a situation where a leader, even at the summit of power, should not try to decide everything on his own, but should rely on the resources of others. Up to now, of all position holders, the one at the fifth position seems to be given the most favorable assessment regarding the relative lot in what everyone can take out of this specific situation. Of course, no one would find himself in a particularly unfortunate position under this situation of the great harmony.

Then, how about the remaining one at the top position? The *I Ching* seems to have the only exceptional and interesting opinion about this particular position. The line statement on this position says, "a dragon that overreaches should have cause for regret" (Lynn, 1994:138). Placed at the top of the hexagram, the sixth yang represents one who is in the most honored position, yet lacks an official position that has a formally endowed power. Thus, Wang Bi comments on this line, "standing alone, he makes move, and no one will go along with him" (Lynn, 1994:138). By the nature of the situation in which the action field is full of dragons (i.e., strong-willed actors dynamically interacting with one another), if the one at the sixth position tries to exercise influence over others, he will be rebuffed because he lacks a formal power base to back up his move.

At the end, the *I Ching* sums up the characteristics of this situation with the following statement; "when one sees a flight of dragons without heads, it is good fortune" (Lynn, 1994:139). There seems to be some variations or disagreements among commentators about what the above statement means.[3] But, to this author, Wang Bi's commentary seems to sound the most convincing in that it allows a clearer interpretation than others do. He explains:

> The nines [yang lines] all signify the virtue of Heaven. As we are able to use the virtue of Heaven [for all the lines], we see the concept of a flight of dragons in them. If one were to take up a position of headship over men by using nothing but hardness and strength, that would result in people not going with it . . . . This is why the good fortune of *Qian* resides in there being no head to it. (1994:139-140)

The point Wang Bi tries to emphasize seems to make sense enough. Since a social organization represented by the hexagram *Qian* consists only of the "yang" types of individuals armed with progressive and aggressive spirits, any attempt to stick out one's head high over others may lead to internal dissension. Thus, it is said, "without heads, good fortunes." In other words, a powerful unitary leadership would not be compatible with an organization under this specific type of situation.

At this point, some readers may be doubtful about the nature of knowledge the *I Ching* is said to contain. Of many possible questions, I consider two as having the utmost significance, a methodological one and a theoretical one. The methodological question concerns how we know that any given social organization is in such and such a specific situation at a particular point in time. The theoretical one, on the other hand, concerns how a specific situation comes into existence or changes into another. Thus, with respect to the ideal situation represented by the hexagram *Qian*, we can raise the two questions as follows. First, how do we know that a given social organization is in a specific situation that can be characterized with the hexagram *Qian*? Secondly, what will bring about such an ideal situation?

The first of these two questions would not be raised if a functionalist position on social integration were at issue. It is simply because the functionalistic theory, in general, assumes functional integration to be a normal and universal feature of the social system. In other words, functional integration is generally expected to be observed throughout all the "non-pathological" societies. Nevertheless, since the *I Ching* posits the situation represented by the hexagram *Qian* as one of many possible situations, the first question becomes rather critical: how do we know that a given social organization at a certain point in time is in such an ideal situation? And, a rather simple answer to the second question, a theoretical one, can also be found in the theoretical perspective of functionalism. If a social system were successful in maintaining its existence, it would be so because it is in some way fulfilling all the necessary functions required for its existence. That is, the fulfillment of necessary functions would provide an explanation about how a functional integration of the social system, an ideal state, is maintained. However, if the ideal situation represented by the hexagram *Qian* is thought to be only one of many possible types of social situations, the answer to the second question should now require a perspective on social changes. In other words, the theoretical question now turns into, "How does the *I Ching* view the mechanism of social change in which a certain type of social situation changes into another one?" This question involves a crucial issue concerning how viable and thorough the *I Ching* is as a system of knowledge. But, we will stop here just to avoid an unnecessary breakage in proceeding with discussions on individual hexagrams. We will return to the two questions, both the theoretical and methodological ones, later to conduct a more thorough examination.

The hexagram *Kun* (☷ ☷, Pure Yin)

The line formation of the hexagram *Kun* consists solely of six yin lines and is the direct opposite of the previous hexagram *Qian*. However, the *I Ching* confers this hexagram with a privileged standing equally comparable to the hexagram *Qian,* seemingly with a belief that it possesses quite opposite yet equally ideal characteristics. The typical characteristics of a situation represented by this hexagram are described with such various terms as "constancy," "compliance," "quiescence" and "simplicity" (Lynn, 1994:142-144). Thus, this situation can be characterized by a tendency to conserve, or comply with, an existing order — an attribute sharply contrasted with such progressive characteristics as "dynamism," "change" and "transformation" used to describe the situation signified by the hexagram *Qian.* If we subtract "change" from the concept of "equilibrium," we obtain the idea of an "equilibrium without change." Dahrendorf (1969) was particularly critical of this kind of a "static" image of society in the Parsonian conception of social order, and the situation represented by the hexagram *Kun* seems to express exactly the same image of society, a "static equilibrium" (Parsons, 1951:36n). The statement in the *Commentary on the Words of the Text,* "*Kun* is perfectly compliant, but the way it takes action is strong and firm; it is perfectly quiescent, but its virtue is square and solid" (Lynn, 1994:144) supposedly conveys the same idea as the characteristic situation of this hexagram. At the first glance, however, the terms "strong," "firm," "square" and "solid" may sound contradictory to the overall characteristic of this hexagram that represents a static equilibrium that, in some important aspects, reminds us of Pareto's "residues of group persistences (Class II residues)"[4] (1935:599-646). But, does a high-degree conservatism not go together with a particular kind of a firm resoluteness to preserve an existing order or a rather strenuous effort to get it to full fruition? It seems exactly in this light that the following advice of Wang Bi makes good sense: "action that is square and straight is incapable of doing evil, but to be so compliant that one becomes irresolute will lead to the deterioration of the Dao. When the virtue is perfectly quiescent, that virtue must be 'square and solid'" (Lynn, 1994:144). Thus, the *I Ching* compares the characteristic quality of this hexagram to a "mare," an obedient yet persistent animal symbolizing one who is required to work strenuously yet stubbornly under a given order

Under a situation where a faithful adherence to habitual modes of behavior is emphasized as an appropriate norm of the time, the bottom line represents a person who, being the newest member at the lowest position, has to be taught compliance to the norms and rules of the organization to which he belongs. For this reason, the line statement given to the first yin line emphasizes a virtue of docility by invoking the possible outcome of early-learned behavior leading to either a "blessing" or "disaster" in the future. Let us look at what the

Commentary on the Words of the Text has to say about this line:

> A family that accumulates goodness will be sure to have an excess of blessings, but one that accumulates evil will be sure to have an excess of disasters. When a subject kills his lord or a son kills his father, it is never because of what happens between the morning and evening of the same day but because of something that has been building up for a long time and that should have been dealt with early — but was not. When the Changes say "the frost one treads on reaches its ultimate stage as solid ice," is it not talking about compliancy [with the Dao involved]? (Lynn 1994:146)

The above passage emphasizes a simple truth: in a conservative social organization or a social situation, whose nature is characterized by the hexagram *Kun*, an individual would have unfortunate outcomes unless successfully socialized into the established order from the very beginning. This raises the interesting hypothesis that there would be no uniform criterion to assess the probable outcomes of a socialization process that people pass through. Rather, it all depends on the specific type of a social organization for which he is socialized. In other words, the success or failure of a socialization process can only be determined in context of the type of social organization to which the individual must be adjusted. Thus, for the person who is placed under the situation characterized by the hexagram *Kun*, the *I Ching* offers advice by saying that to have the greatest blessing in the end, a newcomer must be taught faithful compliance with existing norms and values of the social organization.

Given the overall situational characteristic of the hexagram *Kun*, a particularly favorable judgment is rendered to the one at the second position. The statement given to this line, "he is straight [*zhi*], square [*fang*], and great [*da*], so without working at it, nothing he does here fails to be fitting" (Lynn, 1994:146), overlaps in content, if partly, with the overall characteristics of the hexagram as a whole. Thus, in a sense, the one in the second position possesses the "virtues" characterizing the entire hexagram as a whole. The reason for attributing such an ideal characteristic to the second position can be explained in terms of the typical logic that the *I Ching* applies when interpreting the meanings of the lines in reference to the specific line composition of a hexagram. Recall that the four middle positions represent the formal structure of a social organization. This is made of "incumbent" positions actively taking part in the operation of the organization with more or less amounts of effective power formally assigned to each of them. In this formal structure, the second position is characterized as occupying the "yin" (i.e., subordinate) position in the periphery (again, subordinate) structure represented by the lower trigram. Now, the second position of the hexagram *Kun* is "appropriately occupied" by a yin line because that position is most "appropriate" for someone with a yin action orientation. Moreover, when a conservative mood prevails over the entire group, the second yin line due to the nature of his position and actual action orientation comes to reflect the typical characteristic and spirit of the group as a whole. Wang Bi comments on the second line by stating: "Here, finding oneself at the center and obtaining his correct position there, he perfectly realizes in himself the qualities inherent in the Earth"[5] (Lynn, 1994:146).

Then, compared to the second yin line, how is the yin line located at the third, leadership position of the periphery group interpreted? The line statement of this line reads, "one who effaces his own prominent qualities here will be able to practice constancy" (Lynn, 1994:147). Wang Bi comments on this line statement as follows:

> One who occupies the very top of the lower trigram yet does not excite the suspicions of yang personages [sovereign, superiors] is someone who stays in harmony with the meaning [yin] involved here. He does not involve himself in initiating anything but must respond to the lead of another and must wait for orders before he starts to act: this is someone who effaces his own excellence and in so doing keeps himself correct. (Lynn, 1994:147)

The position holder at the third position is described as a person who does not take the lead and only acts on orders from superiors although he "occupies the very top of the lower trigram," and thus is "someone who stays in harmony" with the prevailing trend of conformity. Here some sociologists may be led to think of the "organization man" (Whyte, Jr., 1956). It is interesting to note that, in contrast to a largely negative image that Western scholars tend to have about the organization man, here in the *I Ching* and Asian societies in general, the conformity and devotion to an existing order or superiors is considered to be a noble man's "correct" demeanor. At the same time, however, it has to be emphasized that there is an ethical ideal underlying the *I Ching* that may be called a situational ethic. In this ethical view, a value becomes relevant or efficacious in the context of a situation to which the value applies as relevant or efficacious. Thus, for instance, if a situation is such that a good outcome would not be expected to come about by practicing conformity, the *I Ching* will not mention conformity as virtuous or advantageous under the given situation.

The meaning of the line statement given to the fourth yin line will be much easier to understand if the fifth line is explained first. At the first sight, the line statement for the fifth yin line, "a yellow lower garment means fundamental good fortune," contains such unintelligible symbolism that it does not seem likely to yield an easy interpretation. What does "a yellow lower garment" symbolize after all? As far as the fifth yin line of the hexagram *Kun* is concerned, Cheng Yi's commentary provides the most meaningful explanation. The following is his comment on the fifth line:

> Although receptivity [which is symbolized by this hexagram] is the path of service, the fifth line in a hexagram stands for the position of the leader. Yellow is the color associated with the center, so a yellow lower garments stand for keeping to a middle course and being humble, understanding the position of leadership as itself one of service, and therefore not becoming overbearing. In other hexagrams when it is in the fifth position, the position of leadership, sometimes yin stands for flexibility and docility, sometimes for culture and civilization, sometimes for ignorance and weakness. In this hexagram, the Receptive, yin stands for the way of administrators, workers, and also women in general. Administrators, workers, and women are at times in positions of leadership, and this is not abnormal. They are only cautioned to be balanced and to avoid arrogance. (Cheng Yi, 1988:4-5)

Cheng Yi makes his point clearly. Under a situation in which conservatism and conformity prevails, the leadership position is occupied by an administrative type of leader who "understands the position of leadership as itself one of service." He is a faithful administrator who works according to established rules and norms, not one who makes rules and rules over the ruled. Like everybody else under this situation, the leader is also an organization man, a team player.

Then, given the presence of this type of the leadership, how does the *I Ching* describe the specific situation confronted by the one at the fourth position? The line statement of the fourth yin line says, "tie up the bag, so there will be no blame, no praise" (Lynn, 1994:148). According to Wang Bi's explanation, " 'tie up' [*gua*] means 'bind up' [*jie*] — to keep confined. A worthy person should stay hidden here, and only exercising caution can he get by . . . ." (Lynn, 1994:148). Wang Bi's above explanation should be appreciated in view of a possible question that may be raised in relation to the leadership characteristic in this type of situation. Given the presence of the type of leadership described as an "administrator," we may ask, "what kind of a situation will the one at the fourth position, himself in an administrative position, face under the leader who attends closely to administrative works?" The *I Ching*'s answer to this question seems to contain a practical wisdom: there would be nothing much to do for the one at the fourth position, and therefore he, by just staying there and doing little, would be free from any unnecessary suspicion or censure from the one above.

All the descriptions thus far concerning the hexagram *Kun* may give the impression that a social situation represented by this hexagram is a modal case of a harmonious yet static equilibrium where everything operates on established rules and norms with little impetus for change or dynamic progress. Conformity and conservatism are two key words that epitomize this situation. Considering a characterization such as this, the line statement of the top position may be viewed as something quite unexpected. It reads, "dragons fight in the fields, their blood black and yellow" (Lynn, 1994:149). What is most obvious is that the big bloody fight suggested by this line statement does not seem to describe the specific condition of the actor in the sixth position of the hexagram *Kun*. And, as a matter of fact, as the statement itself is not subject to easy interpretation due to its lack of clarity in reference, it has yielded a variety of different interpretations among commentators including Wang Bi, Cheng Yi, and other scholars (Lynn, 1994:151n8, n9, n10). However, although the interpretations differ in detail, we may be able to narrow down on an important common theme underlying the varying interpretations. The common theme states that a social organization, whose members display a high degree of conformity and reach the height of integration, may "at the peak of its strength" (Lynn, 1994:150, 151), challenge, or be challenged by, anyone (or group) who is encroaching upon it with an aggressive (yang) intention. Keeping this common theme in mind, let us read Kong Yingda's sub-commentary supplementing Wang Bi's commentary:

> As yin has reached the peak of its strength, it comes under the suspicions of yang, which then takes action, wishing to extirpate this yin, but since yin is already at the peak of its strength, it is unwilling to take evasive action. This is why 'it must fight.' (Lynn, 1994:151n8)

Other commentators such as Cheng Yi and Zhu Xi suggest that when integration is at the highest point, i.e., "at the peak of its strength," "there is sure to be a fight" because it tends to think of itself as "an equal match for yang" (Lynn, 1994:151n8). At any rate, the above interpretations seem to advance a very interesting and seemingly convincing hypothesis. A highly conservative social organization (perhaps, a state or political organization) whose members are characterized by a high degree of conformity and collectivist orientation will oftentimes turn into an aggressive fighting organization warring with outside forces.

As in the hexagram *Qian*, the explanations on the hexagram *Kun* also end with a short statement that gives advice to all involved actors. It says, "it is fitting to practice constancy perpetually here. What is fitting here is at All Use Yin Lines (i.e. under the situation represented by the hexagram *Kun*) is to practice constancy perpetually" (Lynn, 1994:150). It seems that the character of the situation itself has already implied this advice. One has to behave conservatively when a situation filled with a highly conservative mood requires him to behave as such.

Summary of theoretical and empirical propositions

Now, let us briefly summarize what we have gathered from the examinations thus far on the two primary hexagrams. The propositions listed in the following only sum up what we have obtained from examining the two hexagrams, the hexagram *Qian* and the hexagram *Kun*.

1) For any social organization, there can exist two "ideal" modes of integration, the modes of integration respectively represented by the hexagram *Qian* and the hexagram *Kun*. The former type of integration can be characterized as a "moving (or dynamic) equilibrium." "Dynamism," "change," "progressivism" and "balance of power among actors who are engaging actively in creative works" are key words to express the typical attributes of a social organization under this specific mode of integration. The latter type of integration is viewed as the direct opposite of the former in that it can be characterized as a "static equilibrium." "conformity," "persistence," "conservatism" and "stability" are key words to express the typical attributes of a social organization under this latter type of integration.

2) The two situations are regarded as "ideal" because they represent respectively "dynamic change" and "constancy (stability)" — states that had been highly valued by the people of the old Chinese civilization.

3) However, although the overall effect of the situation as a whole is regarded as ideal in both situations, it may not bring about an equitably balanced outcome to all the actors involved. The life chances, the "fortunes" or "misfortunes" of the actors, differ depending on two factors: their social positions and how they "choose"[6] to behave.

4) In a dynamic situation where all the involved actors are vying with one another to have a voice or play an active role in doing things, a strong unitary leadership would not help much in promoting the integration of a social organization characterized as such. The *I Ching* by implication seems to suggest that "dragons without heads," or an organization run democratically, would do better to maintain a peaceful harmony under this specific type of situation. Thus, we may say in a more general context that there will be no uniform principle regarding leadership effectiveness because the effectiveness of a certain type of leadership will vary from situation to situation.

5) There is no universally valid criterion to determine the most appropriate method of socialization. The appropriateness of a given mode of socialization will be judged differently from one type of situation to another.

6) When an administrator who attends to the details of administrative works is in the leadership position, the latitude of power that functionaries or officials at administrative positions can exercise will be limited considerably.

7) A high degree of collective orientation or conformity among the members of a social organization would bring about a high level of integration for an organization. This tight integration may in turn inspire a valiant spirit in this organization and lead it into conflict with outsiders.

2) Six Yang-Centered Hexagrams: Yang-Centered Modes of Integration

A yang-centered hexagram as named here refers to a type of hexagram which has a yang line as its "constituting ruler" (Wilhem, 1967:364). The concept of constituting rulership was already explained in the previous chapter. The hexagrams are comprised on the basis of the two crucial variables, social positions and the action orientations of individual actors. According to the *I Ching*, social positions are organized in a hierarchical order as depicted by the vertically arranged line structure of the hexagram. Out of all the positions in the formal hierarchical order, the *I Ching* marks out a specific position as corresponding to the leadership position for an organized group represented by a specific hexagram. Usually, the fifth position stands for such position. Wilhelm (1967:364) calls a person who is at this position of formal leadership the "governing ruler." Thus, regardless of whether there is a yang line or a yin line, the line at the fifth position would be interpreted as representing the governing ruler. On the other hand, as Wang Bi (1994:26) points outs, if one hexagram has five yin lines and one single yang line, the single yang line will be called the "master," or to use Wilhelm's term, the "constituting ruler," of that hexagram. The reverse is also the case. That is, if a hexagram contains a single yin line and the other lines are all yang lines, the yin line will be the constituting ruler. The logic underlying this distinction between the governing and the constituting rulerships of the hexagrams, or the *de jure* and the *de facto* rulerships, respectively, were discussed in the last portion of the previous chapter. To recapitulate, let us simply say that although a position bestows upon its occupant(s) a formal power vested with that position, an individual's actual potential to influence others will not always be derived solely from the institutionally granted right to exercise the formal power as such. According to the *I Ching*, a position holder's potential for power or influence is also dependant upon an additional factor, what may be called an "informal" power, which will be determined in relation to the actual action orientations of all the actors involved in a given collective situation. The constituting rulership then refers to one's *real* ability to exercise mastery over others; an actual influence potential accruing from a situationally specific configuration of the action orientations of all the involved actors. Thus, for many hexagrams, both types of rulers, the governing ruler and the constituting one, will be present at the same time within a social organization represented by a hexagram. The hexagram *Shi* (☷☵, The Army) provides an example for these types of hexagrams. As we can see from the graphic figure, whereas the fifth line would be marked out as the governing ruler for this particular hexagram, the constituting ruler that is indicated by the single yang line is also present at the second position. So it may be said that these kinds of hexagrams have a "double leadership structure." In other cases, like the hexagram

Bi (☵☷, Closeness or Holding together), however, the governing rulership at the fifth position overlaps with the constituting rulership that is also present at the same, fifth position. We may characterize these kinds of hexagrams as of having a "single leadership structure."

In light of the notion of the constituting rulership as a concept in itself, the "constituting rulerships" can be classified into two types. In the first type, a yang line assumes the position of the constituting ruler. In the other, a yin line assumes the position of the constituting ruler. It was pointed out in the previous chapter that the constituting, or *de facto*, ruler plays the key role in the integration of a group represented by a given hexagram. Thus, we can classify social organizations involving the constituting ruler into two categories, the yang-centered integration type in which a yang line occupies the position of the constituting ruler and the yin-centered integration type in which a yin line is in that position. Since there are six lines for each hexagram, the number of hexagrams involving either the yang-centered mode of integration or the yin-centered mode will be six respectively. In this section, we will deal with the six yang-centered types of integration listed as follows:

1) The hexagram *Fu* (☷☳, Return) (Hexagram No. 24)[7]

2) The hexagram *Shi* (☷☵, The Army) (Hexagram No. 7)

3) The hexagram *Qian* (☷☶, Modesty) (Hexagram No. 15)

4) The hexagram *Yu* (☳☷, Contentment) (Hexagram No. 16)

5) The hexagram *Bi* (☵☷, Closeness) (Hexagram No. 8)

6) The hexagram *Bo* (☶☷, Peeling) (Hexagram No. 23)

The Hexagram *Fu* (☷☳, Return)

Compared to the two hexagrams that we have examined in the

previous section, the hexagram *Fu* seems to belong to a somewhat different breed. To understand the meaning of this hexagram, we need to know first that there is a certain prior assumption underlying the accounts of the text and commentaries on this hexagram. The meanings attributed to the hexagram *Fu* and its lines by the *I Ching* are not something that can be directly or logically inferred from the line formation of the hexagram. However, most of the written accounts related to this hexagram seem to converge on a certain common theme with respect to the core characteristic of the situation indicated by this hexagram. To get at the common thematic concept running through the narrated accounts of the hexagram *Fu*, we first have to imagine a social organization that has ceased normal operation or is dying out due to either weakening spirits among its constituent members or to a seizure of the organizational mechanism. Lee (1997[I]:300) describes this kind of situation as "a disorderly state that a society falls into as a prolonged existence of a dictatorial regime and resisting movements by the people to recover a democratic rule give rise to intense conflicts." Some readers may hold some reservations about interpreting the hexagram in such a way that its meaning is stretched as farthest as to accommodate contemporary sociopolitical situations. Notwithstanding we may raise doubt about the soundness of Lee's "modern" version of interpretation, it is with this background assumption of the existence of a malfunctioning organization in a problematic state that a more or less meaningful understanding can be extracted from all the symbolic accounts given to the hexagram *Fu*.

The hexagram *Fu* represents a situation in which a movement to "return" to an "orderly" normal state is beginning to take place within a social organization that has been malfunctioning for some time. As we can see from the line formation of the hexagram, the one that plays the leading role in this "return" movement is the one at the first, bottom position. Thus, the characteristic of the hexagram as a whole is described as a situation in which most position holders are responding in their own particular manner to the "return" or "revival" movement initiated by the bottom layer or the "grass-roots" level of the organization. Notice that the bottom line is a single yang line, which signifies the constituting rulership for this specific hexagram, and all the other lines are yin, yielding lines. This indicates that the one at the bottom position is initiating the trend of the time characterized by the hexagram, while all others in the positions above him are in conformity with the bottom position. Cheng Yi describes the one in the first line more succinctly as "the vanguard of return" (1988:73).

Let us look at how the *I Ching* describes a specific role played by the actor(s) at the bottom position under the situation. The line statement for the first yang line states: "this one returns before having gone far, so there will be no regret here, which means fundamental good fortune" (Lynn, 1994:287). Regarding this, the *Commentary on the Images* explains, " 'return before going far' provides the way one should cultivate his person" (Lynn, 1994:287). What is the key idea underlying the line statement and the explanation stated above? In interpreting the meaning of a specific situation that the actor at the bottom position finds himself, two possibilities have to be considered. One is that the yang line at the first position represents a person who carries out a "return" or "revival" movement when such an action is urgently needed to revive a social organization *before* it falls into a totally hopeless situation, a state totally disorganized to such an extent that any attempt to remedy the situation would be futile. So it is said, "this one returns before having gone far." The other possible interpretation is that the *I Ching* offers a moral lesson for the one at the first position: it teaches him to cultivate himself to "return before having gone far," probably for the good of both himself and his own group that is in need of a "revival." Thus, out of the line statement given to the first yang line we draw two different interpretations, each of which seems equally compatible with the line statement and related commentaries. One is a descriptive one and the other a prescriptive one. According to the descriptive interpretation, the line statement is understood as stating that the one at the first position is initiating a revival movement for a social organization at the time when such action is badly needed to restore proper order for the malfunctioning organization. Here we may raise a question; why is the one who leads this sort of revival movement at the bottom position? The *I Ching* gives no answer to this but a possible explanation may be that the one at the bottom position holds no formal position so that he is relatively free of interests vested in the established old order. If we follow the other interpretation, i.e., the prescriptive one, the line statement is interpreted to make an injunction on the involved individual to "cultivate himself (i.e., the one at the bottom position)" so that he can "return before having gone far." Judging from several commentaries written by such major figures as Cheng Yi, Wang Bi and Wilhelm on this specific line statement, it is my assessment that interpretation can be made either way. For instance, let us read the following commentary by Wang Bi (1994:287):

> Located at the very first position of the *Fu* [Return] hexagram, First Yang represents the beginning of the process of Return. If one here did

not make this Return with all haste, it would inevitably lead to the misfortune of getting lost, but this one makes his Return before he has gone far, which means that with the onset of regret he starts back. If one were to "cultivate his person" in terms of what is meant here, disaster and trouble would indeed be kept away! And, if one were to utilize this in the conduct of one's affairs, would that not be just about the perfect way to act? This is why there is "fundamental good fortune."

The line statement on the second yin line is translated into English (including Lee's Korean translation) in many different ways. If one reads many versions of it, he would feel a bit perplexed and wonder how a short sentence made up of only a few Chinese characters could possibly yield such a variety of translations carrying different meanings. The reason for this lack of agreement among the translators (Cheng Yi, translated by Cleary, 1988:73; Lee, 1997[I]:300; Legge, 1963:108; Lynn, 1994:288; Wilhelm, 1967:507) lies in the fact that in Chinese, a word can be used with a variety of functions, such as a noun, verb, adjective, adverb and so on. In regards to this and in line with the stated purposes of this book, wherever this kind of occasion arises, I have exercised my discretion to choose an appropriate translation, for which I have applied two criteria: clarity and meaningfulness. That is, I have used the one that best allows a clearer and more meaningful interpretation. In view of this consideration, Lee's translation, "If the person at this position supports with delight the return movement (made by the one at the bottom position), there will be good fortune"[8] (this English translation is by this author) (Lee, 1997[I]:300-301), seems to square far better with the overall meaning of the hexagram and also with the commentaries supplemented by Cheng Yi and Wang Bi[9] themselves. The line statement, as translated above, is then interpreted to offer the position holder at the second position the advice that under the situation implied by the hexagram *Fu*, it would be beneficial for him (and perhaps for the good of a group involved in this situation) to support the returning movement going on at the grassroots level to resurrect the collective unit represented by the hexagram. But again, there is one thing that we have to be careful about in drawing a definite conclusion regarding what the line statement actually means to say. Both Wang Bi's and Cheng Yi's commentaries seem to engage a somewhat different perspective over this troublesome account on the second yin line. Let us look at what Cheng Yi (1988:73) says about this line:

Here return means return to order. Return to order is good. The return of the first yang is return to goodness. The second is close to the first, and is humble toward it. Therefore it is good and auspicious.

The above passage is not stated in the mode of an "if . . . . then . . . ." statement as in Lee's translation. This means that the statements cited above are *describing* the *existing* condition of someone who occupies the second position. That is, the line statement of the second yin line is interpreted as stating that the one at the second position is in support of the movement at the grassroots level to "return to an orderly state." Such a posture taken by the second yin line is judged as "good" in view of the urgent state of the situation calling for a movement towards recovery. Thus, this latter interpretation is describing rather than prescribing a situation in which a movement of the populace at the grassroots level to revive order from a malfunctioning social organization is making advance by gaining sympathetic support from the position holder(s) represented by the second yin line. Here some readers may come to realize that Chinese words and sentences, especially in classical writings, can bear out quite different meanings as one varies his underlying perspective towards what they are supposed to mean. Or it may be said that we have to make some underlying assumption about the original writer's real intention to get at a *correct* interpretation. At any rate, we have to choose a way for the case at hand; the prescriptive one or the descriptive one? Due to the peculiar nature of Chinese classical writings, this problem will continue to arise. Before I continue, therefore, I at this point will lay down a rule for an appropriate interpretation regarding this problem related to the meanings of the Text. In most cases, I will give preference to the *descriptive* interpretation for it usually corresponds better with the principle I already set down. That is, doing so renders a *clearer* and more *meaningful* interpretation in that it informs what the situation in question is like *as a matter of fact.* The prescriptive one, however, tells little about the present state of the situation itself. At any rate, by setting up the rule as stated above, we can also speed up our discussion without repeatedly belaboring the problem associated with interpreting Chinese classics.

With respect to the line statements attached to the next four yin lines — the third, the fourth, the fifth and the top lines — many readers may experience some difficulty in discerning any clear or meaningful linkage between what each of the line statements tells about the situation of the position holder at a specific position and the possible range of interpretations that can be logically inferred from the position itself. In other words, it does not seem immediately obvious how the line statements are related to the respective characteristics of the positions that can be understood in terms of the positional variation of the lines in the hierarchical order. Then, first, let us look at the line statements of the four upper positions that are presented together below:

> *Third Yin*: This one returns with urgency, so although there is danger, there will be no blame.
>
> *Fourth Yin*: It is by traveling a middle course that this one alone returns.
>
> *Fifth Yin*: This one returns with simple honesty, so there will be no regret.
>
> *Top Yin*: This one returns in confusion, which means misfortune. As it would involve utter disaster, if one were to set an army on the march here, it would in the end result in great defeat, and in terms of what it would do to the sovereign of one's state, it would mean misfortune. Even if it were as much as ten years, no attempt at recovery would ever succeed. (Lynn, 1994:288-290)

What is each of these line statements trying to say? Why is the position holder at the third position making a returning movement "with urgency" while the one at the fourth position is doing it "alone"? How about the fifth one who is said to "return with simple honesty"? And, why does the top one "return in confusion"? How does each of these different modes of "returning" relate to a specific situation that can be inferred by taking into account both the characteristic of a specific position that an actor occupies and his action orientation symbolized with a yin line? As far as this author sees, there seems to be no understandable or ostensibly justifiable rationale for attributing such varying modes of return movement to each position holder under the situation. Nevertheless we may be able to identify a general assumption underlying the line statements of this hexagram, which will apply equally throughout all the other hexagrams. This assumption concerns the effect of the social structure on the response patterns of involved actors towards a specific social situation. The assumption states simply that, depending upon the positions they occupy respectively in a given social organization, actors will react differently to a given social situation. This will sound familiar to social scientists of today. Sociology has also long asserted people act and think differently depending upon where they are located in the ranking order of a social stratification system. Nevertheless, we can point out two ways the distinction is made between what is suggested by the line statements of the hexagram *Fu* (and, by those of all the other hexagrams as well) and the differential effects of social positions on individuals' behavioral orientation as viewed in modern social sciences. The first one is that while the focus of modern social sciences in this respect is mainly on variations effected by *class-related* interests, the thinking of the *I Ching* operates at a more detailed level; it focuses on variations in response patterns as related to *positional* characteristics. Secondly, as far as the hexagram *Fu* is concerned (and, later I will also include many other hexagrams in this category), I can hardly think of any clearly understandable rationale with which each position holder is viewed to exhibit a specific response pattern that the corresponding line statement describes. Seen from the modern rational mind, a problematic aspect of the *I Ching* such as this may be simply understood as characteristic of the ancient classic containing knowledge presented with little systematic argument for its justification.

But again, a careful examination coupled with a little bit of imagination may reveal another interesting perspective underlying the narrated accounts on the lines of the hexagram *Fu*. As it was pointed out already, the hexagram of *Fu* symbolizes a situation in which a back-to-order movement starts out from the populace at the bottom level with the other members coming along in support of the movement. A movement from below and an accommodation of the movement by the upper strata are indicated here. In this situation, those at the first yang and second yin lines form a dyadic pair in close contact with each other. The nature of the relationship between these two position holders is described as a "close companionship." As Wang Bi explains in his commentary, "it (the second yin line) has benevolence for its close companionship and delights in the goodness of its neighbor (the first yang line)" (Lynn, 1994:288). This interpretation by Wang Bi must have been derived from the yin-yang principle, the principle that a person with a passive and receptive action orientation tends to be paired with a person with an active and superordinate action orientation since their action orientations as such are complementary to each other.

Meanwhile, the position holder represented by the third yin line is described to "return with urgency."[10] Why should the one at the third position show a tendency of hurrying up to jump into the undergoing back-to-order movement? It seems that a simple psychological principle is implied here — the band-wagon effect. That is, as the two lower position holders are held together and work together as an closely related dyadic unit, the third yin line, having little influence potential on its own under the situation despite his formal position at the top of the subordinate group, will not want to be alienated from the situational trend led by the lower dyadic unit. So he will hurry up to join the key actors at the driver's seat of the day's wagon. Understandably, Wang Bi (Lynn, 1994:288) comments on the situation of this third yin line, "although what is meant here results in 'no blame,' if anything else were involved, such a one would find it impossible to maintain this [good fortune]." That is, considering the overall characteristic of the situation as a whole, the "urgent return" made by the third yin line will be judged as an opportune movement, but such a move will not be evaluated as a happy one for him in view of his position of a formal leadership.

The fourth yin line is described to act in the midst of yin lines. Most commentators interpret this as implying that there is no one nearby with whom he can form a dyadic or triadic relationship (Cheng Yi, 1988:74; Lynn, 1994:289; Wilhelm, 1967:507-508). There is one yang line at the bottom with whom he can seek for a union, yet the one represented by the first yang line already has formed a close companionship with the second yin line and also is joined by the third yin line, the leader of the subordinated group. We may say that a more or less closely integrated triadic group is in formation at the lower stratum of a social organization. Thus, under this situation of the hexagram *Fu* the fourth yin line is characterized as an element acting in isolation from the rest of the members; "This one alone returns."

For the fifth line, I again will take Lee's translation, "If the person at this position supports the return movement with magnanimity, there will be no regret" (this English translation is by this author) (1997[I]:303). Notice the difference between the line statements of the second and the fifth yin lines. Instead of "good fortune," a favorable judgment rendered to the second yin line, the situation of the fifth yin line is judged to be "no regret," a less favorable one. Of this difference, Wang Bi (1994:289) explains:

> Although it has not sufficient means to attain the good fortune that the Return "with delightful goodness" [Second Yin] has, since it effects its Return in accordance with the maintenance of magnanimity, "regret" can be avoided.

What "sufficient means" actually signifies is not clear. What is clearly suggested by Wang Bi's above comment is an assertion that whatever actual outcome is brought, this situation, as experienced by the one in the position of formal leadership, is not a particularly good one. It is possible, however, he may be able to keep himself out of trouble by maintaining a magnanimous attitude towards the dominant trend of the time.

Finally, Lynn's translation of the line statement for the top yin line, "this one return in confusion, which means misfortune," departs a good deal from other versions of translation. For example, Wilhelm's translation reads, "missing return. Misfortune" (1967:508). Similarly, Cleary's translation has it that "straying from return bodes ill" (1988:75). Although the translation itself depends upon one's interpretation of the situation as a whole, I will follow in this case the opinion of the majority as meaning "missing return" or "straying from return." Then, the line statement of the top yin line can be interpreted as that which applies to "those who wind up astray and do not return" (Cheng Yi, 1988:75). An interesting prognosis given here is that, in this delicate process of turning back to an order from a disorderly state, those who refuse return may "seek(s) to attain (their) objective by force." In the process, resorting to an armed campaign "will in the end suffer a great defeat .... it loses for a long time all possibility of recuperation" (Wilhelm, 1967:508). Judging from the statements as they stand, it is not clear for whom the warning of a potential conflict is exactly uttered. It only suggests the possibility that some people may instigate an armed conflict in reaction to the return movement and the conflict, should it occur, will have disastrous outcomes for a long time.

The hexagram *Shi* (☷☵, the Army)

The descriptions of this hexagram commence with the hexagram statement, "if an army's constancy is subject to a forceful man, there will be good fortune and with no blame." Wang Bi comments on this statement by saying "a 'forceful man' is a designation for someone who is stern and resolute.[11] It is good fortune when there is such a forceful man to maintain the rectitude of an army" (Lynn, 1994:177). To grasp the meaning of the situation represented by the hexagram *Shi*, we have to visualize an urgent situation that forces a social organization to mobilize in such a way that it develops an army-like formation with a strong field commander at the helm. In light of this, as we can see from the structure of the lines, the second yang line represents the constituting rulership of this hexagram, the *de facto* leader exercising the dominant influence over the rest of the members represented by yin lines. The one called out as a "forceful man" refers to the one represented by this second yang line. The main characteristic of this situation therefore lies in the fact that the position holder in the second position, denoting middle-positioned officials attending to field services or field generals at the front line, plays the most active role guiding the operations of the social organization in question.

Now, the social organization has transformed into an army-like formation with someone who commands the entire operation located at the field area or front line. Under this situation one who performs the key function is the second position holder. Then, the first yin line would be interpreted as representing masses or people at the lowest stratum who are supposedly subject to the commandership exercised by the second yang line. Thus, Wang Bi comments on this line; "it is by means of regulations that mass troops are held in order. If such regulations are disregarded, the troops will come apart in confusion. This is why the text says, 'The Army should campaign according to regulations'" (Lynn, 1997:178).

As can be expected from the line composition of the hexagram, the line statement given to the second yang line is a favorable one; "here in *Shi*, one practices the Mean, so he has good fortune and so suffers no blame. His sovereign confers a threefold commendation on him" (Lynn, 1994:179). The second line is the only yang line while all other lines including the fifth line at the position of the governing ruler are yin lines. This implies an emergent situation under which the power and authority of the sovereign has been delegated to the one at the second position who is assigned to conduct some sort of very urgent and crucial field campaign. Wang Bi's following explanation illustrates the nature of this situation by making a specific reference to a feudal state that has gone into military campaign in face of a serious crisis:

> To obtain the good fortune that an army campaign offers, one can do no greater good than to win the support of the other states. To have the other states grant their support and the masses their submission, nothing is more important than how the sovereign confers his grace and favor, so this is why he [the general represented by Second Yang] obtains the perfect commendation here. (Lynn, 1997:179)

In addition, the hexagram statement on this hexagram *Shi* involves the advice that "if an army's constancy is subject to a forceful man, there will be good fortune and with no blame." This advice suggests that the second position under this situation should be given to a 'forceful man,' "a man with practical skills, strong body and will power, but not a type of person who is talented in abstract thinking or in theoretical reasoning" (Lee, 1997[I]:140). Thus, the *I Ching* sets down two crucial conditions for the successful operation of the kind of mission suggested by the hexagram *Shi*. First is the total support from the top leader of the organization. Second is that the one who is chiefly responsible for the field operation has to be a man of practical orientation coupled with strong body and will power.

Regarding the meaning of the line statement of the third yin line, most commentators side with Wang Bi's interpretation which translated the line statement into, "the Army perhaps use carriages to transport corpses, and this would be misfortune" (Lynn, 1994:179). The only exception is Cheng Yi whose view yields a quite different interpretation and subsequently a different version of translation, "it bodes ill for the army to have many bosses" (1988:17).[12] I do not know exactly why Cheng Yi took the secondary meanings instead of taking the primary ones as rendered by Wang Bi and other commentators. Yet, his interpretation as such seems to make much better sense than those rendered by others. The line statement seems to contain a warning for the position holder in the third position to avoid interference with the affairs being carried out by the one represented by the second yang line. "The third line is on the top of the lower trigram, in the position of responsibility for a leadership, but not only is it weak, it is not balanced correctly" (Cheng Yi, 1988:17) means that he is not suitable to carry out the responsibility in view of the situation characterized by the hexagram *Shi*. So he is warned not to press on with his formal position as a boss; and if he does, there will be "many bosses" that will suffer unfortunate outcomes under this situation of *Shi*.[13]

The line statement for the fourth yin line also raises some difficulty in interpretation; commentators come up with varying interpretations over the short passage consisting of only a few Chinese characters.[14] In my opinion, however, Lee's interpretation seems to be the most reasonable choice in that it fits more squarely with the characteristic of the situation as a whole and with interpretations rendered to other lines thus far. It reads, "if one camps his army at a lower place, there will be no blame" (Lee, 1997:143, this English translation is by this author). According to Lee's explanation of his interpretation, the fourth yin line represents a high ranking official in this particular situation, usually an official on civilian service rather than a military one, sent from the central government to oversee the conduct of the army operation. Thus, he is the figurehead commander ranked the highest among all personnel in the field operation. And, considering the circumstance that will be encountered by the one in the fourth place as such, the character "left" (左) has to be interpreted as meaning "low." Thus, the line statement of the fourth yin line is interpreted as containing advice given to the one in the fourth position to refrain from curbing the authority of the one (the second yang line) in the field operation by showing off his lofty presence.

After reading the line statement of the fifth yin line, we will grasp more fully the characteristic of the situation represented by the hexagram *Shi*. According to Wang Bi's interpretation, in view of the situation where a weak and passive leadership is incumbent in the position of the governing ruler, a state of mass mobilization, for example, a military operation, implied by the hexagram would be largely defensive in nature. Let us examine Wang Bi's views about the situation represented by the fifth yin line and the hexagram as a whole:

> This one finds himself here in a time of *Shi* [The Army], but it is a weak person who has obtained this noble position. However, being yin, he does not lead the singing, and, being weak, he does not commit aggression against others. If he responds only after having suffered aggression, when he sets out to deal with it, the corrective measures he takes are sure to succeed. This is why the text says, "when there is game in the fields." It is because these others have initiated aggression against him that he can "seize it then, and this will incur no blame." The weak are not ones to make hard warriors, thus they should not personally involve themselves, but others must be appointed instead. (Lynn, 1994:180)

And, since he is not a suitable person to lead the army himself, the *I Ching* warns, the success of the operation will wholly depend upon how suitable a person he appoints to the command post. It is in this context that Wang Bi goes on with his comment as follows:

> If the one appointed does not obtain his sovereign's support, the troop will not obey him. This is why it is right that "the elder son take[s] command of the Army" and why the misfortune pertaining to the younger son is certainly appropriate. (Lynn, 1994:180)

In the above passage, the older son symbolizes a person who could be seen as having competence and legitimacy by the troop. Recall here that the hexagram statement for this hexagram says, "if an army's constancy is subject to a forceful man, there will be good fortune and with no blame." The idea of a "forceful man" carries the same meaning symbolized by the "elder son" here. But, what will happen if "the one appointed is unsuitable" (Lynn, 1994:181)? The *I Ching* gives a grave warning by saying, "the younger son would use carriages to transport corpses."

The line statement attached to the top yin line does not seem to refer specifically to a situation the one at the top position is expected to encounter. As is the case with many other hexagrams, it explains how the given situation will come out at the end or how involved actors have to deal with the situation at its final stage to bring out a good outcome.[15] The line statement of the top yin line in this situation of *Shi* itself is rather straightforward: "he whom the great sovereign orders is either to found a marquistate or to establish a lesser feudatory, but if it is a petty man, he must not so employ him" (Lynn, 1994:181). Thus, Wang Bi's commentary on this merely paraphrases what is stated in the text: "in the orders that the great sovereign issues, he does not overlook those who have achieved merit but has them 'found marquistate[s]' or 'establish . . . . lesser feudator[ies]' in order to maintain the realm at peace. 'If it is a petty man, he must not so employ him,' for this task is incompatible with such a dao as his" (Lynn, 1994:181).

The hexagram *Qian* (☷☶ , Modesty)

Compared to the other hexagrams we have examined so far, the hexagram *Qian* seems to belong to a type that contains a rather different level of meaning. All the position holders are described as behaving modestly in playing their respective roles. Why all the position holders under this situation, including the one represented by the third yang line, the constituting ruler of the hexagram, are interpreted as displaying modest behaviors is not clear at all. Cheng Yi's commentary on this hexagram supposedly provides an explanation as to why the hexagram carries the meaning "modesty":

> The image of the hexagram is a mountain (represented by the lower trigram *Gen*) under the earth (represented by the upper trigram *Kun*); the earth is lowly, and a mountain is high, yet the high mountain dwells under the lowly earth. The meaning of humility is to have noble qualities yet remain lowly. (Cheng Yi, 1988:44)

Cheng Yi's comment cited above suggests that an ethical property of human behavior, modesty (or humility), as represented by the hexagram, was originally taken from natural imageries that were used to symbolize the meanings of the two trigrams constituting the hexagram. That is, the natural imageries of the hexagram had turned into the meaning of a human situation as indicated by the hexagram name. It is typical of the traditional Chinese thought to believe that people can make themselves aware of and thereby teach themselves certain moral virtues such as benevolence or wisdom by carefully observing principles on which natural objects like water or mountains are operating. Here no rigid distinction is made between natural laws and moral principles on human relations. Thus, as the hexagram *Qian* carries the symbolic image of a mountain lying low under the earth, it is thought to illustrate the virtue of modesty that is then equated with a human situation having a characteristic as such. This kind of an associative reasoning relating two classes of things categorically different from each other is strange and illogical to us. But, we have to bear with, if only for some hexagrams, such a peculiar mode of thinking if we are going to delve into the conditions of the social world as conceived by the *I Ching*.

To get at the unique idea conveyed by the hexagram *Qian*, there are two lines which require specific attention, the third and the fifth lines. First, let us read the line statements of the third and the fifth lines and Wang Bi's comments related to them:

> *Third Yang*: Diligent about his Modesty, the noble man has the capacity to maintain his position to the end, and this means good fortune. {Wang Bi's commentary: Third Yang occupies the very top of the lower trigram and so manages to tread on the territory of its rightful position [as a yang line in a yang position]. There is no yang line either above or below to divide off one's people here, and Third Yang is venerated as master by all the yin lines. In nobility none takes precedence over this one. When one finds himself here in this world of Modesty, how can one keep his nobility secure? One carries those above and reaches out those below, is diligent about his Modesty, and is not lazy: this is how he has good fortune.}
>
> *Fifth Yin*: One does not have to use wealth on them to gain access to neighbors here, and, as it is fitting to attack with military force, nothing will be to one's disadvantage. {Wang Bi's commentary: Fifth Yin occupies the position of nobility and does so with Modesty and compliance, thus it can have access to its neighbors without using wealth on them. In spite of its Modesty and compliance, it still attacks with military force, but in all such cases those whom it attacks are scornfully rebellious.} (Lynn, 1994:231-232)

The reason these two position holders are described as displaying modest behaviors was explained. The attribute of this situation and, consequently, the attributes of individuals' action orientations constituting the situation were taken from the ethical idea (or ideals) evoked by the natural imagery that the two constituent trigrams together impart in combination. In addition, to make sense out of the passage quoted above we need some prior knowledge about an ethical orientation so typical of the Confucian culture. In Confucian morality, modesty is considered one having a primary importance. Where the virtues of the leader are at issue, modesty is considered as not only an ethical principle that a leader has to comply with in conducting himself as a leader but also a source of influence or personal resource that enables one to amass heart-felt loyalties from others. Thus, the *I Ching* says the fifth yin line — the governing ruler described as practicing modesty here under the situation of *Qian* — "does not have to use wealth on them to gain access to neighbors here." In other words, just by behaving modestly, he will attract followers in large even without the use of material incentive. Basically the same diagnosis is also given to the one at the third position. He is the constituting ruler of a social organization represented by the hexagram *Qian.* Wang Bi explains in his commentary "there is no yang line either above or below to divide off one's people here, and Third Yang is venerated as master by all the yin lines. In nobility none takes precedence over this one." As far as one's actual influence potential is concerned, the one represented by the third yang line is described as the key person who holds the entire organization together. And, at the same time the third yang line is depicted as a leader who is diligently practicing his modesty. Therefore, the *I Ching* renders to this one also a favorable judgment equally comparable to the fifth one by saying, "he has good fortune."

We here can raise doubt as to whether this situation of *Qian* intends to describe any objectively conceivable situation or this hexagram is merely utilized as an occasion to teach concerned individuals the virtue of modesty. My impression is that the line statements of this hexagram were written with an ambivalent motive that can go either way. This also seems to apply to most commentaries written on this hexagram. After all, as far as the hexagram *Qian* is concerned, to say that all involved actors behave modestly under the situation involves a very ambiguous proposition. Did the author(s) of the *I Ching* believe that a situation where everybody behaves modestly was a real possibility that could come to existence whenever a social organization met the defined condition characterized by the hexagram?

Or, did they simply write down an ethically ideal situation into the line statements of the hexagram? To retrieve a sensible meaning from this hexagram of a somewhat problematic nature, let us pick out an empirical proposition from the *I Ching*, although we cannot say anything for sure of its validity. This can be stated as, "modesty is a valuable personal resource or a good strategy in interpersonal interaction which will bring about profitable outcomes in the long run." I think that this proposition lays down the main theme of this hexagram in that it explains the reason why a social organization under this situation is viewed to form a happy community,[16] i.e., a well-integrated situation.

But, before we settle down on the overall characteristic of the hexagram, we need to deal with a passage that seems contradictory to what is said above of the characteristic feature of the situation. Why does the *I Ching* describe the fifth yin line "as it is fitting to attack with military force, nothing will be to one's disadvantage"? This passage sounds contradictory to the meaning of the situation in which all involved actors are said to behave modestly. Of this line, Wang Bi adds a short explanation; "in spite of its Modesty and compliance, it still attacks with military force, but in all such cases those whom it attacks are scornfully rebellious." Yet, Wang Bi's explanation only paraphrases the line statement in a bit more detail, and, therefore, leaves the question still unanswered. Why does it become necessary for him to quell "scornfully rebellious" people by using military force? Cheng Yi who says the effectiveness of political leadership requires a balance between modesty and show of might forwards an answer to this question:

> However, the Way of leadership does not allow only humility and flexibility to be valued; it is necessary to have awesome might to balance it, before it is possible to really win the people over. Therefore "it is advantageous to invade and conquer to the benefit of all" ("it is fitting to attack with military force, nothing will be to one's disadvantage" in Lynn's translation). When power and virtue are both manifest, then the proper conditions for the Way of leadership are fulfilled, to the benefit of all. This principle is brought out here because it is appropriate to guard against excess in the humble yielding of the fifth yin line. (Cheng Yi, 1988:46)

Cheng Yi is quite straightforward in his commentary quoted above. The effectiveness of leadership is derived from a leader's moral virtues, but so as not to make modesty a weakness "it is necessary to have awesome might to balance it." So from time to time a leader has to stage a show of force by punishing those who are "scornfully rebellious." This seems to be good yet coldly calculated advice to be given to a person in leadership position if he is in fact known to be a person who behaves modestly. However, considering the nature of this situation titled "Modesty," who would be the target person to be dealt with "awesome might" for his "scornfully rebellious" behavior? According to Lee (1997[II]:215), the line statement of the third yang line should be translated as stating, "this line represents one who is in a position to practice modesty diligently, so only the noble man can carry out it till the very end. Then there will be good fortune." Translated in this way, the line statement can be interpreted to suggest the possibility that if the constituting rulership at the third position is not occupied by a noble man truly qualified for that position, the leader of the subordinate group, the one at the third position surrounded by compliant (yin) individuals, may become "scornfully rebellious" as time passes by. And, Lee (1997[II]:215) in fact interprets the line statement as containing, if implicitly, such a warning. Interpreted as such, a simple truth is proposed by the *I Ching* regarding the way the minds of ordinary people work. It will be extremely difficult for a person who "is venerated as master by all the yin lines" to keep on his modest posture "to the end." So it is said, "only the noble man can carry out it till the very end." Then, a question may again be raised. Considering the formation of the situation represented by the hexagram *Qian*, does the fifth yin line of the governing rulership have a real potential to "attack (the one at the third position who is venerated as *de facto* 'master by all yin lines' under the situation) with military force"? It may sound contradictory to say that a weak leader "attacks with military force" a strong subordinate. However, it is not if one considers the "Oriental moral logic." [17] As Cheng Yi points out in his commentary, "those who are leaders yet who remain humble and receptive gain the allegiance of the whole world" (1998: 45), and such allegiance gained through modesty becomes a source of power.

Lastly, the line statement of the top yin line makes the following perplexing observation: "expressing humility, it is beneficial to mobilize the army to conquer one's land"[18] (Cheng Yi, 1988:46). Of the specific situation of the top position holder, Wang Bi and Cheng Yi give partly similar and partly different interpretations:

> Wang Bi's commentary: "Top Yin does not share in inner governance. Thus, one has nothing more than his reputation, and 'one's

ambition to accomplish things remains unfulfilled'." (Lynn, 1994:233)

Cheng Yi's commentary: "Even if they have no rank or position, and are not in charge of affairs of national importance, nevertheless what people do should have a balance of strength and flexibility." (Cheng Yi, 1988:46)

Yet, both commentators seem to converge on a similar interpretation regarding the concluding remark, "it is beneficial to mobilize the army to conquer one's land." According to the explanations offered by the two commentators, the behavioral maxim applied to the fifth line is again equally applied here — humility, not to become a weakness, has to be balanced with strength. However, as Chung Yi points out, "they (the position holder at this position) here have no rank or position, and are not in charge of affairs of national importance." Thus, according to Cheng Yi, "conquering one's land" means here a use of strength only in one's own sphere of influence or towards oneself (1988:46); this gives a portrait of a disfranchised former leader or intellectual with no formal position who therefore has no choice but to perform a task limited to his own house management.

The hexagram *Yu* [☷ ☳, Contentment; Enthusiasm[19]]

For this hexagram, I will start with the fourth and the fifth lines that represent the constituting and the governing rulers of this hexagram respectively, since it seems that the situational characteristic of the hexagram rests mainly upon the relationship between these two lines. First, of the fourth yang line the line statement states, "the source of enthusiasm. He achieves great things. You gather friends around you as a hair clasp gathers the hair" (Wilhelm, 1967:70). Here the fourth yang line is described as "a great minister" (Cheng Yi, 1988:49) around whom people gather with enthusiasm, probably expecting him to lead a new age with a new leadership. The enthusiasm that the strong leader at the fourth position arouses among the people is explained by the characteristic of the fifth yin line who is described as a "weak leader" (Cheng Yi, 1988:49); he is too weak a leader to exercise effective leadership over the social unit represented by the hexagram *Yu*. Thus, Wang Bi comments on this as follows:

Fourth Yang acts with hardness and strength and is the master of the *Yu* hexagram. As Fourth Yang exercises control as absolute ruler, it is not something on which Fifth Yin can ride. Thus it does not dare to contend with Fourth Yang for power. However, since it also abides in the Mean and occupies the noble position, it cannot possibly run away. This is why it is constantly forced to go so far as to do nothing but "maintain constancy in the face of such harassment" and just "persevere in warding off death." (Lynn, 1994:238)

The above passage renders a portrait of a top leader who barely maintains a contemptible existence under a strong subordinate whom people enthusiastically support. Thus, the fourth yin line is the star under this situation, the center of the enthusiasm, shadowing the weak formal leader standing behind him.

Now, what about the other positions? To begin with, each line statement of the other lines seems makes good sense in itself, although how they relate to the attribute of the respective position to which they are appended is not immediately clear. The author(s) of the *I Ching* may have thought out the various modes of possible behavior that people may exhibit under the leadership pattern characterized as above by the *Yu* hexagram and then assigned each of them to the first, the second and the third yin lines respectively. However, the rationale with which the *I Ching* assigns a specific mode of behavior to each position holder is not immediately clear as we try to grasp it from the surface meanings of the line statements. Thus, for instance, the line statement of the first yin line reads, "if one allows one's Contentment (Enthusiasm) to sing out here, there will be misfortune" (Lynn, 1994:236). Commentators converge on the interpretation that this statement describes a low status person who is "singing out (like a bird)" his enthusiasm for the one in power (as represented by the fourth yang line), perhaps with egoistic ambitions (Cheng Yi, 1988:47; Lee, 1997[I]:223-224; Legge, 1963:92; Lynn, 1994:236; Wilhelm, 1967:69). The *I Ching* gives a warning, "this leads to the misfortune of having the will obstructed" (Wilhelm, 1967:468). But, the *I Ching* does not explain clearly why the person represented by the first yin line tends to display the described mode of enthusiastic behavior and why the behavior has to bring about unfortunate outcomes. Apparently, the behavior itself is not viewed as a commendable one. As such, the outcome predicted for the behavior of the first yin line may be explained by an Oriental moral logic that both the author(s) of the *I Ching* and commentators apply more or less implicitly. Cheng Yi sets forth this moral logic in a explicitly written statement: "shallowness like this inevitably runs one into trouble" (1988:47). According to this instructive advice of Cheng Yi, expressing openly and loudly an enthusiastic support for a leader having dubious legitimacy will bring about no good outcome in the long run.

Concerning the mode of behavior displayed by the second yin line, the line statement reads, "harder than rock, he does not let the day run its course. Constancy means good fortune" (Lynn, 1994:236). Commentators generally agree in their interpretations on this line statement. The person here is interpreted as behaving with a great deal of caution under the situation of Enthusiasm; comments rendered to it are mostly quite similar in content to what Wang Bi says about this line:

> This is someone who, being secure in his practice of constancy and rectitude, does not seek thoughtless Contentment (enthusiasm). If one is compliant but does not follow thoughtlessly and is content without violating the Mean (a balanced posture), he will therefore conduct relationships with superiors without sycophancy and with subordinates without insult. (Lynn, 1994:236)

Thus, in short, the second yin line represents a person who conducts relationships with the man in power at the fourth position with the proper measure of compliance, yet balanced with some reserved uprightness. This is the portrait of a man who knows how to keep subtle balance between the trend of the time and his independent self. Of course, as I said a little earlier, it is not clear why there is a difference between the position holders at the first and the second positions in their modes of behavioral orientation under this situation. A typical reasoning applied by the *I Ching* and commentators as well is related to the "appropriateness" of one's position. The second position, being a yin position, is said to be "appropriately occupied" if a yin line occupies that position. Therefore, the second position under the situation of *Yu* is in fact "appropriately being occupied" by a yin line and has to be interpreted to depict someone who behaves in "appropriate" manners. But still, I think, there seems to be no logically inevitable linkage between the line of reasoning that the *I Ching* applies and the specific behavioral orientation that is said to be displayed by the second yin line under the situation of the hexagram *Yu*.

Compared to the "ideal" mode of behavior displayed by the second yin line under the situation of *Yu*, the line statement of the third yin line describes a person who is thrown into an uneasy situation. Listen to what Wang Bi says of this line:

Here one is located at the very top of the lower trigram, that is, at the boundary between the two trigrams. Where this one treads is not its rightful position [because it is a yin line in a yang position], yet it supports the actions of the master of the *Yu* [Contentment, or enthusiasm] hexagram [Fourth Yang]. When one [Fourth Yang] enjoys Contentment (or, enthusiastic supports from others) with eyes so haughty with pride as this, regret will surely come of it [for Third Yin], but if [Third Yin] is too slow to follow, he will suffer Contentment's [i.e., the master of Contentment's, or Forth Yang's] ire. Third Yin's position is not one he can secure, yet he uses it to pursue Contentment, so it is perfectly appropriate that such a one here encounters regret whether he advances or retreats. (Lynn, 1994:237-238)

The above passage by Wang Bi suggests, if implicitly, the source of the uneasiness experienced by the one at the third position. Being close in position to the man in power "with eyes so haughty with pride," he may be compared to a frog within reach of a stone that may be thrown at any time if the former wishes to vent his anger. Yet, why does the man of *de facto* rulership in the fourth position have "eyes so haughty with pride"? Of course, the reason is not difficult to see; he enjoys a monopoly of power so overwhelming even the formal leader above him merely ekes out a bare existence "in the face of such harassment." Compared to the line statement of the second yin line which seems to have some logical gap between its situational meaning attributed and its formally defined positional attribute in the hexagram, the line statement of the third yin line puts us in a better position to grasp the reason why such a mode of behavior is displayed by a person(s) represented by the line at the position.

Lastly, the top yin line entails a line statement for which interpretations rendered by commentators differ from one another so much that no common theme is discernible.[20] Allowed to make a choice for the most meaningful interpretation, however, I would say the line statement seems to express a view that the enthusiastic situation depicted by the hexagram *Yu* is not desirable in the long run and that a change has to take place as the situation draws near to the end. I would like to point out that Asian people in general would not favor a situation of "the lower dominating the upper" implied by the hexagram *Yu*. Emphasizing its undesirable state of affairs of people's "enthusiasm" for the powerful second ranking man as understood above, Cheng Yi's commentary on the top yin line says:

> Because this is the end of delight (enthusiasm), ignorance has already occurred; if you can change, then you can be faultless. This has the

meaning of being able to change at the end of delight (enthusiasm). When they make mistakes, if they can change by themselves, people can become faultless. So even if ignorance is already established, if they can change, that is good. (Cheng Yi, 1988:50)

If we were to interpret the line statement of the top yin line only in this way, it seems obvious that the line statement has nothing to do with the individual situation of someone who occupies the top position. It rather contains an evaluation of the situation as a whole and at its ending stage and gives advice judged appropriate for this time stage.

The hexagram *Bi* (☵ ☷, Closeness, Holding Together [Union][21])

The nature of a situation represented by the hexagram *Bi* can be easily understood from a simplified structure of its leadership: the governing rulership overlaps with the constituting rulership while all other positions are occupied by yin lines indicating that they are all compliant with the one at the fifth position. Thus, a social organization as a whole is "held together" under a strong leadership solely present at the position of the formal leadership. The *I Ching* offers a brief statement on how this kind of a tightly integrated situation under a strong leadership comes to existence: " 'Those in places not at peace then come': all in the upper and the lower trigrams respond to it [Fifth Yang]" (Lynn, 1994:184). To this passage in the *Judgment* Wang Bi adds a rather long commentary:

> There is no other yang line in either the upper or the lower trigram to divide off the folk under separate sovereignty, and, since Fifth Yang alone occupies a position of nobility, none fail to pay it allegiance. Since all in the two trigrams are in resonance with it, they find both cordiality and security there. As Fifth Yang represents security, the insecure entrust themselves to it. This is why "those in places not at peace then come" and why "all in the upper and the lower trigrams respond to it." It is those who have not who seek out those who have; those who already have do not need to seek out others to provide them. It is those who are in danger who seek out security; those who already enjoy security do not need to seek out others to protect them. Fire has its flame, so those suffering from cold draw near to it. Therefore it is because they would find security there that "those in places not at peace then come." (Lynn, 1994:184-185)

The situation that Wang Bi explains in the above passage seems to reflect a historical experience in political process that should be commonly witnessed by history watchers. First, assume a turbulent political situation where large and small feudal states or tribal states are ridden with armed strif against one another; no one is secured if he is not strong enough to protect himself. Now a strong leader emerges and rises up to a promising figure to bring unity and peace by subjecting the entire nation to his strong rule. Consequently, "those in places not at peace then come" to him for "security." This kind of situation recognized by Wang Bi would not be one unfamiliar even to historians in the West. The following accounts by Toynbee (1963,7A:69) seem to provide a fairly relevant instance in this respect:

> A universal state is imposed by its founders and accepted by its subjects, as a panacea for the ills of a Time of Troubles. In psychological terms, it is an institution for establishing and maintaining concord; and this is the true remedy from which a broken-down civilization is suffering as the penalty for its breakdown is that of being a house divided against itself, and this schism in society is a double one. There is a horizontal schism between contending social classes as well as a vertical schism between warring states, and a universal state is born of a paroxysm which exacerbates this twofold strife to an unprecedented and intolerable degree of intensity and, in the same act, puts a sudden stop to it for the time being. The immediate and paramount aim of the empire builders, in making a universal state out of the Power that emerges as the sole survivor from a war of annihilation between the parochial states of the preceding age, is to establish concord among themselves and with their fellow members of the minority of their society who are survivors of the former ruling element in those parochial states that have succumbed in the fratricidal struggle.

To grasp the relevance of the above accounts to the situation represented by the hexagram *Bi*, let us visualize a power that has enormously expanded through a process of military struggles by founders of a universal state. In fact, this had been the case in establishing many great empires including the successive dynasties in the history of China. In such process, all contending parties engage in wars against one another mobilizing all available resources, human and material. Perhaps, the one that would come out victorious at the end would be the one who had done the best in supporting the fight of its founders against other warring states, and the victory will enable its leader to amass unchallengeable power into his hands. When a universal state emerges upon the ashes of destroyed states that have lost the struggle, there appear the psychological phenomena that Toynbee points out to be the case in the passage quoted above. That is, there emerge the governed, "shapeless mass" who are eager to accept the "panacea" of peace, yet lacking "active (yang)" spirit to resist the terms of peace imposed by the victorious ruler. The hexagram *Bi* represents this kind of union.

Now, let us examine how the *I Ching* views specific situations that individual position holders at their respective position would find themselves under the situation. First, the line statement of the first yin line reads, "if there is sincerity, joining in Closeness (union) will not lead to blame. If the sincerity one has keeps the earthenware filled, it will always exert an attraction, so there will be good fortune brought on by others" (Lynn, 1994:185). What the above statement tells about seems straightforward: it gives advice to a person at the lowest position that it would be beneficial for him to let himself merge into a social organization unified under the sole leadership at the fifth position with a simple mind.

The line statement of the second position also is not much different from the above. It states, "here one joins in closeness from the inner trigram. Constancy results in good fortune" (Lynn, 1994:186). Wang Bi's comment on this simply recapitulates what is already said in the line statement: "therefore this one manages to bring about its Closeness from the inner (lower) trigram and can have nothing more than the good fortune derived from practicing constancy [toward Fifth Yang]" (Lynn, 1994:186).

Meanwhile, the line statement of the third yin line involves meaning which yields no easy interpretation. The line statement itself is stated with little ambiguity: "here one joins in Closeness but not with his own people." Although it seems sensible to interpret that the statement refers to the fact that the third yin line pointing to the leader of the subordinate group seeks out for union with the fifth yang line rather than anyone in his own group, most commentators including Wang Bi excludes such interpretation (Cheng Yi, 1988:21; Lee, 1997[I]:152; Legge, 1963:75; Wang Bi, 1994:186-187; Wilhelm, 1967:38). They merely suggest a possibility that the third yin line may go into union with people who are not suitable to associate with under this situation, yet without mentioning specifically who the people unsuitable to be associated with are. So let us leave this ambiguity as it is as this kind of difficulty might be encountered quite frequently in the *I Ching*.

The line statement of the fourth yin line is straightforward again: "here one joins in Closeness from the outer (upper) trigram. Constancy results in good fortune" (Lynn, 1994:187). This statement yields an easy interpretation: as a constituent element of the dominant group at the center of power the position holder represented by the fourth yin line joins in "holding together" with the fifth yang line and, since his faithful service rendered to his superior as such is consistent with the nature of his duty as implied by his formal position, he will have good fortune.

Thus, the situation of the hexagram *Bi* is characterized with the strong power concentrated on the top leader on the governing rulership. There would be no one who could challenge his leadership under this situation, and submission to his authority is made a norm of the day. Nevertheless, the *I Ching* warns of a danger involved in using the unlimited power without restraint and caution. Let us read the line statement of the fifth yang line: "Manifestation of holding together. In the hunt the king uses beaters on three sides only, and foregoes game that runs off in front. The citizens need no warning. Good fortune" (Wilhelm, 1967:38).[22] What is suggested by this line statement seems straightforward if expressed metaphorically. The advice given to the leader possessing the almighty power is that he should not abuse it by trying to crush out every single soul who comes in the way of the drive toward the "unification (holding together)" under his leadership. There is an Oriental proverb that says, "even a rat will turn back and bite a person if driven to a corner." And, after all, some generosity would be a "kingly attitude" that would attract a greater multitude of willing subjects.

Commentators do not differ to any considerable degree in interpreting the meaning of the top yin line, although the statement, "he finds no head for holding together. Misfortune" (Wilhelm, 1967:39), itself sounds somewhat incomprehensible at first reading. Wang Bi describes this one as "the latecomer" who "finds himself shunted aside by the moment" (Lynn, 1994:188). Legge (1963:76) reproduces the interpretation of Wang Bi by offering the following explanation:

> A weak line being in the 6th place, which is appropriate to it, its subject is supposed to be trying to promote union among and with the subjects of the lines below. It is too late. The time is past. Hence it is symbolised as 'without a head,' that is, as not having taken the first step, from which its action should begin, and go on to the end.

Cheng Yi's and Wilhelm's interpretations also do not diverge significantly from the above as rendered by Legge. This kind of situation itself may be understood as a commonplace affair taking place quite often in everyday life. After all, it would be an ordinary experience for many politicians to find out belatedly that they, hedging their political fortune with a camp which only later has turned out to lose, have been left out from the marching parade of the victor. A question, however, may be raised; why does one who is at the top position have to represent anyone who has fallen into such "unfortunate" situation? Or, what sort of structural attribute associated with the top position under this situation of *Bi* makes one at that position fall into such "misfortune"? Neither the *I Ching* nor later commentaries provide any satisfactory answer to this question.

The hexagram *Bo* (☷ ☶ ,Peeling. Splitting Apart[23])

Bo, the name of the hexagram, as used here means decay, disintegration or destruction (Lynn, 1994:280-281; Wilhelm, 1967:93). Cheng Yi (1988:69) reads from this hexagram a situation in which "erasing and negating rectitude," i.e., decay in morality, takes place among individuals as its typical symptom. Looking only at the line formation of the hexagram itself and also considering the ways in which most hexagrams examined so far have been interpreted, the reason why this hexagram is interpreted as representing a disintegrating or morally degenerating situation may not be immediately clear. My own guess is that the meaning of the hexagram as a whole and specific conditions of individuals that are said to be determined in the context of the overall situation might have been derived from a seasonal imagery that are conveyed by the graphic image of the hexagram. Notice that the pictorial image of the hexagram may be viewed as if it represented a withering tree with its only living energy preserved in fruits hanging at high branches. Then, it does not seem difficult to see that the situational meaning of the hexagram as representing a morally degenerating or socially disintegrating situation might have been developed by analogy from the image of physical deterioration conveyed by a withering plant life.

As understood as above, under this situation represented by the hexagram *Bo*, the top yang line is assumed to represent one who has not yet fallen prey to the overwhelming trend of the time in which decay in morality permeates into every social stratum. Thus, the line statement says of this line, "Here the biggest fruit is not eaten. If it be a noble man, he shall obtain a carriage, but if it be a petty man, he shall allow Peeling to happen to humble huts" (Lynn, 1994:283). Notice that the top position represents that which lies outside the formal line of the hierarchical order. This means that the influence potential of the top yang line, although he is described as being in a position to exercise the *de facto* leadership under the situation, is quite limited because he lacks a legitimate power that usually comes with a formal position. Thus, if he is able enough to lead well the "common folk" represented by yin lines under him, it would help them to "obtain shade and protection." If he is a less suitable person who is not capable of carrying out the job as such, a disastrous outcome may happen "to that which provides those below with shelter" (Lynn, 1994:283). This kind of a delicate leadership based on informally established prestige or authority to influence people does not seem to be a totally unfounded idea that is created out of some irrational imagination. I would like to compare, if only in some limited aspect related to the specific social condition of old China, the leadership function formed under the situation of *Bo* to the position that some topnotch intellectuals or ideologues enjoy even in modern days under a certain situation. A hopeless situation of a decaying society makes people look forward to a "spiritual" leader who is not tainted by the ills of the time, and they may get quite vulnerable to influences from anyone who is outside the established order and, as they see, carries signs of new hope. The *I Ching*, however, seems to view that this kind of a spiritual leadership has mixed potentials. Cheng Yi explains about such mixed possibilities involved in the role of the top yang line in this situation as follows:

> And when disorder comes to a peak, then we will naturally think about remedying it. It is why the heart's desire of the multitudes bear enlightened leaders, so the enlightened "get a vehicle (carriage)." In the hexagram this is symbolized by the yins respectfully regarding the yang as their leader and providing collective support. The small person is deprived of a house in the sense that at the apogee of stripping way (disintegration), in the case of the small person it strips away the house (a social organization as represented by the hexagram *Bo*),[24] so there is no place for the body. (1988:71)

Cheng Yi's above comment suggests that depending upon how "enlightened" the leadership represented by the top yang line actually is the situation will develop into either one of two opposite situations, integration or disintegration.

Then, how would the fifth yin line, the governing ruler, be getting along under the situation of *Bo*? The line statement of this line says, "as if they were a string of fish, here court ladies enjoy favor, so nothing done here fails to be fitting" (Lynn, 1994:283). Of this statement, Cheng Yi offers the following explanation:

> The fifth yin is the leader of the yins, and yins are symbolized here by fish. The fifth yin can make the group of yins in an orderly fashion and so win the favor of the yang above, like a courtier; therefore it is beneficial to all.

Commentaries rendered by Wang Bi (Lynn, 1994:283) and Wilhelm (1967:96) do not differ to any significant extent from Cheng Yi's interpretation cited above. It will be interesting to notice that the five broken lines lining up one upon the other look like a string of fish hung from a ceiling. Although we do not know for sure whether the line statement of the fifth line in fact had do to with the graphic image of the hexagram as such, it seems nevertheless the case with the *I Ching* that at least some of its text accounts are related to picture images of hexagrams. Of course, it would certainly be appropriate to think that by relating the two logically unrelated elements — i.e., what is figuratively suggested by a graphic appearance of a hexagram and the substantive meaning of a line to be analytically interpreted from the line formation of a hexagram — the *I Ching* pushes itself to a brink of irrational reasoning. Nevertheless, in this specific case the analogy between a string of fish and a group of passive and lethargic individuals suggested by the situation of *Bo* seems to make a quite reasonable match. Seen in this way, the role that the fifth yin line plays under the situation is not evaluated positively. After all, it will be informative to know that the terms like "court lady" or "strung fish" carry little positive meanings, or more or less belittling ones especially if they refer to traits of a male person in Asian societies. He is viewed merely as the head figure of strung fish, the leader of a group of the yin lines the most of whom are described as "being stripped away," i.e., being in a process of "erasing and negating rectitude" (Cheng Yi, 1988:69) in their morality. Thus, according to Wang Bi (Lynn, 1994:283), if a group consists of people going down on degenerative path as represented by a string of the yin lines of the hexagram *Bo*, one has to "grant favor to (them) in such a way that this would be strictly limited to palace ladies" (Lynn, 1988:283). Being interpreted as by Wang Bi, the line statement of the fifth yin line involves, at least as long as an Oriental perspective of this author is concerned, a quite interesting psychological maxim; under a certain situation where a people of a certain sort as represented by the hexagram *Bo* are prevailing, it would be much more appropriate to treat them with personally engaging favoritism rather than with strict formal rules or moral principles. Thus, here the line statement is interpreted as involving advice given to the top yang line concerning how he has to deal with the people with the characteristic trait represented by the yin lines below him.

The line statement itself, however, leaves some room for ambiguity concerning who is the proper subject to whom the advice contained in the line statement is addressed. If we follow Cheng Yi's version of interpretation as quoted already, the line statement involves a rather different meaning. What the line statement purports to say now is interpreted as directed to the fifth yin line itself: "The fifth yin can make the group of yins follow in an orderly fashion and so win the favor of the yang, like a courtier; therefore it is beneficial to all" (1988:70). In an additional note, Cheng Yi explains also, "speaking in terms of yin, the meaning here is of gaining appreciation and favor." Viewed in this way, the line statement of the fifth yin line yields a somewhat different interpretation from that rendered by Wang Bi: if the person represented by the fifth yin line, while "making the group of yins to follow in an orderly fashion," behaves appropriately so that he can win appreciation and favor (like a court lady) from the top yang line, a social organization represented by the hexagram would be benefited as a whole. Which interpretation of the two different versions presented above we may adopt, however, the meanings interpreted as such seem to make sense, for either of them can be made consistent with the overall meaning that the hexagram *Bo*, having the top yang line as its constituting ruler, has as a whole.

To the rest of the lines, i.e., the first, the second, the third and the fourth lines, the *I Ching* adds statements which vary progressively in line with the respective ranks of the positions that the lines occupy in the hexagram structure. For example, the line statement of the first line states, "the bedstead has suffered Peeling (stripping away) to the legs; so does constancy meet with destruction" (Lynn, 1994:281). For the line statement of the second yin line, only "the legs" from the above line statement of the first yin line is replaced with "the frame"; thus, the line statement for the second yin line reads, "the bedstead has suffered Peeling (stripping away) to the frame; so does constancy meet with destruction" (Lynn, 1994:281). And, passing over the third line, the line statement of the fourth yin line, "the bedstead has suffered Peeling (stripping away) to the skin. This means misfortune" (Lynn, 1994:282), repeats the same pattern. Only exception is the third line. In its line statement, the subject at this position is described as also suffering "Peeling," but, in contrast to the three lines as described above, no diagnosis indicating a particularly misfortunate outcome is rendered. Now, to understand the line statements of the first, the second and the fourth lines mentioned first, it would be necessary to understand the symbolism in which a social organization represented by the hexagram is compared to a human body lying on a bed. Then, it will be easy to imagine that each of the line statements is describing a part of the bedstead and the body going down on a process of decay. That is, the line statements describe a decaying society at its various parts. But, why does the *I Ching* view that although the subject represented by the third yin line also is not exceptional by its being involved in that process, he still is exempted from unfortunate consequences arising from the degenerating trend of the time? According to most commentators including Wang Bi, the reason is found in that the third yin line forms a "corresponding" relationship with the top yang line rather than associating himself with other yin lines located near to him (Legge, 1963:107; Lynn, 1994:282; Wilhelm, 1967:95). In other words, if the top yang line represents a flag bearer to lead the group to get out of the decaying situation, the third yin line is viewed as most receptive to such a hopeful call sign from the top yang line.

I would like to conclude this discussion on the hexagram *Bo* by pointing out a few things that particularly draw my attention. First, it seems that the situation represented by the hexagram *Bo* is the weakest one among all the yang-centered types of integration in terms of the degree and quality of integration it displays as that of a social organization. This weakness in integration is obviously related to two factors: the absence of an effective leadership and degenerative qualities of constituent members. This does not mean that there is no leading element in this situation; the top yang being the sole yang line in the hexagram is occupying the constituting ruler's position. Nevertheless, he has no position in the formal hierarchical order, and due to such a lack of a formal power he has to exercise his influence through an indirect channel, i.e., through the fifth yin line who is described as "leading the fish" (Cheng Yi, 1988:70). The other factor that makes this situation the weakest of all the yang-centered type of integration is, as pointed out, that a social organization represented by the hexagram *Bo* is for the most part constituted of people who are morally or, say, spiritually degenerating. The second thing I would like to point out is that, being interpreted as set down by authoritative commentators, the accounts of the *I Ching* seems to involve some inconsistency. The fifth yin line is described as one who leads the "fish" "in an orderly fashion" and thus gets appreciation from the top yang line. On the other hand, the third yin line is said to represent one who form a "corresponding" relationship with the top yang line. In the *I Ching*, a corresponding relationship means a formation of a close social tie between two actors who are drawn to each other due to mutually felt needs or compatibility. Thus, while the line statement of the third yin describes its subject to form a close companionship with the leading element of the situation at the top position, the line statement of the fifth line describes its situation rather differently by stating that it is one of the strung fish led by the fifth yin line.

The third point I would like to raise is also related to the line statement of the third position. As I see it, the idea of the formation of a corresponding relationship between constituent members of a social organization itself is quite an interesting and plausible one. To take a simple example, if a leader and members at various ranks form a group, within-relationships among the members will take various forms. Sometimes the leader may form a closer relationship with certain members who are steps apart from him than someone who is ranked immediately next to him. A corresponding relationship in the *I Ching* refers to this type of companionship formed between individuals who are not supposed to interact directly and closely with each other in capacity of their formal positions. I think that this idea itself points to a real possibility in the sense that it may be experienced actually as facts of life. The problem with the line statement of the third yin line, however, as far as I see, the *I Ching* provides no explanation about why under the situation the third yin line other than anyone else forms a corresponding relationship with the top yang line.

One possible explanation may be sought in that the *I Ching* views the two positions, the third position and the top position, as being placed in somewhat ambivalent situations. The top position is a position of high prestige yet possesses no formal power. The third position represents that of the leader for the subordinate group, yet is subject to the authority of those at upper echelons. Cleary (1988:xiii), following the tradition established for the interpretation of the *I Ching*, characterizes the typical condition that the position holder of the third position faces as follows

> The third line, at the top of the bottom trigram, represents those at the head of the lower echelons. Being at the top, it is technically considered a strong position, but being in the lower echelons it is still subordinate to the higher positions. Many tensions and conflicts arise at the border between the power and upper ranks, for this is where there exists the

greatest differences between the status of the line in the context of its own trigram and its status in the context of the hexagram as a whole.

It is perhaps because of this ambivalence that, as far as the *I Ching* views it, the third position under usual situations is not tightly knit into neighboring elements or, say, has some difficulty in securing a stable position in its relationship with neighboring ones at the positions immediately lower and higher to him. Thus, The *I Ching* states, "the third usually concern misfortune" (Lynn, 1994:92). The ambivalence and insecurity associated with the third position are frequently expressed in line statements of the third position in many other hexagrams. And, the same may be said of the top position. So it is said, "in this line there is great potential for trouble and sorrow, so there are many alerts found in the top lines, to help people avoid unnecessary grief at the extreme limits of situations" (Cleary, 1988:xiii). It is perhaps due to this similarity in their positional attributes that the *I Ching* views that the position holders at the third and the top positions tend to form an alliance with each other under certain situations.

Summary of theoretical and empirical propositions

1) When a situation involves a single position holder with an active and superordinate action orientation with all others displaying a passive and conforming action orientation, the single actor with the uniquely active action orientation will exercise the *de facto* (constituting) leadership over the group characterized as such by a hexagram.

2) Since a social organization as a rule includes the position of the formal leadership, two types of leadership, the governing ruler and the constituting ruler, may be present at the same time for some social organizations. It is due to this reason that the social organizations under situations characterized by the yang-centered integration patterns differ from one another with respect to their leadership structures: ones that have a single leadership structure and ones that have double leadership structures.

3) As social organizations differ from one another in their modes of integration, there will be differences from one type of social organization (situation) to another in patterns of within-relationships among position holders. (Compare this perspective to that of Western sociology in general which is interested in

"general" features of structural relationships among or between social classes).

4) When the lowest stratum of a social organization holds an initiative in leading the main situational trend for the organization as shown in the hexagram *Fu*, it will also bring a band wagon effect into play. That is, even the people at upper strata may be forced or attracted into a situational trend led by the people at the lowest stratum. This means that as such a situation arises, even people at higher strata fall into situations in which they are compelled to go along with those at lower levels.

5) There are two conditions for the situation represented by the hexagram *Shi* (a situation in which a social organization is organized to cope with an emergent field operation) to end up with a successful outcome: a total delegation of power and trust by the top leader to the man at the commanding post in charge of the field operation and an appointment of a suitable man to the post responsible for it. According to the *I Ching*, for this particular type of responsibility a man of practical reasoning, physical strength and will power would be better suited than a "person who is talented in abstract thinking or theoretically reasoning."

6) Under the emergency situation represented by the hexagram *Shi*, to have too many bosses will result in a disastrous outcome. This implies that the decision making power has to be concentrated in the hands of the person chiefly responsible for presiding over the field operation.

7) Modesty is not only a moral virtue for a leader but also a personal resource that, by winning over the minds of people when properly exercised, can be turned into a potential for power. Yet, lest his modesty be perceived as a weakness by subordinates, he sometimes has to stage a show of force by punishing those who "are scornfully rebellious."

8) When the morality of people decline and, therefore, where a certain type of people with low moral quality prevail, a personally engaging favoritism rather than strict moral principles or formal rules would be a much more effective means to govern them.

9) Depending on types of situations, a social alliance (corresponding relationship) may be formed between strata of people who are far apart from each other in their social ranks.

3) Six Yin-Centered Hexagrams: Yin-Centered Modes of Integration

Yin-centered hexagrams as named here refer to a type of hexagrams which have a yin line as its "constituting ruler." As was explained already in the previous section, if a yin line is the only yin line in a hexagram whereas all other lines consist of yang lines, the yin line is interpreted as occupying the position of the constituting ruler for that hexagram, and this means that one who is represented by the yin line exercises mastery over a situation in terms of his influence potential in relation to others involved in that situation. The reasoning underlying this mode of thinking with respect to the position of the constituting (*de facto*) rulership was also already explained in the previous section. Since a hexagram consists of sex lines, there will be six different yin-centered types of hexagrams. They are as follows:

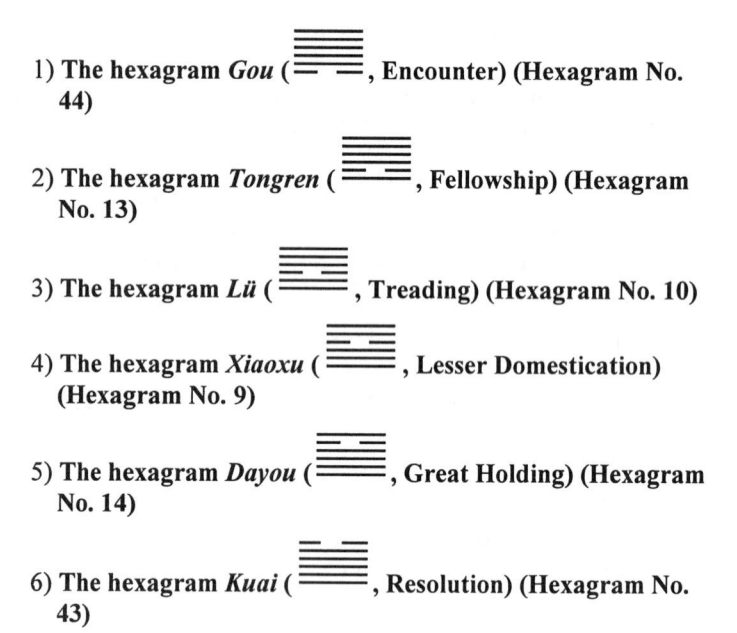

1) The hexagram *Gou* (☰/☴, Encounter) (Hexagram No. 44)

2) The hexagram *Tongren* (☰/☲, Fellowship) (Hexagram No. 13)

3) The hexagram *Lü* (☰/☱, Treading) (Hexagram No. 10)

4) The hexagram *Xiaoxu* (☴/☰, Lesser Domestication) (Hexagram No. 9)

5) The hexagram *Dayou* (☲/☰, Great Holding) (Hexagram No. 14)

6) The hexagram *Kuai* (☱/☰, Resolution) (Hexagram No. 43)

The hexagram *Gou* (☰/☴, Encounter)

The situational characteristic of this hexagram is described symbolically as that of many men (represented by yang lines) who are attracted to one woman (represented by the single yin line at the bottom). Thus, of the specific position of the first yin line under this situation Wang Bi comments: "When we apply Encounter to humankind, it refers to a woman meeting men. Here there is but one woman, yet she meets five men, which signifies utmost strength; thus one must not marry her" (Lynn, 1994:411). More detailed descriptions on the first yin line are given in its line statement and Wang Bi's commentary appended to it:

> This one should be tied to a metal brake, and for him to practice constancy would mean good fortune. But if one here were to set forth to do something, he would suffer misfortune, for it would be like a weak pig [sow] that but strives to romp around. {Wang Bi's commentary: Metal is a tough, hard substance. A brake [*ni*] is a governor that controls motion, which here refers to Fourth Yang.... It (the first yin line) is a single soft and weak [yin] line, yet carries five hard and strong [yang] lines. Such a one embodies an impatient nature, so that when he meets with opportunities, he tends to go through with them, to go every which way with no one in control, utterly at the mercy of his own inclinations.... The text here talks about a yin person who does not practice constancy and thus breaks away from the one who should be doing the leading. To express the ugliness of this lascivious behavior, the text likens it to the willfulness of the "weak pig" that "but strives to romp around."}

The line statement of the first yin line and Wang Bi's interpretation of it impart, implicitly and explicitly, several pieces of information concerning the nature of the situation as a whole and the specific characteristic of the first yin line under that situation. First, the presence of the five yang lines and a single yin line suggests a situation in which the combination of actors with such action orientations gives rise to potential rivalry among those dynamic (yang) individuals who, due to their active nature geared to an acquisition of power and also due to the nature of their positions, try to gain support or allegiance from the only subject at the lowest stratum who, as dictated by his action orientation as expressed by a yin line, submits himself to others' influences. Wang Bi compares this kind of a situation to that of a woman sought for by many men. Second, under this kind of situation, the one represented by the first yin line will find himself in a strong bargaining position so that no one above him may be able to exercise a strong control over him.[25] As Wang Bi says, he "breaks away from the one who should be doing the leading." And, the *I Ching*, to stress the same point, compares the first yin line to "a weak pig [sow] that but strives to romp around."[26] Thirdly, the *I Ching* emphasizes that a proper measure has to be taken to control the "lascivious behavior" of the first yin line so as not to bring out unfortunate outcomes for both himself and others.

Now, in a way to delve into this somewhat curious conceptualization of a social reality, let us begin with raising several questions regarding the last proposition; why did the author(s) of the *I Ching* and later commentators including Wang Bi think it necessary to control what they thought to be a "lascivious behavior" of the people at the lowest position? Why did they think that the strong bargaining position enjoyed by the first yin line would bring out a rather unfortunate outcome? And further, if we take note of the situational characteristic of the hexagram as a whole, the advantageous position that the first yin line enjoys should be thought as what is brought about by the very nature of the situation itself. In other words, the situation in which the first yin line finds himself is rendered by those individuals who are in positions to exercise control over him yet, contrary to what is expected of their formal positions as such, are vying one another for his favor and support. Then, let us ask again; why is this kind of a situation which seems to be enjoyable to the one represented by the first yin line considered to be a rather undesirable situation? To the eyes of people in this modern age in which democracy is accepted as one of the prime values, such an advantageous position of people at the grassroots may be viewed as a desired state of affairs. Nevertheless, we here have to be reminded of the fact that the *I Ching* was written in a remotely old age with cultural values quite different from ours and what it said should have been understood likewise by successive generations of the native people who had been raised in the essentially same cultural tradition. The message conveyed by the line statement of the first yin line, therefore, merely reflects the long-held traditional value in stating in effect that a lower class people like women or common subjects have to behave obediently to their superiors and otherwise will be viewed as "breaking away" from a proper track of the morality dictated by the tradition that they are expected to tread on. It seems in this culturally specific context that we can understand why the situation that may be considered as favorable to the subject represented by the first yin line himself is given a meaning charged with a negative attribute and an unfavorable judgment.

Turning our eyes to the line statement of the second yang line, however, few will fail to notice that there is some discrepancy between what the line statement of the first yin line describes about the situation of the position holder represented by that line and the role that is said to be played by the second yang line under this situation of *Gou*. The line statement reads, "in this one's kitchen, there is a fish, about which there is no blame. It is not fitting to entertain guests"[27] (Lynn, 1994:412). Here the fish refers to the first yin line. Commentators do not differ much in their interpretation of this line statement a modal version of which may be found in Wilhelm's following commentary: "The inferior element is not overcome by violence but is kept under gentle control. Then nothing evil is to be feared. But care must be taken not to let it come in contact with those further away, because once free it would unfold its evil aspects unchecked" (1967:172). Considered apart from the line statement of the first yin line, this interpretation by Wilhelm involves no ambiguity. It means that under the situation the one represented by the second yang line is in position to exercise control over the first yin line so that the "those guests further way" (those position holders represented by all other yang lines above the second line) are to be protected from possible "evil" influence from the first yin line. Here the first yin line is likened to a woman having a promiscuous intent with which she throws herself to any available male partners. As pointed out already, this kind of situation is viewed by the *I Ching* as rather undesirable, for the subject at the lower rank is in an influential position to sway over a plurality of individuals entitled to exercise formal authority. A questionable aspect of what the line statement of the second yang line says, however, is found in that it does not seem to square well with what is said in the line statement of the first yin line. After all, why should the one represented by the second yang line among all others have an ability to prevent the first yin line from playing havoc with the hierarchical ordering of the group? From the line statement of the first yin line, the subject of the first yin line is described as a woman who possesses "utmost strength" because she is sought after by five men. Then, why should she, being in such a strong bargaining position, have to yield herself particularly to the subject at the second position? Neither the *I Ching* nor later commentaries offer any convincing explanation. It is probably with this consideration that Legge (1963:157) says that an explanation said under this second line "seems farfetched." If this author is allowed to add a comment, the image of the second line as described as such does not seem particularly illuminating as to what it actually implies in terms of social relations at a more general level, other than conveying simply an image of a male who has succeeded in taking in a woman who otherwise might have gone out with many other suitors.

However, once the above interpretation for the second yin line is taken for granted, we can proceed more or less smoothly with the line statements on other lines without encountering a similar kind of difficulty as above. The line statement of the third line reads, "This one's thighs are without skin, and his walking falters. Though in danger, he incurs no great blame" (Lynn, 1994:413). About the reason for the third yang line to be described as having no firm and stable footing in his position, Wang Bi explains, "as it cannot lead any line to come to its support, all it can do is keep tightly to its own place" (Lynn, 1994:413). Recall that the third position represents that of the leader for the lower, subordinate group and yet the second yang line is described as already having taken the first yin line into his own sphere of influence. "So, Third Yang does not obtain security here." And, the *I Ching* suggests further that although the third yang line finds himself in a disadvantageous position owing to the type of social formation under the situation, his situation as such does not necessarily incur a gravely misfortunate outcome, of which commentators offer various reasons different from one another (Cheng Yi, 1988:146; Lee, 1997[II]:117; Legge, 1963:157; Lynn, 1994:413).

Similarly, the subject represented by the fourth yang line is also pictured as one who "make(s) a move without the support of the common folk" (Lynn, 1994:413). The attached judgment with respect to how the subject is likely to fare under the situation, however, contains a word of warning, "misfortune." An interesting proposition is suggested here. Recall that according to the *I Ching* the fourth position represents that which provides assistance to the top leader at the fifth position; it is a position with staff functions rather than leadership. Thus, it is thought to be "appropriately" occupied if a yin (receptive or yielding action orientation) line is incumbent at that position. Meanwhile, under the situation represented by this hexagram *Gou* the fourth position is not "appropriately" occupied by a yang line and this indicates that it is occupied by someone who tries to "make a move" on his own initiative. Under this situation, the *I Ching* seems to think, the subject at the fourth position, if he is going to "make a move" as he is likely to do so as his "active" action orientation is indicated by a yang line, should have "the support of the common folk." Unfortunately, however, the social formation represented by the hexagram *Gou* shows no such social support coming from the common folk who have already paired with the second yang line and, therefore, its line statement says, "in this one's kitchen, there is no fish, which gives rise to misfortune" (Lynn, 1994:413).

The line statement of the fifth yang line is interpreted from quite divergent perspectives by individual scholars and, accordingly, its translations differ so much from one version of the text to another that it will be hard to capture a common theme among the various versions of interpretation.[28] This kind of disagreement among scholars, in many cases, as I pointed out previously several times, has to do with the fact that the interpretation of the symbolically narrated accounts of the *I Ching* cannot help but be influenced by differences in individual scholars' philosophical, moral or personally unique outlooks or preconceptions toward the basic conditions of human society or individuals' lives. Thus, as my own logic sees it to be more consistent with the overall meaning of the hexagram as a whole, I am more or less inclined to side with Lee's interpretation with which the line statement of the fifth yang line is translated as follows: "This one may attempt to wrap (cheap) cucumbers with (rather precious) willow leaves. But, if he (giving up such a vain effort) behaves gracefully, he will be showered with blessings coming down from the heaven " (Lee, 1997[II]:118, translated from Korean by this author). In the attached commentary Lee explains that since it would not be wise for the top leader to compete with subordinates to win support from the common folks (to do so will be like wrapping cucumbers with willow leaves), a magnanimous concession would be a wiser policy that would bring him a far better outcome in the end. Here Lee inserts his own interpretation that if the top leader at the fifth position should push himself into a position to compete for the support of the people with his subordinates (especially the second yang line), his behavior as such may give rise to a tense state of confrontations among group members involved in that situation. Of course, as we can guess, the situation in which the leader has to see the common folk to throw their support onto someone who is under his command would not be a comfortable one. But, the *I Ching* advises, he has to bear with it by gracefully exercising tolerance.

The "symbolism" of the line statement of the sixth line, "here one encounters the horns, and, though this is a base situation, it does not incur blame," as Legge (1963:157) also points out, "is difficult to understand." Interestingly enough, however, commentators somehow seem able to converge on similar perspectives with which the top yang line is interpreted as representing a person who is isolated from the rest of the world. Wang Bi (Lynn, 1994:414), for example, comments on the subject at this line position as follows:

This one advances, but there is no one to meet, so all such a one can do is suffer resentment in isolation, but, as he does not contend with others, his Dao here will not lead to harm, thus there is no misfortune or blame.

Wilhelm (1967:173) and Cheng Yi offer similar explanations regarding the reason for which the one at the top position comes to find himself isolated from the rest of the people involved in the situation represented by the hexagram *Gou*. Both of them describe the subject at the top position as a person who maintains such a "high, proud and extremely obdurate" posture (Cheng Yi, 1988:147) that no one would like to be associated with him. This interpretation seems to be derived from the positional characteristic of the sixth line and the property of the sixth yang line determined in terms of the overall line formation of the hexagram. First, we may be reminded of the fact that a position holder at the sixth position represents someone who enjoys a high prestige but holds no official position in the formal hierarchy of a social organization. In this particular hexagram, the action orientation of the sixth line is described as that of a yang quality (of superordination), and yet the occupant of the position is said to have found no willing partner who would submit himself to form an alliance with the former. It seems due to a situation of this kind that commentators saw from the sixth yang line an image of a "proud" but "isolated" person having fallen into such a situation by virtue of his social position and particular action orientation under the specific situation represented by the hexagram *Guo*.

The hexagram *Tongren* (☰, Fellowship)

Wilhelm's brief note added at the end of the section dealing with this hexagram (1967:456) includes a remark that provides a clue for us to understand the core characteristic of a situation represented by this hexagram. It says, "none of them attains the great success that the hexagram as a whole envisions." As the line structure of the hexagram suggests, every yang line will seek companionship with the second yin line and the hexagram as a whole is characterized as a situation where the spirited pursuits of "fellowship" prevail over the entire members of the group. However, as Wilhelm points out, despite the prevailing motives among the "active" components of the group, each of whom is seeking an alliance (fellowship) with the only "passive" component in the hexagram, the situation will not yield "the great success" for any specific position holder. This is due to the type of social formation constituted by the situational components as shown by this hexagram *Tongren*. In other words, the majority of the people involved in this situation have active and competitive spirits eager to expand their sphere of influence and competitively seek companionship with those who would support them. Despite this, however, their pursuits of "fellowship" as such will not be an easy task due to the overall structural condition of the situation.

Now, looking at the overall structure of the hexagram we know that there are two rulership lines in this hexagram, the constituting ruler at the second position and the governing ruler at the fifth position. If taken into consideration by itself, apart from all other lines, the subject represented by the fifth yang line may be thought of as the most influential person since he occupies the formal leadership position and also displays a suitable characteristic (yang, i.e., active and superordinate) in his behavioral orientation for the position. But notice that in the *I Ching*, in addition to the formal position and one's action orientation, there is another factor determining a person's power potential, the patterns of association, characterized as "riding," "carrying" or "correspondence," among constituent members of a social organization. "Who is held together with whom in what kind of mutual dependency," or the relational patterns formed among the group members, will be read, as we have done so far, from the overall line formation of each individual hexagram and the line statements appended to each line. Therefore, also in this hexagram, the actual power potential of the fifth line will be determined in terms of what kind of relationship it forms with others and thus has to be judged in that context.

As pointed out above, the specific situation that the fifth yang line is in under this situation is read from its line statement, "for fellowship here there is first howling and wailing, but afterward there is laughter, for with the victory of the great army, they manage to meet" (Lynn, 1994:219). To get at what is implied by this line statement, we have to understand that the gaining of the support from the second yin line (in other words, establishing a "fellowship" with the second yin line) is crucial for the top leader to maintain effective leadership. Here the second yin line is interpreted as representing a devoted official(s) working in compliance with what is expected of his (their) role. But at the same time, the overall feature of the situation suggests that other individuals, with the only exception at the second position, will use maximum efforts to increase their power potential over others, and, therefore, strive to gain the support (fellowship) from the only yin (yielding or compliant) element at the second position. Notice now that there are two yang lines in between the second yin line and the fifth yang line. From the perspective of the top leader, these position holders at the third and fourth lines pose a hindrance to his aim of obtaining complete loyalty from the second yin line. That is, they are objects to be overcome and forceful means may have to be employed. This is why Legge (1963:87) characterizes the third and fourth lines to be "powerful foes that oppose the union." The line statement of the fifth yang line can now be understood as describing the difficulties in overcoming (covertly or overtly staged) resistance from the third and forth lines while trying to establish a firm alliance with the second yin line and as predicting a success in the end. As Wang Bi concurs, the *Commentary on the Judgments* (Lynn, 1994:217) observes that the core meaning of the hexagram *Tongren* is derived mainly from the fact that the integration of a social organization is achieved through the formation of a strong alliance between the centrally located two core components, each respectively from the upper and the lower groups.

Let us now examine how the specific situation of the second yin line is described through its line statement. The line statement reads briefly, "to practice fellowship just with one's clan is base" (Lynn, 1994:218). For this line statement, Cheng Yi (1988:39) offers a seemingly clear and meaningful interpretation as follows:

> The second and the fifth lines are proper correspondents, so that the text speaks of 'association with people in the clan.' To assimilate only to those with whom one is involved in correspondence is to have bias in association. Accordingly to the way of association with others, this is personal narrowness and therefore regrettable.

What Cheng Yi emphasizes in the above passage seems clear. Although a social organization represented by the hexagram may be said to maintain some degree of integration with its two core components forming an alliance with each other, there are a number of other components left alienated from the association. Therefore, it should be judged as "regrettable."

Each of the line statements of the third, the fourth, and the sixth positions equally make sense in light of what is explained above. The line statement of the third yang line states, "here one hides armed troops in a thicket and ascends his high hill, but even after three years he does not stage his uprising" (Lynn, 1994:218). According to Wang Bi's commentary, this line statement conveys an image of a person who in the presence of the strong "opponent [Fifth yang]," "dares not reveal his arrogance .... (and) looks at things from a distance but dares not to advance" (Lynn, 1994:218). In other words, as a potential opponent about to compete with the top leadership position in pursuit of dominance over the group, the subject at the third position is keeping an eye on the second yin line to induct it into his own sphere of influence. However, such hidden intention would not be fulfilled and has to be given up because such an ambitious task of rising up to the most powerful figure in the group "has already been fulfilled" by the more powerful, governing ruler of this hexagram (the fifth yang line). The two main figures, the fifth yang line and the second yin line, forming a dyadic pair still play the key roles for the unity of the group.

The fourth yang line is again described as another component that has the ambition for power but finds himself in an impossible situation to realize his intention. Thus, the line statement of this line says of its subject, "although he rides the top of the wall, he fails in his attack, but this means good fortune" (Lynn, 1994:219). Notice that the third yang line may be compared to a "wall" standing in between the fourth yang line and the second yin line that the fourth yang line wants to approach. This symbolism makes the fourth yang line a person who "rides the top of the wall." The fifth yang line is too strong a figure for the fourth yang to contend with in winning the support of the second yin line. It is an impossible situation for him to stage a fight for gaining control over the second yin line. But why does the *I Ching* judge that such an impasse to be experienced by the fourth yang line involves "good fortune"? The *Commentary on the Images* provides a simple explanation: "His 'good fortune' is due to the fact that when he found himself in such difficulties, he returned to principled behavior" (Lynn, 1994:219). Although this does not seem to provide an adequate reason for why "he returned to principled behavior" instead of pushing himself forward with his intended goal, most commentators, including Wang Bi (Lynn, 1994:219) and Cheng Yi (1988:40), seem to be satisfied with this explanation.

Both Wang Bi and Cheng Yi share the same opinion on the line statement of the top yang line that describes the subject at the sixth position as an outsider totally dissociated from what is going on in the rest of the world. The line statement says, "if one practice Fellowship in the countryside, he will remain free of regret" (Lynn, 1994:320). As for explaining this line statement the following commentary by Cheng Yi (1988:41) seems quite sufficient by itself and thus requires no further explanation:

> The countryside is far away, whereas if you want to associate with people they must be nearby. The top yang is in the position of an outsider, and has no correspondent, so in the end has no one to associate with. If there is association in the beginning, then by the end there may be falling out and regret. Being far away, without company, though one have no associate, at least one has no regrets. Even though one's aspiration for association may not be fulfilled, one winds up without anything to regret.

We are now left with the first yang line. Although its line statement seems to impart no clear meaning to us, major commentaries such as Cheng Yi (1988:39), Legge (1963:87) and Wang Bi (Lynn, 1994:217) were somehow able to converge on interpretations not much different from one another. For example, Wang Bi's commentary offers the following interpretation that the other two scholars echo:

> As it does not have a resonant relationship with any line above, so one's heart and mind here should not be bound by particularism. Instead one thoroughly identifies with the great community, so when one goes out of this gate, he treats all with fellowship. This is why the text says, "One practices fellowship at his gate." If one practices fellowship upon going out of his gate, who could find him worthy of blame? (Lynn, 1994:217)

With respect to one's behavioral orientation, it is reasonable and thus understandable to propose that there are possibly "cosmopolitan-type" individuals who practice their communal relationships far beyond a narrow circle of some close associates. There would, in fact, be a type who "thoroughly identifies (themselves) with the great community." But doubt may be raised about why this position holder at the bottom position is viewed as displaying such a specific action orientation described above. This question may become more obvious if we remember the interpretation given to the top yang line. The top and the bottom positions share similar characteristics; they are out of the formal hierarchy and their action orientations are equally characterized with the yang line. Moreover, under the situation represented by the hexagram *Tongren,* both are characterized as having no "resonant" relationship (close alliance). Here, perhaps, the author(s) of the *I Ching* might have applied some sort of reasoning that could make sense in view of his own experience or cultural tradition. But, as far as what can be read from the text, no understandable reason is offered for the obvious discrepancy in the accounts given by the line statements of the bottom and the top lines.

The hexagram *Lü* (☰/☱ , Treading)

Before we look at the line statements of this hexagram, it would be helpful to understand the overall characteristic of this hexagram as a whole and recognize that it involves a somewhat peculiar structure. Notice that the second yang, the third yin and the fourth yang lines are not "appropriately" occupied. In other words, position holders who do not have proper characteristics that fit these positions occupy the positions. The fifth yang line at the governing ruler's position is the only line that is appropriately occupied. However, as we will see in the following discussion, it has developed no firm corresponding relationship with any other line or a composite of lines. As the two other lines located outside the formal line of the hierarchical order are also yang lines, this makes the entire hexagram consist of five yang lines except for the one yin line at the third place. When a hexagram consists mostly of yang lines, it is usually interpreted as a social organization consisting of strong-willed individuals competing with one another for leading roles. Because of this, their influence potentials may be balanced out against one another and unless any of them forms an alliance with another, no strong, unitary leadership will emerge. Therefore, there is no strong, leading component that plays the key role for the integration of a social organization represented by this hexagram.

The only possible line that can assume such a role then is the third yin line, the constituting ruler of the hexagram. However, the subject at this position, not being appropriately occupied and being sandwiched in the middle of the strong lines, is said to be in a very unstable situation. Let us look at the line statement given to the third yin line: "The one-eyed may still see, and the lame may still tread, but when such a one treads on the tiger's tail, it will bite him, and he shall have misfortune. Here, a warrior tries to pass him off as a great sovereign" (Lynn, 1994:202). The *Commentary on the Images* explains that the third yin line is facing a very delicate and vulnerable situation in which it is difficult not only to make a clear judgment on the situation at hand but also to maintain an appropriate posture in dealing with others. In other words, under this situation he would be quite vulnerable and prone to misjudgment and misbehavior. This interpretation seems to be related to a unique condition suggested by the hexagram *Lü* — a basically ambiguous situation in which no definite pattern in power relations with respect to "who is in charge of the entire social organization in question" has settled clearly. Without strong leadership that is clearly visible under the situation, the third yin line, a leader of the subordinate group, may misconceive the situation. Wang Bi comments on this line accordingly:

> He wishes to use aggression to intimidate others with his military prowess and would pass himself as a great sovereign, but his actions cannot help but bring him misfortune. Thus to have his will focused on Fifth Yang's position in this way is the height of stupidity. (Lynn, 1994:202)

In contrast to the foregoing line at the third position, the fourth yang line is characterized as being "fearfully cautious" so that "in the end he will have good fortune," although he is also said to "tread on the tiger's tail" (Lynn, 1994:203). Why the *I Ching* interprets the third yin and the fourth yang lines differently from each other is not clear. It seems that there is no obvious convincing reason to have us completely accept such opposing interpretations rendered to the two lines. Of course, it may be undeniable that a dangerous path demands cautious treading, but there are also some people who act unscrupulously and get into trouble. There are also others who act very cautiously so that they can stay out of unnecessary troubles. But this seems to be a mere truism. The key question here is, what in the line structure of the hexagram and the characteristics of the lines justify the *I Ching* yielding such contrasting interpretations to each line? Neither the text nor commentators have come up with reasons that are sufficient or convincing.[29]

Since both the third and the fourth lines are described as "treading on the tiger's tail" and this symbolism defines the main characteristic of this hexagram, let us examine what "treading on the tiger's tail" refers to. Commentators have no disagreement in that the tiger points to the fifth yang line, the governing ruler of the hexagram. It seems without doubt that the expression "tiger" is used to indicate that the subject at the fifth position has a capability to exercise the power assigned to his formal position as the ruler of the entire group. In this case, the fifth yang is appropriately occupied since a yang line is occupying a yang position. This means that he has real power potential (strength) matching his formal status as the leader. Thus, the line statement of the fifth yang line says of the position holder at this position, "Tread resolutely here, and practice constancy in the face of trouble" (Lynn, 1994:203). But why does it say, "in the face of trouble"? What is the source of trouble that the fifth yang is facing? No explicit explanation is given in the *I Ching*. The best possible explanation we can get is from Wang Bi's commentary as follows: "The Dao of *Lü* is adverse to worldly success, and as Fifth Yang is located in this noble position, danger is inherent in it" (Lynn, 1994:203). The above comment by Wang Bi may be understood to mean that no one under the situation of *Lü* is able to secure a wholly advantageous position or garner absolute supremacy in power due to the situationally determined matrix of power relations among the members of a social organization. As a matter of fact, all the accounts on this hexagram and its constituent lines seem to indicate that although the fifth yang line may be powerful enough to hold sway over the entire group members, no other line is in close association with this line under the situation. Thus, as Cheng Yi (1988:29) utters words of warning for the position holder at this position, there may be a danger ("even if they are correct, they follow a dangerous path") if the leader "take(s) charge alone."

Before we proceed to other lines, let us examine the overall characteristic of this hexagram, i.e., the meaning of *"Lü* (Treading)." *Lü* means "treading" or "conduct," "with the secondary meaning of good manners" (Lee, 1997[1]:167; Wilhelm, 1967:439). But the hexagram as a whole has to be viewed as carrying an added meaning, "cautious treading" or "cautious conduct," and, therefore, the secondary meaning of "cautious conduct done in good manners." What is implied here is a situation in which position holders have to tread carefully on rather narrow paths set down by some standard norms. In other words, actors involved in this situation have to conduct their behavior with extra care as if treading on a tiger's tail. What sort of structural attributes of the situation makes it necessary for the actors to behave in such a cautious manner? Two things can be pointed out. One is that the single yin line at the third position, unlike other yin-centered hexagrams, does not seem to contribute one way or another to an integration of a social unit represented by the hexagram. Rather, its line statement implies that it poses a potential source of conflict. Secondly, as pointed out a little while ago, although the strong governing ruler is present at the fifth position, he is described as a tiger that may have to be feared rather than as a center of integration or a source of attraction. Thus, the hexagram as whole does not imply a well integrated situation, but rather a somewhat tense and uncertain situation which involves potential for some, if not an all-out, conflict.

The line statement of the second yang line can make better sense in the context of the overall meaning of the situation as presented above. Note that the subject at this second position is described as "one secluded here" (Lynn, 1994:201). For some reason, the *I Ching* sees the second yang line being as secluded from the troubles of the time indicated by the hexagram. Since he is not in relationships with any of the two leaders — the constituting ruler at the third position and the governing one at the fifth position — he will be able to remain relatively free of troubles that may arise from an association with either of them. At any rate, as described as in their line statements respectively, neither one of them would be the type of leader with whom one could comfortably get along with. Therefore, in this case, such seclusion means freedom and good fortune unless he himself brings in misfortune by behaving inappropriately.

In view of the above interpretation, let us look at the line statement of the second yang line: "The path to tread on is level and smooth, and if one secluded here practices constancy, he will have good fortune." On this line statement, I have some reservation. Why is this particular actor at the second position viewed as being secluded from the rest of the world so that he "is free of dangerous obstacles" (Lynn, 1994:202)? Wang Bi offers some explanations for it but they seem to be couched upon somewhat dubious principles from which a modern social scientist can make no clear sense. Perhaps a better explanation may be found in that since the line structure of the hexagram, as analyzed by the *I Ching*, indicates no strong interdependent relationship formed between or among the lines, the second yang line is interpreted as enjoying a certain measure of independence from those at upper strata. Its independence as such is related to a view commonly found in the *I Ching* in which an isolated *yang* (firm) line, if it is located at lower positions, is interpreted as having room for independence.

In contrast to the line statement of the second line, that of the first yang line simply gives a briefly stated instruction on how the one at this position has to behave under the situation: "If one treads with simplicity, to set forth will bring no blame" (Lynn, 1994:201). Yet the *Commentary on the Images* supplements it with an explanation that says, "The progress of simple conduct follows in solitude its own bent" (Wilhelm, 1967:437). To this, Wilhelm adds his own explanation as follows:

> This line is at the beginning of the hexagram, hence simplicity is the right thing for it. It progresses independently. Not being related to the other lines, it goes its way alone, but since it is strong, this agrees exactly with its inclination.

Here it may be noticed that the first yang line is described in a similar position as the second yang line. That is, "not being related to the other lines," it acts alone and "this agrees exactly with its (yang, i.e., independent) inclination." But why does the line statement emphasize *simplicity* to be duly observed by the first yang line? It may be that the position reflected in this line statement is nothing more than an announcement of a traditionally cherished value of the Chinese and East-Asians in general. Cheng Yi expresses such a position quite clearly in the following commentary that he adds to the line statement of the first yang line:

> The first yang is in the lowest position, but he has the positive strength to rise. If one in that position remains humble and simple, and goes on in that way, there will be no blame. When they cannot rest in the simplicity of the poor and lowly, then people will act greedily and impetuously, their only motive to get out of poverty and lowliness, not to accomplish something. Then when they manage to advance, they will overflow with self-indulgence. Therefore they will err if they go on in that way .... (1998:27)

Simply put, although the people in the lowest position possess some "positive strength" to act free of restraints from others overseeing them, they, nevertheless, have to exercise self-control to avoid unfortunate outcomes. Here we seem to have more Oriental moral logic where a moral inculcation is given as regards what can be expected to happen if one obeys or violates a certain behavioral norm.

Returning now to the overall meaning of the situation depicted by the hexagram *Lü*, we still may wonder: what can we get out of this hexagram in terms of the characteristic meaning it conveys as a whole? Since commentators, including the text itself[30], present a confusing array of different or even inconsistent accounts, any conclusive interpretation is difficult to draw in this respect. But as a sociologist, I can notice, as compared to other hexagrams we have dealt with so far, one particular thing peculiar to this hexagram. It is that this hexagram, judging from its line statements, lacks any integrative tie between or among all its component lines. This implies that this hexagram consists of autonomous individuals acting independently from one another to some degree. From a different angle it may be said that most components possess a certain measure of "strength" to secure their autonomy. So the hexagram as a whole seems to depict a delicate situation in which each has to take extra caution to keep treading on his own trodden trail but not on that which belongs to others, especially to the one at the fifth position described as "the tiger." A somewhat tense but delicately balanced situation is implied here.

The top yang line was left out from the above discussion. This is mainly because it seems to contain a different sort of message from those given by the other lines. The line statement of the top line advises all the actors involved in the situation to "observe what was done, to consider whether it was good or bad, whether it will bring good or bad fortune" (Cheng Yi, 1988:29) when a situation nears its end. But as Legge points out, this is merely a "truism" (1963:81). In other words, it is advice that sounds good, but is nothing more than saying, "observe what was done to know what will happen."

The hexagram *Xiaoxu* (☰☴ , Lesser Domestication, The Taming Power of the Small[31]**)**

The fourth yin line, the constituting ruler as the only yin line of the hexagram, represents the "taming power of the small." The hexagram statement and line statements taken together describe the subordinate group (represented by the lower trigram *Qian*, ☰) as a strong triadic group that consists of dynamic individuals who are pressing their wills hard against the dominant group. The idea that the lower group will show such aggressive behavior seems to be related to the fact that a yielding, weak (yin) line is present at the fourth position that assumes the role of exercising control over the former. Appropriately, the hexagram is called *Xiaoxu*, the "taming power of the small," which refers to one whose controlling (restraining) power is "less than effective" (Lynn, 1994:192). Thus, we come to know here the situational characteristic of the hexagram. It is made apparent by its name, taken from the attribute of the fourth yin line that is determined in the context of the overall line structure of the hexagram.

Let us look at what the line statement of the fourth yin line has to say about the condition of the position holder at this position. It states, "If there is sincerity, blood will be kept away, and apprehension purged, and one will not incur blame" (Lynn, 1994:194). On this line statement, Wilhelm (1967:434) explains as follows:

> The fourth place is that of the minister. It has the difficult task of controlling with weak powers the upward-striving lower lines. This is necessarily associated with danger and fear, but because the line is sincere (yielding in a yielding place, and empty within) the prince, the nine in the fifth place, stands by it and gives the needed support.

Both Wang Bi's and Cheng Yi's commentaries are not much different from Wilhelm's above interpretation. But there is one aspect in which Cheng Yi's interpretation differs from others. Cheng Yi does not seem to view "sincerity" as a situationally determined attribute of the position holder at the fourth position, but rather as a normative orientation required of a weak person to cope with hard-pressing, aggressive individuals. Regarding this view, let us listen to what Cheng Yi (1988:25) has to say:

> This hexagram has one yin alone, restraining and nurturing a group of yangs. The aims of the yangs depend on the fourth yin; if it wants to restrain the yangs by force, the fourth yin will be hurt, as it is alone and weak against a group of strong opponents. Only by perfection of sincerity and truthfulness in dealing with them can the yin move the yangs. If harm is seen from far off the danger can be avoided; in this way one can avoid fault. Otherwise, there is no avoiding harm. This is the way of using flexibility to restrain and nurture strength. If powerless employees can restrain the desires of those of the authority and majesty of leadership, it is because they move them with sincerity and truthfulness.

Yet, to understand more fully the reason for which the fourth yin line is called the "taming power of the small" we have to examine the line statements of the three yang lines of which the lower trigram is composed.

According to the *I Ching,* the first and the second yang lines will turn back without persistently resisting the fourth yin line who tries to restrain their high flying spirit to encroach upon what may be rightly recognized as the domain of their superiors in the upper group. The essential meanings of the line statements for the two lines are almost identical to each other. "In returning, one follows the appropriate Dao [path], so how could there be any blame involved? This means good fortune" is the line statement given to the first yang line. The line statement of the second yang line reads, "Drawn along, one returns, and this means good fortune . . . ." (Lynn, 1994:193). Both of these two actors who display the "upward-striving," aggressive behavior are described as being held back by the "taming power" of the fourth yin line. One can take a reasonable guess as to why the fourth yin line is said to be able to hold back the two coming up against their superiors. After all, the fourth yin line has formal power accruing from his position. And this yin line appropriately occupying a yin place represents a faithful minister (or any position equivalent to it) serving the strong governing ruler represented by the fifth yang line. Recall that

Wilhelm points out in the passage already quoted, the one at the fourth position has the support of the ruler. Thus, the fourth yin line is viewed to possess the "taming power," but also being weak, "of the small," or a "not so effective one."

Why the power exercised by the fourth yin line is viewed as not effective in controlling all the lower elements with yang (unyielding, hard-striving) energy is quite well expressed in the line statement of the third yang line, the leader of the subordinate group. It states, "the carriage body would be separated from its axle housing, so husband and wife turn their eyes against each other." According to the *Commentary on the Images*, "this means that it is not possible to put the house in order" (Lynn, 1994:194). There seems no doubt about what the line statement itself suggests. Some serious dissension or conflict has occurred between two parties that resulted in a breakage of order. However, concerning which particular components in the hexagram the conflicting parties refer to, commentators show some disagreement. Wilhelm's interpretation goes as follows: "The yielding fourth line represents the wife who allows the spoke of the wheels, belonging to the third line, her husband, to get broken. The man looks at her fiercely in his rage, and she returns the look" (1967:433). Interpreted in this way, the house in disorder would refer to an outcome brought about by this dissension, the state in the subordinate unit in which the two lower yang lines and the third one fail to hold together as an integrated unit. Wang Bi's interpretation (Lynn, 1994:194; refer also to Kong Yinda's commentary in Lynn's Note, 1994:198) differs from this. The opposition is interpreted as occurring between the third yang line and the upper group as a whole, which is said to possess a female (yin) quality.[32] Here the entire group is experiencing a state of internal disharmony. This arises primarily from the one, the third yang line, who is displeased with the effort of the upper group to have him "drawn along" into subjection. As I have emphasized, there is no objective criterion to decide which interpretation is closer to what is truly intended by the text. Regardless, the situational meaning implied by the third yang line seems to be clear. It indicates a conflict situation that arises from a rivalry between relatively strong subordinates and superiors with relatively weak controlling powers. Then, what would be the final outcome of this confrontation? To find an answer to this question, we have to look at the fifth and the sixth lines.

The line statement of the fifth yang line conveys an image of a strong leader who "lends a helping hand" to its neighboring elements to end the conflicting situation. Of this, Wang Bi explains that Second Yang's being drawn along is something to which Fifth Yang lends its own helping hand" (Lynn, 1994:195). In other words, it is the position holder of the governing ruler who makes the second yang line turn back and help the forth yin line succeed in separating the second yang line from the third yang line, the leader of the subordinate group. A different interpretation that may be more squarely in line with the statements of other lines is offered in Lynn's additional remark made on Wang Bi's interpretation:

> Both Cheng Yi and Zhu Xi think that the word neighbors (*lin*) here has nothing to do with Second Yang but refers to Fourth Yin and Top Yang, the lines contiguous with it and with which it makes up the upper *Sun* trigram. The joint purpose of these three lines, as Zhu Xi puts it, is to "pool their strength and garner the lower *Qian* trigram." Thus the "helping hand" is extended not to Second Yang but to the other two lines in *Sun*. (1994:199n13)

As interpreted in the passage above, the line statement of the fifth yang line explains that the governing ruler at the fifth position plays the central role in holding together the members of the upper group to deal with the aggressive subordinate group represented by the lower trigram *Qian*.

The final outcome of the confrontation between the upper group acting in unison and the aggressive lower element is stated in the line statement of the last, sixth yang line. It says, "This one not only achieves rain but also secure its place. It is esteemed for the way it carries virtue, but even a wife's constancy here means danger, and as the moon is almost full, so if the noble man goes forth and acts, it means misfortune" (Lynn, 1994:195). From the above passage, "achieving rain" and "securing its place" mean that the lower trigram *Qian* and the upper trigram *Sun* interact, produce rain, and therefore the confrontation settles down. The dominant group represented by the trigram *Sun* draws along the lower, subordinate group represented by the trigram *Qian* and so the tense situation is brought to rest. The next line, "it is esteemed for the way it carries its virtue," is interpreted by most commentators (with an exception in Wang Bi who interprets it otherwise) as referring to the esteem that the position holder at the fourth, not the top, place comes to enjoy for the role he plays in the taming of the lower yangs. However, the *I Ching* adds a warning; if he, being buoyed by such a successful reversal of the situation, would come forward and act like a leader, he will meet with an unfortunate outcome. On the other hand, Wang Bi (1994:195) compares the role held by the fourth yin line, of controlling the aggressive subordinate group, to a wife controlling her husband or a minister his sovereign. This implies the difficulty involved in the task of weak, administrative types of supervisors or managers at a superior level who must control strong subordinates. Wang Bi explains, "although they practice constancy, they still place themselves on the edge of danger" (Lynn, 1994:196).

The hexagram *Dayou* (☰☲, Great Holding)

In its structure, this hexagram is the exact reverse of the hexagram *Bi* (☷☵, Holding Together). Nevertheless, for this hexagram also, the governing rulership overlaps with the constituting rulership, which indicates a strong integration centered around the top leader. A difference is found in that while the hexagram *Bi* has a strong leader that is dominant over yielding, weak subjects, this hexagram *Dayou* has a receptive and embracing leader responsive to the needs or wills of the rather demanding subjects. Thus, on this hexagram Wang Bi (1994:223) comments:

> Fifth Yin fills the noble position with its yielding nature and achieves greatness through abiding in the Mean. As there is no other yin line in the entire hexagram with which it has to share the resonance of the yang lines, all the lines above and below respond to it, and of these there is none that it does not welcome. This is the meaning of the *Dayou* hexagram.

In the sense that the fifth yin line occupies the central place of integration represented by the hexagram, the hexagram name "Great Holding" seems to indicate that every member of the group with active spirits is accommodated by the leader who is eager to facilitate their active participation. Thus, if integration by "submission" to a strong power characterizes the hexagram *Bi*, the integrative situation of this hexagram *Dayou* may be characterized as "participation through accommodation."

We will first look at the line statement of the fifth yin line, the integrative axis for the hexagram. It states, "their trust in him swings back and forth, and, therefore, it is with a display of his awesome majesty that there will be good fortune" (Lee, 1997[I]:208, translated from Korean by this author).[33] The line statement tells us that since the leadership position is occupied by a person who has a receptive and accommodating personality, it may be interpreted as weakness by others, and they may have some distrust in his leadership quality. Thus, the *I Ching* advises the position holder at the fifth position to ward off such possibility by displaying his awesome majesty.

All other lines also accompany line statements that describe features of position holders as being more or less well integrated into the pattern of union represented by this hexagram. However, it will be instructive to notice that the nature of the leadership indicated by this hexagram is quite opposite to that for the hexagram *Bi*. In the hexagram *Bi*, the leadership is characterized by a monopoly of power amassed solely in the hands of the top leader. Here in this hexagram, the quality of the leadership is characterized as of a receptive and yielding nature, which implies that a great deal of power and authority is delegated to officials at the lower echelon. Keeping this in mind, let us turn our eyes to the other individual line statements.

The line statement of the first yang line reads, "No relationship with what is harmful; There is no blame in this. If one remains consciousness of difficulty, One remains without blame" (Wilhelm, 1967:458).[34] In this hexagram, what "what is harmful" refers to is not clear. Lee (1997[I]:203) explains that under the situation of the hexagram *Dayou* "what is harmful" is related to the weakness of the top leadership as perceived by strong subordinates. In other words, there may be a possibility of a planned coup to overthrow the leader who is perceived as weak. Thus, as interpreted by Lee, the line statement contains advice to the first yang line to not get involved in such a harmful thing. But no other commentary seems to render support to Lee's interpretation as such. The next portion of the statement can be explained more easily in view of the characteristic of the lowest position occupied by the first yang line. The first position is the lowest position located outside the formal hierarchy. But as Wang Bi points out, being represented by a yang line, it is "filled with strength" for which he may not "refrain from overflowing." This is why the *I Ching* advises that the subject represented by the first yang line should "remain conscious of difficulty" (Lynn, 1994:224).

As mentioned earlier, in this hexagram, the receptive leadership will delegate a great deal of power and authority to officials at the lower echelon. Accordingly, the line statement of the second yang line describes its subject as "a great wagon carry(ing) things," as "one entrusted with duties by Fifth Yin" (Lynn, 1994:224-225). Since the second yang line occupies a stable position (the second position in general is considered as a secure position because it is centrally located in the lower trigram) under a strongly integrated situation, it is energetic and entrusted with duties and authority by the top leader. The line statement goes on to say, "one should set forth, for there will be no blame." Of this, Wang Bi explains; "Although the duties so borne are heavy, they present no danger, so this one can go as far as possible without getting stuck in the mud" (Lynn, 1994:224-225).

An equally favorable judgment is also given to the third yang line: "When a duke uses this position, he enjoys prevalence along with the Son of Heaven, but a petty man is not equal to it"[35] (Lynn, 1994:225). The Son of Heaven is a term referring to the supreme ruler (emperor) of the Chinese Empire, which is represented by the fifth yin line. Thus, as far as this hexagram is concerned, the leader of the subordinate group is said to enjoy a powerful status comparable to that of the top leadership. The following commentary of Wang Bi gives a more detailed account of the specific situation in which the third yang line is entrusted with a power and prestige comparable in magnitude to that of the fifth yin line:

> As it shares with Fifth Yin the same merit, it represents the utmost measure of martial force, which none can surpass. When a duke uses this position, he succeeds in sharing in the Dao of the Son of Heaven, but a petty man is not equal to this, and he can expect calamity to come of it. (Lynn, 1994:225)

The latter portion of the above passage seems to be a truism. It emphasizes the obvious fact that since the position holder at this position has to carry out a role of such magnitude, only a truly able person can bear the responsibility.

The line statement of the fourth yang line states very briefly, "If one rejects such plentitude, there will be no blame" (Lynn, 1994:225). According to Wang Bi's commentary on this line statement, "such plentitude" refers to "that of the third yang" (Lynn, 1994:226). Hence, the line statement is interpreted to contain advice to the subject at the fourth position not to abandon "Fifth Yin (the weak top leader)" to join with "Third Yang" who enjoys a powerful status (i.e., plentitude) comparable to that of the top leadership under this situation of *Dayou* (Great Holdings). Compared to this, Cheng Yi (1988:43) offers a simpler interpretation which, I think, makes more sense. According to Cheng Yi, the line statement is to advise the subject at the fourth position that it would be unwise for him, being in an enjoyable position under the yielding ruler, to seek for "aggrandizement" taking advantage of his position as such.

Lastly, the line statement of the top yang line, "Heaven will help him as a matter of fact; this is good fortune, and nothing will fail to be fitting" (Lynn, 1994:226), is not difficult to understand. It means simply that the subject at the top position is in such a fortunate situation that there will be nothing to undermine the happy situation he is allowed to enjoy. However, no specific rationale is offered for giving such an auspicious judgment for the particular position holder at this top position. Commentators offer various explanations, but to this author, none seems thoroughly convincing. None of them seems to be logically consistent with what is stated in other line statements, and none coheres well with the interpretive schemes of the *I Ching* that we have applied so far.

The hexagram *Kuai* (☰☱ , Resolution)

In its line structure and its meaning, this hexagram is the opposite of the hexagram *Bo* (☷☶ , Peeling). The only yin line is present at the top position while yang lines occupy all other positions. When we discussed the hexagram *Bo*, it was pointed out that its pictorial image can be seen as representing a withering tree with its only living energy preserved in fruits hanging at high branches. And, it was also pointed out that the situational meaning of the hexagram *Bo* represented a morally degenerating or socially disintegrating situation. This kind of analogy-like reasoning seems to apply equally to the hexagram *Kuai*. Here the hexagram *Kuai* can be seen as conveying an image of the high spring season filled with newly growing trees and plants, yet covered with dry weeds left over from the last season. The yin line at the top position represents the only remaining element from the old order. Sociologically speaking, it represents the remnants of the old order that are still present at the high echelon of a social organization denoted by the hexagram.

The situational meaning represented by this hexagram is clearly expressed through its hexagram statement (the *Judgment*):

> Kwâi (*Kuai*) requires (in him who would fulfill its meaning) the exhibition (of the culprit's guilt) in the royal court, and a sincere and earnest appeal (for sympathy and support), with a consciousness of the peril (involved in cutting off the criminal). He should (also) make announcement in his own city, and show that it will not be well to have recourse at once to arms. (In this way) there will be advantage in whatever he shall go forward to. (Legge, 1963:151-152)[36]

From the above passage, we can see easily that the situation represented by the hexagram is characterized by the presence of two camps with contrasting fortunes, victors taking over with a new regime and remaining elements from the old order. The hexagram name "Resolution" as used here, therefore, refers to the situational characteristic of a stage in a political process in which a decisive (resolute) measure by the winner is about to take place to purge out the remnants from the old order. Then, first, let us look at the line statement of the sixth line whose subject represents those who have been left over from the old order, "As no cry will do here, it will end in misfortune" (Lynn, 1994:409). The message here is simple and clear: his day is over and has no choice but to go out in disgrace.

The line statement of the fifth yang line, the governing ruler who is supposed to bear the primary responsibility for the task implied by the hexagram, also can be easily understood in view of the line statement at the top line. It reads "The pokeweed is dispatched with perfect Resolution. If this one treads the middle path, he shall be without blame" (Lynn, 1994:408).[37] Wang Bi adds an interesting comment to this line statement. He seemed to have thought that the elimination of losers who have been deprived of power and the will to resist is not a commendable enterprise. Thus, he says, "Here we have the most noble matching itself against the most humble. Although victory is had here, it is not really worth very much . . . . one here is up to avoiding blame but nothing more than that; this is not enough to bring one glory" (Lynn, 1994:408). In my opinion, Wang Bi's commentary points out well the mixed characteristics of the political purge — once victory is won, it may be necessary to root out the old elements left over from the old order, but, as a rule, the political purge as such would not bring out desirable outcomes.

The line statements for the rest of the lines can be understood also in the situational context in which the political purge is about to take place. The line statement of the first yang line reads, "Mighty in the forward-striding toes. When one goes and is not equal to the task, One makes a mistake" (Wilhelm, 1967:605).[38] This particular line statement reminds me of the Red Guard who spearheaded the Great Cultural Revolution in China during the 1970's and thereafter has been blamed for all its faulty outcomes. It was a mass movement led by the strongly motivated lowest stratum of the society that was "striding forward" to get rid of the old, "anti-revolutionary" elements left at the higher echelon.

The line statement of the second yang line is also interpreted in many different ways from one commentator to another. As I see it, however, Lee's interpretation seems to fit far better with the overall meaning of the hexagram and those rendered to other line statements. It reads:

> The second yang line is in a situation in which he, while being deeply aware of danger involved, keeps on crying out slogans (for rooting out the old order represented by the top yin line). Although he fights until late at night, he should refrain from showing sympathy. (Lee, 1997[II]:106, translated from Korean by this author)

Interpreted in this way, the line statement portrays the second yang line as a campaigner who stands out in the front of the purge movement. The last portion of the statement is simply to emphasize that under this kind of situation, sympathy toward the one at the top position will bring out nothing beneficial to the subject at the second position.

In essence, the line statement of the third yang line does not seem to be much different from that of the second yang line. It states:

> To put strength into the cheekbones would mean misfortune, but the noble man acts with perfect Resolution. But if one here were to travel alone, he should encounter such a rain that he should be as if sunk in water, and, though he feel anger, there will be no one to blame. (Lynn, 1994:407)

If we follow Wang Bi's interpretation, the above line statement contains a warning for the third yang line not to "assist the petty man" at the top position (1994:407). The detailed account of Wang Bi's interpretation on this is quoted in the following:

> If a noble man occupies the position of Third Yang, he will surely be capable of casting off any entanglement with Top Yin; that he should be decisive about this he has no doubt. This is why the text says that he "acts with perfect Resolution." However, if Third Yang does not associate with the other yang lines but instead travels alone in pursuit of different ambitions and responds to the petty man [represented by Top Yin], he will suffer hardship and distress by doing so. "He should encounter such a rain that he should be as if sunk in water," and he should feel resentment but would have no place to lay blame.

Regarding the above interpretations rendered to the line statements of the second and the third lines, however, a question may be raised; why does the *I Ching* see a possibility that the subjects at the second and the third positions would be inclined to show a sympathetic attitude toward the one at the top position? Unless it envisions such a possibility, it would not have included the warning in the line statements. Presumably, the reason may be found in that human beings in general have mixed emotions about killing off enemies already in a state of a near death. However, we do not find in the text a clear explanation about why it sees the possibility of the position holders at the second and the third positions having some inclination to show sympathy toward the top position holder who is said to have run out of any chance for survival.

Commentators also offer a confusing array of interpretations for the line statements of the fourth yang line. The line statement itself involves descriptions that are expressed so symbolically that it leads to no straightforward interpretation: "This one's thighs are without skin, and his walking falters. If he were to allow himself to be led by the ram, regret would disappear, but he might hear what is said but not trust it" (Lynn, 1994:408). But, somehow most commentators have derived a common theme from it. The fourth yang line is portrayed as a position holder who displays a "superordinate" action orientation that does not fit the requirements of the fourth position — there is no one, either above or below him, who will yield to his action orientation as such. Notice that there is a strong governing ruler above him at the fifth position and below him a strong subordinate group represented by the trigram *Qian* made up of three yang lines. And, according to Wang Bi (1994:408), the "ram" symbolizes the fifth yang line that represents the governing ruler of the hexagram.[39] Viewed in this way, the line statement contains the advice that the fourth yang line should yield himself to the leadership of the governing ruler at the fifth position and, only in doing so, can he make the best out of this situation represented by the hexagram *Kuai*. But, still, the *I Ching* adds a rather sarcastic remark on the nature of the position holder at this position by saying that this one possesses such a recalcitrant and cocky characteristic that "he might hear what is said but not trust it."

Summary of theoretical and empirical propositions

1) Up to now, judging from the ways that the *I Ching* analyzes various types of social situation, we can identify the four sources of power. The first one is, of course, the formal position that a person or category of individuals occupies in the hierarchical order of society. The second one is the action orientations of individuals, expressed with either a yang or yin line. The third one is rooted in

the concept of Oriental moral logic: certain moral virtues of individuals such as modesty can be cashed into power by attracting large followings among people. Now, in this section, we are going to add another source of power: patterns of association or alliance between or among the constituting members of the group represented by a given hexagram. This reflects a simple perspective that has been largely absent from the theoretical perspectives in the sociology or political science of the West, perhaps with a rare exception to be found in Simmel. Power seeking involves support seeking. In other words, since a person will have little power without another that is willing to render support to his power, a source of power necessarily involves a formation of social associations from which the needed support is derived. In the *I Ching*, the concept of *corresponding* (*resonant*) relations reflects this perspective where the support-dependent power relationships formed between or among position holders is expressed.

2) For the reason stated above, gaining the support of subordinates is an essential requirement for a leader to maintain an effective leadership.

3) The situation represented by the hexagram *Lü* suggests that a social situation due to its essential characteristic may require a careful and tense posture from its constituent members; or, it can be viewed as such from the perspective of some people at certain positions. Judging from the hexagram *Lü*, this careful posture imposed upon concerned individuals is related to the fact that although the situation permits a certain degree of independence to individuals, this independence, at the same time, will be operated as a right to prevent others from stepping into what rightly belongs to an individual. And, note especially that the leader has a strong self-defensive power to exercise punitive measures whenever the others step over a certain forbidden limit. A tense situation involving a group of individuals who act more or less independently from one another but are treading carefully in rather narrowly set limits is depicted by this hexagram *Lü*.

4) From what is said in the above passage, an additional proposition may be derived: the subordinate position does not always involve a dependent relationship in which the subordinate person is placed under the control of someone at a superior position. Depending on situations, people at subordinate positions may be allowed, or have

enough strength, to enjoy independence to more or less degrees.

5) As indicated through the hexagram *Xiaoxu*, the dominant group does not always possess enough power to control the subordinate group if the latter possesses the strength to press its will against the former and the dominant does not have enough power potential to exercise control over the subordinate group. Thus, in this sense, as far as the *I Ching* is concerned, the term "dominant" or "subordinate" will not be used as referring to some "real and general" properties invariably found in actual relationships among position holders. They are only "formal" properties of social positions, which is one, although perhaps the most important, variable in determining one's power. Thus, in reality, a person or group in a "dominant" position may not possess effective power to fully exercise his formal position-endowed power.

6) When the hexagram *Bi* and the hexagram *Dayou* are considered together, the *I Ching* suggests that there can be two possible types of leadership style, a yang type and a yin type. As indicated by the hexagram *Bi*, a yang type of leadership exists where power is concentrated in the hands of a strong, unitary leader who holds all the subordinates together as loyal subjects. On the other hand, a yin type of leadership exists where, as shown by the hexagram *Dayou*, a leader rules by delegating both power and duties, inducing active participation from appropriate position holders rather than forcing one-sided submission to his power.

7) When a newly emerging force wins victory over the old camp, there will be always a clean-up operation conducted by the new camp. However, as a norm, the political purge will not bring out desirable outcomes.

4) Other Types of Integrated Situations

Six hexagrams that we will analyze below are put together here with two considerations. One consideration is that, as some may have noticed already, they have relational structures that are more complex than the previous ones. Let me say frankly that these six hexagrams were left out when I classified the hexagrams with the criteria that I applied in the previous section. The other consideration, which seems more important to me than the above, is that they share some important characteristics which allow them to be called "integrated" situations.

"Integrated" situations denote more or less harmonious situations of a society that is characterized by "orderly," "peaceful," or "cooperative" relations among people involved. They are represented through six hexagrams as follows:

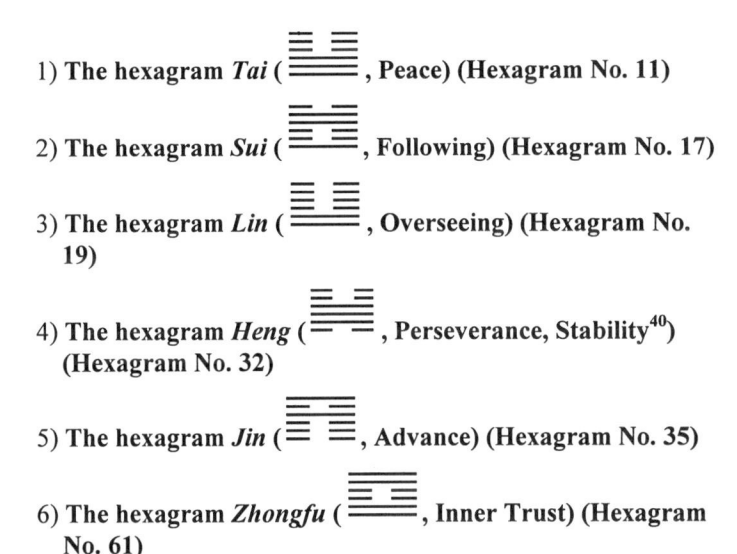

1) The hexagram *Tai* (☷☰ , Peace) (Hexagram No. 11)

2) The hexagram *Sui* (☱☳ , Following) (Hexagram No. 17)

3) The hexagram *Lin* (☷☱ , Overseeing) (Hexagram No. 19)

4) The hexagram *Heng* (☳☴ , Perseverance, Stability[40]) (Hexagram No. 32)

5) The hexagram *Jin* (☲☷ , Advance) (Hexagram No. 35)

6) The hexagram *Zhongfu* (☴☱ , Inner Trust) (Hexagram No. 61)

The hexagram *Tai* (☷☰ , Peace)

A hexagram name itself does not tell much about a situation represented by the hexagram unless its hexagram statement and all the attached line statements are carefully examined. Hexagram names in general do not refer to abstract properties in human situations as seems to be the case with abstract concepts in social sciences in the West. Since they refer rather to much more concrete characteristics of human situations that can be defined in terms of unique patterns of relations among people occupying unequally ranked social positions, the core idea of a hexagram then will rest upon the specific pattern of human relations depicted by that hexagram. In this hexagram, therefore, the appropriate question is regarding what kind of specific relational patterns is in formation in view of which the situation represented by this hexagram is characterized as being in "peace"?

Then, first, let us examine what specific sort of peaceful situation in social relations is depicted by the hexagram *Tai* with its particular line structure. Although the *Commentary on the Judgments* (Lynn, 1994:205) allows room for more than one way of interpreting the meaning of this hexagram, the reading of the line statements leads us to one particular way of looking at this hexagram: a peaceful situation achieved through a perfect union of the upper and the lower groups. An important point to note is the manner in which the union is achieved. As we can see, the subordinate group is represented by the trigram *Qian* while the upper group is represented by the trigram *Kun*. The former characterizes an active and superordinate action orientation and the latter is a rather passive and yielding one. Therefore, the hexagram as a whole presents a situation in which a union is achieved between a strong and assertive subordinate group and a dominant group who accommodates the action orientation of the former by delegating or rather relegating its authorities to those below. Thus, the *Commentary on the Judgments* explains, "Those above and those below interact perfectly, and they will become one" (Lynn, 1994:205).

The line statement of the first yang line states: "When one pulls up the rush plant, it pulls up others of the same kind together with it, so if one goes forth and acts, there will be good fortune" (Lynn, 1994:206). The first yang line belongs to the lower group whose members (being represented with the trigram *Qian*) "share the same aim" and, therefore, "if one goes forth and acts," "the others will follow" (Lynn, 1994:206). In other words, the subordinate group represented by the trigram *Qian* is described to be a highly integrated group acting together in unison. The *Commentary on the Images* supplements an additional meaning to this line by stating that "here one should keep his aim on outer things [the public world]" (Lynn, 1994:206). Considering under ordinary situations the lowest, first position is given the advice not to get involved with "outer things" such as political activities, the *I Ching* must have conceived this situation as quite an exceptional one, or an advantageous one as far as the first position is concerned. As Wang Bi points outs in his commentary, the reason the first position is placed in such an advantageous situation will be found in that "the (yin) lines of the upper trigram respond compliantly and do not become disobedient or contrary, so when the yang lines advance, all of them achieve their purpose" (Lynn, 1994:206). The situation where the weak upper group is under the influence of the strongly integrated subordinate group allows room for the first position holder to stage politically oriented activities.

The line statement of the second yang line describes the subject at the second position as the key figure who acts in the best possible way for the integration of the group under the situation represented by the hexagram *Tai*. The manners that he is said to behave are so well balanced that they are regarded as model behavior exemplifying what is called the Doctrine of the Mean in the Confucian ethics. The line statement itself poses no difficulty in the sense that it conveys quite clearly the ideal mode of behavior: "One here embraces the uncouth, makes use of those who wade rivers, and does not leave out who are far away, thus cliques disappear, and he succeeds in being worthy of the practice of centrality [the Mean]" (Lynn, 1994:207). But, why is the one at the second position under the defined situation viewed as practicing such an ideal mode of behavior? According to Cheng Yi (1988:31-32), the modes of behavior described by the line statement involve "elements" that "government in tranquility (peace) has." "Tolerance," "broadmindedness," "firm decisiveness" and "non-partisanship" are virtues that are instrumental in bringing the peaceful state of government indicated by the hexagram *Tai* into reality. And, the line statement of the second yang line suggests that the subject at the second position carries these virtues in his action orientation and, therefore, assumes the key role for maintaining the condition represented by the hexagram. But, again, why should the second yang line be the one who carries out such crucial role? The *I Ching* may explain that it is because the second position, rather than the third one, as a rule is likely to perform a more crucially important role in creating a situation. Undoubtedly, this perspective concerning the functional importance of the second position applies generally to most hexagrams. In view of the overall characteristics of the situations represented by most hexagrams, the second position that is said to engage in administrative functions, rather than the leadership function that is said to be exercised by the third position, is assumed to play a more important role for maintaining a situation. But, notice that this principle applies only to the lower trigram. For the upper trigram, the fifth position, the top leadership for the entire group, occupies the central location, not only in terms of spatial location in a trigram but also in terms of functional importance. An interesting proposition is put forth here. Whereas the core function for the subordinate group is performed by the second position, for the dominant group it is done by the fifth position. Therefore, the actions of the position holder at the administrative position in the lower unit are of the most strategic importance in its operation, but how the regulative, dominant unit operates depends mostly on the performance of the position holder with the leadership function. In this sense, the *I Ching* seems to make a distinction between the ranking order in statuses and the importance in functions. This is particularly true of the lower trigram which, in terms of function, the subject at the second position, in most occasions, is considered to assume a more important role than the one at the third position who is placed at a higher rank in the hierarchically ordered system.

As far as the line statement of the third yang line is concerned, we can read no clearly stated indication of what kind of specific situation the position holder at this position would face. Yet, judging from the moralistic lesson rendered to the subject of the line position proper, it seems clear, the *I Ching* is assuming that the position holder at this position would be in a difficult situation. The line statement itself, as suggested above, is largely a prescriptive one: "There is no flat that does not eventually slope; there is no going away that does not involve a return, but one who practices constancy in the face of difficulty will be without blame. Grieve not over your faithfulness, for there are blessings in the salary that sustains you" (Lynn, 1994:207). The line statement, first of all, as Cheng Yi explains, points out that there is no such thing as permanent "tranquility (peace)" (1988:32). And, the line statement suggests that when things change, the subject at the third position may enter a difficult situation. Why is this? The line statement itself offers no explanation. A clue, if still hard to decode, may be found in the *Commentary on the Images*, which states, " 'There is no going away that does not involve a return': this is at the boundary between Heaven and Earth" (Lynn, 1994:208). Wang Bi's explanation (Lynn, 1994:207) on this is not of much help either. Forced to make a reasonable guess, I would venture that the reason why the third position holder falls into such a difficult situation is that, being placed at the leadership position for the strong subordinate group bearing forcefully upon its superiors, he has to take primary responsibility for what takes place until the situation changes into a new one.

Now regarding the line statement for the forth yin line, it is easier to capture what is meant by its line statement if the line statement and the attached *Commentary on the Images* are introduced together:

> The line statement: He flutters down, not boasting of his wealth (*all of them have lost what is real*), /Together with his neighbor, /Guileless and sincere (*he desires it in the depth of his heart*). (Wilhelm, 1967:444)[41]

By supplementing a few words to the *Commentary on the Images*, the meaning of the line statement is much easier to understand. All the members of the upper group have lost what is real (in power); he desires it (i.e., peace) in the depths of his heart. I will paraphrase this again by adding Legge's commentary: since the upper group has lost the power to hold sway over the subordinate group, the subject at the fourth position will seek "to maintain the state of Thai (*Tai*, peace) . . . . giving them (the lower group), humbly but readily, all the help in their power" (Legge, 1963:83).

The above comment supplied by Legge applies equally to the fifth yin line, although the line statement of the fifth yin line involves a narration stated in symbolic words of a different kind. It reads, "The sovereign Yi gave his younger sister in marriage. As a result, there were blessings and fundamental good fortune" (Lynn, 1994:209). "The sovereign Yi gave his younger sister in marriage" refers to a historical episode that is supposed to actually have taken place in China, although it has not been documented to which individual sovereign Yi refers (Legge, 1963:83-84; Lynn, 1994:211). But, regardless of what actually had happened in history and who the actual personnages were, what the line statement tries to say seems clear. In ancient China, giving sisters of an emperor for marriage to powerful subordinates is one way of buying peace for a sovereign in a weak position. Thus, as Legge explains, the fifth yin line, "while occupying the place of dignity and authority in the hexagram, is yet a weak line in the place of a strong one; its subject, accordingly, humbly condescends to his strong and proper correlate in line 2" (1963:84). With the help of these line statements, the peace of this hexagram can now be understood clearly. It is a peace bought with patience and compliance by the weak dominant group that does not possess enough power to exercise control over the strong subordinate group.

Lastly, the line statement of the top yin line states, "The city wall falls back into the moat. Do not use the army now, and only in one's own city issue commands, otherwise constancy will be debased" (Lynn, 1994:209). Wang Bi (Lynn, 1994:209) and Cheng Yi (1988:34) agree that the line statement for the top yin line refers to the final stage expected to take place as the peaceful situation represented by the hexagram draws closer to an end. That is, the line statement says that as the peace constructed through the way indicated by the hexagram *Tai* is wearing away, "there is lack of communication between those above and those below" (Cheng Yi, 1998:204) or "those above and those below do not interact" (Lynn, 1994:209). The points out briefly that the army should not be used under this situation because "commands here will result in confusion" (Lynn, 1994:210). "Commands here will result in confusion" develops from the situation in which "there is lack of communication between those above and those below" or "those above and those below do not interact," people "do not follow the leadership," and, consequently, a mobilization of the army may only result in "disorder" (Cheng Yi, 1998:34). In this context the last portion of the line statement also seems to make sense. It issues advice, probably to the person at the leadership position, that his commands will not go through to anyone but a narrow circle of people closely associated with him. At this point, a question may be raised, Why should the peaceful situation maintained through the way depicted by the hexagram *Tai* finally end up with this rather disorderly outcome? The *I Ching* provides no clue to answer this question.

The hexagram *Sui* (☱☳ , Following)

First, let us look at the way in which the lines are arranged in the hexagram *Sui*. Viewed from the perspective that the *I Ching* reads the line structure of the hexagram, the first yang line is paired with the second yin line, the third yin line with the fourth yang line, and the fifth yang line with the sixth yin line. Every element finds a proper associate to form a harmoniously matching (i.e., yin-yang) pair. Thus, it is interpreted, everyone under the situation finds someone to "follow" or "is followed" by someone. Hence, the hexagram name, *Sui* (Following), is given. This is a well integrated, stable situation where no one finds himself alienated from social networks, due to which no serious misfortune or grave warning sign except a mild reminder for possible hazards is rendered to everyone situated under the situation.

Since, in this hexagram, the first yang line and the second yin line make up a pair in a corresponding relationship, it will be better to introduce together the line statements of the two lines at the same time. They read as follows:

> *First Yang*: One's self-control has the capacity to change course, so his practice of constancy means good fortune, and, when he leaves his own gate, he relates to others in such a way that he achieves merit.
>
> *Second Yin*: This one ties itself to the little child and abandons the mature man. (Lynn, 1994:243)

Let us look at the line statement of the second yin line first. According to Wang Bi, "the little child" refers to the first yang line and "the mature man" refers to the fifth yang line (Lynn, 1994:243). Thus, the line statement is interpreted as refering simply to the fact that the first yang line and the second yin line are paired together to form an alliance of a certain sort. Nevertheless, the subject at the first position, the lower position, holds the initiative in their relationship. In terms of the overall meaning of the situation represented by the hexagram, the subject at the second, higher position is the follower. This makes the subject at the first position having, as is characterized by the line statement, the capacity for "self-control," i.e., "the capacity to change course." Although the subject at the first position occupies the lowest place of the hierarchy, he possesses "the capacity for self-control"; he is allowed to exercise a good deal of freedom in doing things of his own choice or introducing changes, perhaps to social standards or institutions. And, as the line statement of the second line implicitly suggests, the subject at the second position will comply with the situationally determined condition in which the subject at the first position exercises such autonomy or initiative. An interesting yet perplexing aspect of the line statement of the first yang line concerns the last verse, "he leaves his own gate, he relates to others in such a way that he achieves merit." According to Legge (1093:94), what the above verse intends to indicate is "the public spirit" of the subject at the first position which is not related to "selfish considerations." Cheng Yi (1988:51) accords with this interpretation and explains that people's prejudices in general tend to be associated with limited associations confined narrowly within "his own gate"; they occur when people limit their associations to a narrow circle of people closely related to themselves. Thus, in the line statement, "when he leaves his own gate, he relates to others in such a way that he achieves merit" means that one goes beyond his private realm to involve himself with the public welfare. Regarding the line statement and its interpreted meaning rendered above, it does not seem to be an unreasonably conceived possibility that the common people, represented by the bottom line, work to bring about changes to society and have enough potential to do so under certain circumstances. Considering that this book is a product of an archaic society, however, this may be viewed as a remarkably sober and candid observation on a possibility that might have appeared impossible to most people who had lived in the old Chinese Empire. But, a question may be raised as regards the actual existence of the intellectual tradition from a perspective of which the subject at the first position is viewed to act rather with "the public spirit" than with much more narrowly limited group interests. It appears pretty obvious that the question raised above exposes us to a shadowy alley of the *I Ching*. A clear answer to it is not available at present, or rather, as we can see in some hexagrams, the opaque symbolism of the *I Ching* is open to leeway for its readers to see what they would like to see.[42]

The following two line statements also indicate that the two subjects at the third and the fourth positions constitute a pair of components that are in close association with each other.

> *Third Yang*: This one ties itself to a mature man and abandons the little child. By following in this way, one should obtain what one seeks, so it is fitting to abide in constancy.
>
> *Fourth Yin*: This one has success at garnering a Following, but constancy will still result in misfortune. The sincerity he has is there in the path he follows, and, as it is brought to light in this way, what blame will he have? (Lynn, 1994:244-5)

In the above line statements, the beginning verse of the third line statement, "This one ties itself to a mature man and abandons the little boy," corresponds in meaning with that of the fourth line statement, "This one has success at garnering a Following." The mature man refers to the subject at the fourth position and the third position holder is the follower to the fourth one who "has success at garnering a Following." The reference to the third position as one who "should obtain what one (he) seeks" simply refers to the fact that as he "abandons the little child (the subject at the bottom who belongs to his own group)" and seeks for an alliance with the fourth yang line instead, he will be accepted. However, why does its line statement say that, on the part of the fourth yang line, "constancy will still result in misfortune"? According to Legge's explanation, the fourth position represents "the place of a great minister next the ruler in 5," and, therefore, "his having adherents may be injurious to the supreme and sole authority of that ruler" (1963:94). Coupled with this, the fourth place, a yin position, is occupied by a yang line; this mismatch is interpreted as the subject's displaying a superordinate action orientation, instead of a "subordinate" one as expected of his position, and may raise suspicion from the top leadership. Wang Bi in accord with the above interpretation explains in more detail:

> "This one has success at garnering a Following." Fourth Yang abides in the territory of the subject minister, so where it treads is not its rightful position [it is a yang line in a yin position]. To use this to seize control over the people is a violation as far as the Dao of the subject minister is concerned, and such a one is in violation of what is right. (Lynn, 1994:245)

Of the verse that follows next, Legge's translation, "If he be sincere (however) in his course, and makes that evident, into what error will he fall?", seems to permit a much easier and clearer interpretation. It contains a simple yet, given the situation, seemingly sound advice for the subject at the fourth position by saying that he should behave as sincerely as possible so that he can deflect the risk involved in his present situation.

The remaining pair of line statements, those for the fifth yang line and the sixth yin line, are as follows:

> The fifth line, undivided, shows us (the ruler) sincere in (fostering all) that is excellent. There will be good fortune.
>
> The topmost line, divided, shows us (that sincerity) firmly held and clung to, yea, and bound fast. (We see) the king with it presenting his offerings on the western mountain. (Legge, 1963:94)[43]

The line statement for the fifth yang line can be understood in the light of the familiar logic with which the ruler's position is interpreted as being occupied by someone whose personal quality or action orientation matches with that position (i.e., a yang line is present where a yang line is supposed to appear). The subject at the topmost position, being a yin line with the strong ruler in incumbency, is described as a faithful follower who is "firmly held and clung to, ... bound fast" to the subject at the fifth position. The next line stating, "the king with it presenting his offerings on the western mountain," symbolizes the union achieved between the subjects at the two positions, the fifth and the sixth positions. According to Legge (1963:95), the western mountain refers to "mount *Khi*, at the foot of which was the original settlement of the house of *Kau*," to which king *Wen* and the duke of *Kau* known as the authors of the *I Ching* belonged. Thus, "to present offerings on the western mountain" should refer to a symbolic ritual commemorating a happy union achieved by a political community.

The hexagram *Lin* (☷☱ , Overseeing)

The situation denoted by the next hexagram *Lin* (Overseeing or Approach) can be understood differently depending upon how we analyze the hexagram. The hexagram consists of the trigram *Dui* (the Lake) below and the trigram *Kun* (Earth) above. Thus, on the basis of the arrangement of the trigrams as such, the *Commentary on the Images* explains: "Above the Lake, there is Earth: this constitutes the Image of *Lin* [Overseeing]" (Lynn, 1994:254). If viewed in this way, the hexagram is interpreted as symbolizing a situation in which the group at the upper echelon is overseeing (or caring for, managing, governing) the group at the lower echelon having a characteristic represented by the trigram *Dui*. On the other hand, the situation represented by the hexagram may be inferred from the characteristics of individual lines: above two yang lines at the first and the second positions there are four yin lines at the four high ranking positions. Since individuals or things with yin and yang characteristics are complementary to each other, they will "approach" each other to form a union. It is with this notion of integration achieved on the basis of complementary traits that the hexagram *Lin* is understood to signify an "approaching" situation.[44] Legge combines the two ideas, Overseeing and Approach, and explains that "*Lin* denotes the approach of authority — to inspect, to comfort, or to rule" (1963:98). As far as it denotes a mode of a social integration, I think, the concept suggested by the hexagram *Lin* would not be significantly different whether we translate it to mean "Overseeing" or "Approach," and, in this sense, the way that Legge defines the meaning of *Lin* seems to provide a quite handy way to resolve the difference. In the following interpretation, therefore, I will take the two ideas as mutually interchangeable or nested in each other.

The line statements of the first and the second yang lines repeat nearly the same theme, and, therefore, are presented together:

First Yang: This one prompts Overseeing, and constancy here means good fortune.

Second Yang: This one prompts Overseeing, which means good fortune such that nothing fails to be fitting. (Lynn, 1994:255)

According to Wang Bi's commentary, "prompt" in the above line statement carries the same meaning as "provoke" or "provoke a response." Considering the fact that "Overseeing" is done by the ruling group represented by the upper trigram and also that the first and the second yang lines are in corresponding relationships with the fourth and the fifth yin lines respectively, the line statement, "this one prompts Overseeing," can be read as saying that the subjects at the first and the second positions put pressures on the governing elites at the upper echelon to oversee (look after or take care of) them. Notice that the ones below are represented by yang lines and those above by yin lines. This combination of the lines suggests that those in the lower positions have enough potential to "prompt" wanted responses from those above. As both the line statements indicate, the *I Ching* seems to consider this kind of situation as favorable to the subjects at these two lower positions.

The subject at the third position is described as one who "does Overseeing" but "with sweetness." According to Wang Bi, "sweet refers to seductive, wicked flattery" (Lynn, 1994:256), which means that the one at the third, leadership position governs the people under his rule with flattery. He may not be said to "govern" in the correct sense of the word as understood in the cultural perspectives of Asian societies. He merely tries to gain popularity by currying favor with the people under his leadership. Thus, the *I Ching* renders quite a negative assessment saying, "there is nothing at all fitting." And, in view of the assessment made above, the line statement, ending with a phrase, "but once one becomes anxious about it, there will be no blame," seems to involve a good piece of advice that makes perfect sense. Here, however, a question may be raised; why is this subject at the third position interpreted as one who "does Overseeing with sweetness"? The *Commentary on the Images* offers a simple explanation; "for the position is not right for him," indicating that a yin line occupies inappropriately the third position, a yang position. As I have pointed out several times before, this rule of interpretation does not seem sufficient to explain why this one does it particularly "with sweetness." The logic behind reading "sweetness" from a misplaced yin line is difficult to follow. And, as I think, the personal experiences of the author(s) of the *I Ching* might have played quite a heavy role here.

The subject at the fourth yin line is described as one who does "perfect Overseeing" (Lynn, 1994:256). The logic with which a favorable judgment is rendered to his situation is the same as that for the third line; a yin line occupies appropriately the fourth position, a yin position, and, therefore, the subject at the fourth position is interpreted as behaving correctly as required under the situation. Thus, to explain, this subject, prompted by those who are in a position to exercise strong influence from below, will do a perfect job in Overseeing and rendering services to the people under his administrative jurisdiction.

The line statement of the fifth yin line is similar in essential content to that of the fourth yin line except that what it says takes into account the specific position of the fifth yin line. It states, "This one does Overseeing with wisdom, which is the wherewithal for a great sovereign and means good fortune" (Lynn, 1994:257). Wang Bi's commentary adds to this line statement a more detailed description on the complementary relationship formed between the subject at the second position and the sovereign at the fifth position:

> It (the leader at the fifth position) knows how to receive the hard and strong [Second Yang] with decorum and thereby strengthen its practice of rectitude. Fifth Yin does not dread the growth of Second Yang's strength and so is able to employ Second Yang in its service. It is by employing others in order to extend one's abilities, while doing no wrong in the process, that the precarious can extend his power of sight and hearing to the utmost and the one empowered with wisdom can fulfill his ability to plan. (Lynn, 1994:257)

The above commentary in fact describes an ideal mode of a cooperative relationship between a weak leader and a strong subordinate. Yet, it is under the situation denoted by the hexagram *Lin* that such an ideal complementary relationship meets a real chance to come into reality.

Now, the last line statement reads, "This one does Overseeing with simple honesty, which results in good fortune and no blame" (Lynn, 1994:257). From the arrangement of the lines in the hexagram where the yin line at the sixth position finds no complementary line (yang line) at the third position, it may be thought that it is isolated from the others under this situation. However, commentators explain that the overall orientation of the ruling elites represented by the trigram *Kun* (signifying receptivity and simplicity) makes the top position holder a part of the group as a whole with no separate motive; therefore, "this one (also) does Overseeing with simple honesty."

Before I finish with this hexagram, I would like to add a brief note on the nature of this hexagram. If we follow a common sense notion of democracy, the type of integration featured by the hexagram *Lin* may be characterized as depicting that which is based on a democratic principle. This is because we see the receptive governing elites who work for people who are powerful enough to "prompt" the former to respond to what they want. It is interesting to note that the *I Ching*, a product of ancient Chinese society, views a democratic integration of this kind as a favorable situation in which everyone, except the leader who rules the populace with flattery, would enjoy "good fortune."

The hexagram *Heng* (☷☴ , Perseverance, Stability)

The situational meaning of the hexagram *Heng* (Stability) can be understood in reference to two things associated with its line structure.

First, the hexagram *Heng* consists of the trigram *Zhen* above and the trigram *Sun* below. As we may remember, the trigram *Zhen* is represented by a variety of symbolic images which include as one of its major symbols "the Eldest Son," whereas "the Eldest Daughter" is one of the major symbols that is used to represent the situational attributes of the trigram *Sun*. Thus, the upper group that has an attribute of a male is positioned above the subordinate group with the attribute of a female. As Wang Bi puts it, "the hard and strong is in the exalted position, and the soft and yielding is in the humble." And, according to Wang Bi's interpretation, such an arrangement of an organization "means that a proper order is maintained" (Lynn, 1994:32). The meaning of the situation, expressed through its title name *Heng* (Stability), reflects a typical mode of thought in Chinese culture where stability in the order of an organization is viewed to exist whenever everyone occupies his own proper place as prescribed by the prevailing normative standards of the society. The second thing taken into consideration in understanding why a hexagram represents a stable organization is the patterns of relationships among individual lines. As we can see, the yin line at the bottom position is matched with the yang line at the fourth position, the yang line at the second position with the yin line at the fifth position, and the third yang line with the yin line at the top position; therefore, every line in the lower trigram finds in the upper trigram a favorable partner having a complementary trait suitable to form a union. Thus, as the *Commentary on the Judgments* succinctly expresses this situation, "the hard [yang] and soft [yin] lines are all in resonance, so Perseverance (Stability) is had" (Lynn, 1994:335). In terms of both its constituent trigrams and its component lines, the hexagram is composed of a pair or pairs of components that have complementary traits, and, therefore, "Stability" as represented by this hexagram refers to a type of a social integration achieved through well matched combinations. But, we notice here an inconsistency — an annoying aspect in the above interpretation regarding the "stable" integration of an organization that the line structure of this hexagram is said to represent. In terms of its component trigrams, an organization represented by the hexagram is said to maintain a stable order because the upper and the lower trigrams are integrated into a properly ordered unit according to the principle of duality between a yang (dominant one) and a yin (submissive one). Notice that the upper trigram with a male attribute is positioned above the lower trigram with a female attribute. This means that one with a dominant behavioral orientation or trait occupies the dominant position while the other with a submissive behavioral orientation or trait occupies the lower position that requires submission. However, if we examine the line structure in terms of individual lines, a rather different picture emerges. For instance, a yin line is located at the fifth position, and this is matched with a yang line at the second position. Since these two positions are regarded as having a specific affinity to each other and there exists a yang and yin complement between these two positions, we may say that an arrangement of the lines as such contributes to a stable order that is said to exist under the situation. For this combination, however, notice that the yin-yang complement is reversed in its positional arrangement: a yin line lies above and a yang line below, respectively at the fifth and the second positions. Can this be considered a stable or "proper" relationship? There is no indication that either the *I Ching* or later commentators had taken into consideration the fact that changing the levels of analysis from trigrams to individual lines may force us to accept, if unintentionally, inconsistent rules or perspectives in the interpretation of any given hexagram. Of course, although this kind of problem is found not only in this hexagram but also in many other hexagrams, our interpretation has been proceeding largely on the basis of the meanings of individual lines. Thus, let us put this problem aside simply as some incomprehensible aspect of this extremely old classic.

Judging from the composition of individual lines and attached line statements, the subject at the second position is considered the ruler of the hexagram, the one who plays the central role in maintaining stability as implied by the hexagram (Wilhelm, 1967:545). Its line statement says briefly, "Regret vanishes" (Lynn, 1994:337); nevertheless, of all the line statements in the hexagram this is the most favorable one. The reason why the subject at the second position settles into his position is explained in view of two factors. First is that the second position, of low ranking officials at operative levels, is viewed as a stable position. The other is that he is in a corresponding relationship with the fifth yin line, which means that he has a close tie with the top leader responding to his will. Then, the line statement of the fifth yin line would be expected to correlate with what is said in the line statement of the second line. As a matter of fact, it describes the situation of the fifth line as one in which its subject is in some sort of a dependent relation with the subject at the second position. It reads: "If one perseveres in virtue here and practices constancy, it would be good fortune for the woman but misfortune for the man" (Lynn, 1994:339). This line statement states that the subject at the fifth position is in a weak position relative to others under the situation and this requires him to comply with the will of his subordinate at the second position who has the upper hand at the present time. If he attempts to put down strong subordinates with force, he may suffer unfortunate outcomes. However, a cooperative relationship between the two actors at the second and the fifth positions would be insured in so far as the latter behaves in accordance with his limited ability imposed by the given situation. Thus, here we can see that the subjects at the second and the fifth positions held together in a "reversed" dependent relationship (a yang below and a yin above it) constitutes a primary relationship that allegedly brings about the situation of Stability indicated by the hexagram.

Although the hexagram as a whole represents a situation whose overall characteristic is noted by its name *Heng* (Stability), the judgments of all other lines except the two lines discussed above do not seem to pertain much to a "stable" situation. Then, first, let us look at the line statement of the bottom line: "The first line, divided, shows its subject deeply (desirous) of long continuance. Even with firm correctness there will be evil; there will be no advantage in any way" (Legge, 1963:125-6).[45] Being expressed as a yin line at the lowest place, the first position is described as being "deeply desirous of long continuance (a stable relationship)," especially with the fourth position due to a specific and complementary affinity with regard to both their positional and situational attributes. But, why does the line statement give a rather negative appraisal on its subject's prospect for securing such a stable relationship? According to Legge's interpretation, the presence of two strong lines, the second and the third yang lines, lying between the two (1963:126), poses, if not willfully, obstacles to a union between the first and the fourth positions. Of course, it may happen in real life situations that people, in an attempt to prevent an emergence of a strong rival party, try to wedge themselves between potential opponents whose strength may become greater through a union. Legge, or rather commentators on whose interpretations he relies, commenting on the adverse role of the two middle yangs against a possible alliance between the bottom and the fourth positions, may have seen a typical human situation in which people play against one another, strategize and plot for an advantageous and more secure position.

Then, skipping the third yang line for the moment, let us look at the line statement of the fourth yang line that is said to be the mostly likely alliance for the first yin line, but resulting in no successful outcome. It states briefly: "In the field there is no game" (Lynn, 1994:338). The *Commentary on the Images* describes this line as being "out of place" (Lynn, 1994:338) and refers to the fact that a yang line is in a yin place. And, this line at the same time is left isolated as his most likely partner at the bottom position is held in check from siding with him. Thus, the line statement simply says that the subject under the situation has no prospect for favorable outcomes.

Both the third and sixth lines are described by their line statements as displaying rather unstable or inappropriate behavior. Considering that this situation as a whole is characterized as a stable one, why these two particular lines are viewed to behave in such inappropriate manners is not clear. The marked differences in commentators' perspectives seems to indicate that their commentaries are largely *ad hoc*; that is, with the ambiguity of the given line statements, each commentator might have to "construct" or "invent" some sort of reasonable explanation. Despite a divergence in explanations concerning why the two position holders behave inappropriately under the situation, however, there is one agreement amongst commentators: under the situation represented by the hexagram, the position holders at the third and the sixth positions can be considered as the most likely pair to seek a partnership with each other; these two actors are judged to be in a close relationship, for they occupy positions having a specific affinity and, at the same time, possess situational attributes (as a yin and a yang) that are complementary to each other. In addition, also consider the fact that these two positions have been generally considered "unstable" ones. The third position is considered an unstable position because it has the ambivalent status of being located at the highest position in the lower group that has not yet entered the upper echelon. Perhaps this is why it is often said that the third position is "at the point of transition from the lower trigram to the upper trigram" (Wilhelm, 1967:548). And, it is also why native scholars of the *I Ching* somehow saw a greater deal of insecurity associated with this position than any other position. The sixth position is a highly honored one, yet out of the formal office, which means that it carries no formally vested power. Thus, in most ordinary situations, favorable judgments are not rendered to the subjects at this position. Now, does the above explanation lead us to accept what the line statements tell about the specific situations of the subjects at the third and the top positions as sufficiently convincing? Perhaps, from the line structure, related line statements, and appended commentaries, it is possible for us to imagine a situation in which people whose positions involve inherent insecurities seek one another to form a union. Nevertheless, an important question may be raised regarding the above interpretation: how does this sort of corresponding relationship between the two subjects with equally unstable positions and, therefore, rather unstable or inappropriate behaviors contribute to the "Stability" of the situation taken as a whole? Is this simply a case of blatant inconsistency between the hexagram statement and the individual line statements in the accounts of the *I Ching*? I looked over available documents in search of clues with which to shed light on this issue, but have found none.

The hexagram *Jin* (☷ ☲, Advance)

The hexagram *Jin* (Advance) consists of the lower trigram *Kun* (the Earth) and the upper trigram *Li* (Fire or Brightness). Thus, the hexagram is described to convey an image of "Brightness appearing above the Earth" while the line structure of the hexagram is said to "constitute(s) the image of advance" (Lynn, 1994:350). Nevertheless, the text does not explain clearly what the specific nature of the "advancing" situation is. Judging from a passage in Wang Bi's sub-commentary on the *Commentary on the Judgments* which reads, ". . . . when one comes to enjoy his sovereign's favor by advancing with softness and yielding," "to advance" may be interpreted to mean simply "to submit" oneself to his sovereign or "to come forward to serve" his sovereign. This interpretation is based on the idea that since the lower unit is represented by the trigram *Kun* (a symbol of obedience), all the subjects in the lower group partake of the group trait as such. Regarding the sovereign who is represented by the middle yin line (at the fifth position) of the upper trigram *Li*, the *Commentary on the Images* also points out that he possesses a main attribute of the trigram *Li*, a man who "illuminates himself with bright virtue" (Lynn, 1994:350). Thus, this hexagram represents a situation in which, under an intelligent and gentle leadership, there also are conforming people who submit themselves voluntarily to such leadership. It would be undoubtedly in this context that the *Commentary on the Judgments* says, "It is obedience that allows one to adhere to this great brightness, and it is a soft and yielding advance that allows one to move up" (Lynn, 1994:350). A peaceful situation thereby is featured by the hexagram.

The line statement of the first yin line describes its subject as someone who is not fully trusted so that his wish to serve the leader (or the country) may not be realized. It reads, "The first line, divided, shows one wishing to advance, and (at the same time) kept back. Let him be firm and correct, and there will be good fortune. If trust be not reposed in him, let him maintain a large and generous mind, and there will be no error" (Legge, 1963:132). Why the subject at the first position is not trusted so that his "advance" is "kept back" is not clear. Of course, when many people try to "advance" and offer themselves for service to the government, not all of them will be trusted and offered the chance. Undoubtedly, the line statement of the first yin line intends to refer to such people whose wishes for "advancement" have been denied for some reason. Yet, as said already, the reason for which they are not trusted is not clearly explained anywhere in the text. This is probably why Lynn's text based on Wang Bi's interpretation translates the passage, "If trust be not reposed in him, let him maintain a large and generous mind, and there will be no error" instead of as "One is not yet trusted here, but if he were to let his resources grow rich, there would be no blame" (1994:352). I think that both the above translations fit with the overall meaning of the situation as I have explained. With Legge's translation, the line statement is interpreted to involve the instruction that when one fails to realize his wish to make "advancement" and experiences frustration, he has to "maintain a large and generous mind" not to commit a mistake. Lynn's translation renders a reading a little different from the above; it teaches that one has to use the situation as a chance for his personal development. Either way, judging from its line statement, the first yin line in this hexagram seems to represent a more narrowly defined range of people than generally interpreted in many other hexagrams: it represents young people who aspire to serve the government, yet are given no appointment due to lack of trust.

The line statement of the second position reads, "The second line, divided, shows its subject with the appearance of advancing, and yet of being sorrowful. If he be firm and correct, there will be good fortune. He will receive this great blessing from his grandmother" (Legge, 1963:132).[46] First, the subject at the second position is described as advancing, yet feeling sad. According to Cheng Yi, the subject "has the qualities of gentleness and harmony, representing those who are not strong in advancing. Therefore there is something sad in advancing, meaning that there is difficulty in making progress" (1988:111). That is, due to his "yin (gentle and passive)" qualities, he does not push hard enough to have his presence or wishes felt by those at the higher echelon so that he may be left in the "sad" state of being neglected or ignored. Legge's interpretation does not seem much different from the above one. According to Legge, a weak line at the second position is correlated with another weak line at the fifth position, and this combination of two weak lines is interpreted to indicate that the subject is left in "obscurity" (1963:133). Regardless of this initial difficulty, however, the line statement offers a favorable judgment on the final outcome of the subject's situation; if the subject acts firmly and correctly, he will be rewarded with a "great blessing" from the leader at the fifth position and thereby end up with good fortune.

The line statement of the third yin line states briefly: "All trust, so regret vanishes" (Lynn, 1994:353). "All trust" means that there is consensus among the lower group (the three lines of the trigram *Kun*) regarding their willingness to work for the leadership represented by the fifth yin line. And, as the leader of the subordinate group, the subject at the third position represents someone who leads a group with the same intention to devote themselves to the service of the governing leadership. He is an obedient middle-leader in the loyal subordinate group. Of course, as the line statement suggests, he may have some "regret" about his position as such. This "regret" is believed to stem from the fact that a yin line occupies inappropriately a yang (leadership) position. Nevertheless, the line statement anticipates the "regret will vanish," for the characteristic of this position under this situation is quite compatible with that of the subordinate group as a whole.

The line statement of the fourth yang line describes its subject as someone who displays a different mode of behavior from the others. It reads, "Now advancing like a flying squirrel, this one should practice constancy in the face of danger" (Lynn, 1994:353). Commentators have different views on what the mode of behavior symbolized by "a flying squirrel" specifically refers to, and, accordingly, they interpret and translate it differently as any of various kinds of rats such as "marmot" or "rat" (Legge, 1963:132), "hamster" (Wilhelm, 1967:562), or "big rat" (Cheng Yi and Zhi Xi, in Lynn, 1994:356n10). According to Kong Yingda (quoted in Lynn, 1994:356n10), "flying squirrel" is an animal that possesses several skills of minor importance but no significant ability to achieve great things, and, therefore, symbolizes "Someone who . . . . lacks the wherewithal to keep safe" (Wang Bi, in Lynn, 1994:354). Thus, the subject at the fourth position is interpreted to represent officials or ministers who display talents and skills in small things but with no significant ability to manage important matters. Cheng Yi views it differently (1988:111-2), and explains that, "squirrels," greedy and fearful animals, symbolize people who, out of both greed and fear, try to secure their positions or interests against others. Both interpretations seem to make sense in that both types of people may be found to exist under the situation represented by the hexagram or even in many other situations. However, why is the subject in the fourth position viewed to display such a mode of behavior described by the line statement? Why is he described to have such a negative character by the line statement? Neither the text nor any later commentary offers any clear answer to this question except that a yang line inappropriately occupies the fourth position, a yin position.

The subject at the fifth position is the constituting and governing ruler of the situation and is described in the *Commentary on the Images* as "the sovereign" who "illuminates himself with bright virtue" (Lynn, 1994:351). As far as the line statements is concerned, there is no challenging figure against this subject's authority and the people in the lower echelon, represented by the trigram *Kun,* symbolize "obedience" or "conformity" in behavioral terms to this "sovereign." Thus, the hexagram as a whole indicates that the subject would be in quite a comfortable situation. In fact, the line statement reads, "Regret vanishes, and one should not worry about failure or success, for to set forth here means good fortune, and nothing shall fail to be fitting" (Lynn, 1994:354). The above line statement suggests that the situation initially poses some problem for its subject to elicit "regret." This kind of judgment is often given to anyone whose characteristic does not fit with the requirements of his position; in this case also, as Cheng Yi explains, "The fifth yin has weakness in the position of honor, so there should be regret" (1988:112). Nevertheless, as explained already, "regret vanishes." Two reasons can be pointed out for his happy turn of events. First, the subject, who is situated in the middle position of the trigram *Li* (Fire, or Brightness), is interpreted as representing a weak but intelligent leader. The other reason is found in that there are loyal subjects whose blind obedience to the leader itself constitutes the essential characteristic of the situation represented by this hexagram. The situation thus is described as an extremely favorable one for the subject at the fifth, leadership position. But, why does the line statement advise him "not to worry about failure or success"? Cheng Yi believes this is because the subject is likely to think too much about the possibility of "failure or success" in his actions. Thus, he interprets the subject at the fifth position as someone who is thoughtful but excessive in seeking "clarity too much, to the point of becoming picayune, and losing the way to delegate responsibility" (1988:112). Cheng Yi's above interpretation suggests that the yin line, if only in this hexagram, is interpreted as representing a specific type of personality — someone who over-analyzes all likely outcomes before going into action. This interpretation involves an interesting view on personality types. But, no other commentator seems in accord with Cheng Yi in this respect. And, as a matter of fact, Wang Bi's interpretation is diametrically opposed to that of Cheng Yi and says that the subject at the fifth position, being a bright leader, would be able to "avoid recourse to scrutiny" (1994:354) so that he does not have to worry about failure or success. Interpretations of this line statement offer further evidence of the effect of one's subjective viewpoints or value orientations on the reading of the lines, a problematic aspect of the *I Ching*.

The sixth yang line entails a long line statement that reads, "Making progress with the horns is permissible / Only for the purpose of punishing one's own city. To be conscious of danger brings good fortune. No blame. Perseverance brings humiliation" (Wilhelm, 1967:563).[47] As pointed out before, the line statement of the sixth line is often understood to contain a concluding remark given specifically to the ruler of the situation. Thus, since the subject at the fifth position is described to be the ruling figure in the situation, he is the person to whom the line statement is addressed. The beginning verse, accordingly, can be interpreted as indicating that under the situation in which the subject at the fifth position enjoys a highly advantageous position, he may be tempted to take hard-headed actions against enemies, internal and external. But, the line statement advises him that it "is permissible only for the purpose of punishing one's own city." Although it is not explicitly stated, the advice seems to have an understandable reason: he is a weak leader and the people who follow him (as represented by the three weak lines of the trigram *Kun*) also lack the ability to carry out warfare beyond their own border. His leadership is judged to possess such limited strength that it can only punish internal enemies. He should be aware of this limitation of his power. Thus, it is stated, "To be conscious of danger brings good fortune." And, the line statement adds, "Perseverance brings humiliation." To interpret, the essence of his leadership function does not lie in strength, but in gentleness and intelligence; therefore, it would not be advantageous for him to strive forward with persistence.

The hexagram *Zhongfu* (☴☱ , Inner Trust)

Regarding the hexagram *Zhongfu* (Inner Trust), it is not clear why the line structure with two yin lines inside and four yang lines positioning outside gives rise to the idea of "Inner Trust." Taken together, however, all the accounts in the *Judgment*, the *Commentary on the Judgments*, and Wang Bi's commentary on them converge on one important message that is expressed quite clearly: inner trust of people in one another is an essential condition for uniting them together. After all, faith in the power of trust for social unity constitutes the core theme of the *Commentary on the Judgments* on the hexagram *Zhongfu*; this is epitomized so well in a short passage, ". . . . the sense of trust reaches even fishes and swine." Wang Bi echoes the same opinion in his commentary: "When such a state (inner trust) exists, none will engage in artful competition, and actions based on honesty and substance will be the rule" (Lynn, 1994:521 - 522). Thus, as we can see from the above account, the hexagram intends to represent a situation in which trust among people exists as the prevailing condition in social relationships and, consequently, a specific type of unity is achieved on that basis. We, nevertheless, may note an interesting fact from what the line statements tell about individual situations. When the line statements are read and evaluated as a whole, there emerges the underlying idea that a situation where everybody has a trusting relationship is impossible. The *I Ching* seems to think, if implicitly, that trust means commitment and commitment in turn brings about exclusion to a certain extent. In other words, if a person has a trusting relationship with someone, it embodies a commitment through which he may exclude other persons from his circle of trusted people. For this reason, therefore, it may be said that unity based on mutual trust can never be perfect as a principle of integration; it will necessarily entail internal divisions to some extent. Then, let us look at the line statements.

The line statement of the first yang line states, "This one's devotion is such that he has good fortune, but if he were to extend it to others, he would suffer disquiet" (Lynn, 1994:524). Of this line statement, Cheng Yi explains that "Once you have found the trustworthy you should be sincere and single-minded. If there is another, you do not find peace" (1988:205). Interpreted in this way, the line statement offers advice to anyone under this situation; it is good to devote oneself to a relationship with a trusted person, but if he tries to extend such relationship to a large circle of people, the harmony or "peace" in his social relationship may be disturbed. Of course, Cheng Yi's interpretation involves one additional aspect that is absent from Lynn's translation. As Lynn also notes, Cheng Yi "glosse(s) *yu* (concern, or devotion) as *duo* (measure)" (Lynn, 1994:528n5), and, therefore, the line statement is interpreted as emphasizing a need for "assessing people as worthy of trust" before we put trust in them (Cheng Yi, 1988:205). Whether we give additional weight to Cheng Yi's interpretation or not, the line statement seems to involve an interesting perspective already suggested: if not carefully managed, the formation of trusted relationships may give rise to exclusion and division among the people involved.

The line statement of the second yang line seems to portray how inner trust, once it is formed, operates among people involved with each other. The line statement reads, "A calling crane is in the shadows; its young answers it. I have a fine goblet; I will share with you" (Lynn, 1994:524). "A calling crane is in the shadow; its young answers it" is a metaphoric expression used to denote the invisible, yet powerful function of trust in maintaining the ties among people. In this sense, Legge's explanation that "the subject of the paragraph is the effect of sincerity (i.e. inner trust)" seems quite appropriate. Cheng Yi accords with a similar view that "This represents people with hearts' desires in common" (1988:205). However, as I see it, it is not particularly clear whether the line statement specifically describes the situation of the second position or merely recapitulates the main theme of this hexagram emphasizing the important function of mutual trust in social unity.

A yin line that inappropriately occupies a leadership (yang) position represents the subject at the third position. The line statement of this line is interpreted quite differently depending upon how individual commentators view this line statement in the overall context of the hexagram. Regardless of whether any particular interpretation fits better with what was originally intended by the text, Cheng Yi's interpretation coupled with his commentary seems to offer the most meaningful choice. His interpretation is based on an idea called the dysfunctional aspect of mutual trust. First, let us look at the line statement as translated on the basis of Cheng Yi's interpretation: "Gaining a counterpart, one sometimes drums, sometimes stops, sometimes weeps, sometimes sings" (1988:202). Of this line statements Cheng Yi comments:

> Sometimes drumming, sometimes stopping, sometimes weeping, sometimes singing, those in this state are active or passive, sad or happy, all according to their object of trust and belief. Since everything depends on the object of trust, it is not known whether the outcome will be good or bad. In this case, this is not the behavior of enlightened people. (1988:202)

As was the case with the line statement of the second line, it is not clear whether the account presented above applies to the behavior of the subject of the third position or points to a dysfunction that blind trust among people can have in general. Regardless, the line statement reminds us of one important thing: trust performs an essential function in promoting social integration, yet at the same time it can have the dysfunction that makes people blindly follow those they trust even when "it is not known whether the outcome will be good or bad." The line statement of the third line contains such warning or describes the type of people for whom such warning is considered appropriate.

The line statement of the fourth yin line differs from other lines in that it deviates somewhat from the theme of inner trust. The line statement itself is expressed with such symbolism that it poses some difficulty to read: "The moon is about to wax full here, and, as this horse abandons its mate, there is no blame" (Lynn, 1994:526). Read on its own, the line statement contains two seemingly unrelated ideas. First, as Wang Bi explains, the subject at the fourth position represents one who is in an advantageous position to realize his potential to the fullest extent. And, the other is that although he "abandons his mate" (thereby violating the trust invested upon him by his mate), he will not be criticized for that violation of trust. Wang Bi (1994:526) combines these two ideas into one and interprets that under the situation it is desirable for the subject at the fourth position to abandon his mate (either the subject at the first or third position depending upon how one reads the alliance pattern indicated by the hexagram). And, this severance of the relationship is required for the fourth position holder so as to realize his potential to the fullest extent by aligning himself with the ruler at the fifth position. Wang Bi's interpretation, I think, carries a certain merit in that it suggests a convincing proposition. In social relationships, Wang Bi seems to maintain, whom we give our commitment to is a matter of choice related to the issue of what or who comes first or next in importance under given situational exigencies.

The line statement of the fifth yang line presents its subject as one who "maintains trust secure as a tether." Since this subject occupies the leadership position under the situation of *Zhongfu* (inner trust), he is the central figure who plays the vital role to "bind people to one through trust" (Lynn, 1994:526). Since this situation is characterized as one in which people are bound together through inner trust, it is understandable that the subject at the top leadership position plays the most vital function in the process.

In contrast to those represented by all the other lines below, the subject at the sixth position is described as one who has high reputation ("high flying sound") but little substance that equals his "high flying sound," thus suggesting he would lose trust from others. Why this sixth position holder is the one who behaves in opposition to the dominant mood of the time is not clear from the accounts of either the text or later commentaries. Of course, it is not strange that someone might act otherwise even though the prevailing mood of the time dictates that most people get along with others. And, by the same token, it is not strange that some degree of deviancy always exists even under a tightly integrated situation. However, if the line statement of the sixth is not a statement of a general fact, and rather aims at describing a pattern of behavior expected of the specific subject at the sixth position, an explanation is in order: why is the actor at the specific position likely to act differently from others under the situation?

Summary of theoretical and empirical propositions

1) The six "integrated" situations examined above denote cohesive or stable situations that exist in a society or social organization due to the way people interact or are interrelated with one another. What attracts our attention, however, is that each of the situations is "integrated" under its own unique principle that differs from the other "integrated" situations. Of the six situations we have examined, the two situations represented by the hexagram *Tai* (Peace) and the hexagram *Lin* (Overseeing) may be said to share a similar characteristic. Both hexagrams seem to represent a type of political integration based on what we can call a democratic principle — a political community integrated by governing elites who comply with the needs or demands of the people at the lower strata. In contrast, the hexagram *Jin* (Advance) represents a different type of situation in which integration is effected by conforming subordinate people who are eager to render their services to the governing leader. In the hexagrams *Sui* (Following) and *Heng* (Stability), the constituent members of the units are viewed to form cohesive or stable organizations through the possession of characteristics compatible with, or complementary to, one another. The remaining hexagram, the hexagram *Zhongfu* (Inner Trust), represents a situation that is integrated on the basis of what may be called a social-psychological factor, mutual trust. Overall, the various modes of integration differ from one another in the principle or the factor on the basis of which integration is achieved.

2) Although the situations are characterized as "integrated" in view of the overall condition of each situation, the examination conducted above reveals that no specific situation is perfectly or ideally integrated in the sense that there are always certain members who are alienated from, less fortunate, or less secure than, others.

3) Trust plays an essential role in promoting integration. Yet it can be dysfunctional if people blindly follow those they trust with little careful consideration of the outcome.

5) Situations Characterized by Internal Conflicts or Disunity

The following six hexagrams included under the heading above can be viewed as sharing a common characteristic in that they all represent situations involving meanings opposite of the "integrated" situations discussed in the previous section. In modern social sciences, the term "conflict" or "disunity" has been used to denote situations featuring social conditions that contrast such terms as "consensus," "integration," or "unity." This contrast is exactly what I had in mind when I chose to group the six hexagrams together here in this section. The six hexagrams included here are as follows:

1) The hexagram *Song* (☰☵, Contention) (Hexagram No. 6)

2) The hexagram *Pi* (☰ ☷, Obstruction) (Hexagram No. 12)

3) The hexagram *Mingyi* (☷☲, Suppression of the Light) (Hexagram No. 36)

4) The hexagram *Kui* (☲☱, Contrariety) (Hexagram No. 48)

5) The hexagram *Gen* (☶ ☶, Restraint, Keeping Still) (Hexagram No. 52)

6) The hexagram *Feng* (☳☲, Abundance) (Hexagram No. 55)

The hexagram *Song* (☰☵, Contention)

According to the *Commentary on the Judgments*, the meaning of the hexagram *Song* (Contention) is derived from the attributes of the two component trigrams, the upper trigram *Qian* signifying strength and the lower one *Kan* danger, which yields an idea of conflict between forces with uncompromising strength and contentious disposition. Regardless of the logic applied in formulating the meaning of the hexagram as a whole, however, it seems obvious that the specific situation of each position holder is not predicated on the premise that conflict is occurring between the upper and the lower groups. An overview of the line statements will reveal that all the position holders under the situation are described to have propensities for conflict with others, probably due to the prevailing mood of society at the time. The conditions of respective position holders are described primarily in terms of one's potential to garner an advantageous outcome from a conflict in which he may get involved, and such potential is evaluated by both the positional and the situational attributes of each position holder in their overall context of the hexagram.

Then, let us look at the line statement of the first yin line. It states, "If one does not perpetuate the case involved, it might slightly involve rebuke, but in the end, good fortune will result" (Lynn, 1994:172). Since "the place and the character of the line are too weak" (Wilhelm, 1967:418), the line statement explains, the subject at the first position would not be able to engage in a prolonged conflict, and, therefore, has to give up contending with others.[48] What is said in the following verse is an obvious conclusion drawn from the preceding line: if one calls a quick stop to the conflict, he will draw a little criticism but not with bad consequences. The main idea conveyed by this line statement seems to be common sense wisdom that involves a warning against engagement of a prolong conflict by a weak subject at a low position.

The subject at the second position is described as someone who "from below . . . . engages one that is above [Fifth Yang] in Contention" (Lynn, 1994:173). This is interpreted from the fact that a strong (yang) line is present at the second position and indicates a presence of a subject who has a strong will to engage in conflict as the overall trend of the time may give rise to such propensity. Yet, the line statement renders the judgment that "Not victorious in Contention, one escapes by returning home" (Lynn, 1994:172). Why is the second position holder not victorious in Contention, as viewed by the *I Ching*? Regarding this question, notice simply that another subject represented by a strong line also shows its powerful presence at the ruling, fifth position. The line statement then offers that if the leader is powerful enough to fend off the contentious subordinate, it would be very difficult for the latter to come out victorious, and, consequently, there is no way for him but "to escape by returning home." The line statement ends with interesting advice given to the subject involved: "If his city consists of fewer than three hundred households, there will be no disaster" (Lynn, 1994:172-3). The number of households refers to one's potential resources that will support his return to the fighting ground if he in fact is to make such a movement. It is exactly in this sense that Wang Bi comments on this portion of the line statement as follows: "if his city surpasses three hundred households, it will not be a place of refuge for him, for calamity is never avoided by escaping and then relying on strength" (Lynn, 1994:173). This advice seems to contain an age-old wisdom of seasoned politicians (probably that of King *Wen* of the *Zou* (1171-1122 B.C.) known as the author of the *I Ching*) (Lynn, 1994:4) in the old Chinese society. If one loses in a political battle and still tries to show off signs of strength, calamity certainly will befall him.

The subject at the third position is described as someone who, in spite of the conflict-prone environment, is mainly interested in subsisting on what is already in his possession instead of actively engaging in conflict with others. Notice that a yin line is present at the leadership position of the subordinate group; thus, this line is interpreted to represent a functionary who has position and benefits but no powerful drive or capability to pursue quarrel with others. This one, favoring a preservation of the status quo, is not contentious. He, the subject of this position, would only "Subsist on old virtue"[49] (Lynn, 1994:173). The line statement continues: "If one exercises constancy in the face of danger, in the end, good fortune will result. He might attend to his sovereign's business, but he has no opportunity to accomplish anything of his own." The diagnosis of danger to this subject refers to the fact that he is positioned between two neighboring lines above and below that possess the strong propensity to engage in conflict with others. However, as also suggested by the line statements of the second and the fourth yang lines, they are not in advantageous positions to secure profitable outcomes through involvement in conflicts; thus, the subject at the third position, if he behaves correctly, would not be drawn into contention with any of them. The meaning of the last line, "He might attend to his sovereign's business, but he has no opportunity to accomplish of his own," does not seem clear. According to Wang Bi's commentary, it is related to the sixth yang line that is interpreted as having a specific affinity with the subject at the third position. This interpretation, however, does not seem consistent with what is said of the subject at the sixth position, which we will see when examining the sixth line later. Hence, interpretation would be easier if we instead adopt Wilhelm's translation as follows: "If by chance you are in the service of a king, / Seek not works" (1967:418). Given the line statement rendered above by Wilhelm, it can now be understood as a prescriptive one; it advises the subject at the third position that he had better refrain from pursuing great accomplishments considering that he can hardly do anything beyond subsisting on what he already has.

Now, let us look at the line statement of the fourth yang line: "The fourth line, undivided, shows its subject unequal to the contention. He returns to (the study of Heaven's) ordinances, changes (his wish to contend), and rests in being firm and correct. There will be good fortune"[50] (Legge, 1963:70). The surface meaning of the line statement seems clear by itself as translated above. But, why is the subject at the fourth position judged to have no sufficient capacity to contend with others? The perspective employed by Legge to explain this is familiar to us. The yang line at the fifth position represents the presence of a strong ruler with whom the subject at the fourth position is unable to contend. And, immediately below him, there is an evasive subject who is trying to keep distance from any contention. Even at the first position where he may expect to find someone to look toward for some help, as its line statement indicates, the first line also is a subject who shows no interest in getting involved in prolonged conflict. Thus, in the face of the surrounding conditions that work against the engagement of contentious conduct, the subject at the fourth position "changes (his wish to contend), and rests in being firm and correct."

Most commentators except Legge interpret the line statement of the fifth yang line as describing the top leader's role as the judge's seat dealing with contentions arising within his domain. Only Legge interprets it as describing its subject as a potential contender who may involve himself in conflict. Here I will go along with Legge's interpretation for one good reason; it is the only one that seems to be, if not entirely, in agreement with what has been said in other line statements. In line with the interpretation rendered as such, Legge's translation reads as follows: "The fifth line, undivided, shows its subject contending; — and with great good fortune" (1963:70). And, Legge adds a brief comment on this line statement: "Line 5 has every circumstance in favor of its subject." The favorable circumstances referred to by Legge seem to point to two things at once. First is that the subject at the fifth position occupies the highest position in the formal hierarchy of the hexagram, and, at the same time, he, being represented by a yang line, is interpreted as having the appropriate characteristic or actual ability required of the subject at the position. This makes him not only the *de jure* but also the *de facto* leader of the group, against whom nobody else is able to contend.

Lastly, concerning the sixth yang line, I find its line statement to involve a very interesting viewpoint. Let us look at the line statement: "One might be awarded with a leather belt, but before the day is over he will have been deprived of it three times" (Lynn, 1994:175). The line statement suggests that, under the situation where the prevailing mood of the society is conducive to contentions among people, the subject at the sixth position is the ablest contender, the most likely to come out as winner. Thus, "he might be awarded with a leather belt (symbolizing a victory like a champion belt)." Here, let us be reminded of the positional attribute of the sixth line, which represents that of "former leader(s) in retirement" or "leading intellectuals (sages)," as has been acknowledged widely among the readers of the *I Ching*. It may be said that the function performed by the position holder at this position is largely of an intellectual sort, associated mainly with what may be called "pattern maintenance."[51] Interpreted as above, the line statement seems to advance an interesting hypothesis. When members of a society, affected by a situation in which disputes among them have become the prevailing trend, are disposed to engage in contest with others, the subject at the sixth position engaged in the "pattern maintenance" function would be the one most likely to win. However, the line statement then adds a warning, "before the day is over he will have been deprived of it three times." The idea of victory taken away "before the day is over " seems to imply what may be called occupational hazards associated with the privileged role of Chinese intellectuals whose primary duties were to raise voices protesting against injustices or social ills, especially when connected with privileged people including even the emperor himself.

Before I turn to the other hexagrams, I would like add one final note on this hexagram concerning its major theme. Although the hexagram *Song* (Contention) describes a social situation in which the people involved are bent on contending with one another, the line statements taken as whole may be regarded as an essay on conditions affecting outcomes of contention. Throughout all the line statements, it is only the fifth yang's line statement that offers its subject a victorious result. And, we can see that in the hexagram the fifth yang line is the only line that is "appropriately occupied." This seems to imply that in a conflict situation, the winner must satisfy two conditions. First, he has

Hexagrams: Types of Social Situations 181

to be in a strategically advantageous or powerful position such as the fifth one. Secondly, he must be the person whose action orientation or ability suits what is expected of that position. The line statements of all the other lines, except the third yin line, tell about contentions that are carried out with certain handicaps or under adverse conditions, which the *I Ching* sees little merit to engage in. Thus, in effect, the message that the *I Ching* wants to convey to parties involved in such a contentious situation as represented by the hexagram *Song* may be expressed summarily as follows: do not engage in or prolong conflicts unless you are quite sure of the prospect of victory in view of both the position you occupy and the real power potential you have come to possess under the situation.

The hexagram *Pi* (☰ ☷ , Obstruction)

A passage in the *Hexagrams in Irregular Order* says, "*Tai* [Peace, Hexagram 11] and *Pi* [Obstruction, Hexagram 12] are opposed in kind" (Lynn, 1994:212). As we have seen in the previous section, since the hexagram *Tai* represents an integrated situation in which the upper and the lower groups are united together in peace, the hexagram *Pi* should stand for a situation in which the two fail to hold together presumably due to a breakdown in communication or interaction. However, the underlying reasoning behind the interpretation of the line structure of the hexagram (the trigram *Kun* below and the trigram *Qian* above; ☰ ☷) as indicating a breakage of harmonious interaction between the governing unit above and the subordinate one below may not make sense to social scientists of today. Reasons proposed by commentators find a typical expression in Cheng Yi's commentary (1988:34), which reads as follows:

> The hexagram is formed with *heaven* above and *earth* below. When heaven and earth commune, so yin and yang harmonize; this is tranquillity (peace). When heaven remains above and earth remains below, then heaven and earth are separated and do not commune; therefore it is a state of obstruction.

And, the reason for which they do not commune is found in that "the trigram *Ch'ien* (*Qian*) above withdraws always farther upward, and *K'un* (*Kun*) below sinks farther and further down" (Wilhelm, 1967:446). Wang Bi (Lynn, 1994:212) characterizes this situation as one in which "there is no true polity in the world." Out of the two interpretations presented above regarding the overall meaning of the hexagram, one thing may sound reasonable. Since harmonious interaction or communication between the governing unit and the governed one is an essential condition to bring about a true polity in society, a lack of interaction between the two means a "state of obstruction," or a society with "no true polity." But, what would statements such as "heaven remains above and earth remains below" or "the trigram *Ch'ien* (*Qian*) above withdraws always farther upward, and *K'un* (*Kun*) below sinks farther and further down" specifically mean when applied to human situations? They would make sense if they simply propose that there exists a state of little interaction or communication between the upper and the lower units for some reason or another. But, what kind of reasoning is available here for us to accept an assertion that since the hexagram carries the image of heaven and earth moving away from each other, it also involves an idea of human groups moving apart from each other? Neither the *I Ching* nor any individual commentator comes forth with a reasonable explanation on this seemingly unjustifiable mode of associative thinking. Meanwhile, if the trigram *Qian* and the trigram *Kun* represent respectively a quality of a powerful leadership and of conformity, isn't it far more reasonable to interpret the hexagram *Pi* as a state of integration achieved through a strong leadership exercised by the dominant group over the subordinate one yielding "appropriately" according to its lowly position? Thus, doubt still remains. Why is the line formation of the hexagram *Pi* interpreted as representing a disintegrated situation, a state of little interaction between the two constituent units? Probably, the logic involved here might have been rather simple. It might be thought that since the hexagram *Pi* has a line structure inverse to the hexagram *Tai* (a highly integrated situation), a situational meaning opposite to that of the hexagram *Tai* also had to be attributed to the hexagram *Pi*. But, this has yielded an outcome that does not fit well with principles of interpretation applied generally to other hexagrams. As a matter of fact, the text accounts on the situational meaning of the hexagram *Pi* seem to be out of tune with the ways in which hexagrams and their component elements are generally interpreted throughout the *I Ching*.

Leaving aside this issue, which arises rather frequently here and there in the *I Ching*, for some other investigations, let us examine each individual line statement. The line statement of the first yin line states, "When one pulls up the rush plant, it pulls up others of the same kind together with it, but if one practices constancy, good fortune will prevail" (Lynn, 1994:212). As one may remember, this line statement is the same as that given to the first yang line in the hexagram *Tai* except a section that states, "if one practices constancy" instead of "if one goes forth and acts." Like the first yang line in the hexagram *Tai*, the starting line, "when one pulls up the rush plant, it pulls up others of the same kind together with it," describes the subordinate group represented by the trigram *Kun* as a highly integrated group acting together in unison. The crucial point in which the first yin line of the hexagram *Pi* differs from the first yang line of the hexagram *Tai* is found in that whereas the latter is said to meet with more fortunate outcome "if one goes forth and acts," the former is advised to maintain "constancy," or faithfully adhere to normatively correct behavior. Thus, to explain, under the situation of obstruction signified by the hexagram *Pi*, passive and conservative behavior rather than active engagement in worldly affairs is recommended so as to bring about a better outcome for the "yin" subject at the first position.

The line statement of the second yin line is not much different in its essential meaning from that of the first yin line. Here the subject of the second position is described to be one who is "bearing up under orders" (Lynn, 1994:213). That he displays "patient and obedient" (Legge, 1963:84) behavior under the situation is explained by the fact that the second position, which will be considered "appropriately occupied" if a yin line occupies it, is in fact occupied by a yin line. However, although this interpretation accords a scheme of interpretation generally accepted by later commentaries, how the behavior pattern of the second position holder as described by the line statement is related to the overall meaning of the hexagram, "obstruction," does not seem obvious at all. After all, how does the behavior of the occupant of the second position relate with the situation characterized as "obstruction"? Wang Bi (Lynn, 1994:213) and Cheng Yi (1988:36) as well explain that the second position holder is able to garner good fortune by being "patient and obedient" or "bearing up under orders" (from the ruler at the fifth position) and obtain the most desirable outcome for him under the situation of *Pi*. But, if he behaves patiently and compliantly, as indicated by a yin line at a yin position, why or how should his behavior as such give rise to the breakage in interaction between the upper and the lower groups after all? The *I Ching* seems to provide no adequate explanation for this. Meanwhile, the line statement taken as whole, "Bearing up on orders here means good fortune for the petty man, but, although it means obstruction and stagnation for the great man, he will prevail" (Lynn, 1994:213), seems to be merely a restatement of a Chinese cultural cliché. This cliché offers that "patience and obedience" are proper virtues for the low-quality man, and, therefore, adherence to such virtues will result in better outcomes for them, whereas the same orientation in action may not be appropriate for the superior-quality person whose mission is to lead people. Of course, the *I Ching* seems to concede that even if the subject at the second position were a "great man," he would have no choice but, as dictated by the given situation, to act contrarily to his nature. This will explain why the line statement says, "it means obstruction and stagnation for the great man."

The line statement of the third yin line is brief: "He bears his shame" (Lynn, 1994:213). But, Lynn's translation presented here is but one of varying ways in which the short sentence composed only of two Chinese characters is interpreted and translated by commentators. Still, we may be able to pick up a common underlying theme in the various versions of translation. It is understood that the third position is not "appropriately occupied" as a yin line in the leadership position of the subordinate group. However, commentators do not seem to agree among themselves in explaining the specific reason for which the subject of the third position is viewed as one with such an inadequate (or "shameful") characteristic. The *Commentary on the Images* explains that "he bears shame" because "the position is not appropriate" (Lynn, 1994:213). But, there is a jump in reasoning to say that the subject at the position is someone who has fallen into a state in which "he (has to) bear(s) his shame." Obviously, it might be due to this reason that commentators tried to fill in the gap with various explanations.[52]

The line statement of the fourth yang line, "He who is issued commands here will be without blame, and his comrade will share in his blessings" (Lynn, 1994:213), has also rendered varying interpretations that differ from one commentator to another. Concerning the first portion, "he who is issued commands here will be without blame," however, commentators seem to share a similar opinion. It is viewed that "he who is issued commands" refers to the subject of the fourth position himself. But, in the second portion of the line statement, divergence arises. Why is the fourth position viewed as being without blame? Of this, Wang Bi offers a somewhat plausible and thus interesting interpretation:

> The reason one cannot issue commands while situated in Obstruction is that those who answer them will be petty men: when commands are issued to petty men, this deteriorates the Dao of the true sovereign. Now here for the first time is someone with his ambitions dedicated to his sovereign but situated in a humble and obscure position; thus he can be issued commands and remain

without blame .... (Lynn, 1994:213)

Above all, the passage by Wang Bi points out that although commands are issued from the leader at the fifth position, there is no one in the subordinate group who can effectively or faithfully carry out the commands. If we express it in Wang Bi's own words, there are only "petty men" who will yield results that "deteriorate(s) the Dao of the true sovereign." In this sense, the situation *Pi* (obstruction) means, as far as Wang Bi interprets it, a frustrating situation in which the political goal pursued by the leadership is not adequately communicated to, and consequently is not carried out by, the subordinate group. It is only with the one at the fourth position, an acting member of the dominant group, that the one in the leadership position finds a truly suitable individual to whom his commands can be issued with an expectation for desirable outcomes. Therefore, under a breakage in effective communication or interaction between the upper and the lower groups, the only reliable companion to whom commands can be issued is found in someone within his own group. Yet, who is the person that is referred to as "his comrade"? Wang Bi views that "his comrade refers to the first line" (1994:214). Wilhelm views otherwise and explains that "here again .... minister and ruler are united" (1967:450). According to this interpretation, "his comrade" then refers the ruler at the fifth position. I personally incline to side with Wilhelm's interpretation, for his interpretation as above seems to be more compatible with the overall meaning of the situation represented by the hexagram *Pi*.

The line statement of the fifth yang line states that "he brings Obstruction to a halt, and this is the good fortune of the great man" (Lynn, 1994:214). Without doubt, this line statement describes this subject as one who can bring about some improvement to the situation of obstruction. Of course, the *I Ching* adds a warning of the difficulties that the situation of obstruction poses for the person occupying the position here. These difficulties are associated with the situational characteristic and the line statement goes on to say "(But let him say), 'We may perish! We may perish!' (so shall the state of things become form, as if) bound to a clump of bushy mulberry trees" (Legge, 1963:85).[53] The line statement above emphasizes that extreme care must be taken by the one at the leadership position in overcoming the situation of obstruction. However, what specific kind of difficulty he may encounter in this situation of *Pi* is not mentioned clearly either by the text or by any other commentary.

Lastly, the line statement of the sixth yang line simply states that the situation of *Pi* will end sooner or later and turn into another situation, a happier one. The statement itself seems to be a simple restatement of the principle of cyclical change that is typical of the Chinese view on the process of change. In accordance with this perspective, Cheng Yi (1988:37) comments on this line statement and says "According to natural principle, when things come to a peak or culmination, they inevitably reverse; therefore when tranquillity culminates there is obstruction, and when obstruction comes to an end there is tranquillity."

I would like to add a brief note before I finish this discussion on the hexagram *Pi*. From a sociological viewpoint, it is an interesting idea to think of the possibility that there can occur a breakdown in effective cooperation between the governing and the subordinate units. There is a real possibility that this can occur in any existing group or society. Now, given this as an actual possibility, we may raise a number of questions concerning the conditions under which this kind of "obstructed" situation comes to existence, how constituent members would react respectively to this situation, and possible measures to be taken to bring this situation to a resolution. In view of these questions and other possible ones, all the text accounts and commentaries connected with the hexagram *Pi* seem to be gravely deficient and must be recognized as falling short of our expectation, a limitation of the *I Ching* as such an ancient book. Nevertheless, what about the idea itself that a social organization may suffer from a breakage of interaction or communication between the governing and the subordinate units? It seems to me that the situation represented by the situation *Pi* is an ever-present possibility that poses a great hindrance to the healthy operation of any human organization. Then, why has modern sociology shown relatively little interest in the possible malfunctions of social organizations? We do not know exactly. But, at any rate, it seems that the *I Ching* leads us to many interesting and important issues that broaden the areas of our concerns beyond what we have been holding to either by habit or by collective commitment to familiar ideas.

The hexagram *Mingyi* (☷☲ , Suppression of the Light)

The hexagram *Mingyi* (Suppression of the Light) has its ruling line in the sixth position whose subject is described as the dominant figure responsible for suppressing the light. "The light" in this hexagram refers to the goodness or excellence residing in the people ruled by the top leader. The situation depicted by this hexagram figures a dark period of a society that suffers from a bad leader suppressing, or inflicting damages upon, what is good or excellent among his governed subjects. It is not clear why the one at the sixth position, instead of the fifth one, stands for the incumbent ruler in this particular hexagram. As we will see, the line statement of the fifth position carries an account of the "viscount of *Ji*" who is known to have made every effort to save his country from falling down under the rule of his nephew Zhou, the last king of *Shang* (C.f., Legge, 1963:137; Lynn, 1994:361n2,3). Zhou has been known as one of the worst tyrannical rulers throughout the history of China, and, therefore, there might have been some reluctance on the part of the author of *the I Ching* to relate such a wicked, thus illegitimate, ruler as Zhou to the fifth position, the formally recognized position of the leader.

In the face of the seemingly hopeless situation of a deteriorating society described roughly above, the people at various strata would have showed different modes of adaptation or response to the situation. It seems that this is what the author of the *I Ching* wanted to reconstruct from sources that were gathered from either his personal experiences or historical records.

Now, perhaps the best way to look into the essential feature of the situation represented by this hexagram would be to start with the line statements of the sixth yin and the third yang lines. Let us look at the line statement of the sixth yin line: "Not bright but dark, this one first climbed up to heaven but then entered into the earth." The *Commentary on the Images* explains about this line statement as follows: "This one first climbed up to Heaven and cast light on states in all four directions. The reason such a one later into the earth [i.e., perished] was that he had lost the right way to rule" (Lynn, 1994:360-1). The above commentary involves little ambiguity. It states clearly that the subject at the topmost position would first have great success in rising up to the powerful leadership holding hegemony over the entire country ("states in all four directions") and later would be driven out of the position as the result of his tyrannical rule. There is little doubt that the account presented in the above line statement is related to the historical episode of King Zhou known as one of the worst tyrannical rulers throughout the history of China. Then, we are led to expect, there should be a line in this hexagram that represents the ruling family of the Zhou state, or King Wu who actually took action to force out the tyrannical ruler. We find this one at the third position. The subject who represents the hero is represented by the third position for the two following reasons. First, since the Zhou State was a vassal kingdom under hegemony of the Shang, its leader is assigned to the third position that represents the leadership position for the subordinate group. Secondly, since the lower trigram *Li* symbolizes "light (brightness)" opposing the "darkness (tyranny)" of the incumbent ruler at the sixth position, the top line of the trigram, the third yang line, is interpreted as a leader carrying out the task of bringing back the country to the light and into rightful leadership. Then, keeping the above points in mind, let us look at the line statement of the third position: "Suppression of the Light finds this one on a southern hunt. He captures the great chief but must not be hasty to put constancy in practice" (Lynn, 1994:359). "The great chief" refers to the subject at the sixth position, the ruler whom the subject at the third position goes to hunt. Wang Bi's following commentary on this line statement summarizes:

> Third Yang occupies the top position in the lower trigram, so it is located at the apex of cultivation and light. Top Yin represents the darkest dark, something that has gone into the earth. Therefore this one at Third Yang suppresses his brilliance so he can succeed in going on a southern hunt, where he captures the great chief [Top Yin]. With this southern hunt he manifests his brilliance. Once he has killed the ruler, he can go on to rectify the people. But the people have been misled for such a very long time that their transformation ought to take place gradually; one must not try to rectify quickly.... (Lynn, 1994:359)

The line statement of the hexagram *Mingyi* and later commentators' comments give us an interesting clue as to how the line statements of the *I Ching* were written into the lines of the hexagram and subsequently interpreted in later commentaries. On the one hand, there are the graphic symbols made of six yin or yang lines that the author of the *I Ching* inherited from prior generations; the symbolic figures had yet to be filled in with more detailed meanings regarding certain social situations. On the other hand, he should have been equipped with a rich amount of historical knowledge and personal experiences in social and political affairs of his society. An example would be his knowledge or personal experience of the historical episode figured into the hexagram *Mingyi*, i.e., the downfall of the Shang that occurred in due course following the tyrannical rule of King Zhou. The line statements of the hexagram *Mingyi* should have been composed by combining the ideas associated with the yin-yang lines, the six positions of the hexagram and the episode that actually took place in history. Or, we may say, they were composed by extrapolating the sociological ideas associated with the graphic symbols of the hexagram upon the mentioned historical episode. Of course, there is no clear evidence that this is generally the case of all the hexagrams.

Now, excluding the two lines explained already, we start from the bottom line. The line statement of the first yang line states, "Suppression of the light finds this one in flight, keeping his wings folded. This noble man on the move does not eat for three days. Whenever he sets off to a place, the host there has something to say about it" (Lynn, 1994:358). To understand this line statement, we must know that the lower trigram as a group represents the emancipating force that will save the country from its tyrannical ruler. The lower trigram represents a noble group, having the third yang line leading at the front, that stood up to the evil force represented by the sixth yin line. Thus, the line statement presents an image of someone with a noble personality who is on the move fleeing from the evil force, yet still "renounces the idea of sacrificing its principles in order to secure a livelihood; it prefers going hungry to eating without honor" (Wilhelm, 1967:567).

The characterization of the subject at the first position as one hurt by the oppressive rule of the tyrant and, therefore, in flight from it also extends to the second yin line. The line statement of the second position reads, "Suppression of the Light finds this one wounded in his left thigh, but he is saved by a horse's strength and as a result has good fortune" (Lynn, 1994:359). According to Legge, this line statement "gives the idea of an officer, obedient to duty and the right," who "finds means to save himself" and thereby will overcome the adverse situation in the end (1963:136). Once we are given the interpretation that the lower trigram represents the subordinate group who suffers under bad leadership, yet rises up and overturns it, Legge's above interpretation of the second line statement seems to make perfect sense. The subject at the second position is described as someone who, despite sufferings inflicted upon him by the tyrannical ruler, manages to survive and will come out victorious in the end.

On the line statement of the fourth yin line, interpretations by commentators yield no common theme and translations differ likewise from one version to another. Here I will pick up just two versions that seem to make some sense to me considering the nature of the situation suggested by the hexagram. First, let us read the line statement as translated by Wilhelm: "He penetrates the left side of the belly. / One gets at the very heart of the darkening of the light, / And leaves gate and courtyard." In this version, the line statement talks about someone who "stands near the lord of darkness (the sixth yin) .... thus .... finds out his inmost sentiment and can take itself out of danger in time" (1967:568). According to this interpretation, the subject at the fourth position is described as a wise defector who had served the ruler in close proximity but later would flee in time from the sinking ship. The other interpretation offered by Cheng Yi views the subject as "those . . . . (who) gain the hearts of the leadership. (And, then) . . . . do what they want in the outside world"; they are "dishonest ministers (who) serve ignorant rulers, ... (who) poison the minds of the rulers . . . ." (Cheng Yi, 1988:115-6). Both interpretations can make sense in that the behavior described in both of them seem highly likely to be observed among high ranking officials under the situation depicted by the hexagram, the fall of an empire.

The line statement of the fifth yin line describes its subject as displaying a mode of behavior that is in contrast to that of the fourth yin line. It reads, "Suppression of the Light as a viscount of Ji experiences it means that it is fitting to practice constancy" (Lynn, 1994:360). The mentioned viscount of Ji refers to an uncle of King Zhou, who is known to put out every effort to stop his nephew from misruling the country, but without avail. Thus, the subject at the fifth position is described as someone who, unlike the subject at the fourth position, is staging a rightful but losing fight to prevent the downfall of the country. But, the actual outcome that the viscount of Ji experienced was that he saw the country being overtaken by the army of King Wu (the son of King Wen, known as one of the authors of the *I Ching*). It would be understood in this historical context that the *Commentary on the Images* appended to this line statement says, "The constancy of a viscount of Ji is such that his brilliance cannot be extinguished" (Lynn, 1994:360). This commentary seems to have been written in tribute to the patriotic gentleman, the viscount of Ji, whose devotion and sacrifice for his country shows a model example for Confucian virtues. This hexagram as a whole seems to provide a panoramic picture of people who respond in various ways to a disintegrating kingdom. The manner in which the viscount of Ji behaved is, of course, also included here as the most praiseworthy that one can possibly take under the circumstance.

The hexagram *Kui* (☱☲, Contrariety)

The hexagram *Kui* (Contrariety), as its name suggests, represents a situation where "division and mutual alienation" (Legge, 1963:140) among the members of a group prevail as the dominant trend of the time. Terms such as "discord" and "turning outward (estrangement)" (Lynn, 1994:369) used in the text to characterize the situation denoted by this hexagram all point to divisive and discordant relationships existing among people under the situation. However, there is one unique feature about this hexagram that distinguishes it from ordinary "conflict" situations in which opposing camps face each other with hostile intentions to defeat the other side. All the accounts in the text suggest that the situation depicted by the hexagram is characterized as a milder sort of discordant relations such as a family dispute. In a family disputes sometimes occur among family members due to differences in opinions or interests, yet as members of the same family they share a common spirit or goal to seek reconciliation. Of course, it seems obvious that this situation represents a conflict situation; but, we may call this a controlled conflict situation in the sense that the shared goals of the people involved will bring them to seek reconciliation before they take the conflict to an extreme. Perhaps, this is why the *Judgment* says of this situation, "In small matters, there is good fortune" (Lynn, 1994:368). Then, let us look at how this overall situation is related to specific situations of individual position holders.

The line statement of the first yang line states, "Regret disappears. If one here loses his horse, he need not pursue it, for it will come back as a matter of course. As he meets with evil man, he avoids blame." According to Wang Bi, the subject at the first position is "without a line to resonate with and has to stand alone" and, therefore, "should feel regret" (Lynn, 1994:369). In the logic of the *I Ching,* the situation of an individual subject is read from the line composition of a hexagram — the first yang line is next to a yang line at the second position and the fourth position that has a specific affinity with the first position is another yang line. This arrangement of the lines should have rendered the reading that the first yang line has no appropriate partner with whom he can unite and, therefore, "has to stand alone," which is regarded as a regretful situation. Yet, why does the regretful situation disappear, or, in other words, why does one's lost horse "come back as a matter of course" although he does not pursue it? Two things can be considered to answer this question. First, under this kind of controlled conflict situation, time is considered to be the best remedy to cure dispute with others. Unless one tries to resolve the dispute by exposing his counterpart's wrongdoing, things will turn out fine as a matter of course. This is a situation in which disputing people in a normatively regulated conflict situation, owing to shared common goals, are committed to reconciliation or peaceful resolution. The other factor to be considered is related to a passage in the line statement that reads, "As he meets with evil man, he avoids blame." Most commentators interpret this passage to carry the same kind of message as the one above. The phrase "he meets with evil man" is interpreted to mean that he "communicates with them" (Cheng Yi, 1988:212; c.f., Legge, 1963:140), and, accordingly, the passage is interpreted to suggest that if the dispute is solved through communication or mutual understanding, he will not be blamed for conflicts that may result from pursuing his opponent till the end.

The line statement of the second line is brief and yet involves symbolism that seems difficult to understand. It reads, "This one meets his master in a narrow lane, so there is no blame" (Lynn, 1994:370). To begin with, commentators show no disagreement in that "his master" refers to the leader at the fifth position. Then, a question is raised regarding the significance of the "narrow lane." Commentators respectively come up with different explanations, and their explanations diverge so widely that they only leave an impression that the interpretation of this particular line statement is nothing but a product of each one's personal imagination or predisposed mode of thinking. Here, I will utilize Legge's interpretation because it yields an easier and more meaningful understanding of the line statement than others. First of all, the two lines at the second and the fifth positions can be said to be in a corresponding relationship because they, constituting a yin-yang pair, have complementary characteristics. However, the arrangement of the lines, a yin line at the fifth position and a yang line at the second position, is not what is expected of a normal relationship between the sovereign and his officials. So, "they might meet openly," but, under the situation fraught with discord and alienation, the relationship between the weak ruler and the strong subject may lead to conflict. A meeting in a narrow lane, signifying an informal meeting, or behind-curtain talks, to promote "a better understanding," is proposed here as a means to deflect the potential conflict between two inappropriately positioned subjects (Legge, 1963:.141).

To understand what the line statement of the third yin line says, we first have to look at the arrangement of the third line itself and the lines around it. As we see, there are two yang lines above and below the third yin line. The second and the fourth positions, both yin positions, are occupied inappropriately by yang lines, and the third yin line itself also occupies inappropriately a yang position. This kind of combination in which each position is inappropriately occupied makes for incompatible relationships. Moreover, the overall trend of the situation conducive to disharmony among people does not contribute to peaceful cooperation among them. Accordingly, whatever the subject at the third position sets out to do will be obstructed by the strong subjects above and below him. Then, let us read the line statement: "Here one has his wagon hauled back and oxen controlled. This one has the forehead tattooed and nose cut off. But, whereas nothing good here happens at the start, things end well" (Lynn, 1994:370). One's "forehead tattooed and nose cut off" refers to the way criminals were punished to prevent them from repeating criminal acts (C.f., Lynn, 1994:374n9). In conjunction with the overall meaning of the hexagram, this line statement is interpreted to emphasize the fact that the subject at the third position would be criticized and obstructed by the two subjects at the neighboring positions who interfere with whatever the former attempts. To be situated between individuals intent on inflicting injuries on weak people would indeed be a unbearably difficult situation for the weak ones. "Nothing good . . . . happens" to them under the situation. But, why does the *I Ching* view that "things end well" for them? Regarding this question, I first would like to point out that no one under this "normatively controlled conflict situation" represented by the hexagram *Kui* is pushed into such a desperate state to lose every thing or fortune one can possibly have. In dispute, people in less fortunate positions have to suffer losses, yet under this situation, they will end up with no gravely misfortunate consequences owing to the nature of the situation in which disputes among people tend to patch up with mutual understandings in the end. It is important to remember that this is a conflict situation, yet one that is "normatively" controlled by the common goal or feeling of unity shared by the people involved.[54]

The subject at the fourth position also is described as being "isolated" in the midst of disharmony. This is a reading obtained from the fourth yang line as its positional and situational characteristics are interpreted in the overall context of the line composition of the hexagram. Thus, a rather unfavorable situation is indicated for the position holder at this position, too. However, the theme of a possible reconciliation among people, the underlying spirit of the time, is expressed again for the subject at this position. So, the line statement narrates the situation of the subject at the fourth position: "Isolated by disharmony, when you meet a good man, if you communicate sincerely, there is no fault even in danger" (Cheng Yi, 1988:122).[55] Reconciliation achieved through mutual understanding is suggested clearly here as a means to overcome one's alienation. In most commentaries, the mentioned "good man" (translated as "a like-minded man" by Wilhelm) is interpreted to refer to the subject at the first position. For instance, Wilhelm commenting on this line statement explains: "The companionship found is the strong line at the beginning, which is of the same character as the nine (yang) in the fourth place.

Both have the will to overcome the misunderstandings, and thus succeed" (1967:577). As I see it, the idea that the subject at the fourth position seeks reconciliation with the one at the first position by overcoming some misunderstanding between them fits with the overall theme of the situation.

The line statement of the fifth yin line involves such ambiguous symbolism that there practically seems to be no agreement among commentators on its intended meaning. So, here again I apply the rule that has been applied consistently up to this point; to choose a version of interpretation that is the simplest, the clearest, and coheres the most with the main theme of the hexagram. First, I will present the line statement as translated by Lee: "Regret disappears. Which one would be picked out to blame if clansmen bite each other's skin (i.e., if contentions arise among clansmen)?"[56] (1997[II]:60, translated from Lee's Korean text by this author). According to Lee, the line statement contains advice for the ruler at the fifth position to refrain from taking sides with any specific contender if the situation should give rise to contentions among people under his leadership. This interpretation seems to be consistent with the overall theme and with the line structure of the hexagram in two respects. First, interpreted as such, the line statement views the overall situation as one in which disputes occur among close-knit people. The other is that the leader at the fifth position is in a weak position himself so that it would not be wise for him to take sides with anyone in the midst of internal feuds among his own people. The line statement of the second yang line suggests that all he can do under the situation is covert talks with disputants to induce reconciliation among them. The *Commentary on the Images* states that the leader in the fifth position "would be blessed" by doing as advised, and this also indicates the belief that a conciliatory approach is an effective way to attain peace under a normatively controlled conflict situation represented by the hexagram.

The line statement of the sixth yang line contains an interesting metaphor that epitomizes the main theme of the hexagram. It reads: "Isolated by disharmony, you see pigs covered with mud, a wagon full of devils. Before, you drew the bow; afterward, you relax the bow. You are not enemies, but partners. Going on, if you meet rain, that is auspicious" (Cheng Yi, 1988:123).[57] This line statement is a bit longer than the average length of most other line statements, but the message that it carries is quite clear and effective in depicting the situation of the subject at the sixth position in relation to the main theme of the hexagram. First, the line statement describes its subject as being isolated amidst conflicts prevailing among group members under the situation. When an individual, including the subject at this position, is filled with hostile feelings against others, the others would be looked at as if they were "pigs covered with mud, a wagon full of devils." Although they try to inflict injuries upon one another, due to the common goal and the identity shared among them, they will realize eventually that they are partners, not enemies. "You (therefore, afterward) relax the bow." To "meet rain," according to the *Commentary on the Images*, "means that all suspicions will disappear" (Lynn, 1994:373). This passage provides a concluding remark for this situation that says everything will turn out fine as people come to a realization that they belong to the same community with a shared goal.

The hexagram *Gen* (☶ ☶, Restraint, Keeping Still[58])

Two factors relate to the situational meaning of the hexagram *Gen* (Restraint or Keeping Still). One is that the two *Gen* trigrams composing the hexagram *Gen* indicates a static situation; no progressive movement or change takes place under the situation characterized by this trigram. The other factor accounts for the situational meaning of the hexagram. Every line in each of the two *Gen* trigrams has no corresponding line to form a partnership; no yin-yang pair is found between any pair of corresponding positions, i.e., between the first and the fourth, the second and the fifth, and the third and the sixth positions. This is not a social formation where cooperation among people is facilitated. The line structure of the hexagram read as above also explains the stasis indicated by its constituent trigrams. Now, since there is no conditional factor to facilitate progressive movement, everyone in the situation is described as being forced to remain still or inactive. Or, to interpret the line statements from a slightly different perspective, everyone is advised to remain still or inactive wherever he is, for the given situation would not help him to gain anything by taking action to bring about change to his situation. Then, let us examine the individual line statements.

The subject at the first position is described as "toes," the lowest part of the body, which seems to be an appropriate metaphor considering that it refers to those at the lowest stratum of the social hierarchy. The line statement thus reads, "Restraint takes place with toes, so there is no blame, and it is fitting that such a one practices perpetual constancy" (Lynn, 1994:468). Although the *I Ching* advises this one to "practice constancy (act correctly)," it also seems to assess that the situation represented by the hexagram *Gen* is not likely to work against the welfare of this particular subject at the first position.

The line statement of the second yin line differs from the line statement of the first yin line in one notable aspect; he is described to find his heart in an unhappy mood. The line statement reads, "Restraint takes place with the calves, which means that this one does not raise up his followers. His heart feels discontent" (Lynn, 1994:468). He is described as the "calves," a higher potion of the body than "toes" and therefore signifies his status at a higher stratum in the social hierarchy. Implicitly suggested by the line statement is that the subject at the second position wants to mobilize the one below him ("toes"), probably because with the help of the latter he may able to free himself from his paralytic situation. But, to "raise up" the toes, he himself has to make movement, yet, as Wang Bi explains, "as this one has his calves restrained, his toes do not get raised up" (Lynn, 1994:468). This explains why "his heart feels discontent." When Wang Bi's interpretation as above is considered, the symbol of the "calves" seems to involve more significance than just the social position of the subject. The calves are the organs that perform the most active function in the mobilization of the body. In terms of a social organization, the second position represents that of administrative workers who play a pivotal role in the operation of a system, thus can be compared to the "calves" of the body. Considering the vital function of the subject at the second position, what the line statement says about his situation makes sense; the "restrained" or lethargic situation in which he finds himself makes him feel discontent.

The third position is compared to the midsection (loin) of the body. By implication the loin connects the lower and the upper parts of the body, and, therefore, if it does not function properly under the situation, the whole body may split into two parts causing them move separately. This warning seems to be the message conveyed by the line statement of the third position as it states, "Restraint takes place with the midsection, which may split the back flesh, a danger enough to smoke and suffocate the heart" (Lynn, 1994:469). Of this line statement, Wang Bi explains, "If restraint were applied to the muddle of the body, the body would split at that place, and if a body were to split so that it had two masters, the great vessel [*daqi*][59] would indeed perish" (Lynn, 1994:469). "Danger enough to smoke and suffocate the heart" emphasizes the seriousness of the danger involved in the role of the subject at the third position under this situation. As the leader of the lower echelon of the group, he is an intermediary between the upper and the lower echelons of the group; he is at the joint section between them. But, the situation indicates a possibility that his function as an intermediary may be reduced to a state of complete paralysis. Thus, the line statement says that in view of the possibility of upper and lower organizations drifting apart from each other, the subject would be full of worries that burn and suffocate his heart.

The fourth position is compared to the torso of the body as we see in its line statement, "Restraint takes place with torso. There is no blame" (Lynn, 1994:469). Unlike the subjects at the second and the third positions to whom rather unfavorable judgments are given, a favorable judgment is rendered to the subject at this position. Why then is the paralytic situation represented by this hexagram judged to work favorably for this particular position holder? Wang Bi (Lynn, 1994:469) in his commentary explains that it is because a yin line is present appropriately in a yin position. But, the above explanation seems to involve a logical inconsistency because it does not apply equally to the second yin line that also occupies appropriately a yin position. It seems more likely that the line statement is based on a metaphoric reasoning associated with a view on the function of the body part: unlike either the calves or the loin, the torso is not a part of the body that functions through locomotion. Thus, even if "Restraint takes place with the torso," it will not impair the function of the body system, so "there is no blame." Although the rationale of this explanation may be questioned, additional support for the above interpretation itself can be found in the line statement of the fifth line.

The line statement of the fifth line compares the fifth position to "the jowls." Why the fifth position is compared to this specific body part is not clear except that the jowls are located higher than that of either the loin or the torso. At any rate, once the position is identified with the symbol of the jowls, metaphoric reasoning can again be applied; "Restraint takes place with the jowls, so this one's words have order, and regret vanishes" (Lynn, 1994:470). In Asian cultures, to keep one's mouth heavy indicates both virtue and wisdom, especially for one who is in the leadership position; thus, as Wang Bi explains of the line statement, "This one applies restraint to the jowls . . . . thus, his mouth stays free of arbitrary words, and he can banish his regret" (Lynn, 1994:470).

The idea of restraint as having a positive function extends to the line statement of the sixth yang line. The line statement reads: "This one exercises Restraint with simple honesty, which will results in good fortune" (Lynn, 1994:470). The subject at the sixth position is the only yang line in the upper trigram *Gen* (Mountain) and symbolic of the top of a mountain, the most dominant figure in possession of the lofty and solemn virtue like that of a mountain. We again will see here that the metaphoric reasoning that a natural symbol can give rise to an idea or ideal in human situation is exemplified by Wang Bi's explanation that "Top Yang abides at the apogee of restraint, so it represents one who practice the most extreme restraint" (Lynn, 1994:470). Now, we here again may raise doubt about the rationality of the metaphoric reasoning that we have examined above. Do they make any sense? To this question most readers will be inclined to give a negative response. However, unless the author(s) of the *I Ching* held a previous notion about the desirability of exercising restraint by members of the dominant group under the situation, would he have used the same symbolism as is read in the text? I doubt he would have. "To stand still as a mountain" or "to remain restrained as a mountain" has long been regarded as a virtue for learned elites in Asian societies, therefore, even though we may disregard the strange metaphor of body organs, it does not seem unusual for the *I Ching* to render favorable judgments to all the subjects in the upper echelon provided that they remain restrained under the situation.

The hexagram *Feng* (☲☳ , Abundance)

Although "*Feng* (Abundance)" is indicated as the main feature of the situation by its title name, the situation in itself involves shady areas where some people are denied abundance. Thus, the line statements as a whole are regarded as descriptive of a situation in which different strata of people have different life styles or unequal chances under the state of abundance. This hexagram, as I see it, involves a very interesting symbolism in which brightness and darkness are sharply contrasted. We may say that darkness looks even darker when contrasted with bright light, and the same may be said that prosperity will make those who are less prosperous even more miserable. To explain this symbolism, we had better start with the *Judgment*: "Abundance means prevalence, which the true king extends to the most. Stay free from worry, and you shall be fit to be a sun at midday" (Lynn, 1994:487). As Wilhelm points out (1967:669), "the true king" described as "a sun at midday" refers to the position holder at the fifth position. Then, let us look at the line statement of the fifth position: "This one arrives here and manifests himself, which gains him blessings and praise, and this means good fortune." The line statement is straightforward involving little obscure symbolism. As the *Commentary on the Images* paraphrases it, "The good fortune of Fifth

Yin is such that he gains blessings" (Lynn, 1994:491) under this situation with abundance. Thus, under the situation represented by the hexagram, the subject at the leadership position is one in the most fortunate situation ("gain blessings and praise"). Here a question may be raised; why is a yin line occupying inappropriately a yang position judged to be in a fortunate situation particularly in this time of abundance? I presume that the author(s) might not have applied the yin-yang logic of the *I Ching* to this particular case, and instead decided to follow common sense experience with which the leader of a time of prosperity is judged to enjoy the most favorable condition.

Now, the line statements of the first and the fourth yang lines will be examined together because the *I Ching* treats the subjects represented by these two lines as partners cooperating closely with each other in producing abundance.

> *First Yang*: This one meets a master who is his counterpart. Although they are alike, there is no blame. To go forth here would mean esteem.
>
> *Fourth Yang*: This one has his abundance screened off, so the polar constellation could be seen at midday. He meets a master who is his equal, which means good fortune. (Lynn, 1994:489-92)

In the above line statements, the subjects at the first and the fourth positions are described as co-workers in a cooperative relationship due to a certain need or difficulty contingent upon the situation of abundance. Notice that both are yang lines that are not likely to form a union under ordinary circumstances. Of this, Cheng Yi explains:

> Through their mutual sustenance they become useful. When they are in the same boat, people of conflicting views are of one mind; when they share difficulty, enemies cooperate. It is the force of events that makes this happen. (1988:187)

The need arising from the situation creates an odd couple. However, there is no passage in either the text or Cheng Yi's commentary that will give us hint about what the urgent need is. The line stating that "This one has his abundance screened off, so the polar constellation could be seen at midday" seems to provide the only clue. Here the subject at the fourth position is described to be in a state of such darkness that "the polar constellation could be seen at midday." But, what aspect of the situation of abundance puts this one into such a difficult situation is unclear. Although abundance characterizes this situation as a whole, the line statements suggest rather that for certain groups of people, this situation is fraught with many difficulties. To put this in a metaphoric expression typical of the *I Ching*, although the situation "is good to be as fully illumined as the sun at midday" (Cheng Yi, 1988:186), it will create shadowy areas which look much darker when placed in contrast to areas illumined with light.

The line statement of the second yin line involves an equally unfavorable judgment as that given to the fourth position: "This one has his Abundance screened off, so the polar constellation could be seen at midday." And, it goes on: "If he were to set forth, he would reap doubt and enmity, but if he were to have sincerity and develop accordingly, he should have good fortune" (Lynn, 1994:489). Why the subject at the second position is given an unfavorable judgment as above under the situation of abundance is not clear at all. Under usual circumstances, if a yin line is located at a yin position, the situation is judged favorable for the subject at the position. Moreover, the second position is considered to be quite stable so that whether its position is appropriately occupied by a fitting line or not, its subject in most cases is rendered favorable judgments. What factor or factors under this situation representing prosperity has made the yin line at the second position an exception to the general rules on interpreting the lines of the hexagram?[60] No clue for this question is found in either the text or any later commentary. All we can say or know is merely the fact that, as also was the case with the fourth yang line, although abundance features this situation as a whole, this situation will be fraught with many difficulties for the subject at the second position. This may explain why the *Hexagrams in Irregular Order* says of this hexagram, " 'Abundance means many occasions,' that is, occasions for care and sorrow" (Wilhelm, 1967:670).

The line statement of the third yin line repeats the theme of darkness, although the yang position is appropriately occupied. It reads: "This one has his Abundance shaded, so that even the dim could be seen at midday. If he should break his right arm, there would be no blame." According to Wang Bi, the line statement depicts the subject at the third position as someone who "still lacks the wherewithal to free himself from obscurity" (Lynn, 1994:490). And, his lack of capacity explains why he may break his right arm if he attempts great things. However, since his limited capacity is not his own making but rather caused by external circumstances related to the situation, his failure (breaking his right arm) will not be considered his own fault. Then, again, we are pressed with a question; what in the situation brings the subject at this position down to such a powerless state? Or, more broadly, what about this situation causes people at various strata to fall into rather unfortunate situations? Judging from the line statements, this seems certainly true: the prosperity in this situation is not experienced as happily by all involved. Yet, the text offers no explanation as to why.

With respect to the question raised above, the line statement of the sixth yin line may shed some light. The line statement reads: "This one keeps his Abundance in his house, where he screens off his family. Where he peers out his door, it is lonely, and no one is there. For three years he does not appear, which means misfortune" (Lynn, 1994:491). In the above line statement, the subject at the sixth position is described as someone who has accumulated wealth, but hides it only in his house, and therefore is isolated from the rest of the world. This gives the typical image of the selfish rich. Of course, it seems reasonable to think that prosperity produces the type of individuals represented by the sixth yin line. But, why should the subject at the sixth position stand for persons with such a selfish orientation? Commentators do not offer satisfactory explanations. As I see it, the most reasonable explanation seems to be that the author(s) of the *I Ching* might have negative feelings about certain affairs occurring in the state of prosperity and the type of people described by the sixth line statement might be the object of such feelings.

Summary of theoretical and empirical propositions

1) The hexagrams examined above suggest that conflict or disunity in a society occurs for various reasons and in various forms. Under a certain condition, a society or social organization can produce contentious people who are highly prone to engage in conflict with others. Disunity may occur as the governing and the subordinate groups fail to operate as a harmoniously cooperating unit due to a breakdown in communication or interaction between them. Implicitly suggested by the hexagram *Pi* (Obstruction) is an idea that this kind of disunity can occur when a social unit has an operative unit that is not capable enough to carry out roles assigned to them. In the hexagram *Mingyi* (Suppression of the light), a tyrannical rule of a bad leader is recognized as the main source that causes the ruled to turn their backs and go into armed strife to overturn the ruling regime. The conflict situation represented by the hexagram *Kui* (Contrariety) features a disputing situation of a much milder sort such as that among family

members. The distinctive feature of this type of situation is that conflict is controlled within normatively set limits and, thus, an all-out conflict to get rid of one's opponent will rarely occur under this situation. The hexagram *Gen* (Restraint) depicts a situation in which a society falls into a state of paralysis due to the fact that its constituent members do not possess characteristics supportive of, or complementary to, one another. The state of "Abundance" that the hexagram *Feng* represents is described as a situation where a blessed state of material abundance exists yet most of its constituent members live in "shaded darker places." Thus, the hexagram is understood to be descriptive of a situation in which people, especially those at the lower positions, suffer deprivation in the midst of abundance. The situations featured by the six hexagrams are grouped here because they all show conditions that may be called "disintegrated situations" in modern social sciences. However, the fact that the *I Ching* classifies them into different types of situations suggests the idea that conflict and disunity in a society occur for various reasons and in various forms, a view that seems obvious to our everyday experience but worth examining for its theoretical implication in modern social sciences:

2) Under the "conflict" situation, it would not be advantageous for one to engage in a prolonged conflict unless he is quite sure of victory in view of both the position he occupies and the real power potential he possesses under the situation.

3) As indicated by the hexagram *Pi* (Obstruction), a society or social organization under certain circumstances may function badly and fall into a situation in which there occurs a breakdown in effective cooperation between the governing and subordinate ones.

4) Even tightly knit organizations such as a family whose members share a high sense of common identity and welfare may be drawn into conflicts. The *I Ching* views this kind of a conflict situation as normatively controlled in the sense that the people involved will not take the conflict to an extreme due to the sense of unity shared among themselves.

5) Darkness looks even darker when it is contrasted with bright light: this symbolizes the principle of "relative deprivation"; the state of prosperity (Abundance) will make those who are less prosperous feel even more deprived.

6) Situations in which order is established or reestablished for a newly emerging state or society that has undergone disintegration

Included here are situations in which a society or social organization undergoes order-building processes. A new order has to be instituted either when a new political regime comes into power or after a society has disintegrated for some reason or another. Reading the following discussions on these situations, we will notice that the *I Ching* adheres to a commonsense idea about the order building of a political community. The idea is simple indeed: the task of building order in a political community is complicated and therefore requires a great deal of caution and care from those who engage in the task. In this sense, the *I Ching* seems to tell a seemingly obvious truth that because order building is a human endeavor, difficulties may arise due to human error. One distinctive way that this simple view is distinguished from that of modern sociology would be that, as far as the *I Ching* is concerned, an order comes into existence because there are processes in which people exert effort to have the order instituted. The following five hexagrams represent the situations undergoing such processes through which a society or social organization strives to recover order.

1) The hexagram *Zhun* (☵☳, Birth Throes) (Hexagram No. 3)

2) The hexagram *Xie* (☳☵, Release) (Hexagram No. 40)

3) The hexagram *Ding* (☲☴, The Cauldron) (Hexagram No. 50)

4) The hexagram *Huan* (☴☵, Dispersion) (Hexagram No. 59)

5) The hexagram *Jie* (☵☱, Control) (Hexagram No. 60)

The hexagram *Zhun* (☵☰, Birth Throes)[61]

First, from the line structure of the hexagram *Zhun*, notice that a yang line in the bottom position is lying under three broken lines that together make up the trigram *Kun* (Earth) and another yang line is also present at the fifth position. As Legge explains, a line structure such as this might have made the author(s) of the *I Ching* conjure an image of "a plant (struggling) with difficulty out of the earth, rising gradually above the surface." The idea of difficulty or "Birth Throes" suggested by this natural imagery then should have elicited the idea of "the rise of a state out of a condition of disorder, consequent on a great revolution" (Legge, 1963:63). On the other hand, Wang Bi found the overall pattern of relationships among its line elements to be the primary source of the difficulty indicated by this hexagram. As we can see, there are two yang lines in the hexagram, one at the first position and the other at the fifth, and all other lines are yin lines. According to Wang Bi, "the weak cannot take care of themselves, so they must rely on the strong" (1994:36). And, the need for dependence will be more acute when people look forward to a recovery of stable relationships that broke down as their society fell into disorder. However, an absence of stable relationships per se is not what constitutes the difficult situation characterized by this hexagram. The difficulty lies in that there is a certain structural factor that poses an hindrance to the formation of ordered social relationships. The chief factor is the presence of two yang lines that "are pulling (yin lines) at odds." In more familiar terms, there are competing forces of power that have no definite supremacy over each other in drawing support from those between them; a double rulership structure is in existence here so that no definite pattern of dominance or alliance yet has formed under this situation. As Wang Bi puts it, "Unsuccessful at finding a master, they have no one on whom to rely" (Lynn, 1994:36). An unconsolidated authority structure in which people are in "Birth throes" or experiencing "difficulty" in establishing stable relationships is indicated here by this hexagram.

Then, let us read the line statement of the first yang line, one of the ruling figures in the situation: "One should tarry here. It is fitting to abide in constancy. It is fitting to establish a chief" (Lynn, 1994:153). "Chief" translates *hou* (侯). However, depending upon how the meaning of the line statement is interpreted as a whole, the word *hou* is translated differently as "supervisors," "helpers" (Cheng Yi, 1988:5-6;

Wilhelm, 1967:400) or "feudal ruler" (Legge, 1963:62). If the overall situation meant by the hexagram as a whole is taken into account, it seems to me that the meaning of the line statement can be rather straightforwardly understood in terms of what it says. Although the bottom position holders may seek to win influence over those above them, the intention as such would have little chance for success due to the relational patterns indicated by the line structure of the hexagram. So "it is fitting to" keep on doing things according to correct moral standards. And, "it is (also) fitting to" bring a unity to themselves by "establishing a chief."[62]

The line statement of the second yin line is stated in such obscure symbolism that it is not likely to mean much on its own. However, by recalling that the situation represented by this hexagram is characterized by "difficulty" in forming stable relationships in terms of the establishment of a firm leadership over the collective unit represented here, we would be able to get a relatively clear idea about what it intends to say. The line statement states: "Here *Zhun* [Birth Throes] operates as impasse, as yoked horses pulling at odds. She is not one to be harassed into getting married but practices constancy and does not plight her troth. Only after ten years will she plight her troth" (Lynn, 1994:154). Here the subject at the second position is described as one who is in the dilemma of being "pulled at odds." Along with this, the line statement also implies that there is no single dominant figure that holds enough influence to co-opt the second position into one's own sphere of influence. This impasse is predicted to be resolved somehow, but only after a quite long period of time.

This situation brings down the same predicament upon the subject at the third position. Why this one is in need of establishing stable relationships is indicated by the fact that a yin line is incumbent in the position where a yang line is expected to appear. As we know well by now, a presence of a yin line at a given position indicates that the position is occupied by one whose action orientation is to comply with others in dominant positions or in possession of authority. Considering what is required of the position holder of the third position, however, the action orientation indicated by a yin line will pose difficulty in establishing stable relationships with others under this particular situation. That is, it is interpreted that no prospect of social support is indicated for the "weak" subject — a tragic situation for the leader of a group. In view of this circumstance, the line statement of the third line compares the condition of its subject to that of a person who is destined to failure whenever he tries to manage things of his interest on his own. Now, with reference to what is said above, the following line statement of the third yin line may be understood more clearly as delivering a meaningful message: "To go after deer without a forester would only get one lost in the depths of the forest. The noble man, then, is aware that it would be better to refrain, for if he were to set out he would find it hard going" (Lynn, 1994:155).

Compared to the "difficulties" of the others, what is the situation of the subject at the fourth position? The line statement of this position starts with the verse that involves the same description as the second yang line; "Although it involves yoked horses pulling at odds, one seeks to get married here" (Lynn, 1994:155). The passage above alludes to the situation in which there are rival camps trying to co-opt the subject at the fourth position into each one's own side and, accordingly, he would seek an alliance by siding with one of them. Then, with whom does he form an alliance, the subject represented by the first yang line or the fifth one? Following a general rule of interpretation established in the native tradition, most commentators agree on the view that since the subject at the fourth position has a specific affinity with the first position, he can have his will fulfilled as wished if he sets out to align himself with the first yang line. We here again come across one of the major perspectives of the *I Ching* regarding the basic conditions of human life. It is obvious that the *I Ching* sees the life chance of an individual as determined by the social position that he occupies at a given time. The yin-yang dualism of the *I Ching* adds another dimension of reality that affects his life chance. In addition to these two factors, there is still another dimension of reality to which the two dimensions mentioned above, in operating together, give rise. It is relational patterns that are formed among individuals with respect to "who aligns with whom." As far as this particular dimension of social reality is concerned, isolation or lack of support from others would be the worst predicament that an individual could possibly suffer. It is exactly in this sense that the *I Ching* describes the situation of the fourth yin line as a "fortunate" one. That is, the line statement, "to set out means good fortune, and all will be fitting without fail," offers the positive prognosis that if the subject at the fourth position sets out to align himself with the first position, the outcome will be fortunate.[63] And, as was said above, whether or not one can find someone with whom he can associate is one of the most crucial conditions that, as far as the *I Ching* is concerned, will make him "fortunate" or otherwise.

Under the situation where many people experience difficulties "being pulled at odds," the power potential of the top leader should be limited to a much narrower extent than normally expected from his position under ordinary situations. Thus, the line statement for the fifth yang line starts with a verse saying, "Benefaction here is subject to the difficulty of *Zhun*." The *Commentary on the Images* on this line explains, "this means that it is not yet the time to extend one's power in a grand way" (Lynn, 1994:156). He will not be a powerful leader capable of exercising the leadership function to the fullest extent. The continuing portion of the line statement contains a piece of advice that can be judged appropriate for the subject at the fifth position under the situation: "To practice constancy in small ways means good fortune, but to practice constancy in major ways means misfortune" (Lynn, 1994:156). The above passage advises that since the subject's power is limited, he should not attempt to engage in grandiose enterprises, but only in projects of limited scales. The situation of the one at the leadership position is evaluated as such because of the arrangement of lines. Remember the *I Ching* regards the second yin line as the most likely partner to render support to the one at the fifth position. First of all, in view of what its line statement describes, the subject at the second position is a reluctant partner who hesitates to commit himself to either the one at the first position or the other at the fifth position. Thus, looking over the entire situation, as far as we read it from the line statements of all the individual lines of the hexagram, we find no one who will render strong support for the leadership. Of course, the overall situation also shows no other overwhelming figure that is powerful enough to make the top leader utterly powerless. Thus, the situation of the subject at the fifth position is judged as that having a limited power potential. It is not a situation where he can expect gainful outcomes by setting out to do great things.

Although everyone, perhaps except the subject at the fourth position, suffers "difficulties' to varying degrees under this situation, it is the subject at the sixth position who will suffer the most serious difficulty. Its line statement reads, "As one's yoked horses pull at odds, so one weeps profuse tears of blood." Of this line statements, Wang Bi explains: "Here one is trapped in the most dire of predicaments and has absolutely no one on whom to rely" (Lynn, 1994:156). That is, under the situation where everybody is experiencing difficulties in building up reliable relationships, the subject at the sixth position is said to suffer the most, presumably for two reasons. One reason is found in that, as Wang Bi reads from the relational patterns shown by the line structure of the hexagram, "there is no one to respond to help." And, the other reason is that since he is located outside the formal power structure, his marginal position is likely to make the condition of his alienation even worse.

The hexagram *Xie* (☵☳, Release)

"*Xie* (Release)," the name of the hexagram, means release from troubles or danger (Lynn, 1994:380-2). It is not entirely clear from what specific sort of troubles or danger one is to be released. Judging from the line statements, however, it may be guessed, roughly at most, that they refer to difficulties of a political nature. That is, they are connected with people posing obstacles to an effectively functioning government. The hexagram then represents a situation in which people obstructing the establishment of an effectively functioning government are taken care of so that a political community is "released" from a disorderly state. In this particular hexagram, however, the line statements are written with such vague symbolism that most of them yield no easy interpretation, and, as a result, even later commentaries do not seem to provide much help in extracting clear or sensible meanings out of them. It is clear, however, that the second and fifth positions are the position holders who are primarily responsible for carrying out the task of "releasing" the country from difficulties. The line statements of these two positions describe them as the main agents working in unison to bring to realization the situation represented by the hexagram. Thus, we had better start with these two lines:

> *Second Yang*: This one hunts down three foxes in the fields, obtaining a yellow arrow. Constancy here means good fortune.
>
> *Fifth Yin*: Only the noble man could bring about Release here and have good fortune, for he would even inspire confidence in petty men. (Lynn, 1994:382, 384)

The line statement of the second yang line describes its subject as an active agent working to remove obstacles ("foxes") standing in the way of bringing order to the country. "A yellow (gold) arrow" seems to signify an authority delegated to this subject by the leader at the fifth position with the backing of whom he carries out the purge campaign (C.f., Lee, 1997[II]:75-6). The line statement also contains advice for the subject to be firm and correct in carrying out the task. The subject at the fifth position is also described as an agent to bring about release from difficulties. However, notice here that a yin (weak) line occupies the fifth position, a yang (leadership) position. Being in a weak position, the line statement suggests that the subject would not be able to deal with the task at hand by forceful means. Thus, the line statement states that the task requires him to be a noble man who "would even inspire confidence in petty men." This subtle yet heart-winning tactic to gain influence as opposed to the exercise of an awe-inspiring power should have carried an air of ideality in the eyes of Chinese intellectuals. It would be the only and ideal way with which gentle people either lacking or disliking strong means influence others.

The line statement of the first yin line states simply that "there is no blame" (Lynn, 1994:382). With a brief statement such as this, whatever explanation one may come up with would be nothing more than a matter of personal opinion. My simplest interpretation would be that the common folk, as conventionally represented by the first position, in this situation are not likely to become a target for the purge movement. They will not be blamed for creating the difficulties present in this situation and, therefore, will come out uninjured throughout the process of removing the difficulties.

The subject of the third yin line is one of the sources causing the difficulties from which the collective unit represented by this hexagram is to be released. The line statement reads as follows: "The third line, divided, shows a porter with his burden, (yet) riding in a carriage. He will (only) tempt robbers to attack him. However firm and correct he may (try to) be, there will be cause for regret" (Legge, 1963:145).[64] What the line statement says does not seem difficult to understand. A wrong person who is not qualified for the position is incumbent at it; so, however hard he may try to do well and correctly in his position, little good outcome will result from such futile efforts. Thus, we may have a reading, if not explicitly stated, that this subject at the third position is the one causing difficulties for the collective unit referred to by the hexagram, and would be the target that has to be removed. How plausible this interpretation is can be assessed in light of what is stated in the line statement for the fourth yang line, which has a meaningful connection with the third line statement.

Then, let us look at the line statement of the fourth yang line: "Release your big toe, for a friend will come and then place trust in you" (Lynn, 1994:383). Commentators offer varying interpretations regarding the two subjects mentioned in the line statement; what is the "big toe", and who is the "friend," respectively? I will take the version offered by Wilhelm (1967:588), for it seems more consistent with the interpretations of the other lines presented already. According to Wilhelm, the big toe refers to the subject at the third position; this is the one who has to be released from the relationship that is sought for by both the subjects at the third and the fourth positions due to their complementary characteristics (being contiguously located and forming a yin-yang pair). By disengaging himself from the third yin line who figures as a source of trouble under the situation, the subject at the fourth position will join a friend, the one at the second position, who according to Wilhelm "jointly (renders) loyal help to the ruler in the fifth place." Of course, although it may make a morally laudable story that two strong subordinates work together to serve a weak ruler, one may wonder if such a touching affair could really occur in the world of politics? To this question, the *I Ching* may answer that it depends on the overall situational context in which relationships among individual position holders come into formation.

Lastly, concerning the sixth yin line, Wang Bi views that "it (the subject at the sixth position) represents one who will bring about Release from gross disobedience and do away with abominable revolt" (Lynn, 1994:384). Legge also interprets this line from a similar perspective (1963:147). Understandably, their translations are in line with the above interpretation. In contrast, Wilhelm offers an interpretation diametrically opposed to the above. In his translation, "The prince shoots at a hawk on a high wall. He kills it. Everything serves to further," the sixth yin line is described metaphorically as the "hawk," a "highly placed evildoer" who will be "shot from below, where the trigram K'an (arrow) is situated" (1967:588). According to this interpretation, the subject at the sixth position is one of the sources causing the troubles indicated by this hexagram, and, therefore, the release from the problem that the country faces will be completed by removing this element. I prefer Wilhelm's interpretation to the other version proposed by both Wang Bi and Legge for one good reason; it seems more consistent with what is stated in the line statement of the second yang line where the subject at the second position is described as one who shoots three foxes with a golden arrow. And, there is also the consideration that, in this hexagram, the yang lines assume the role of active agents working to release the concerned social unit from troubles and that all other yin lines stand for those playing opposite roles.

The hexagram *Ding* (☲☴, The Cauldron)

Now, looking at the hexagram *Ding* (the Cauldron) having a line structure inverse to the hexagram *Zhun*, it may be presumed that the former would carry a situational meaning directly opposite to the latter. Contrary to this seemingly reasonable expectation, the meanings of these two hexagrams involve little opposition. And, in a certain aspect, even some similarity may be viewed to exist between them. This indicates that the meanings of hexagrams in many cases might not have been derived analytically from their line structure. As a matter of fact, the meaning of the hexagram *Ding* seems to have been derived from its pictorial image that resembles the shape of cauldrons used in ancient China.[65] Still, the cauldron itself is but a symbol to represent a certain category of social situation. Then, what does the cauldron represent in terms of a specific category of social process or a pattern of social relationships? It would be helpful to know that the hexagram *Ding* comes right after the hexagram *Ge* (Radical Change) in the sequential order of the hexagrams as customarily presented in the text. According to the *Hexagrams in Irregular Order*, whereas "*Ge* [Radical Change] means 'get rid of the old'," "*Ding* means 'take up the new'" (Lynn, 1994:445, 453). That is, after getting rid of the old, a new order takes the place of the old. The hexagram *Ding* refers to a societal phase in which social reconstruction goes on to establish a new order.

However, the line statements of this hexagram, as Legge points out, are "difficult to interpret" (1963:171). It seems that this difficulty is related to two things. One is that although the line statements in the *I Ching* are narrated mostly in symbolic words, the line statements of this particular hexagram involve more difficult symbolism, far from people's ordinary way of thinking. The other thing is that it is not easy to understand how each line statement is related to the overall meaning of the hexagram *Ding*, which symbolizes a society at the stage of putting a new order into effect. I think that Legge would have in his mind exactly this kind of problem when he, commenting on a line statement in the hexagram, says, "The above is what is found in the best commentaries on the paragraph. I give it, but am myself dissatisfied with it" (1963:172). So, here we have a hexagram that allows no easy access. Nevertheless, I would like to adopt a unique perspective in interpreting this hexagram, with which I think we can render a reasonably sensible interpretation. The interpretation and translation that I am going to adopt here is that rendered by Lee in his *Lectures on the I Ching* (1997[II]). How Lee interprets and translates each line statement of this hexagram is shown below. For now, let me just point out that a uniqueness of his perspective lies in that he views the ordered series of the line statements of the hexagram as different kinds or levels of tasks required to build a new order.

The line statement of the first yin line reads, "If the subject at the first position turns the cauldron upside down having its legs turned upward, it will help him to expel what is bad inside. Although one takes up a concubine, there will be no blame if it is for the sake of having a son" (Lee, 1997[II]:173, translated by this author from the Korean text). Understood as translated above, the line statement acquires a clearer meaning in reference to the overall situational meaning of the hexagram. To fill up a system with a new order requires first of all a cleansing job to empty out remnants from the old regime; and, it has to be done as thoroughly as "turning the cauldron upside down having its legs turned upward." In the process, however, it may be necessary to resort to extraordinary means (like taking in a concubine) that deviate from normal standards accepted by society; yet, "there will be no blame" if it is done for a justifiable purpose such as "having a son." As interpreted above, the line statement seems to give reasonable advice to those undergoing the process of building a new order. Of course, a question remains here: why should such an advice be given specifically to the subject at the first position? Perhaps it is because the job of cleaning out remnants from the old order would have to be carried out by the common people at the bottom layer of the society. Or, the line statement may simply make reference to the task that people in general, rather than the specific subject at the first position, are required to do at the initial stage of social reconstruction. Interpreted either way, the line statement offers meaningful advice in view of the meaning of the situation represented by the hexagram. Regrettably, no definite evidence is available in either the *I Ching* itself or later commentaries to assist us in making a choice between the two different explanations.

The line statement of the second yang line states, "The second yang line represents one who fills food stuff into the cauldron. He will have good fortune if his ailing companion is kept away from where the cooking is done" (Lee, 1997[II]:174, translated by this author). In this line statement, the subject at the second position is compared to a person who puts foodstuffs into the cauldron, an important job in preparing a feast. Comparing the task of building a new order to preparing a communal feast and considering an important job required for the occasion is to fill food stuffs into the cauldron, it make some sense that the subject at the second position is recognized as one who will perform such an important job. And, as Lee explains, when persons at this position plan, organize, or execute things, they should try to keep away close associates who may approach them with ill intentions (1997[II]:174).

The line statement of the third yang line states, "if the cauldron's ears are changed, the process will be obstructed and peasant fat will not be eaten. As rain falls, regret will be diminished; So in the end, there will be good fortune" (Lee, 1997[II]:174, translated by this author). The above translation itself is not much different from other versions of translation including Lynn's. What makes Lee's interpretation of this line statement unique is the way in which he interprets the word, "the cauldrons' ears." According to Lee, "the cauldron's ears" refers to a person (or persons) who is responsible for implementing a new working system into the collective unit represented by the hexagram. The starting verse of the line statement could be read to say that if the third position is replaced with others (probably being held responsible for ill management of the ongoing project), the reconstruction process may come to a halt and the goal of developing a new system would be frustrated. The next verse, "As rain falls, regret will be diminished," indicates that as the subject at the third position is able to get over the difficulty task of building up a new working system, his tough situation will improve into a better one. However, why is the situation seen to improve? And, first of all, why is the subject at the third position judged to have fallen into a difficult situation in which he has to wait for "rainfall"[66]? Why does the situation of *Ding* develop in this specific way for the subject at the third position? It seems that the rational ground for this sort of deterministic thought cannot be clearly understood by us. Of course, the kind of leadership task that the subject in the third position has to perform under the situation represented by the hexagram *Ding* may not be an easy one. And, therefore, he may be replaced with another person if things do not progress well. Understood the way that Lee interprets it, the line statement does not seem to carry us into a world of ideas too unfamiliar for the organized lives of our modern days.

The line statement of the fourth yang again presents no easy case in seizing on its meaning and understanding how its meaning is related to the line structure of the hexagram. The line statement states, "if the cauldron's leg is broken and the prince's meal is spilled, a punishment by decapitation will be called for for such a grave mistake. This means disastrous misfortune" (Lee, 1997[II]:176, translated by this author). One thing that seems obvious from the above line statement is that the subject at the fourth position is seen to perform such a crucial task that failure in handling that task will result in grave consequences for him. Of course, given that the subject at the fourth position is assigned a critical role in installing the new working order, it is not unreasonable that his failure to do the job would be met with a severe punishment as the line statement says. But, here again, we may ask; what sort of logical connection exists between what the line statement says about the position holder at the fourth position and the attributes of the line, its position and the property of being a yang line, as understood in the context of the overall line structure of the hexagram? Commentators including Wang Bi make attempt at some explanation concerning this question (Cheng Yi, 1988:171; Legge, 1963: 172-173; Lynn, 1994:455; Wilhelm, 1967:645). Their explanations differ from one another in detail, yet there is an underlying idea on which they seem to converge. According to this idea, the subject at the fourth position is viewed as a person who, due to the position he occupies under the situation, is assigned a crucially important role, yet possesses certain weaknesses that may cause problems in carrying out his assigned role. This is because as a yang line occupying a yin position, he is judged to be a person whose personal characteristic or action orientation does not match what is required of the position. Another weakness is a relational one: for reasons that are not clearly illuminated, commentators (Cheng Yi, 1988:171; Legge, 1963: 172-173; Wang Bi, in Lynn, 1994:455; Wilhelm, 1967:645) view that the subject at the fourth position fails to develop good working relationships with either one or both of two potential co-actors, the first and the fifth yin lines. Of course, it seems plausible to think that the two factors pointed out above, if they should occur, may work against anyone who performs an important role in an organized setting. However, here we encounter once again the chronic problem concerning the interpretation of the *I Ching*. We have three elements, the line structure of a hexagram, the statements appended to the hexagram and the individual lines, and commentators' commentaries on the above two materials. Obviously, some kind of logical linkage should exist among these three elements. But, in many cases including the line statement at hand here, a logical connection does not appear to us as obvious enough.

The fifth and the sixth line statements only give an indication, stated in vague symbolism at most, that the subjects at both positions are in happier situations than the other position holders. Commentators, here again, attempt some explanations as to why the situations of the two particular position holders are viewed as such, yet, as far as this author sees it, with no success. Nevertheless, if the *Commentary on the Images* and the line statements are considered together, we may find an exception in Wilhelm's interpretation: his interpretation does not seem to sound so exotic as to go beyond our ordinary understanding. Then, let us look at the line statement of the fifth yin line as translated by Wilhelm: "The *ting* (*Ding*) has yellow handles, golden carrying rings. Perseverance furthers" (1967:645). Of this line statement, Wilhelm explains:

Hexagrams: Types of Social Situations   215

The carrying rings (which in ancient Chinese vessels are usually linked together) are no doubt represented by the strong line at the top . . . . the handle is hollow and can therefore receive the "real" (i.e., firm) carrying things, and the vessel can be carried. / In the language of symbols this means a great deal. The line is the ruler of the hexagram and has over it a sage (the nine at the top), with whom it is connected by position and complementary relationship. The ruler is "hollow" [receptive], hence capable of receiving the power, that is, the teachings of this sage . . . . Thereby he makes progress. (1967:646)

In the above passage, the subjects at the fifth and sixth positions are described to be in a complementary relationship in which the one at the fifth position is eager to receive the teachings of the sage represented by the sixth yang line. This is not a strange idea, as this may happen oftentimes as a matter of fact, that a person at the top leadership displays a specific receptivity or willingness to listen to whatever intellectuals with no official position have to say about issues of the day. A problem with this interpretation, however, is that such a complementary relationship that is said to exist between the two actors seems to carry no relevant meaning with respect to the overall situational meaning of the hexagram. In other words, it does not seem clear at all what kind of specific meaning the above stated relationship has in the context of the overall situation in which a new working order is being instituted. Perhaps, we can fill the gap by supplying an invented idea that the one at the top leadership position carries out his role for implementing a new order in close consultation with intellectuals who are out of office. Although the line statements do not seem to contain anything against this interpretation, we may wonder how far ideas of our own invention would be justifiably allowed to make play in interpreting the symbolism of the *I Ching*.

The hexagram *Huan* (☴☵, Dispersion)

The hexagram *Huan* consists of the two trigrams, the trigram *Sun* (signifying wind) above and the trigram *Kan* (signifying water) below. Thus, the wind blowing over water gives an idea of dispersion, the theme of this hexagram. However, perhaps because the structure of the hexagram conveys the idea of motion or transition from a certain state to another, the theme of the hexagram seems to refer to a process, rather than a fixed structure of social formation, in which the components of an organized unit represented by the hexagram are striving for a unity while it is in a state of dispersion or disintegration. In this sense, I think, the overall meaning of the hexagram may be expressed more adequately if it was named "reintegration," for the term reintegration seems to include the idea of dispersion (or disintegration). In recognition of this duality involved in the meaning of the hexagram, Wilhelm points out, "As against this process of breaking up (dispersion), the task of uniting presents itself; this meaning also is contained in the hexagram" (1967:690). It also would be instructive to note that the *Judgment* on this hexagram emphasizes reintegration as a required task that must be fulfilled by certain position holders under the situation of dissolution. It reads:

> *Huan* [Dispersion] is such that prevalence is had, but only when a true king arrives will there be an ancestral temple. It would then be fitting to cross the great river and fitting to practice constancy. (Lynn, 1994:511)

"An ancestral temple" represents a ceremonial location symbolizing the continuity and unity of a kingdom. One interesting thing we can note from this then is that the situation of Dispersion involves inside itself the mutually opposing situational characteristics of disorder and recovery toward a stable social order. As one is threatened with disorder or separated from others with whom he might have expected an intimate relationship,[67] he will strive for new companionship. This hexagram thus describes a moving, interactive process in which dissolution or disintegration exists as an ongoing condition, and a counteracting movement, reintegration, takes place at the same time. Now, let us look at the individual line statements.

The line statement of the first yin line states, "He brings help with strength of a horse. Good fortune" (Wilhelm, 1967:690).[68] A strong horse refers to the subject at the second position because the second yang line is the only yang line with whom the subject at the first position seeks a union. The line statement suggests that the situation of dispersion is recognized as a threatening one by the individuals involved; they have to reach out for help to escape possible isolation resulting from social relations undergoing dissolution. The subject at this particular position will find the one at the second position to be the most suitable partner with whose help he can get out of a difficult situation in the process of dissolution.

In view of what is said in the first line statement, the line statement of the second yang line is expected to involve a related topic. The second line statement reads, "At the dissolution / He hurries to that which supports him. Remorse disappears" (Wilhelm, 1967:691).

Regarding the meaning of this line statement, however, Wilhem explains that "that which supports him" refers to the ruler at the fifth position. We may question how the first line statement's message coheres with what the second line statement says? It is perhaps due to this inconsistency that other commentators such as Legge (1963:196) and Cheng Yi (1988:200) interpret the line statement differently and explain that the one who "supports him" refers to the one at the first position. Viewed with this latter interpretation, the subjects at the first and the second positions form a complementary pair who remain together against the situational trend threatened with dissolution.

The third yin position at the top of the trigram *Kan* is symbolized by water and is in contact with the upper trigram *Sun* which is symbolized by wind. The natural imagery of this line is vaporization; it is disassociated from its own group, goes up, and joins with someone at a higher level. There is no doubt that the line statement of the third yin line is derived from such natural imagery. It reads, "He dissolves his self. No remorse." And, the *Commentary on the Images* adds, "His will is directed outward" (Wilhelm, 1967:692). Notice that this is the only line in the lower trigram that has a corresponding line in the upper trigram, a yang line at the sixth position. According to the logic of the *I Ching*, the yin line at the third position will have a resonant relationship with the yang line at the sixth position because the two positions have a specific affinity and their subjects under the present situation, as represented respectively by yin and yang lines, have characteristics complementary to each other. Thus, what the line statement says also conveys an idea associated with the main theme of the overall situation: while a disintegrative process in a given pattern of relation goes on, a new integration emerges out of it.

The line statement of the fourth yin line repeats the same theme: "He dissolves his bond with his group. Supreme good fortune. Dispersion leads in turn to accumulation. This is something that ordinary men do not think of" (Wilhelm, 1967:692). By most commentators, the subject at the fourth position is interpreted as referring to a minister (or ministers if referred to a collectivity of people engaging in similar functions) who works together with the ruler at the fifth position to bring about "a large gathering ('accumulation') in a time of dispersal and separation" (Cheng Yi, 1988:201). But, regarding the beginning line stating, "He dissolves his bond with his group," commentators interpret and thereby translate it differently. For example, Legge's translation reads, "The forth line, divided, shows its subject scattering the (different) parties (in the state) . . . ." (1963:195). Thus, its subject is figured as one who, in cooperation with the subject at the fifth position, achieves reintegration of the country by breaking up factional groups counterproductive to the unity of the country. On the other hand, in Wilhelm's translation, the subject at the fourth position is interpreted as someone who has "dissolved its bond with its (own) group" (1967:692) and then works with the ruler at the fifth position for the integration of the entire group. These two interpretations differ from each other, but both seem consistent with the main theme of the hexagram, due to which we find no definite reason to favor one over the other.

The line statement of the fifth yang line also is interpreted and translated differently, depending upon the commentator. Considering the main theme of the hexagram and the interpretation of the fourth yin line presented already, Cleary's translation rendered with reference to Cheng Yi's interpretation appears most fitting. It reads, "In a time of dispersal, make the great order reach everywhere. In dealing with dispersal, the abode of the king is blameless" (Cheng Yi, 1988:201). Of this Cheng Yi comments:

> This is the way to remedy dispersal; it is a matter of making the remedy reach people's hearts, so that they obey and follow. It is imperative to make directives reach all the people's hearts, so that they accept them and go along with them. Then it is possible to save society from dispersal. To be in the position of kingship is appropriate here, so there is no blame.

In the above commentary, the subject at the fifth position is described as the leader who takes a far reaching measure that is geared to integrating all the people of his country. That is, he is the ruler who with the help of a faithful minister (ministers) takes action to reintegrate his country facing a difficult situation threatened with disintegration. An effective leadership is present at the leadership position (a yang line is present at a yang position) and the presence of the leadership as such explains exactly why this situation of dissolution includes the counteracting force of reintegration.

The line statement of the sixth yang line is reflective of the natural imagery that is conveyed by each of the two component trigrams of the hexagram. One of the signs that symbolizes the lower trigram *Kan* is blood[69] while the upper trigram *Sun* is symbolized by wind. Now, let us look at the line statement: "He dissolves his blood. Departing, keeping at a distance, going out, / Is without blame" (Wilhelm, 1967:693). When we discussed the line statement of the third yin line, it was pointed out that the third yin line dissociates itself from the trigram to which it belongs and joins the sixth yang line in a corresponding relationship. A unity achieved by these two lines, as might have been understood by the author(s) of the *I Ching*, has the positive function of curbing the "disintegrating" trend of this hexagram. The line statement, "he dissolves his blood," is understood to refer to this effect of the union of the two lines.[70] Remaining words such as "Departing, keeping at a distance, going out" can be understood in the same context. The lower trigram *Kan* signifies danger, and the upper trigram *Sun* wind. Since the sixth line is at the top of the trigram *Sun*, that of wind, it gives the image of "departing, keeping at a distance, going out" from the source of the danger. Of course, today this kind of logic will sound incomprehensible. In essence, what the line statement says may be restated as follows: if a man or a group is characterized by "wind," he or they will easily move out of danger just as wind makes an easy escape from any source of danger. This is strange metaphoric reasoning, indeed, and it seems undeniable that the *I Ching*, an ancient classic, is not free of mystic thinking.

The hexagram *Jie* (≡≡ , Control)

The hexagram *Jie* (Control) features a situation in which the members of the group or organization represented by the hexagram are governed by Control, i.e., the strong measures employed to bring order to the system in question. Judging from a passage in the *Judgment*, the fifth and the second positions are recognized as key actors who are responsible for exercising the Control under the situation. However, the line statements yield a little different reading where although the ruling figure at the fifth position is depicted as the primary actor to play the key role in exercising the Control, the subject at the second position assumes a supportive role. All the other subjects, except the sixth position, are individuals subject to the Control. The line statement of the sixth yin line is of a rather different sort in that it contains a message that is related to the overall theme of the hexagram rather than a specific situation of a particular position holder. All these distinctions among the lines will become obvious as we examine the line statements.

The line statements of the first and the second yang lines involve directly opposing meanings. Thus, by presenting and comparing them together the difference between their positions and situations can be more sharply contrasted.

First Yang: This one does not go out the door to his courtyard, so there is no blame.

Second Yang: If this one does not go out the gate of his courtyard, there will be misfortune. (Lynn, 1994:520-1)

The immediate question is why the subjects at the two different positions are judged to be in situations that are so opposing? This is because their positions under the situation differ; the subject at the first position represents people subjected to Control, whereas the subject at the second position is the one who exercises the Control. In other words, for the subject at the first position, caution and discretion are required under Control, whereas the subject at the second position must go out and actively engage in his assigned function to put Control into effect. Of course, such an exercise of strong regulations as implied by the line statement of the second yang line should not go beyond a reasonable limit. As a matter of fact, an emphasis on "measured control" constitutes the primary theme of this hexagram as seen in a passage of the *Judgment* that reads, "bitter Control cannot be practiced with constancy." Of the lesson that the short passage above involves, Wang Bi adds a lucidly stated commentary as follows:

> If in applying Control one goes too far and makes it bitter, it will become something the people cannot bear. If the people cannot bear it, one will no longer be able to correct their behavior. (Lynn, 1994:519)

The advice written above seems to be sensible, although we at present are not in a position to assess its practical effects in real politics. However, it certainly reflects one of the typical value orientations of the *I Ching* — moderation.

A yin line occupies the third position, a yang position, and its subject therefore is interpreted as failing in adjusting himself to the situation. The maladjustment of the subject and its unfortunate result are clearly indicated by its line statement: "As this one is in violation of Control, so he should wail, for there is no one else to blame" (Lynn, 1994:520). Contrasted directly to the unfortunate situation faced by the subject at the third position is the situation of the subject at the fourth position. The line statement of the fourth yin line states, "This one is content with Control, so prevalence is had" (Lynn, 1994:520). There seems to be little doubt that the favorable judgment for the fourth position holder is rendered because the fourth position, a yin position, is occupied appropriately by a yin line. Thus, represented by a yin line occupying a yin position, he symbolizes someone who complies with the demand put forward by the situation. And, this is exactly Wang Bi's interpretation of this line statement as he comments: "Fourth Yin obtains its proper place [it is a yin line in a yin position] and is characterized by obedience, so it represents someone who does not try to alter the Control placed upon him" (Lynn, 1994:520).

The subject at the fifth position is represented by a yang line, and, therefore, is described as both the governing and constituting ruler of the situation; he is the primary actor responsible for imposing Control under the situation. Of this subject, the line statement says, "The fifth line, undivided, shows its subject sweetly and acceptably enacting its regulations. There will be good fortune. The onward progress with them will afford ground for admiration" (Legge, 1963:198).[71] Why the subject is seen as "enacting its regulations sweetly and acceptably" is not clearly explained by any account in either the text or any later commentary. If we are to read the characteristic of the fifth yang line only with reference to the overall line formation of the hexagram, at most we see that a strong leader is present at the leadership position with sufficient power to impose Control over the people subjected to his authority. But, the characterization of the fifth position as one who is "enacting its regulations sweetly and acceptably" is possibly related to the ideal type of leadership that the author(s) of the *I Ching* had in mind for the social situation represented by the hexagram *Jie* (Control). Looked at in this way, the line statement may be translated as involving the following conditional: "if the subject at the fifth position acts as ideally as a leader who 'enacts its regulations sweetly and acceptably,' there will be good fortune." The last verse, "The onward progress with them will afford ground for admiration," states the expected reaction of the people to the conduct of the leadership under this situation provided that it is exercised as ideally as stated above.

The line statement of the sixth yin line presents a type of leadership that is directly opposite to the line statement of the fifth line. It describes the subject at the sixth position as someone who "enacts regulations severe and difficult." Understandably, the line statement predicts, "Even with firmness and correctness there will be evil." Therefore, the consequence of the leadership style so described is not judged as auspiciously as that given for the subject at the fifth position. There is, however, an additional remark in the line statement that may sound contradictory to what is stated in previous verses: "But though there will be cause for repentance, it will (by and by) disappear" (Legge, 1963:198). Commentators have offered several explanations to bridge the seemingly inconsistent remarks made by different passages in the same line statement. Of these varying explanations, Legge's explanation seems most appropriate. Drawing from what Confucius says in *Analects* (3·3), he explains that although the effect of severe regulations may be negative as indicated by the line statement, it "is not so greatly a fault as to be easy and remiss. It may be remedied, and cause for repentance will disappear" (Legge, 1963:200). That is, strong regulations may have considerable negative side effects, but the negative effects will wear out and eventually their contribution to restoring order for the system in question will be recognized. This explanation in itself sounds reasonable, although its factual hypothesis may give rise to some doubt about its actual validity. Nevertheless, we here again may ask why the subject at the sixth position is described as one who is likely to show the kind of behavior that is to be thought far less ideal than that of the one at the fifth position? What does this line statement have to do with the situational and positional attributes of the sixth yin line? No hint with which to answer this question is found in either the text itself or any later commentary. The most reasonable explanation is that it simply contains a warning that the person at the leadership position should not give up applying regulations (to enforce law and order) even though he is not able to exercise them as ideally as the fifth position holder. As far as this situation is concerned, even bad regulations would be better than no regulation.

Summary of theoretical and empirical propositions

1) The situations represented by the hexagrams examined above suggest that order-building processes often involve internal conditions that modern sociologists may call "conflict situations." In these situations, social order is built through expelling forces that resist efforts to bring about a given kind of social or political order or through overcoming factors that pose obstacles to the building of a new order. In this sense, we may say, the *I Ching* views conflicts as a basic reality of society.

2) The building of a new order requires a cleansing job to empty out remnants from the old regime or institution. In the process, extraordinary measures that deviate from normative standards of a society may have to be used.

3) The hexagram *Huan* (Dispersion) represents a situation in which new relationships among people emerge where old relationships are dissolving. Opposing yet mutually dependent trends are in progress at the same time. Therefore, the events of the order-

building process and the dissolution of an order are linked. Thus, we are presented with a quite complex and dynamic situation in which a trend toward integration exists while existing relations, if in part, undergo a process of dissolution. According to the *I Ching*, change is the most fundamental reality of both nature and society. In this sense, it does seem not unusual that the *I Ching* presents a dynamic situation where new relationships are in formation while old relationships are disintegrating.

4) In bringing order to a society, it is advisable to refrain from using excessive control measures that are unbearable to the people. However, if time calls for the establishment of order, even bad control would be better than no control although "bitter" control may bring about negative side effects.

7) Situations in Which Movements to Bring About Changes in Existing Orders Take Place

All four hexagrams presented here represent situations in which movements to bring changes in existing orders take place. The four situations are differentiated from one another mainly in terms of who leads the change movement. The two hexagrams, *Ge* and *Sun*, represent situations in which change movements are led by the governing elites: both of them symbolize reform movements initiated and carried out by the people above. Directly opposite to these two situations is the hexagram *Zhen*: it represents a change movement from below, from the lowest tier of a society. The remaining one, the hexagram *Gu*, figures a situation in which most people are involved in engaging tasks to redress problems inherited from previous generations. As these four hexagrams suggest, the *I Ching* views that changes can be brought about not only from above but also from below: who will take the lead in bringing about changes will differ from one situation to another. Considering that one of the main concerns of sociology regarding social change has focused on the source or force of change, the following four hexagrams will present interesting perspectives.

1) The hexagram *Gu* (☶☴ , Ills to Be Cured) (Hexagram No. 11)

2) The hexagram *Ge* (☱☲, Radical Change) (Hexagram No. 49)

3) The hexagram *Zhen* (☳☳, Quake) (Hexagram No. 51)

4) The hexagram *Sun* (☴☴, Compliance) (Hexagram No. 57)

The hexagram *Gu* (☶☴, Ills to Be Cured)

The hexagram *Gu* depicts a situation in which the people involved are engaging in tasks to redress problems ("Ills") inherited from the previous generation. The line statements vary according to each subject's chance for a successful outcome in fulfilling his task, the manner in which each subject deals with the problem, the source from which the problem came about, etc. But, how are all these things related to the positional characteristic of each line? Of course, we cannot immediately reject as wholly implausible an idea that people at different social rankings may differ in the ways or manners in which they deal with "ills." However, I have the impression that each line statement about the activity of the subject involved was written in a very unusual frame of mind or from a very unique frame of reference of which social scientists of today, including myself, have no propensity to partake. For instance, while the subjects at the first, the third, the fourth, and the fifth positions are described as dealing with problems caused by the father, the second position's task is to remedy problems caused by his mother. Why is the subject at the second position viewed as dealing with a problem caused by the mother whereas all the other subjects' problems are related to the father? Regarding this question, Legge, commenting on this hexagram, says that he conducted a thorough examination for possible reasons why the differentiation of the sources of the problems was made among the line statements, but was "unable to account for these things" (1963: 96-7). Leaving this reservation in mind, let us turn to the individual line statements.

The line statement of the first yin line states, "The first line, divided, shows (a son) dealing with the troubles caused by his father. If he be an (able) son, the father will escape the blame of having erred. The position is perilous, but there will be good fortune in the end"

(Legge, 1963:95).[72] From the above line statement, the second verse, "If he be an (able) son, the father will escape the blame of having erred," seems to be nothing more than an obvious conclusion drawn from what is stated in the beginning statement. Meanwhile, why, in the next verse, is the situation evaluated potentially as a "perilous" one for the subject at the position? Legge (1963:96) suggests that the perspective underlying the *I Ching* that accounts for the stated situations of individual position holders can explain this. The "weak" subject at the bottom position (represented by a yin line under the situation) may look for support from the one at the fourth position, the most likely partner with whom to form an alliance, yet the fourth one being a yin line itself is in too weak a position to render any support. And, lastly, although the last portion of the line statement is stated as it is already presented above, most commentators interpret it as if it is stated with a condition requiring that the subject's ability or behavioral orientation should measure up to the task at hand. Thus, the resulting interpretation would be somewhat like what we can see in Cheng Yi's explanation: "if one in this position is able to work hard, it is possible thereby for it to end up well" (1988:54-5).

As pointed out already, the line statement for the second yang line describes its subject as dealing with the problem caused by the mother. And, it ends with the shortly stated advice that "He should not (carry) his firm correctness (to the utmost)" (Legge, 1963:95). The situational context in which the above advice is relevant has become familiar to us. A yang line is incumbent at the second position, a yin place, and a yin line that indicates the presence of a yielding, weak ruler occupies its corresponding position, the fifth position. Thus, in view of what is expected from the second position in its formal capacity, this makes the present position holder too strong a subject; hence, the advice, "He should not (carry) his firm correctness (to the utmost)," is given. That is, although the subject at the second position is in an advantageous position due to the specific condition associated with the given situation, he is advised not to be carried away too far with his superior position as such.

Of the subject represented by the third yang line, its line statement repeats the recurring theme of the hexagram describing him as one who "straightens out Ills caused by the father." Then, the line statement adds a remark, this subject "has slight regret," although in the end he may suffer "no great blame" (Lynn, 1994:251). Commentators' opinions on why the *I Ching* renders this judgment are divided into two lines. Wang Bi's explanation is that the subject's slight regret is due to the fact that "it (the subject at the third position) has no responsive partner." Yet he "suffer(s) no great blame" because the position holder would act appropriately in accordance with what the position requires (a yang line occupies a yang place) (Lynn, 1994:251). On the other hand, Legge views it differently. The subject at the third position is represented by a strong line occupying a yang (leadership) position, and this would signify a possibility that "its subject might well go to excess in his efforts." But, why is he viewed to commit no great error? It is because such tendency "is counteracted by the line's place in the trigram *Sun*, often denoting lowly submission" (1963:97). Wilhelm (1967:480) and Cheng Yi's (1988:55) explanations are very much similar to that offered by Legge. By comparing the two contrasting explanations presented above, we here again encounter an interesting yet, at the same time, troublesome aspect concerning the nature of the knowledge derivable from the *I Ching*. First, to look at the interesting side, we may be able to identify several interesting hypotheses from those explanations that seem to be sociological in nature. One possible hypothesis that draws our attention is related to the question of why a strong line in a strong position is considered to be too strong? This sort of judgment is rarely seen when the fifth position, which is also regarded as a yang place, is involved. In contrast, a yang line is often interpreted as "too strong" when the third position is involved. Above all, the third position, the leadership position of the subordinate group, is basically ambivalent in the sense that a yang line at the third position represents a strong leader who, if viewed from those at the upper echelon, occupies a subordinate position. Such ambivalence inherent in the position,[73] depending upon types of situation, would make a strong leader of the subordinate group too strong. This sets forth a hypothesis regarding the ambivalence and, therewith, insecurity inherent in the leadership of the subordinate group. And, as we have seen, the interpretation adopted by Legge and others is based on this hypothesis. Legge's interpretation also involves an additional hypothesis that a subject's characteristic is mediated in part by the overall characteristic of the group to which he belongs. Therefore, for example, although the subject at the third position is likely to show the tendency of being too strong, the tendency as such will be counteracted by the overall mood of the subordinate group, denoted by the trigram *Sun* which symbolizes Compliance, resulting in a fortunate outcome for him. Meanwhile, the explanation advanced by Wang Bi is based on a different interpretation, which involves a hypothesis still different from the two hypotheses introduced above. Wang Bi explains that the subject at the third position may experience some difficulty because he, under this situation, has "no responsive partner," suggesting that social isolation as indicated by the line structure of the hexagram poses a condition that creates difficulty for the subject involved.

All these hypotheses, I think, seem to involve plausible ideas concerning certain features related to human organizations. There is, however, a troubling aspect of the *I Ching*: anyone with discerning eyes would not have missed the fact that the two different interpretations introduced above are based on totally different, even contradictory, perspectives. Legge's interpretation is premised on the view that since a yang line is present at the third position, this will make the subject at that position "too strong." In contrast, in Wang Bi's interpretation, the fact that a yang line is present at the third position operates as a remedial factor easing the difficulty associated with the subject's situation. Thus, in fact, commentators come up with different, even contradictory, readings from the same passage. Without doubt, the ambiguity associated with the way in which the text is addressed in metaphoric symbolism is chiefly responsible for these divergent interpretations.

The line statement of the fourth yin line reads that "Tolerating what has been spoiled by the father. In continuing one sees humiliation" (Wilhelm, 1967:480).[74] For some reason that I presently cannot locate, the subject at the fourth position is described to take a tolerant attitude towards the problem caused by the father. The next line, "In continuing one sees humiliation," states simply the probable consequence that may result from the subject's continuance in putting off the remedial action. Under the situation in which most actors are engaged in the campaign to heal "Ills inherited from the previous generation" the subject's behavior may evoke negative responses that bring humiliation to him.

The line statement of the fifth yin line, again, returns to the recurring theme of the hexagram; "The fifth line, divided, shows (a son) dealing with the troubles caused by the father. He obtains the praise of using (the fit instrument for his work)" (Legge, 1963:96). The last portion is related to the role that the subject at the second position is supposed to play under the situation. The second yang line is interpreted as representing a subject who is in a corresponding relationship with the "weak" ruler at the fifth position: hence, it represents an official who is entrusted with the task of dealing with the problem at hand on behalf of the ruler. In this context, the subject at the fifth position in turn is figured as one who "obtains the praise of using (the fit instrument for his work)."

The subject at the topmost position is pictured as someone who stands aloof from the ongoing affairs of the time. This idea of his posture distancing himself from those in other sectors of the society is conveyed rather straightforwardly in its line statement which reads, "This one does not concern himself with the affairs of king or feudal lords but works to elevate his own higher pursuits" (Lynn, 1994:252). The image of aloof scholars who separate themselves from worldly affairs and are, instead, in pursuit of loftier spiritual goals is quite a familiar idea among the learned circle of Oriental intellectuals. Intellectuals often considered such self-imposed seclusion to be an ideal way to escape trouble whenever they experience difficult situations as described by Cheng Yi as follows:

> When people of strength and understanding have no assistants, and are in a position where there is nothing to do, this is a situation where wise people and those with leadership qualities do not fit in with the time, so they remain aloof and uninvolved in worldly affairs. (1988:56)

But, why does the *I Ching* view the subject at the sixth position as putting himself in "noble seclusion" as such? Commenting on this line statement, Legge (1963:97) takes note of the fact that the sixth line is a strong (yang) line located at the topmost position outside the hierarchical line of the formal office. At the same time, no line corresponding to it is found under the situation; "Hence, it suggests the idea of one outside the sphere of action, and taking no part in public affairs, but occupied with the culture of himself." Wang Bi's interpretation (Lynn, 1994:252) is not very different from that of Legge.

The hexagram *Ge* (☱☲, Radical Change)

The hexagram *Ge* (Radical Change) represents a situation in which, as suggested by the hexagram name, a radical change takes place. The meaning of the hexagram is derived from its line composition that consists of the upper trigram *Dui* that symbolizes the Lake and the trigram *Li*, a symbol of Fire, which conceives the coexistence of two incompatible elements. Thus, the *Commentary on the Judgments* says of this hexagram: "Radical Change is such that just as Water and Fire try to extinguish each other, so is it when two women live together and find their wills at odds. This we call 'Radical Change'" (Lynn, 1994:444). Wang Bi adds his own commentary to the above as follows:

Whenever it happens that things are incompatible, change consequently arises. The reason that such change arises is due to the incompatibility involved. This is why the text selects images of incompatible things to represent Radical change. (Lynn, 1994:444)

The above passage may remind us of the Marxian notion of contradiction that, as believed by social scientists with Marxist orientations, results in revolutionary change. However, a cursory examination of the line statement of this hexagram would reveal that Radical Change represented by this hexagram is a reversed version of what is meant by Marx; it is not a revolution from below, but from above. This is suggested by the line formation of the hexagram; the upper trigram *Dui* (the Lake, i.e., water) is below the trigram *Li* (Fire) and since water extinguishes fire, the dominant group is the one who brings about a radical change to an old order.[75] But, despite the difference, the hexagram *Ge* shares in an essential aspect of revolutionary change with modern conflict theorists; as *the Hexagrams in the Irregular Order* defines it, "*Ge* [Radical Change] means 'get rid of the old'" (Lynn, 1994:445). Accordingly, this hexagram provides good material through which we can compare how intellectuals of old China and of today understand radical change in society.

Then, let us look at the line statement of the first yang line: it states, "To bind himself tight, this one uses the hide of a brown cow." On this Wang Bi's comment is clear and lucid. He explains, ". . . . First Yang represents someone who makes himself secure inside old, regular ways, as he is incapable of response to change" (Lynn, 1994:446). Of course, when a revolutionary change is attempted from above, there will be people who hold fast to the old order until they are compelled to see the change as an inevitable trend of the time. But, why is it the subject at the bottom position who is conceived as one who shows such a conservative attitude towards radical change? One possibility is that the author(s) of the *I Ching* thought that under the situation represented by the hexagram, the common people would be the most likely to resist the change induced by the ruling elites. There is another possible explanation related to an internal logic of the *I Ching*. The lower trigram has two yang lines and one yin line, and such a line composition could be interpreted to mean that among those subject to change forced upon them from above, the ones at the first and the third positions (yang lines) are most likely to put up strong resistance to the change. To modern social scientists, the first explanation may be more appealing than the latter one because the logic of the *I Ching* based on the yin-yang duality is an idea unfamiliar to them and involves ambiguity in what it actually explains. At any rate, however, the line statements of the second and the third lines seem to be accounted for far better with the latter explanation based on the typical logic of the *I Ching*.

Thus, as might be expected, the subject at the second position represents someone who will go along with the change yet, being in the lower unit, drags his feet until the trend of time makes clearly manifest itself in that direction. Accordingly, the line statement of the second yin line states, "This one falls in with Radical Change only on the day it comes to an end, and if he were to set forth then, it would mean no blame" (Lynn, 1994:446). Commentaries suggest two factors that explain the line statement. One is that the position is occupied by a yin line; someone who complies "appropriately" with what is required of him under the situation is incumbent at that position. The other is found in that he is in a resonant relationship with the fifth yang line, the ruler of the hexagram who leads the campaign to bring about a revolutionary change. Thus, the above two factors explain why the subject at the second position is described as one who is more receptive, if reluctant at first, to the radical change.

The subject at the third position is figured as someone who opposes the change and, therefore, has an inclination to stage rebellious actions against it. The line statement, accordingly, warns him of acting against the inevitable trend of the time and advises him to go along with the change. Let us look at the line statement; "For this one to go out and attack would mean misfortune, and though he were to practice constancy, he would cause danger. Addressing themselves to Radical Change, the three say that they will accede to it; in this he should trust" (Lynn, 194:447). In the above line statement, according to Wang Bi, "the three" refers to those who are at the higher strata represented by the upper trigram *Li*. Then, the latter portion of the line statement suggests quite clearly that it is the dominant group that is leading the radical change; the three position holders represented by the upper trigram are those who "address themselves to Radical Change," who "say that they will accede to it." And, the line statement advises the one at the third position that even if his action to uphold the old order is viewed as correct from a moral standpoint, there will be no chance for him to derive profitable outcomes from putting up resistance under the circumstance. The line statement ends with the verse that "in this he should trust," which means that he should "accede to" the inevitability of the revolution.

As already suggested, the fourth yang line represents one of those components who comes out to promote the radical change. The role that the subject at this position plays under the situation is clearly indicated by its line statement, "Regret disappears, and as this one changes the mandate to rule with sincerity, he has good fortune" (Lynn, 1994:447). He is described as an active agent who is actively involved in the radical change of the old order. But, why is he viewed as having some regret, although it would disappear as time went on? The reason for this is sought again in the logic of the *I Ching* in which the fourth position is viewed as a position with some handicaps. There is a yang line "inappropriately" occupying a yin position, and, as the overall line formation of the hexagram shows, there is no other line in a corresponding relationship with this one. However, it seems to be thought by the author(s) of the *I Ching*, "regret disappears" because, as Wang Bi explains, "this one happens to abide where change may take place and so can act without being charged with obstinacy or basement" (Lynn, 1994:447). In other words, he belongs to the dominant group that, under the situation, is highly motivated to bring about radical change, and, therefore, his action to get involved in the change movement fits with the overall orientation of the group; so "he has good fortune."

A yang line that occupies appropriately a yang place represents the subject at the fifth position. Thus, according to Wang Bi, the subject is interpreted to "be in accord with the disposition of the times": he is depicted as an able leader who undertakes radical change exactly when the time is ripe for it. There is little ambiguity in the line statement, "When the great man does a tiger change, one can trust in the outcome before any divining is done" (Lynn, 1994:448). "Tiger change" is simply another term for a radical change of old institutions: a tiger changes its old coat into a new one "whose patterns [*wen*] shine forth with great brilliance" (Lynn, 1994:451n11).

The sixth yin line entails a rather long line statement: "Whereas the noble man here would do a leopard change, the petty man should radically change his countenance. To set forth result in misfortune, but to stay put and practice constancy would result in good fortune" (Lynn, 1994:448). According to the *Commentary on the Images*, "a leopard change" means a change of one's "pattern [*wen*, meaning 'culture, cultivation']," whereas "to change his countenance" means that "he will follow his sovereign with obedience" (Lynn, 1994:449). This implies that the situation would be utilized differently by the position holder depending upon his personal capacity; if he is an able man, he can accomplish significant changes in his way of living for the better; on the other hand, if he is a petty man, he will change only on the surface and comply with the situation as forced upon him. Or, viewed differently, the subject at this position may have alternative ways of responding to the situation, either he becomes an active part of the changing order or shows only a superficial loyalty to the new order with no serious commitment to it. The line statement continues and warns that the subject should not try to take a lead in promoting the change; it will be sufficient to make only passive reactions to the situation, firmly and in the correct manner, as it unfolds. Why does the *I Ching* judge that the subject at the sixth position is not capable of playing a leading role in carrying out radical change? Regarding this question, note that, according to the interpretation that we have applied so far, the sixth position has to do with the position of intellectuals. It then may be thought that this position carries on a function related to ideology. Now, knowing that ideology provides guiding ideas with which campaigners for radical change set down the goals and the directions of the change, the subject at the sixth position can be thought of as playing a highly significant and active role under the situation. Yet instead of the reasoning above, when the sixth line statement was written, the yin-yang disposition of the line seems to have been a main, if not the main, consideration. The product is as we see it; the subject at the sixth position is advised not to become actively involved in radical change, for it is represented by a yin line and accordingly judged as having weak potential. Why should an "active (yang)" line under the situation of Radical Change not represent the subject at the sixth position instead? This question suggests that since a hexagram has a fixed structure made of a given set of yin or yang lines at respective positions, it imposes a limit on the range of possible meanings. To put this in modern terms, a hexagram may exclude many hypotheses, owing to its line structure, even when such hypotheses seem quite plausible, or even probable.

The hexagram *Zhen* (☳☳ , Quake)

The title name of the hexagram *Zhen* (Quake) is taken from the trigram *Zhen* that makes up the lower and the upper trigrams of this hexagram. Legge (1963:174) points out that the attribute of the hexagram represented symbolically with "quake" or "thunder" "is indicative of movement (such as insurrection or revolution) taking place in a society or in a kingdom." However, considering the *Judgment* of the hexagram that says "If Quake can startle at one hundred *li*, one will not lose control over the ladle [*bi*] and the fragrant wine [*chang*]" (Lynn, 1994:460), the hexagram does not suggest a revolutionary situation of the radical sort as suggested by Legge. According to Wang Bi, the control over the ladle and the fragrant wine signifies "the offering up of sacrificial bounty in the ancestral temple [the prerogative of state power and sovereignty]" (Lynn, 1994:460). Then, the "shaking up" movement indicated by the hexagram should be interpreted as referring to a movement of a less radical kind that occurs within the framework of an existing order to strengthen rather than to destroy it.

Now, who is chiefly responsible for carrying out the movement indicated by the hexagram *Zhen*? Wilhelm points out that "the line at the beginning" should be considered the ruler of the hexagram, implying that "the strong line at the beginning (is) initiating movement from below" (1967:647). Cheng Yi, agreeing on this point, says "the first yang is the thundermaker" (1988:173). Given this interpretation, the line statement as translated by Lynn and Wang Bi's appended commentary render a reading somewhat incongruent with the above meaning as attributed to the first line. Cleary's translation, which seems to match closely with the given interpretation, therefore, is quoted here: "When thunder comes there is fright, afterward laughter, which is fortunate" (Cheng Yi, 1988:173). Concerning this line statement, Lee explains that in order to bring about a profound reform in a lethargic society one has to shake it up so hard that everybody feels frightened or shocked (1997[II]:182). It is exactly in this sense that the first yang line is called "the thundermaker." Yet, why is it said that there will be laughter afterward? The *Commentary on the Images* comes up with an answer to this question: "For later he has constant rules to live by" (Lynn, 1994:461). Putting the above statement into words more familiar to modern social scientists, this hexagram outlines a situation in which the people stage a strong reform or protest movement and thereby succeed in improving the system. Coser (1956), known for his functional theory of social conflict, might characterize this as a function of conflict.

Meanwhile, what is the situation of the second position holder when a hard-hitting reform movement staged by the people down below breaks out arousing "fear" as if a "Quake" strikes? The line statement given to this line can be considered quite exceptional in the sense that there are only a few cases among hexagrams that the second position holder is judged to fall in an extremely dangerous situation as told here in this hexagram. Let us look at what the line statement says about the position holder here: "When Quake comes, there is danger, and this one, alas, loses his cowries. He might climb nine hills, but one need not pursue him, for in seven days he will be taken" (Lynn, 1994:462). Although the above line statement is heavy in symbolism, the meaning can be clearly comprehended with little difficulty. As the purge movement from below goes on, officials who have been in close touch with the people below would be the most directly affected by it, and there will be no way to escape the severe penalties to be inflicted upon them. As Wang Bi comments on this line, "such a one finds himself in danger, loses his wealth and goods, and forfeits the place where he is positioned" (Lynn, 1994:462).

Compared to the second position, the third position is somehow less seriously affected by the purge campaign. Perhaps, since the ongoing movement is not geared toward the total overhaul of the entire ruling structure, one at the leadership position would be blamed less and thus condemned less than those engaging in administrative works. As we will see later, this explanation also seems to draw support from the line statement of the fifth position, another leadership position. At any rate, the subject represented by the third yin line is described also as being affected by the fearful situation that makes him "tremble." But, the line statement involves a less ominous prognosis than that of the second position: "The third line, divided, shows its subject distraught amid the startling movements going on. If those movements excite him to (right) action, there will be no mistake" (Legge, 1963: 173).[76] Regarding the above line statement, notice first that a yin line is incumbent at the third position which is expected to be occupied by a yang (leadership) position. This incongruity implies that present in this position are people who do not act as expected of the occupants of the position (Cheng Yi, 1988:174). Thus, it is in the context of the above idea that the line statement is understood to involve a warning for the subject at the position: the storm will not simply pass away without leaving serious damage unless he brings reformation to himself in this turbulent period.

The line statement of the fourth yang line is short: "Quake comes, so this one gets mired" (Lynn, 1994:463). Although some may wonder how Wang Bi could read a rather complex group situation out of the short line statement above, his commentary itself involves an interesting perspective:

> Fourth Yang is located in the midst of the yin and, finding itself as it does here at a time fraught with fear, it becomes the ruler of all the yin lines. As such, one here should bravely assert himself in order to bring security to all. But if such a one were to suffer Quake himself [i.e., succumb to fear], he would fall into difficulties. If one were to tread

this path of unrighteousness and fail to ward off fear and instead make others provide for his own security, his virtue would "never shine forth." (Lynn, 1994:463)

Since the sweeping reform movement from below may affect everyone in the officialdom, they will look for someone who "will bring security" to them. Wang Bi sees the subject at the fourth position as the only yang line "located in the midst of the yin" and, therefore, he will be looked to as the one who can provide protection for others during the "Quake." However, for some reason that cannot be inferred from either the line structure of the hexagram or any commentary, the line statement says in effect that, given the condition determined by the situation, any effort to protect the existing interests of those in office would fail. Thus, the line statement, "Quake comes, so this one gets mired," can be understood more clearly.

Naturally, the ongoing movement will make the subject at the fifth position, the top leadership position, feel extremely uneasy obviously because as the situation develops, it may pose a threat to both his position and the system itself. This uneasy situation is described in the line statement as follows: "The fifth line, divided, shows its subject going and coming amidst the startling movements (of the time) and always in peril . . . ." Yet, the line statement continues, "but, perhaps he will not incur loss, and find business (which he can accomplish)" (Legge, 1963:174).[77] Here we may be reminded that the situation indicated by the hexagram *Zhen* is not a radical one that aims at overthrowing the entire system or the top leader. Therefore, the subject at the fifth position will weather the situation safely with little "loss." And, the line statement adds the comment that "he will . . . . find business." Is this to suggest that the subject in the top leadership position now will take actions to introduce reforms to his government? Although such an interpretation certainly makes some sense, we may be reading too much into the short passage that involves no further account than that stated in the line statement.

The last position accompanies a fairly long line statement: "Quake comes, so this one is anxious and distraught, his gaze shifty and unfocused. To set forth would mean misfortune. If Quake were not to reach one's own person but only that of one's neighbor, he would be without blame. Even those who joined in marriage here will have words" (Lynn, 1994:464). Commenting on this line statement, Legge expresses doubt that any meaningful interpretation can be made (1963:176). According to him, "(he does) not see anything in the figure to indicate this final symbolism," although "the writer (of the *I Ching*), probably, had a case in his mind, which it suited." However, as far as I see in this instance, this is taking an overly cautious approach in interpreting the *I Ching*. In this hexagram, let us suppose that all the line elements except the first yang line constitute what may be called the Establishment, the target of a reform movement under the situation. Perhaps, "Quake" may not touch directly the one at the top position because he does not hold a formal position; he may not share the responsibility for the ills of the day with others. Still, the ongoing situation in which one is watching "neighbors" and "relatives" being driven into difficulties would not be a comfortable one even to the subject of this position; after all, he is one of the "noble" ones. This, I think, seems to be the main idea concerning the personal situation confronted by the subject of the sixth position, if too vaguely alluded to in symbolism by its line statement.

The hexagram *Sun* (☴, Compliance)

The hexagram *Sun* represents a situation whose meaning contrasts with the hexagram *Zhen* in a couple of important aspects. But, before we go into these aspects, let us examine first what kind of specific implications its name "Compliance" involves in describing the unique characteristic of a social situation. Wilhelm adds to this hexagram's main title name "the Gentle" two supplementary titles, "Penetrating" and "Wind" (1967:679). Combining the above words associated with the hexagram name, the main idea of the situation represented by the hexagram may now be expressed with a longer title, "Compliance like the grass bending before the penetrating wind."[78] Since this title is made up of symbolic words referring to natural objects and not very informative, I again would like to add a more substantive reference as follows: "(people) complying with the penetrating influence of the government exercised 'to remedy what is wrong with (them)'." Compared to the previous hexagram *Zhen*, two aspects can be noticed from this long, expository title for the hexagram *Sun*. One is that under the situation indicated by the hexagram, some actions are taken from above, not from below as with the case for the hexagram *Zhen*, to introduce reforms to the system. The other is that the people who are subject to reform actions are viewed as having no choice but to comply with them. But, why are the people viewed as being so compliant with it? The *Commentary of the Images* gives a clue to answer this question. It reads, "Wind following wind: this constitutes the image of

Compliance. In the same way, the noble man reiterates commands and has endeavors carried out" (Lynn, 1994:502). That is, since both the upper and lower trigrams that make up the hexagram *Sun* are characterized by "wind," a natural symbol used to characterize a property of things represented by the trigram *Sun*, the structure of the hexagram is understood as featuring an image of "wind following wind." Wind is suggestive of the moral virtue or the type of action orientation, "Compliance." This is the way that the logic (or, to say more accurately, the peculiar mode of associative reasoning) of the *I Ching* operates to construct the situational meaning of the hexagram *Sun*. Despite the logical problem related to the way in which the overall meaning of the situation is attributed to the hexagram, however, the idea of the situation itself as described by the *I Ching* seems to depict a real situation. After all, we can easily imagine a situation in which the leader of a troubled society comes forward to remedy the ills of the society and the people, having little power potential to refuse or resist, have no choice but to go along with the reform campaign from above.

Although it is not clearly explained from the line structure of the hexagram, the line statements give us a clear indication that the fifth yang line is the single ruler of the hexagram. He is designated as the dominant figure who leads the campaign suggested by the hexagram. Thus, the line statement of the fifth yang line provides us with the most important clue concerning the situational meaning of this hexagram. The line statement itself is somewhat vague:

> Constancy here means good fortune. Regret vanishes, and nothing fails to be fitting. Whereas nothing good here happens at the start, things end well. If there be three days before a new law is issued and three days after a new law is issued, there will be good fortune. (Lynn, 1994:504)

This rather vague statement is supplemented with a clearer and more meaningful interpretation by Wang Bi's commentary. First, concerning what is implied by the latter portion of the passage, Wang Bi offers his reading as follows:

> In rectifying and delivering the people, one must not be too sudden. If the common folk have been firmly entrenched in error for a long time, correction must not be attempted precipitously. This is why one should issue a new law three days before it goes into effect, wait three days after it is issued, and then issue it again. Only then will the punishment involved not provoke blame and resentment. (Lynn, 1994:505)

Wang Bi's main point emphasizes the need for careful deliberations in formulating and executing reform measures planned and promoted by the subject at the fifth position. For the earlier portion of the line statement, "Whereas nothing good here happens at the start, things end well," Wang Bi also gives a seemingly meaningful interpretation, although his interpretation may give the impression that he reads too much into the short passage. It seems to me that there will be no serious lack in our understanding of the line statement even if the passage is read simply as it says: whereas this kind of reformation from above brings "nothing good at the start," it will result in a desirable outcome at the end. That is, although the reformation undertaken by the top leadership under the situation would bring about beneficial outcomes for the kingdom (or for any social organization as referred to by the given hexagram), it has to start with pains and complaints of those affected by it.

Then, how does the *I Ching* describe the conditions of those who are subject to the "hard corrective measures" (Wang Bi, in Lynn, 1994:505) undertaken by the top leadership? Let us go over the line statements one by one starting from the bottom line. The line statement of the first yin line states, "This one now advances, now retreats, so the constancy of the warrior would be found fitting" (Lynn, 1994:502). Wang Bi interprets this line statement as describing "someone who is unable to obey orders" (Lynn, 1994:502). In other words, the subject at the first position would respond to the corrective measures issued from above in such an indecisive manner as to require a specific disciplinary action.

The second yang line accompanies a line statement that involves highly ambiguous symbolism. Consequently, this single line of narration has yielded many different interpretations. Under this kind of a situation in which there are widely open possibilities for reading "intended" meaning into a line statement, all we can do is to choose or invent one that can be judged as the most "meaningful" interpretation. Then, first, let us read the line statement; "This one practices Compliance as if he were beneath a bed, but if he were to use it in respect to invokers and shamans on a large scale, there should be good fortune and no blame" (Lynn, 1994:503). Both Cheng Yi (1988:194) and Wang Bi (1994:503) interpret the line "Compliance as if he were beneath a bed" as symbolizing one's posture showing "an extreme degree of servile Compliance," with which I find no particular reason to disagree. However, understood this way, this portion of the line statement seems to fit better with what Wilhelm (1967:682) reads out of the portion coming next, the section that includes words about "invokers and shamans." According to Wilhelm, "priests (and magicians) (i.e., invokers and shamans) are intermediaries between men and gods." Their role is to spread the commands of gods to men. It is exactly in this sense that the line statement assigns the subject at the second position an intermediary role that can be compared to invokers and shamans. To put it in Wilhelm's own words, "By submitting to the strong ruler of the hexagram, who is of like kind, the line is able to aid the ruler in spreading his commands." As was pointed out already, the strong ruler under this situation refers to the subject at the fifth position. Interpreted this way, the line statement of the second line pictures its subject as one who faithfully carries out orders from the top leadership to bring needed reforms to realization.

The line statement for the third yang line presents a mode of adaptive behavior that is dramatically opposed to the one at the second position. The position holder is described as one who complies, grudgingly, with the situation, scowling with unhappiness. The line statement itself states straightforwardly that the subject at this position "practices Compliance" with discontent; "This one practices Compliance with a scowl, which means regret" (Lynn, 1994:503). Of course, under the type of situation indicated by the hexagram *Sun*, there would be always people who felt forced into a situation requiring Compliance, thus creating unhappiness. However, as was the case with the two lower positions, why the subject at this particular position is said to be in a forced, thus unhappy compliant situation is not immediately clear from the line-up of yang and yin lines in the hexagram. One thing that does seem clear is that the line statements of the three lines in the lower trigram *Sun* describe respectively different modes of compliant behavior. Yet neither the *I Ching* nor any later commentary seems to provide sufficiently reasonable accounts with which to explain why certain modes of compliant behavior are attributed respectively to given subjects at specific positions.

The short line statement of the fourth yin line reads, "This one's regret vanishes, for in hunting he catches the three categories" (Lynn, 1994:503-504), and again commentators' interpretations differ in detail. Nevertheless, they converge on the interpretation that the fourth position is viewed as ministers who are placed in the somewhat difficult situation of being sandwiched between a strong ruler and strong subordinates (represented by the second and the third yang lines). But, such a regretful situation will pass because the fourth yin line is "appropriately" occupied. In other words, loyal ministers at the fourth position who function properly and well with their roles in assisting the strong ruler at the fifth position will work out an effective partnership with the latter to achieve the task implied by the hexagram.

Meanwhile, the subject at the sixth, top position is pictured as displaying the same characteristic as that of the second yang line, an excessive Compliance. However, although both the position holders are equally described as "practicing Compliance as if [they] were beneath a bed," the fate of the one at the top position is judged to be far worse than the one at the second position. "This one . . . . loses the axe that he uses," a gloomy prognosis for the position holder at this position. According to Wang Bi, to lose the axe means that one "loses the means to cut [i.e., make decisions, pass judgments]" (Lynn, 1994:505). Thus, the line statement is interpreted to say that an extreme degree of Compliance drives the subject at the top position into a state of impotence so that he is unable to make sensible judgments on his own. Of course, a question arises here; considering that both the subjects at the second and the top positions are equally characterized by their excessive Compliance, what brings about such a big difference between them in their behavioral outcomes? The only possible factor that can explain the difference is a variable associated with each of their positions in the hexagram. Yet, regarding this specific variable, no explanatory account that is convincing enough to the eyes of social scientists of today seems to be found in either the text or any later commentary.

Summary of theoretical and empirical propositions

1) There are various forces or ways with which changes are brought about in a society. In the hexagram *Zhen*, the change movement is initiated and carried out from below by the subject at the first position, the common people. In the hexagrams *Ge* and *Sun*, the ruling group, especially the one at the top leadership, is described to be those who lead change movements. The situation represented by the hexagram *Gu* differs still from the above three situations in that the movement to redress problems inherited from previous generations is featured as a prevailing trend of the time. The theoretical significance of the *I Ching's* view of the phenomena of social change thus is found in that the ways in which social change takes place are viewed to differ from situation to situation.

2) Depending upon position and situationally determined characteristics, people will produce different responses when subject to a situation in which change takes place. For instance,

when a radical change is carried out from above, some people will try to hold fast to the status quo while others may go along, if reluctantly, with the change forced upon them. In this aspect, the *I Ching* seems to present an interesting typology on the possible modes of behavior that people exhibit in response to social change.

3) In many situations, the subject at the third position can be regarded as occupying an ambivalent position in that it performs a leadership function but, at the same time, is subject to the command of the upper group. For this reason, a strong leadership exercised by the subject at this position may give rise to some tension in his relationship with the upper echelon. Thus, the *I Ching* regards this position by nature as an unstable one, which means that its subject in most situations would find it hard to perform his double roles as both leader and subordinate with the balance required of his position.

4) Incompatibility (contradiction) between component elements of a society will be brought to a resolution through a revolutionary change. In other words, a social reintegration is achieved through introducing radical change to existing institutions that malfunction due to an incompatibility between component parts.

5) If people shake up the system hard enough by staging a strong reform or protest movement and the condition is right for such a movement, as is indicated by the hexagram *Zhen*, they will succeed in improving the system. In this sense, if such situation as indicated by the hexagram *Zhen* should occur, we may say, the movement has a positive function for those who shook up the society by displaying their discontent with it.

6) Once people have been accustomed to old institutions for a long time, an effort to bring about sudden changes in their way of life will likely result in undesirable outcomes. Under the situation as such, reforms have to be carefully planned and executed prudently, allowing sufficient time.

8) Character Situations: Situations that Are Composed of Types of People with Certain Kinds of Behavioral or Attitudinal Orientations

"Character situations" as referred to here are situations whose characteristics are determined by the presence of people with certain types of behavioral or attitudinal orientations. It is not unfamiliar, even in modern social sciences, that social scientists attempt to characterize a situation of an organization or, more generally, social situations, with the personality types of individuals whose specific behavioral or attitudinal orientations render distinctive characteristics to the social unit to which they belong. For example, the term "organization man" (Whyte, Jr., 1956) refers to a type of person who identifies the goals in his personal life solely with the goals imposed by the organization to which he belongs. At the same time, it is used as a concept to explain the situation of modern society in which big organizations live on the blind loyalty and devotion of their members. Included in this category are situations represented by five hexagrams. Of these five hexagrams, the three hexagrams *Bi*, *Sheng*, and *Dui* describe situations of social units that are composed of types of people who seek for, respectively, elegant living, achievements or upward mobility, and satisfaction. The hexagram *Wuwang* features a situation in which the social unit represented by the hexagram is composed of people whose conduct does not violate appropriate normative standards and who commit no error in morality. The situation represented by the hexagram *Kun* is descriptive of a social unit that consists of two categories of people who either succumb to or win over a difficult situation. While examining the situations to be dealt with in this section we will note one distinctive perspective of the *I Ching* that is distinguished from modern social theories couched upon ideas of prevailing personality types that a dominant social trend of a certain period has produced. It is probably due to the unique conceptual framework of the *I Ching* that whatever behavioral or attitudinal orientations individuals are likely to manifest, their resulting outcomes would have to be examined in relation to the social positions that the individuals occupy. We may say that as far as the *I Ching* is concerned, individuals' actions are inseparable from both the structural and situational contexts of people in respective positions under a given situation. Therefore, although people under a given situation may share a certain common trait in the way they behave, there will be differences in individual situations relative to the structural and situational contexts of the actors.

Individuals' behavioral and attitudinal orientations and their outcomes therefore would be position- and situation-specific as we can see in the following five hexagrams.

1) The hexagram *Bi* (☰☷, Elegance) (Hexagram No. 22)

2) The hexagram *Wuwang* (☰☳, No Errancy) (Hexagram No. 25)

3) The hexagram *Sheng* (☷☴, Climbing) (Hexagram No. 46)

4) The hexagram *Kun* (☱☵, Impasse) (Hexagram No. 47)

5) The hexagram *Dui* (☱☱, Joy) (Hexagram No. 58)

The hexagram *Bi* (☰☷, Elegance)

Before we examine the hexagram *Bi* (Elegance), readers may need some background information on the meanings that the term *Bi* (Elegance) has in the Chinese intellectual tradition. In Confucian ethics, human culture is viewed as consisting of two essential aspects, outer form and inner substance. In its outer form, human culture can be elaborated, refined, and made rich, presumptuous, or elegant. Culture, in this aspect, can be expressed with a lack of internal motive that should constitute the true substance of human morality, considered more important than outer behavior expressed in ritual forms. It is exactly in this context that Confucius says, "If a man be without the virtues proper to humanity (love), what has he to do with the rites of propriety? If a man be without the virtues proper to humanity, what has to do with music?" (Confucian *Analects* (IV, 3), in Legge, 1971:155). "The rites of propriety" or "music" refers to the ritualistic forms of human culture whereas "the virtues proper to humanity (love)" refers to the moral substance of human behavior that man, if he truly wants to be a moral being, is required to have in dealing with other human beings. "Elegance" as referred to by the hexagram *Bi* is to denote specifically an esthetic property of human culture as it is expressed in ritualistic behaviors or ways of livings with refined tastes. The hexagram name "Elegance" is then interpreted to indicate a situation in which the people involved are mainly concerned about pursuing elegance or sustaining an "elegant culture" in the sense said above and in accordance with their specific position and capacity.

The line statement of the first yang line states, "He furnishes his toes with Elegance, discards carriage, and goes on foot" (Lynn, 1994:274). Oftentimes the subject at the first position is described with such bodily symbols as the feet or toes to signify his low status in the hierarchical relationship represented by the hexagram. Thus, the line statement can be interpreted as saying that its subject is doing what he can do to make his humble life elegant within the bound of his limited capacity. The remaining line, stating "discards carriage, and goes on foot," is given a moralistic interpretation by most commentators and the *Commentary on the Images*; the subject is viewed to represent someone who exercises moral consciousness and therefore "is content to go on foot" to do "the righteous thing" (Wang Bi, in Lynn, 1994:275; c.f., Legge, 1963:104; Wilhelm, 1967:497). But, to offer my own interpretation, I rather take a simpler and more logical one: he makes his toes (humble self) elegant and goes on foot to show off his toes furnished with elegant decorations. Interpreted in this way, the line statement simply describes its subject as pursuing elegant life styles in conformity with the dominant trend of the time.

The line statement of the second yin line, "He uses his cheek whiskers to provide Elegance" (Lynn, 1994:275), can be understood to convey essentially the same meaning as the first yang line. This one also represents someone who is doing what he can to make his life elegant. The only difference between the two line statements is found in that the subject at the second position makes his beard elegant whereas the one at the first position does the same to his toes. This difference in the locations of bodily symbols will be understood to denote in symbolism the difference in life styles of the subjects at the two positions in accordance with their statuses. Interpretations of most commentators on the line statement of the second line, however, differ radically from the one offered above. Their interpretations may be more authentic, for they have been regarded as such in the established tradition of the *I Ching*. Thus, although their interpretation seems too fanciful to make any sense to me, I should be obliged to give a brief presentation of it. According to the interpretation agreed upon by most commentators, the subjects at the second and the third positions, having found no proper partner elsewhere, form a mutually dependent relationship; thus, "cheek whiskers" symbolizes such relationship that "they (cheek whiskers) cling to that which is above them [the face] (referring to the subject at the third position)" (Lynn, 1994:275). Interpreted in this way, the line statement will be read as saying, "He uses his whiskers to make the face (i.e., the one above him) elegant"; the subject at the second position is interpreted to represent someone who performs service to make his superior above him elegant. Now, with this interpretation, actors under the situation are divided into two kinds, into those who make others elegant and those who are made elegant by others. From this, I cannot derive any meaningful idea related to social situations.

The line statement of the third yang line is descriptive of a situation that fits the overall context of the situation where the pursuit of refined livings is the dominant mood of the time. It reads, "Such consummate Elegance here, such perfect luster, so perpetual constancy means good fortune" (Lynn, 1994:275). Among those who are in the formal power structure, the third line is the only subject represented by a yang line so, as Wang Bi points out, "no one should encroach upon him" (Lynn, 1994:275). Thus, under this situation, he is understood to be the most influential one surpassing all others so that he can make the most out of the time; he is the one who will enjoy "such consummate Elegance, such perfect luster." The advice, "so perpetual constancy (constant moral rectitude) means good fortune," is typical of the *I Ching* in that it is given generally to anyone who is in a highly advantageous position.

The line statement of the fourth yin line is stated with symbolism whose intended meaning is quite difficult to grasp. Accordingly, commentators interpret it differently and, therefore, render different versions of translation.[79] Offering my own translation, I would rather take a much simpler and clearer route than any existing version: "Elegance or simplicity? If this one should remain as plain (white) as a white horse, (people will come to him) not as robbers but for a matrimonial alliance." The subject finds himself in a dilemma over whether to pursue elegant or simple living. The source of the dilemma is not clear. Commentators explain that it has to do with a strong power that the subject at the third position has over the weak subject at the fourth position under this situation (Legge, 1963:105, Wang Bi, in Lynn, 1994:276). I personally see no obvious reason against this explanation. At any rate, the line statement interpreted as above involves advice that sounds quite reasonable in the sense that when a person is in a disadvantageous position, he is unable to defend himself if his ostentatiously ornate style of living attracts hostility from others.

The fifth yin line represents "the ruler of the *Bi* [Elegance] hexagram," so it "represents the acme of decorative beauty" (Lynn, 1994:276). Under the situation in which the pursuit of elegant living prevails as the dominant mood of the time, the subject at the fifth position can enjoy much of the benefit endowed by the time. Thus, the line statement describes its subject as one who enjoys an extravagantly decorated lifestyle: "This one is Elegance as from a hillside garden, so bundles of silk increase to great number." Of this line statement, Wang Bi explains, "here one's application of adornment is like that of a garden to a hillside, and nothing can reach greater than this." Here, the *I Ching* seems to be concerned about possible harmful effects resulting from this lifestyle. The line statement thereby adds the advice: "If one is sparing, in the end, there will be good fortune" (Lynn, 1994:276-7).

The line statement of the sixth yang line seems to have been written in the same spirit as the fifth line. It states: "Here one turns Elegance into plainness, so there will be no blame" (Lynn, 1994:277). The moral view that elegant living, decorated with rich trappings, always has to be moderated with a certain measure of simplicity or plainness is voiced repeatedly throughout the line statements of all the lines in the upper trigram. One interesting point is that this emphasis on moderation, as some readers may have noticed already, is found also in many other hexagrams, and, in this sense, it may be viewed as constituting one of the primary value orientations held by the *I Ching*.

The hexagram *Wuwang* (☰/☳, No Errancy)

The hexagram *Wuwang* consists of the trigram *Qian* and the trigram *Zhen*. *Qian*, the upper trigram, is said to represent things or characteristics that can be symbolized by Heaven, and *Zhen*, the lower trigram, by Thunder. By the fact that both the hexagrams carry symbols related to heavenly beings or events, the hexagram is given a positive attribute that is free of imperfections or errors. Thus, all the position holders under this situation are said to behave with no error.

The most distinctive feature of this hexagram may be found in that although all the position holders in the group represented by the hexagram are said to act with no breach of moral standards, the situation is not necessarily experienced as a happy one by every one. According to Wilhelm (1967:509), this hexagram has two ruler lines, the one at the bottom position and the other at the fifth position. The rulership of the first yang line is indicated by the fact that there is no other yang line, except this one, in the lower trigram. Thus, it is interpreted that there is no one who can exercise a controlling power over the first position in the subordinate group. It is probably for this reason that a fairly favorable judgment is rendered to the subject occupying the first position. Its line statement states, "If one has No Errancy here, to set out will result in good fortune" (Lynn, 1994:295). In other words, as long as the subject at the position keeps step with the moral ethos that is dictated by the situation, he will have a favorable outcome. An interesting thing is that a somewhat less favorable judgment of the situation is given to the subject at the fifth position, the other position holder occupying a rulership position in the hexagram. Its line statement reads, "If an illness strikes the one who practices No Errancy here, let him not resort to medicine, for then there will be joy" (Lynn, 1994:296). The above line statement may be interpreted to say two things. First, some problem in governing a country or an organization may occur although the leader makes no mistake in his management of the government. Second, this line statement contains the advice that he should not resort to extraordinary measures ("medicine") to deal with the problem if it should arise under the situation. Because the illness (of the government) is not of his own making, "it will pass of itself" (Wilhelm, 1967:513).[80] Here we can raise a question; what specific kind of problem in governing the country can possibly occur under this situation in which all the people involved are said to practice "No Errancy"? Neither the *I Ching* nor any later commentary offers any clue to answer this question.

The line statement of the second yin line highlights the position holder's faithful observance of perfectly compliant and modest behavior.[81] This is a fairly typical characterization of the second position whenever the second position holder is judged to possess suitable characteristics that are required of him occupying that position. A favorable judgment ("good fortune") on his personal situation can be understood in the same context. That is, since he acts appropriately according to what is required of his formal position under the situation indicated by the hexagram, it is judged that nothing harmful to his personal well-being will happen.

The situation for the third yin line, however, differs from the second yin line. The meaning of its line statement seems to be expressed most clearly by Legge's translation, which reads as follows: "The third line, divided, shows calamity happening to one who is free from insincerity; — as in the case of an ox that has been tied up. A passer by finds it (and carries it off), while the people in the neighborhood have the calamity (of being accused and apprehended)" (1963:110-111). The line statement states a simple truth in life: even if one commits no erroneous conduct, he, being the leader at the lower echelon, may be blamed for an outcome that harms his community. Of course, undesirable outcomes may sometimes result although no one commits wrongdoing, and, should such an event occur, the leader may be accused of having caused it even though he didn't. An interesting fact is that, in this hexagram, the two leadership position holders of the lower echelon and the upper echelon are warned of possible unintended, yet undesirable consequences that may happen to them despite their faithful observance of correct normative standards. This, I think, is a possibility that can happen often in reality. However, as I already pointed out, a question similar to that which was raised with respect to the fifth yang line can also be raised here concerning specific conditions or reasons for which events unintended by involved actors can occur under this specific situation.

The line statement of the fourth yang line is short: "If one can practice constancy here, he will be without blame" (Lynn, 1994:296). Commentators offer various explanations on this line statement. Yet, none seems to square well with the meaning of the situation as a whole and the positional characteristics of the line under the situation. On the other hand, the line statement of the top, sixth yang line is a bit clearer in what it tries to say. It states, "If one were to act here in No Errancy, it would mean disaster, as there is nothing at all fitting here" (Lynn, 1994:297). This line statement contains a warning against taking actions of any sort by the one at the top position, for there is no way for him to avoid committing errancy under this situation of No Errancy. To put this into sociological terms, the structural composition of the situation as a whole leaves no room for the subject at the top position to play the active role indicated by his action orientation as represented by a yang line. Therefore, he has to refrain from playing any active role under the situation unless he dares to bear gravely negative consequences. Why does the *I Ching* make an unfavorable judgment on this one? Neither the *I Ching* nor any commentary is particularly clear about the reason. It can be only guessed that it is probably because, as was the case for the top yang line of the hexagram *Qian*, the sixth yang line placed at the top of the hexagram represents one who is in the most honored position, yet lacks an official position with formally endowed power. Being in such an ambivalent position, the subject will face a particularly difficult situation where other actors in formal offices exercise power effectively over the action field as indicated by the upper trigram *Qian*. With this, notice that two strong lines are incumbent at the fourth and the fifth lines. At any rate, as far as I see it, the idea that there can be a situation where an actor is unable to find

Hexagrams: Types of Social Situations   249

any suitable role due to a specific attribute associated with his position and action orientation is an interesting one. A situation in which an actor finds himself being surrounded by "nothing at all fitting" to his action may be considered as a very special kind of alienation, impling a complete breakdown in social relationships.

The hexagram *Sheng* (☷☴, Climbing)

Now, the hexagram *Sheng*, having a structural formation inverse to the above hexagram *Wuwang*, may be thought to involve characteristics directly opposite to the latter. But, contrary to this expectation, the situational meaning of the hexagram *Sheng* is derived from a unique perspective clearly distinguished from that applied to the hexagram *Wuwang*. The meaning of the hexagram signifying the "Climbing (growing)" situation seems to have been derived from a corresponding relationship that is thought to exist between the natural phenomena and the human world. The *Commentary on the Images* explains how the meaning of the hexagram is determined in terms of the characteristics of its component trigrams: "Within the Earth grows the Trees: this is the image of Climbing. In the same way, the noble man lets virtue his guide and little by little becomes lofty and great" (Lynn, 1994:424). Some of us may remember that, of the two trigrams making up this hexagram, the upper trigram *Kun* and the lower trigram *Sun* are represented by many symbolic images. And, the Earth is one of such symbols that are used to represent the properties of the tirgram *Kun* and the Trees for the trigram *Sun*. Since the hexagram *Sheng* consists of the trigram *Kun* above and the trigram *Sun* below, it carries an image of the Trees growing up under the Earth. This imagery then by analogy is carried over to the human situation, thus comes to signify a social situation in which all involved individuals are propelled by strong propensities to grow larger (or, to put it in modern terms, make achievements or upward mobility). Indicated here, therefore, is a group or society that, for some reason that can not be clearly understood from the text accounts, is charged with a shared mentality or a commonly held, strong motivation to "become lofty and great." However, as our discussion continues to examine the line statements, we will find two more specific aspects that characterize this situation. One is that although people involved in the situation share a general characteristic as determined by the overall situational trend, the actual chances of "Climbing (growth)" differ from one actor to another depending upon each one's position relative to others. The other is that the situation as figured out with the line formation of the hexagram works more favorably for the "Climbing" of the people in the lower echelon. It is not unusual situations in the *I Ching* that people at lower levels have more power, or better, more gainful or securer life conditions than ones at higher levels. This hexagram depicts this type of situation with an inverse structure that favors people at the lower strata.

Now, having in mind the above stated aspects of this hexagram, let us turn to the individual line statements. The line statement of the first yin line states, "It is right that this one climbs, and he shall have great good fortune" (Lynn, 1994:425). The *Commentary on the Images* supplements a reason for which one's situation at the first position is judged as such: "for this is the result of combining one's will with those above" (Lynn, 1994:425). The subordinate group represented by the trigram *Sun* is described as possessing the active wills to do Climbing. Thus, as one of the members of the group, it is said that the subject at the first position is also "combining (his) will" with the others (those at the second and the third positions) to accomplish laudable things of any sort.[82]

The second yang line is also interpreted to be in an advantageous position regarding his potential to accomplish his aims under the situation, i.e., to do the Climbing. However, at the same time, the *I Ching* seems to notice that the active action orientation of the position holder pushing forward with a strong will to Climb (to make achievements) does not fit well with the formal function expected of the position. The line statement of the second yang line, "If one is sincere, it would be fitting to perform a *yue* sacrifice here. Such a one will be without blame" (Lynn, 1994:425), can be understood in this context. That is, although he is entrusted with some measure of autonomy to do things on his own initiative owing to the advantage of the situation, he is advised to keep a low profile as the position itself may call for such modesty. Cheng Yi compares the position of the second yang line under this situation to that of "strong ministers working for weak rulers" who, due to their powerful position, "have invariably used pretense and outward show" "since ancient times." And, he continues, the subject at the second position is, therefore, advised "not to use embellishment but to communicate with those above through sincerity alone" (1988:154) so that he can remain blameless.

The line statement for the third yang line simply states that "This one climbs an empty city" (Lynn, 1994:425). An empty city means a city that does not put up resistance to fend off outsiders. Thus, Wilhelm (1967:622) offers, the line statement says that the subject at the third position will meet with no obstacle to stop his Climbing or "progress." This open opportunity to Climb or progress is explained by the fact that whereas the third yang line indicates the presence of strong leadership at that position, the upper group represented by the upper trigram *Kun*, "as though empty and open" (Wilhelm, 1967:622), is shown as a weak unit with no strong controlling power. Then what would people at the high echelon but with weak power do when they saw their subordinates eagerly engaging in progressive activities that press forward? The line statement of the fourth yin line offers an answer to this question. It says, "The function of the king succeeded at Mount Qi. Auspicious, no error" (Cheng Yi, 1998:154).[83] Since the line statement above involves a reference to a historical event in ancient China, Cheng Yi's commentary on this would help our understanding:

> In ancient times, when King Wen [ca. 1100 B.C.E.] was living at the foot of Mount Qi, he obeyed the emperor above, yet wanted to get him to embody the Way; he went along with the wise people in the land, yet he made them rise and advance. He himself was yielding and docile, modest and respectful, never out of place. Such was his consummate virtue — the kingship of the Zhou dynasty [ca. twelfth-third centuries B.C.E.] succeeded by applying this. If people in the position of the fourth line here can do this, they will succeed auspiciously without error. (1988:154)

Cheng Yi's main point in the above passage is to emphasize a situationally imposed condition where the best behavioral strategy for the subject at the fourth position would be accommodation. This interpretation is supported by Wang Bi who comments on this line as follows: "The assemblage at Mount Qi was such that he [King Tai] complied with the innate tendency of the situation and accommodated himself to all without exception" (Lynn, 1994:426).[84] The situation allows no room for the subject at the fourth position to do his own Climbing; all he can do is accommodate with grace the wills of others.

Compared with the one at the fourth position, the subject at the fifth position is seen to be in a better situation. The line statement is interpreted in two different ways. In Lynn's text (and, similarly in Wilhelm's text), it is translated as "Constancy results in good fortune, for this one has climbed in stages" (1994:426). In Legge's and others' texts (Cheng Yi, 1988:155; Kim, 1997:355; Lee, 1997[II]:137; Legge, 1963:160), the latter portion of the line statement is translated as "he ascends the stairs." Regardless of how the literal meaning of this sentence, made up of only two characters, is interpreted and thus translated, there are again divergent opinions among commentators regarding its intended meaning. I will take Cheng Yi's version because his commentary on this line statement renders an interpretation seemingly more congruent with the interpretations rendered so far to the other lines. Cheng Yi comments:

> Stairs are a means by which to climb. When the leadership appoints strong and balanced people of wisdom to assist it to rise to greater heights, this is like climbing stairs, meaning that there is a specific way of doing it, and it is easy. This points to the second yang, the true correspondent and complement of the fifth yin, but all wise people in the lower echelons are stairs by which to rise, and those who are able to employ the wise thus rise through their agency. (1988:155)

In the above passage, the subject at the fifth position is viewed as a dependent leader whose achievements have to rely on the work of "people in lower echelons"; only with their assistance ("stairs"), he can achieve Climbing. Thus, as the *Commentary on the Images* puts it, this kind of dependency is "the way that one here can greatly realize his goals" (Lynn, 1994:426). How can we evaluate this kind of dependent relationship between a weak leader and strong, able subordinates in terms of the costs and benefits incurred by each side? Exchange theorists of modern days may be curious about how this kind of dependent relationship can be put into exchange terms and its possible outcomes predicted. The line statement says simply that the one at the leadership will come out fine if he practices "constancy," i.e., persistent self-control. Nothing more is said either in the text or any later commentary.

Lastly, the line statement of the sixth yin line can be clearly understood in view of the positional attribute of the top position. It reads, "This one climbs in darkness, so it would be fitting if he were to practice unceasing constancy" (Lynn, 1994:427). Considering that the subject of the sixth position is assigned no formal role to play and has no influence over others, the *I Ching* judges that he has no growth potential under the situation. So, if he tries to Climb, it would be as if "one climbs in darkness." Little prospect to realize his intention is predicted here. Thus, the *Commentary on the Images* comments on this line statement: "The one who climbs in darkness may be at the top, but he shall find exhaustion there, not prosperity" (Lynn, 1994:427).

The hexagram *Kun* (☱☵, Impasse)

The hexagram *Kun* represents a situation in which all the subjects involved in it experience difficulties although the exact nature of the difficulties is not explained anywhere in the text. The overall meaning of the situation, as the *Commentary on the Images* explains, is derived from a metaphoric idea that is conjured up by the arrangement of its component trigrams, the upper trigram *Dui* (the Lake) and the lower trigram *Kan* (Water): Water is below the Lake, thus with Water sunk into the Lake, "the Lake has no Water: this is the image of Impasse" (Lynn, 1994:429). Although there is a passage in the *Commentary on the Judgments* suggesting that the difficult situation indicated by the hexagram is related to the pattern of relationships among the lines,[85] the line statements seem to contain no accounts to yield such a reading. In my opinion, the key to understanding the situational meaning, or rather the teachings, of this hexagram lies in the accounts given in the *Commentary on the Appended Phrases*, which reads as follows: "*Kun* [Impasse] is the criterion for distinguishing virtue. *Kun* demonstrates how one who suffers tribulation still stays in complete control of himself. . . ." (Lynn, 1994:429-30). In light of what is said in the above passage, we then may ask what factor or type of behavioral orientation would help us stay in control of ourselves in the difficult time indicated by the hexagram? From the line statements, we can identify one specific factor that distinguishes the subjects clearly into two groups, those who fall into miserable states in the face of the distressful situation and those who endure it and emerge with fortunate results. The factor distinguishing these two groups is whether a line is figured as a yang or yin line. According to Legge, "the three strong (yang) lines in the figure (2, 4, 5) are all held to represent 'superior men'," and this explains why the subjects in these positions are described as having the ability and strength to overcome the distressful situation. Then, the subjects represented by yin lines feature those who "are unable to deal aright with the straightened state indicated by the figure" (1963:164). Being represented by yin lines, they are weak people unfit for their jobs under the situation and will, therefore, fall prey to the tough situation. Thus, it becomes clear by now that the hexagram represents an extremely difficult situation where only the fit survive. Of course, we here should remind ourselves that the meaning of "fit" as used here in the context of Chinese culture is tinged with more moralistic connotations than those applied to the natural world.

Considering the nature of the situation and the different fates of the subjects as described by the line statements, it is best to deal separately with all three yin lines together, and all three yang lines together. Let us look at the line statements of the three yin lines first:

> *First Yin*: This one suffers Impasse in the buttocks here on the root of the tree, so he enters a secluded valley and does not appear for three years.
>
> *Third Yin*: This one suffers Impasse on rocks, so he tries to hold on to the puncture vine for support, and then he enters his home but does not see his wife.
>
> *Sixth Yin*: This one suffers Impasse either in creepers and vines or in danger and perplexity, so he should say to himself, "Take steps that you will regret," for even if it means regret, to set forth here will result in good fortune. (Lynn, 1994:430, 432,434)

All the line statements describe the respective subjects as ones who fall into such helplessly difficult situations that there is no prospective for them to safely emerge out of their distressful situation. An exception may be found in the sixth yin line where the line statement mentions "good fortune." Nevertheless, it sounds more like a consolation for a regretful event than an assurance for good fortune. We may take into account an additional factor contributing to the misfortunes of these subjects — the positions of the subjects. Here in this hexagram, the positions at which yin lines are located share a common characteristic in that they are generally regarded as having certain disadvantages due to which the subjects at these positions, even under ordinary circumstances, are not given judgments as favorable as those at the second, the fourth, and the fifth positions. Thus, the unfavorable judgments rendered to the subjects at the mentioned three positions are due to both their situational characteristic as represented by yin lines and the attributes connected with their positions.

In contrast to the three subjects represented by yin lines, those who are represented by yang lines are described as ones who equally undergo difficult situations, yet persist, and then slowly emerge with good results. It seems because of this that the *Commentary on the Appended Phrases* comments, "*Kun* [Impasse] is the criterion for distinguishing virtue." In other words, the difficult situation represented by the hexagram *Kun* offers an occasion to test one's character or ability (or "virtue") to endure and overcome. And, using its peculiar symbolism of the yin-yang duality, the *I Ching* seems to emphasize that only people equipped with suitably virtuous characteristics or sufficient capabilities (i.e., here denoted by yang lines and advantageous positions) will be able to weather difficult times. Then, let us look at the line statements of the three yang lines:

Second Yang: his one has Impasse in his food and drink. But as soon as the crimson ceremonial garment arrives, it would fitting to offer sacrifice here but to set forth would lead to misfortune, and there would be no one to blame.

Fourth Yang: This one comes slowly, so slowly, for he suffers Impasse at the metal-clad cart. Although there is humiliation, he should bring about a successful conclusion.

Fifth Yang: This one cuts off noses and feet and so has Impasse with the red ceremonial garment, and only when he takes things slowly does he have joys. It is fitting to offer sacrifice. (Lynn, 1994:430-3)

In the line statement of the second yang line, the starting phrase, "This one has Impasse in his food and drink," is read in two different ways that yield directly opposite meanings. One way to read it is that this subject experiences difficulty in securing food and drink (Cheng Yi, 1988:157; Kim, 1997:362). Another way of reading it is that the subject "fares sumptuously" although he is in Impasse (Legge, 1963:164; c.f., Lynn, 1994:431; Wilhelm, 1967:626). The text can be read both ways depending upon how readers interpret the line statement in context of the other line statements. I prefer the first reading because the next verse describes the subject at this position as succeeding in securing a cooperative relationship with the leader at the fifth position, and under normal circumstances, a subject represented by a yang line would not form a union with other yang lines. So, it may be thought, it would be only under extraordinarily difficult situations that this kind of a union between congruous, rather than complementary, lines is formed. Then, let us look at the next verse: "But as soon as the crimson ceremonial garment arrives, it would fitting to offer sacrifice here . . . ." Commentators voice no disagreement in that "the crimson ceremonial garment" refers to the ruler at the fifth position, a symbol of his leadership position. Thus, the line statement is interpreted as suggesting that the subjects at the second and the fifth positions form an alliance to overcome the difficult situation. In dealing with this alliance, the subject at the second position thereby is advised to "maintain his (utmost) sincerity as in sacrificing" (Legge, 1963:162). We will see that the same advice is given to the subject at the fifth position. Why both the subjects are advised to maintain their utmost sincerity is not clearly explained in the text, but may make enough sense if we take into account the nature of the alliance between the two subjects at the second and the fifth positions as one formed between actors with equally strong wills.

The line statement of the fourth yang line should be understood in the context of the tripartite relationship among the subjects at the first, the second, and the fourth positions. Notice that the first line is a yin line and the fourth a yang one. This indicates a possibility that a union is formed between the position holders at these two positions. However, there is yet another yang line right above the first yin line, and this will indicate also that the subject at the second position has an ability to exercise influence over the first position holder who is in its immediate vicinity. Thus, in this tripartite relationship, the subjects at the second and the fourth positions would be understood as being in a rival relationship in pursuit of control or jurisdiction over the first yin line. Competing relationships and conflict among position holders appear often in many hexagrams, and the three lines in this hexagram are interpreted to be in such a relationship. Then, first, let us examine the fourth yang line more closely. Wang Bi's following commentary appended to this line statement is couched exactly upon the idea of the above mentioned kind of rivalry in a social relationship:

> The "metal-clad cart" refers to Second Yang. As it is hard and strong enough to carry others, it is referred to as "a metal-clad cart." *Xuxu* [slowly, so slowly] is an expression that suggests doubt and fear. Fourth yang has his will fixed on First Yin but is blocked by Second Yang, and, as such a one treads on a territory that is not his rightful position [because this is a yin position], he might try awe-inspiring orders, but they will not be carried out. Fourth Yang is incapable of abandoning First Yin, and it might want to go to First Yin, but it fears Second Yang. One at Fourth Yang has a resonate partner but is unable to succor him, thus the text says: "There is humiliation." (Lynn, 1994:432)

And, Wang Bi's commentary goes on to explain, "This one gets the measure of his own powers and so stays put and does not do battle with Second Yang."

The line statement of the fifth yang line describes its subject as having both his noses and feet cut off, which seems to mean that its subject encounters difficulties that come from many directions. Commentators differ in their interpretations concerning where the sources of difficulties lie. Wang Bi's commentary on this line statement

(1994:433) involves a long story in which the subject at the fifth position is said to have suffered the punishments owing to certain problems arising from the ways he behaves. I personally feel that Wang Bi's interpretation on this particular line statement stretches one's imagination beyond what we can sensibly get out of the *I Ching*. According to Legge, the wounds of the subject at the leadership position have to do with the subjects at the sixth and the fourth positions, and, especially more with the latter who is referred to in the line statement as one in the "red ceremonial garment." However, this interpretation also does not seem to fit well with what is stated in the line statement of the fourth yang line. Legge (1963:165) himself concedes that his explanation attempted for the line statement is not satisfactory. In such a case where no sensible interpretation is available by any means, no interpretation would be preferred to a contrived or confusing one. Thus, putting this problem aside, we find from the remaining portion of the line statement a theme similar to those found in the other yang lines of the hexagram: "only when he takes things slowly does he have joys. It is fitting to offer sacrifice."

The hexagram *Dui* (☱☱, Joy)

The next hexagram *Dui* (Joy) is obtained by doubling the trigram *Dui*, hence its name. There is a passage in the *Commentary on the Judgments* that accounts for how "Joy" functions for social integration, thus suggesting its meaning related to a social situation. It reads: "If one leads the common folk with Joy, they will forget their toil, and if one has them risk danger and difficulty with Joy, they will forget about dying. Great is Joy, for it is the motivating force of the common folk" (Lynn, 1994:505). Judging from the above account, "Joy" refers to satisfaction that one derives from a group to which he belongs. In this sense, I see little difference between "Joy (satisfaction)" as used here and the variable "levels of satisfaction" that are measured quite frequently in both psychological and sociological researches of today. In the both contexts, satisfaction is understood and treated as a crucial factor for social integration. If we turn to the individual line statements, however, a rather different picture emerges: each line statement describes the source of the subject's satisfaction or the manner with which one pursues satisfaction, and then renders either a favorable or unfavorable judgment for the described mode of satisfaction attainment. Thus, the line statements considered as a whole may be regarded as involving a typology on various sources of satisfaction or different modes with which people pursue satisfaction in life. Of course, since in this typology each line statement at a given position is descriptive of a type, we may expect that a given type is related to the positional and the situational characteristics of the line. Contrary to this expectation, there seems to be little connection between what the line statements state and the situational and positional attributes of the lines. This is why I think the line statements of this hexagram, taken as a whole, are better treated as a typology with appended moral judgments on the various modes of satisfaction attainment. Then, let us examine the individual line statements.

The line statement of the first yang describes its subject as someone who "achieves Joy through harmony, (and therefore will have) . . . . good fortune" (Lynn, 1994:508). According to Wang Bi, "harmony" means "one . . . . stays free of factional affiliation." (Lynn, 1994:508). Thus, the subject is described as one whose satisfaction is derived from having harmonious relationships with everybody, making no enemies, thus causing little trouble in managing his relationships with others.

The subject at the second position is described as someone who "achieves Joy through sincerity, (and therefore will have) . . . . good fortune" (Lynn, 1994:508). The *Commentary on the Images* explains, "The good fortune that comes to one who achieves Joy through sincerity is due to the fact that he keeps his will trustworthy" (Lynn, 1994:508). The commentary above suggests that due to one's sincerity, others will trust him and his being trusted by others as such will operate as the factor from which he derives satisfaction in his social life. As I assess it, the line statement here carries in essence the same message as that of the first yang line. Through both the line statements, the *I Ching*, in effect, gives forceful moral lessons to persuade individuals to act as "harmoniously and sincerely" as possible so that they can have satisfaction in living with others.

The moral lesson continues in the line statement of the third yin line that states, "This one comes after Joy, which means misfortune." Here, its subject is described as "someone who comes in search of Joy" (Lynn, 1994:509). It seems obvious that the idea underlying this line statement is a belief that satisfaction should not be sought after for its own sake, but should come to us naturally as we tread on virtuous paths as exemplified by the ones at the first and the second positions.

The fourth line also entails a statement that presents its subject as exercising a prudent approach with which he is carefully "deliberating about what to seek his pleasure in, and not at rest" (Legge, 1963:193).[86] It is not clear why he is understood as showing such a cautious and attentive attitude. The succeeding passage in the line statement offers a clue: "He borders on what would be injurious." According to Legge (1963:194-5), "What would be injurious" refers to the subject at the third position who is described as coming in search of satisfaction, thus "might have an injurious effect" on the subject at the fourth position. Therefore, the line statement suggests that the subject at the fourth position, as he looks at the way the one below him behaves in pursuit of joy, will be busy examining various possibilities in attaining satisfaction. Yet, as indicated by the line statement that ends with a favorable judgment, "but there will be cause for joy," he, in the end, will make a rational choice through which he is expected to attain real satisfaction. This line statement, like the previous ones, emphasizes the exercise of careful deliberation before we decide on how to satisfy ourselves and that such a prudent approach under the situation will bring good outcomes.

As a type, the way that the subject at the fifth position seeks for satisfaction is described as an undesirable one by its line statement. The line statement states, "This one puts his trust in one who embodies deterioration, which means danger" (Lynn, 1994:509). Although it may be viewed to involve a moral truism, what the line statement says certainly seems to make sense: if one finds satisfaction in what is going to deteriorate, this will put him into a difficult situation. But, why is it the subject at the top leadership position who seeks satisfaction in "one who embodies deterioration?" Neither the situational nor the positional attributes of the line as interpreted from the line formation of the hexagram gives any particular clue to account for such a reading. Thus, once again, the line statement has to be understood as giving practical advice for anyone under the situation represented by this hexagram: it would not be wise to seek pleasure from what is going to crumble away easily because as the very source of our satisfaction disappears from our sight, our satisfaction would disappear likewise.

Commentators' interpretations of the line statement of the sixth yin line differ so much from one another that two have yielded translations with diametrically opposed readings. Lynn's translation based on Wang Bi's commentary reads, "This one achieves Joy through being led" (1994:510), whereas with Legge's translation the line statement reads, "The topmost line, divided, shows the pleasure of its subject in leading and attracting others" (1963:193). There is another version of translation based on Cheng Yi's interpretation, which reads, "This one tries to draw out Joy further" (Lynn, 1994:511n6; c.f., Cheng Yi, 1988:199). And, there is still another version by Wilhelm whose translation reads briefly, "Seductive joyousness" (1967:688). To my mind, all of the translations presented above make sense in the overall context of the hexagram. This is because each of them represents a type of immoderate pleasure-seeking behavior of which the *I Ching* seems to have a negative opinion. Accordingly, none of them would be particularly incompatible with the typology of satisfaction-seeking behaviors as represented by the line statements of the hexagram.

Summary of theoretical and empirical propositions

1) Individuals' actions are inseparable from both the structural and situational contexts of people at their respective positions under a given situation. Therefore, although people under a given situation may share a certain common trait in the ways they behave, there will be differences in individual situations relative to the structural and situational contexts in which actors find themselves. Individuals' behavioral and attitudinal orientations and their outcomes would be position- and situation-specific.

2) If one is at the position of the top leadership, one of the primary moral virtues he has to comply with would be moderation. Therefore, even when he is placed under the situation in which all people are in pursuit of elegant living decorated with rich trappings, it would not be wise or advantageous for him to follow the trend of the time blindly and do the same. His position as the leader requires him to moderate his elegant living with a certain measure of simplicity and plainness.

3) Undesirable occurrences may sometimes result although no one commits wrongdoing, and, should such an event occur, a leader may be accused of being responsible for it, though he be completely blameless.

4) Some people under certain circumstances may face a situation in which they are unable to find suitable roles to play. The *I Ching* considers this kind of alienation, in which certain people experience a complete breakdown in social bonds with others, as one of the particularly unfortunate situations that individuals in social settings can suffer.

5) People at the upper echelon under certain situations will find themselves unable to use strong and effective means to control powerful subordinates at the lower echelon. Under such circumstances the best strategy that the weak ruling elites can

adopt would be accommodation. That is, all they can do is to make concessions with grace to those under their authority.

6) When a society faces a difficult situation, the ability to cope with the situation will differ among individuals depending upon two factors, what advantage or disadvantage one's position poses in weathering out the difficulty and whether or not he possesses a suitable personal quality for overcoming it.

7) A rivalry may occur between individuals or groups of people when two parties are competing with each other to take the third party into their own side. This kind of competition occurs because the formation of an alliance with others can be utilized as a source of power, influence, or at least, security.

8) "Joy" (satisfaction) operates as "the motivating force of the common folk" with which they will work hard, risk danger, and endure difficulty for the group to which they belong, and, therefore, will lead to a strong social integration.

9) Situations Signifying Patterns of Reciprocal Relationships Centering on Specific Tasks

A common underlying characteristic of the five hexagrams presented here will be found in the dualistic division of roles among the constituent members of the social entities represented by the hexagrams. In carrying out specific tasks that require reciprocal relationships, the constituent members are divided into two groups — those who lead actions and those who are acted upon. In the hexagram *Meng* (Juvenile Ignorance), the members of the social unit represented by it are divided into ones who are in positions of educating or socializing others and others who are being educated or socialized by the former. The situation represented by the hexagram *Shihe* (Bite Through) also involves two types of people — ones who deliver judiciary decisions or punishments to others who pose obstacles to the integration of a group and others to whom the legal sanctions are applied. In the hexagram *Yi* (Nourishment), people are divided into two categories playing opposite yet reciprocal roles — ones who nourish others and others who are nourished by the former. The composition of the members of the social unit represented by the hexagram *Xian* (Influence) is suggested by its title name; its constituent members consist of those who exercise influence over others and those others who are influenced by the former. And, lastly, in the hexagram *Yi* (Increase), people who are assisted in growth by others are paired with others who help them to grow. Thus, as we can see, all the situations represented by the five hexagrams included here have a common feature in that each consists of members with functionally matching roles. Of course, we may question if situations or social structures involving such simple dualistic divisions of roles among people actually exist. My answer is yes. In social organizations such as educational institutions, correctional institutions, and the family, constituent members can be divided along the lines of specific tasks that by their nature involve simple dualistic divisions. Nevertheless, can this idea be applied to more general levels of social situations? I think that the application suggested above is possible in the sense that any social situation as conceived by us is but a theoretical construct built from a specific viewpoint and chosen with a specific interest. In other words, if we look at a society from a limited perspective that is considered relevant in the light of a certain prevailing issue of a period, we may come up with a much simpler picture of the society drawn with only a few characteristic outlines. Thus, the situations represented by the five hexagrams to be examined below may be regarded as involving feasible ideas worth studying.

1) The hexagram *Meng* (☶☵, Juvenile Ignorance) (Hexagram No. 4)

2) The hexagram *Shihe* (☲☳, Bite Through) (Hexagram No. 21)

3) The hexagram *Yi* (☶☳, Nourishment) (Hexagram No. 27)

4) The hexagram *Xian* (☱☶, Reciprocity, Influence[87]) (Hexagram No. 31)

5) The hexagram *Yi* (☴☳, Increase) (Hexagram No. 42)

The hexagram *Meng* (☶☵, Juvenile Ignorance)

The meaning of the hexagram *Meng* (Juvenile Ignorance) must have been derived from its line composition that consists of the upper trigram *Kan* symbolizing the Mountain and the lower trigram *Gen*, the Spring. As the *Commentary on the Images* explains, "Below the Mountain emerges the Spring: this constitutes the image of Juvenile Ignorance" (Lynn, 1994:159), which conveys an image of someone who is at its earlier phase of socialization and therefore needs instructions and guidance due to his "Juvenile Ignorance." Judging from the line statements, however, individual line components do not carry meanings related to what might have been suggested by the meanings of the trigrams as above. A notable feature of this hexagram is found in the simple principle according to which characteristics of the line components are differentiated into two different kinds. Subjects represented by yin lines are described as those who need instructions, guidance, or assistance whereas yang lines are described as ones who are mature enough to be in responsible positions giving instruction or guidance to the former. It would be with this observation that Legge explains that "The object of the hexagram is to show how such a condition should be dealt with by the parent and ruler, whose authority and duty are represented by the second and sixth, the two undivided lines" (1963:66). Thus, as far as this hexagram is concerned, one's positional status itself is not a relevant factor in determining whether he is assigned to a position to give or receive instruction, and, therefore, its line statements seem to bear little relationship with the hierarchical standings of respective position holders. Moreover, the line statements do not seem to be written in such a style as to depict certain ongoing social situations, but rather as an essay to offer some useful lessons concerning the teachings of the immature people. We will see this more clearly as we proceed with the line statements.

The line statement of the first yin line states, "With the opening up of Juvenile Ignorance, it is fitting both to subject him to the awareness of punishment and to remove fetters and shackles, but if he were to set out in this way, he would find it hard going" (Lynn, 1994:160). The subject at the first position is represented by a yin line, and, therefore, is described as someone who needs be freed of his Juvenile Ignorance. The line statement contains an instruction that may draw some interests even today. Although penalty has to be applied whenever necessary, restrictions do not help to bring enlightenment to the mind of the people in need of instruction; both restrictions and free atmosphere are needed in good education or, more generally, in socialization. The line statement ends with a warning that, as Wang Bi comments on the ending line, "the threat of punishment cannot long be used" (Lynn, 1994:160).

The subject at the second position figures one who "treat(s) the Juvenile Ignorance with magnanimity" and thereby is to meet with "good fortune." The second verse, "To take a wife means good fortune," is interpreted by Wang Bi as taking in someone "who serves to complement him and so allows him to perfect his virtue." The theme of treating the Juvenile Ignorance with kindness and of success in the management of a household or a country as implied by the second verse ("to take a wife") are combined. In combination, they yield the last verse of the line statement which reads, "His child will be up to taking charge of the family" (Lynn, 1994:161). As far as I see it, the message that this line statement intends to convey is reduced to one essential point — an essential factor for the success in inculcating Juvenile Ignorance (customarily referring to either children, women, or the common folk) is kindness and understanding, frequently heard from people engaging in teaching even today.

The line statement of the third yin line describes its subject as a woman who "sees a man of wealth" (Legge, 1963:65)[88] and throws herself away. Accordingly, the advice, "It will not do to marry this woman," (Lynn, 1994:161) is given although to whom this advice is given is not clear. It may be thought that the line statement is a precept offered generally to anyone who engages in teaching. Viewed in this way, "a woman who sees a man of wealth and throws away herself" is interpreted as anyone who will do everything to get rich, and the line statement advises that teachers should not take in such persons. This undesirable characteristic attributed to the third yin line may have to do with the fact that a yin line occupies inappropriately the third position, a yang position. However, the text offers no clear explanation concerning why the subject has to be someone acting only with materialistic motives.

Meanwhile, the subject at the fourth position is described as someone who is ignorant and has no one to help him to break out of such ignorance. Its line statement states, "Here confounded by Juvenile Ignorance, one becomes base" (Lynn, 1994:162). Why is the subject at the fourth position judged to remain in a state of ignorance? The explanation offered by commentators is based on logic typical of the *I Ching*: he finds no resonant partner since a yin line, instead of a yang one, is present at the first position that has a specific affinity with the fourth position, and is surrounded by two neighboring yin lines that are incapable of rendering any help under the situation (Legge, 1963:66; Lynn, 1994:162; Wilhelm, 1967:409). Thus, as Cheng Yi puts it, the fourth yin line "represents the case of people who are weak and ignorant, lacking strong, intelligent friends to help them, having no way to develop themselves. They thus get stuck in immaturity" (1988:9).

In contrast to the two yin lines at the third and the fourth positions, the subject at the fifth position is described as the leader who, although he also is identified as one in Juvenile Ignorance here under this situation, "will find good fortune" (Lynn, 1994:162). The reason for this favorable judgment is supplied by the interpretation that the subject is understood as a leader who is ignorant, yet admits his limitation, and delegates his authority to able subordinates (who are represented by the second yang line in this particular hexagram). Interpreted in this way, this line statement also purports to offer a simple and commonsense maxim for those in positions of leadership: if they are not wise or capable enough to do well on their job, it would be better for them to delegate their power to wiser and more able subordinates who will do the job in their behalf.

The sixth line is a yang line and, therefore, the subject represented by it again is described as someone who is in a position to teach the Youthful Ignorant. It states, "Strike at Juvenile Ignorance, but it is not fitting to engage in harassment; it is fitting to guard against harassment" (Lynn, 1994:163). "To engage in harassment" is translated variously as "doing him an injury" (Legge, 1963:66), "to commit transgressions" (Wilhelm, 1967:410), "to be hostile" (Cleary, in Cheng Yi, 1988:10), or "to do it in unlawful ways" (Kim, 1997:66). Nevertheless, the main idea does not differ much from one version to another: even if we may have to apply punishment in educating people, it has to be done with appropriate principles, restraining hostile emotions.

The hexagram *Shihe* (☲☳, Bite Through)

The title name and the situational meaning of this hexagram are derived from its pictorial image — an image of a hard substance (a hard line in the middle) in the mouth to be bitten through by closing the two jaws (the two hard lines located at the top and the bottom). Thus, as Legge points out, *Shihe* "means literally 'Union by gnawing'." To express this in terms of "the body politic," the hexagram represents a situation in which an integration is achieved through "removing (by applying "legal constraints" or punishment) the obstacles to union" (1963:102).

What the obstacles specifically refer to is not clear at all. Yet, there is a picture that emerges from a cursory overview of the line statements; this situation has a notable feature in that recalcitrant elements obstructing integration are located at positions with no official function, the first and sixth positions. Thus, the subjects at these two positions are described as ones who pose some sort of obstacles to a union and, therefore, are about to receive punishment. The rest of the line statements (of those who occupy formal positions) describe various modes or levels of judiciary decisions to deliver punishments. Here we can draw a picture of a social or political situation; the government carries out a reform or clean-up project, largely targeted at the ruled subjects outside the government, through which it wants to rid itself of what is thought to obstruct the unity of society.

Then, first, let us take up the line statements at the bottom and the top positions and examine how their respective situations compare to each other.

First Yang: Made to wear whole foot shackles, his toes are destroyed, but he will be without blame.

Sixth Yang: Made to wear a cangue, his ears are destroyed, and this means misfortune. (Lynn, 1994:267,271)

First, regarding the first yang line, notice that the subject at the bottom position is deprived of freedom of movement, indicating that some punitive actions are taken to prevent the subject at the bottom position from committing further deviations. Yet, since the measure is taken largely for a preventive purpose, the one being punished would not be worse off in the long run. If we are reminded of the fact that the first position refers to the common people, the line statement is interpreted as suggesting that the common people, under this situation, may feel uncomfortable under the government whose rule relies mainly on restrictive measures. But such a rule in the long run would not result in gravely unfortunate outcomes for their welfare.

The line statement for the top yang line differs from the above. Under this particular situation, deviant acts committed by the subject at the top sixth position are regarded as serious criminal acts, and, therefore, will bring about punitive reactions as severe as to put a cangue on one's neck that may result in such serious consequences as having one's ears destroyed. And, consequently, a negative judgment stated straightforwardly, "this means misfortune," is rendered to the subject at this position. Now, we may question why such a crucial difference exists between the two subjects. Neither the *I Ching* nor any later commentary gives any clue to answer this question. Here I would like to attempt an answer based only on my own assumption that seems reasonable enough to me but cannot claim support from any documentary source. My answer is derived from a simple view that the two subjects represented respectively by the bottom and the sixth positions would differ in the seriousness of obstacles that they are likely to pose against the integration of a group. The subject at the top position is generally interpreted as referring to someone who is in highly exalted status yet with no formal position in the government. As was explained earlier in this book, the top line is often interpreted as pointing to "ex-emperor in retirement" (a figure representing the political power of a bygone era) or "sage" (leading intellectuals). Thus, once a subject with such important status puts up resistance against the government's effort to bring unity to the society, it may be considered to have such dangerous implications as to require severe punishment. Meanwhile, obstacles posed by the subject at the first position, by the common people, may not have to be dealt with as seriously as those committed by the one at the sixth, top position. Restrictive measures of a milder degree may suffice to prevent further incidents of deviant behaviors. We may say here, as far as political offenses are concerned, deviant behaviors among the common people will be dealt with far less severely than those committed by the people at upper strata. And, "makig an example" of those highly placed seems to give the law more weight, as we often see in modern times.

From the second position up to the fifth position, all the line statements describe various modes or levels of judiciary decisions to impose punishment. Thus, all the subjects holding incumbent governmental positions are described as those who deliver punishments supposedly to the ones at the bottom and the sixth positions. Nevertheless, all the line statements are addressed with such highly ambiguous symbolism that what they actually refer to, in terms of judiciary decision making, is not clear at all. The line statement of the second yin line, which states that "Biting through soft and tender flesh, he destroys the nose, but he will be without blame" (Lynn, 1994:268), indicates a successful outcome achieved with relative ease through a timely application of decisive sanctions. The successful outcome expected from the punitive measure employed by the second position is explained simply by the fact that a yin line "appropriately" occupies a yin position.

For the third yin line, the line statement depicts the situation of its subject as dealing with such a difficult case that may get him into some sort of trouble. It states, "Biting through dried meat, he encounters something poisonous. He will have small regret but without blame" (Lynn, 1994:269). Since, as Wang Bi explains in his commentary, "'biting through' is a metaphor for meting out punishment to someone" (Lynn, 1994:269), "dried meat" is also a metaphor for the hardship that one will experience in rendering appropriate judiciary judgment to a case. This difficulty to be encountered by the subject at the third position is explained because a yin line is inappropriately occupying a yang position. What specific sort of difficulty the subject is expected to undergo, however, is not clearly explained by either the *I Ching* or any later commentary.

The line statement of the fourth yang line presents its subject's situation as even more difficult than the one encountered by the subject at the third position. It states, "the fourth line, divided, shows one gnawing the flesh dried on the bone, and getting the pledges of money and arrows. It will be advantageous to him to realize the difficulty of his task and be firm, — in which case there will be good fortune" (Legge, 1963:102).[89] As we can see, a notable difference between the line statements of the third and the fourth lines is found in that while the third yin line tells about "dried meat," the fourth yang line "bony dried meat," involving a clear implication that the latter has to deal with tougher cases than the former. The reason for which the subject at the fourth position is viewed as encountering difficulty is the same as that for the third yin line: a yang line occupies inappropriately a yin place, a mismatch between its subject's action orientation and the mode of conduct that is required by the position itself. Hence, the advice, "It will be advantageous to him to realize the difficulty of his task and be firm — in which case there will be good fortune," is offered.

The remaining line statement, that of the fifth yin line, also points out the difficulty ("biting through dried meat") involved in carrying out the task assigned to its subject. Notice that again a yin line is incumbent at a yang position; thus, an inappropriately occupied position explains the source of such difficulty. However, the line statement includes a clause which, despite the difficulty, pronounces a rather auspicious outcome resulting from the subject's handling of cases at his discretion; to quote the line statement, "he obtains yellow metal (or gold)" (Lynn, 1994:270). Why is the subject at the fifth position treated as an exception to others in that he is able to produce a more fortunate outcome than others in similar conditions? The answer to this question is found in a general perspective that underlies, if implicitly, the *I Ching*. The fifth position corresponds to the top leadership position for a society or any collective entity represented by the hexagram. And, since it represents the most powerful position having no higher position above it, even a weak position of the subject, owing to the power matrix of any given situation, would be overcome with the formal capacity empowered by the position itself. Thus, with only a few exceptions among the 64 hexagrams, the subject at the fifth position, regardless of the situational characteristics that vary from one hexagram to another, is given a favorable judgment regarding his personal well-being. This seems to be the case also with the fifth yin line of the present hexagram. Of course, a little warning for possible "danger" is included in the line statement, but with an assurance that "there will be no blame" (Lynn, 1994:270).

The hexagram *Yi* (䷚ , Nourishment)

As was the case with the previous hexagram, there seems to be no doubt that the title name of the hexagram *Yi* also is derived from a pictorial image of its component lines; the hexagram looks like a tunnel entrance formed between the two solid lines, thus resembling a mouth, an organ for taking in "Nourishment." As Wilhelm (1967:522) points out, "The hexagram contains three ideas — nourishing oneself, nourishing others, and being nourished by others." Of course, if nourishment is the characteristic activity engaged in by the people under the situation represented by the hexagram, there is no question that the possible modes of behavior related to nourishment would be reduced to the three modes of nourishment-related activities as suggested by Wilhelm. Nevertheless, what kinds of social relationships or activities does "Nourishment" involve? There seems to be no passage in either the *I Ching* or any later commentary that provides an answer to this question. Perhaps, we only can guess by taking into account the meaning of the situation as a whole as it is represented through the line formation of the hexagram. Thus, Wilhelm's view that this hexagram has two ruling lines, the top yang line and the fifth yin line (1967:519), provides a useful clue regarding the nature of the situation indicated by this hexagram. Then, first, let us look at the line statements of the two positions together:

Fifth Yin: Here one goes off the right path, so to abide instead in constancy will mean good fortune. One must not cross the great river.

Top Yang: They depend on this one for Nourishment. Severity will bring good fortune. It is fitting to cross the great river. (Lynn, 1994:308-9)

The line statement of the top yang line indicates that the subject at this position is one who provides nourishment for others involved in this situation; viewed from a different angle, it may be said that the people below will look toward this one for nourishment. However, what sort of nourishment can the subject at the top position provide for others including the one at the fifth, leadership position? Considering the positional attribute of the position holder who holds no position in the formal office, it may be thought that he nourishes people with what is of spiritual or intellectual substance: a spiritual or ideological leader who is highly influential over all the actors involved in the situation is present at the sixth position. Legge seems to support this interpretation as he comments on this line, "(the subject at this position) feels himself in the position of master or tutor to all under heaven" (1963:116). The second verse of the line statement, "Severity will bring good fortune," which is translated in line with Wang Bi's commentary, may also be considered to make some sense. Of this Wang Bi explains, "As the ruler of all the yin lines, Top Yang must not suffer disrespect, and, therefore, "severity will bring good fortune" (Lynn, 1994:309).[90]

Meanwhile, we may expect that the subject at the fifth position will also take part in providing nourishment for the people down below since he occupies the top leadership position. Contrary to this expectation, under the present situation, he is represented by a yielding, yin line, interpreted to mean that his personal quality or action orientation is not equal to what is required of the position. This explains why the line statement says, "Here (the subject at the fifth position) goes off the right path." It is obviously in view of this condition that the line statement goes on to say, "so to abide instead in constancy will mean good fortune." Here, commentators do not differ much in their interpretations, most of which fall well into a proximate range of what the following commentary of Cheng Yi explains:

The fifth yin represents those in the position of leadership in a time of nourishment, those who are to nourish the whole community. However, their yin weakness makes them unable to nourish the whole community. Above there are wise people who are firm and positive, so they follow them, relying on them for nourishment so as to help the whole community. / The leadership is supposed to nourish others, so when instead it relies on nourishment from others, this is "contravening the norm" (translated as "goes off the right path"). Since the leaders themselves are insufficient, they follow wise teachers. / The top line is the position of the mentors. It is imperative to remain upright and steadfast, sincerely reposing trust in wise mentors, so that they may help the leaders in such a way as to benefit the whole community. In this sense it bodes well. (1988:85-6)

A situation in which the ruling figure of a country looks for intellectual or ideological guidance from "wise teachers" — "sages" or intellectuals who are positioned outside the formal hierarchical line of the officialdom — would not be rare. And, a situation where the informal influence exercised by spiritual or ideological leaders operates as the most powerful factor over a political community does not seem be a wholly unusual idea. It is in this light that Cheng Yi's commentary is viewed as rendering a meaningful interpretation on the line statement of the fifth position.

Now, keeping in mind the nature of the relationship characterized as mentioned above between the two key actors in the hexagram, let us look at the rest of the line statements of the hexagram. The line statement of the first yang line reads, "You set aside your luminous tortoise shell and watch me move my jaw instead: this means misfortune" (Lynn, 1994:306). This line statement is addressed as if a certain person ("me") is giving advice to someone else ("you"). Commentators show little disagreement over interpreting that "you" refers to the subject at the first position. Regarding "me," however, their opinions are divided; Legge (1963:115) and Cheng Yi (1988:83) view that "me" refers to the fourth yin line; Lee (1997:328) and Wilhelm (1967:522) say instead that it refers to the top yang line. I prefer the latter interpretation because it seems more consistent with the statement given to the top yang line. Given Wilhelm's interpretation as such, then, "the strong line (at the first position) below" would be understood to have the capacity to "provide nourishment for itself (the magic tortoise needs no earthly food but can nourish itself on air)." And, Wilhelm goes on to explain the remaining portion of the line statement: "Instead, however, it too moves toward the general source of nourishment and wants to be fed with the rest. This is contemptible and disastrous." As suggested already, "the general source of nourishment" refers to the top yang line. Being understood in this way, the line statement itself seems to leave little ambiguity as far as its surface meaning is concerned.

Commentators also diverge a great deal from one another in

interpreting the line statement of the second yin line. I present Legge's translation together with his interpretation because his version seems simpler and clearer than others. The line statement as translated by Legge reads, "The second line, divided, shows one looking downwards for nourishment, which is contrary to what is proper; or seeking it from the height (above), advance towards which will lead to evil" (1963:114). Looking at the overall line formation of the hexagram, we see two yang lines, at the bottom and the top places. These two yang lines, in the context of the ongoing situation where "weaker" (yin) categories of people seek nourishment, are interpreted by most commentators as sources of nourishment for others to look toward. Then, it may be thought that the subject at the second position is likely to seek for nourishment from either the one at the first position or the other at the top position. Taking into account this possibility, Legge explains why the line statement views the subject at the second position as being in a difficult situation. An inclination to "look downwards for nourishment" is judged inappropriate because it is inappropriate for one in a higher status to seek nourishment from someone below. To seek nourishment from the one at the top is also judged inappropriate because he is not regarded as one with whom the position holder at the second position can properly be associated. Thus, although the subject at the second position has a need for nourishment, due to his condition determined under the situation, there exists no one with whom he can establish a dependable partnership. This sort of helpless situation in which the one at the second position fails to secure a dependable source of nourishment explains why the line statement predicts ill fortune. But, how can we assess the type of situation that is said to impinge upon the subject at the second position? For one thing there seems to be no reason to think it odd that a person will fall into a difficult situation if he fails to satisfy a certain need due to obstacles in an existing social situation. Of course, here again, a question concerning the view that the subjects at the first and the top positions cannot be appropriate partners for the one at the second position to be associated with still remains. What kind of structural factor or factors operate to bar the formation of relationships between, for example, the position holders at the second and the sixth positions? But, in neither the *I Ching* nor later commentaries do I find detailed and systematic accounts that will help us understand why there is such incompatibility or lack of affinity between those positions.

The line statement of the third yin line also renders an equally unfavorable judgment on its subject's condition under the situation. It reads, "This one practices Nourishment in a contrary way, so even constancy here will mean misfortune, and he will have no employment for ten years, for nothing at all would be fitting" (Lynn, 1994:307). The ill fortune that is said to impinge upon its subject is explained by the presence of a yin line misplaced in a yang place. An unfitting person who will "practice Nourishment in a contrary way" is occupying the third position, and, thus, it is interpreted that failure to follow normal patterns of Nourishment assures no prospect for him to derive desirable outcomes from the situation. But, what kind of behavior would be considered as deviating from normal patterns of Nourishment for the actor under this situation? According to Wang Bi, "Nourishment directed upward here is such that its provision to a superior becomes a form of sycophancy" (Lynn, 1994:307). Legge's interpretation characterizes its subject as someone who "considers himself sufficient for himself, without any help from without . . . ." (1963:116). And, Cheng Yi interprets the line as representing "those who are weak and dishonest, and who act wrongly" (1988:84). Wilhelm' view differs again from all of the above (1967:523). All these varying interpretations seem to be symptomatic of the somewhat arbitray nature of deciphering the "underlying" meanings of the *I Ching's* shortly phrased symbolism. Nevertheless, a general sociological perspective that seems to be uniquely characteristic of the *I Ching* still applies throughout all the varying interpretations: if one's actual action orientation and what is normatively required of his formal position are incongruent with each other, such incongruity will bring about no good outcomes for the actor involved. Implicitly suggested in this perspective is its reverse proposition: congruity between them will bring about good outcomes.

Now, we find such congruity from the fourth yin line that properly occupies a yin place, and this explains why the appended line statement renders a favorable judgment for the subject at that position. However, as was the case for the third yin line, the line statement has such opaque symbolism that commentators seem to have had a difficult time finding or, we may say here quite properly, "inventing" any sensible meaning out of it. Then, let us look at the line statement: "To reverse the Nourishment process here means good fortune. Such a one should stare with the ferocious look of a tiger, and his will should be strong and persistent, for then he will be without blame" (Lynn, 1994:308). Most commentators, except Wilhelm who interprets the line statement in a completely different way, share the same view and interpret that "to reverse the Nourishment" means to seek for Nourishment from someone positioned in lower status. Here we will remember that the subject at the second position is rendered a rather unfavorable judgment for the same reason as is stated in the above line statement. Probably aware of this inconsistency Wang Bi explains that not to "suffer disrespect" in establishing "a relationship with someone below him" "such a one (the subject at the fourth position) should stare down with the ferocious look of a tiger" (Lynn, 1994:308). Cheng Yi seems to agree with the above interpretation. However, their interpretations as such do not seem consistent with what is said in other line statements or with the overall theme of the hexagram.

The hexagram *Xian* (☱☶, Reciprocity, Influence)

The hexagram *Xian* (Influence) consists of the lower trigram *Gen* (Mountain) and the upper trigram *Dui* (the Lake), and, thus, the *Commentary on the Images* explains; "The Lake above the Mountain: this constitutes the image of Reciprocity. In the same way, the noble man receives others with self-effacement [*xu*, literally, "emptiness"]" (Lynn, 1994:330). To explain further, the Lake is formed as the empty crater on the mountaintop formed from volcanic activity is filled with water, and then the Mountain is nourished by water it receives from the Lake.[91] It is through this kind of a metaphoric reasoning that the hexagram *Xian* features a situation of Reciprocity between mutually dependent elements. However, the theme of the hexagram as such does not seem to give a particularly illuminating or useful guide, for we may not find it easy to relate it to what the line statements say. A more or less meaningful picture, if not as clear as desired, seems to emerge if we set off the interpretation of the line statements with a recognition that the hexagram embodies a situation in which certain position holders exert influences upon others who are subject to the influence exerted as such. Then, with this recognition in mind, let us examine the line statements.

The line statement of the first yin line is brief: "The first line, divided, shows one moving his great toes" (Legge, 1963:123).[92] It seems obvious first of all that the subject at the first position is compared to the big toes, the lowest part of the body whose movements "[do] not get you anywhere" (Cheng Yi, 1988:98). The line statement ends with this. Thus, all we can say is that the subject occupying the lowest position is represented by a yin line under this situation of influence, and, therefore, he is described as someone who is not in a position to exercise influence over others. Additional information is provided by the *Commentary on the Images*, which states, "his mind is set on what is beyond (himself)" (Legge, 1963:305). According to

Legge, the above passage means that the subject has "the desire to influence" the subject at the fourth position with whom he has a specific affinity. But, as implied by the line statement, the subject is interpreted to have insufficient potential to make his will effective. Of course, this interpretation considered by itself is not strange at all: people, even the common folk at the lowest position in society, may try to influence those at the higher echelon to work for their interests, but more often than not fail, largely due to factors operating against their wishes. However, I repeatedly have questioned why the subject at the fourth position is held to be the only position holder targeted to align with the one at the first position. Besides this troublesome question, the interpretation above nevertheless seems to involve a simple but interesting hypothesis: social influence needs a certain measure of power to make it felt by others.

The second position is compared to the calves of one's leg, and accordingly the line statement says of its subject, "The second line, divided, shows one moving the calves of his leg. There will be evil. If he abide (quiet in his place), there will be good fortune" (Legge, 1963:123). In essence, the line statement is interpreted as containing the same message as the first line; since "the calves cannot move of themselves" and "they (rather) follow the moving of the feet" (Legge, 1963:125), the movement of the calves symbolizes a vain effort to exercise influence that would not be effective due to the subject's lack of ability indicated under the situation. People who are not in advantageous positions to exercise influence should not go out and try to influence others.

The line statement of the third yang line compares the third position to "thighs" and, with use of such metaphor, it describes the situation of its subject as follows: "The third line, undivided, shows one moving his thighs, and keeping close hold of those whom he follows. Going forward (in this way) will cause regret" (Legge, 1963:123). As "one moving his thighs" its subject is described to be in a situation in which he is following someone closely as the thighs move along with other parts of the body. If we understand the subject's behavior to be descriptive of a blind submission to others' influence, then the advice, "Going forward (in this way) will cause regret," makes sense from our commonsense notion of dignity or independence. However, why should this subject at the third position be described as someone who would follow others in such blind conformity? And, who are "those whom he follows"? Regarding this latter question, Legge (1963:126) points to the subject at the fourth position, Wang Bi (Lynn, 1994:331) and Wilhelm (1967:543) the subjects at the lower two positions, and Cheng

Yi (1988:98) the subject at the sixth position. Here again we are witnessing an instance in which the idea of corresponding relationships, carrying or riding relationships, is applied quite arbitrarily depending upon individual commentators' subjective viewpoints. I suspect that the idea itself might not have been a part of the original thought system of the *I Ching*, but rather a product of the later periods, invented as commentators tried to formulate some systematic principles of interpretation to make sense out of the line statements. Notwithstanding their potential merit involving interesting theoretical ideas,[93] however, the ideas of corresponding, carrying, or riding relationships lack specific principles to regulate or guide their actual applications in interpreting the line statements. An outcome of this is what we see here; commentators apply them differently thus yielding different interpretations.

The subject at the fourth position is described as one who enjoys sufficient potential to exercise influence over others. Its line statement reads, "The fourth line, undivided, shows that firm correctness which will lead to good fortune, and prevent all occasion for repentance. If its subject be unsettled in his movements, (only) his friends will follow his purpose" (Legge, 1963:123). Considering the fact that the fourth position, a yin position, is occupied inappropriately by a yang line, the above line statement may be thought of as deviating from what can be ordinarily expected from a mismatched line such as this. However, Legge interprets that as every position in the hexagram is compared to a part of the body, the fourth position represents "the seat of the mind" (1963:126; c.f., Wilhelm, 1967:540). This suggests that the location of the fourth position can be compared to the heart where the mind resides. Following from this metaphor is another metaphoric reasoning that the mind is the source of influence that makes the body move. It is in this context that the last verse, stating, "If its subject be unsettled in his movements, (only) his friends will follow his purpose," makes sense. As is the case with the mind, "if the subject at the fourth position be unsettled in his movements," people except his close friends would not be moved by the influence exercised by him. Considering that the subject is understood to occupy the most advantageous position to exercise influence under the situation,[94] the line statement may be regarded as intending to give practical advice for one who enjoys the strong potential to influence others — unless one acts in a firm and dependable manner and thereby wins confidence from people, he will not be followed.

The line statement of the fifth yang line compares the location of the fifth position to "the flesh along the spine above the heart," and it reads, "The fifth line, undivided, shows one moving the flesh along the spine above the heart. There will be no occasion for repentance" (Legge, 1963:123). The meaning of this line statement is understood differently depending upon how commentators interpret the word *mo* (未) in the *Commentary on the Images*. If it is interpreted as meaning "trivial," the *Commentary on the Images* on this line statement is translated as, "'He (tries to) move the flesh along the spine above the heart:' — his aim is trivial" (Legge, 1963:306; c.f., Lynn, 1994:333). The word has another meaning, "the end." If we take this latter meaning, the same passage is translated as, " 'The influence shows itself in the back of the neck.' The will is directed to the ramifications" (Wilhelm, 1967:544). In Legge's translation, the subject at the fifth position is interpreted to aim at exercising influence, yet what he aims at is nothing more than trying to "move the flesh along the spine above the heart," meaning he tries to use his influence over trivial things. If the leader of a society tries to exercise influence over trivial things, this indeed is a regrettable affair. Yet this reading may be understood as inconsistent with the ending line, "There will be no occasion for repentance." Notwithstanding this issue, why is the subject interpreted as displaying such inopportune behavior in his leadership? Regarding this question, we may notice that the line formation of the hexagram may yield a reading diametrically opposed to the above interpretation: since a yang line occupies a yang place, the subject represented as such may have to be judged to be in an advantageous or favorable situation. I think the above puzzle and question might have led Wilhelm to interpret the line statement quite differently from the views presented above. According to him, the subject at the fifth position is in a crucial position where he controls "the chief organic processes" through which he also "achieves order in particulars as well" (1967:544). An advantage of this latter interpretation seems obvious; the ending line of the line statement is now meaningfully related to what is stated in the preceding line and the subject at the fifth position is now given as favorable a judgment as can be expected from the line formation. Of course, at least in the eyes of native scholars who put great value on the moral lessons that can supposedly be derived from the *I Ching*, there may be one crucial drawback in Wilhelm's above interpretation. As far as the moral lesson of the line statement is concerned, the former interpretation may be viewed as involving more useful advice for those in leadership: it would not be desirable for the leader to use his influence over trivial matters.

The sixth position is compared to "jaws and tongue," and,

accordingly, the line statement describes the subject at the position as "moving his jaws and tongue," which means that he tries to influence people by "means of speech" (Legge, 1963:124, 126). Implicitly suggested here is that this method is far less ideal and effective than such means as "sincerity," a far superior way, morally and practically, to earn trust from others. It is with this belief that Cheng Yi comments, "this (i.e., to influence by means of speech) is the ordinary condition of the petty man; how can it move anyone?" (1988:101). Nevertheless, it is not clear why the subject at the sixth position is described to be a petty man who tries to influence people only (to put it into a modern term) with the use of propagandistic messages. Thus, it may be interpreted to contain a moral teaching for whoever is in a position to exercise influence under the situation represented by the hexagram. Understood from this perspective, the line statement seems to emphasize the point that to succeed in influencing others, one is required to have effective resources such as advantageous position and appropriate moral posture, not merely "jaws and tongues" to persuade others.

The hexagram *Yi* (☴☳, Increase)

The meaning of the hexagram *Yi* (Increase) is derived from the ideas associated with its two component trigrams; the trigrams *Zhen* and *Sun* indicating things at a phase of active development and Compliance, respectively. Thus, as Wang Bi comments, the hexagram represents a situation in which the "One located above and imbued with compliance does not oppose *Zhen*" (Lynn, 1994:396). Hence, a state of dynamic development, or Increase, refers to the situational trend manifested by the subordinate group who is undergoing "Increase" with the support of the upper group. The upper group, in turn, complies with the "growth" oriented activities of the lower. The favorable line statements for the three position holders in the lower group can be understood in the overall context of the situational meaning of the hexagram as explained above: all the members in the subordinate group are growing and the upper group is helping the people below to grow. Regarding the meaning of the situation, however, there is some ambiguity. What kind of growth does the hexagram signify? If it means a growth in power, the hexagram can be interpreted as representing a situation in which the subordinate group is allowed to exercise greater autonomy in managing affairs or in decision making. As a matter of fact, the line statements involve narratives, if only partial, that lead us to such an interpretation.

Considering the meaning of the situation and the line structure of the hexagram, the subject at the first position is considered the governing ruler, one who leads the entire group or occupies the strategic position setting the tone for the group under the situation. Understandably, its line statement contains a favorable judgment, but with some reservation: "It is fitting to use this opportunity to accomplish some great undertakings, but only with fundamentally good fortune will one be without blame" (Lynn, 1994:398). Commentators offer similar explanations as to why the line statement says the subject is in need of "fundamentally good fortune" to avoid blame. I present Wang Bi's explanation as an example:

> Here below where First Yang abides is not a situation for substantial undertakings; this humble place is not a position where one should be entrusted with weighty matters, and a great undertaking cannot be got through with only a small amount of success. (Lynn, 1994:398)

To paraphrase Wang Bi's commentary in words familiar to modern social scientists, the subject at the bottom position has the opportunity to do great things which will enhance his status, yet his chance for achieving successful outcomes will be largely circumscribed by the limitation of his lowly position. Although the situation allows him a great deal of autonomy, he may not be able to garner great benefits due to structurally imposed disadvantages inherent in his low position. With this consideration the line statement says, "only with fundamentally good fortune will one be without blame." Cheng Yi supplements this line statement with his own view peppered with a moral instruction: "When people are in the lowest position but are faced with great responsibilities, a little good will not be sufficient. Therefore great good is necessary to be impeccable" (1988:137).

The line statement of the second yin line is rather long but also carries a message that is consistent with the overall meaning of the situation represented by the hexagram. It reads:

> There are those who increase this one. Of tens of coteries of tortoises, there are none that can act in opposition. The practice of perpetual constancy here will mean good fortune. If the king uses this opportunity to make offering of this one to the Divine Ruler [*di*], there would be good fortune. (Lynn, 1994:398-399)

In the above line statement, "those who increase this one" refers to the subject at the fifth position, the top leadership. Then, the line statement can be understood as saying that the best action for the subject at the fifth position under this situation is to help "this one" (the subject at the second position) grow. The subject at the second position will enjoy great opportunities that may bring about an enhancement in his status or an increase in his personal resources or power potential, and, consequently, the best the one at the fifth position can make out of this situation is showing God ("the Divine Ruler") what he has achieved by demonstrating what the subject at the second position has achieved on his behalf. But, why is the subject at the second position advised to maintain a "perpetually constant" posture? According to Wilhelm, this admonition is considered "necessary because the yielding quality of the line, in combination with the yielding place, might lead to a certain weakness, which must be balanced by firmness of will" (1967:599). In other words, although a yin line appropriately occupies a yin place, the second subject is in too weak a posture to carry out great things; even with help of the fifth yang line, the subject at the second position needs a measure of resolute will power to attain positive outcomes for either his own advancement or the collective welfare of the group. Hence, the advice, "The practice of perpetual constancy here will mean good fortune," is offered to the subject at the second position.

The line statement of the third yin line yields many different interpretations and therewith different translations, indicative of the difficulty in interpreting symbolically narrated verses composed of only a few words with highly condensed meanings. Thus, I would like to pick out only two versions and compare how they differ in interpreting the specific situation of the subject at the third position. We will examine Lynn's and Legge's translations. Lynn's translation of the line statement reads, "This one brings about Increase, but if he were to use it to save a bad situation, he should be without blame. He has sincerity, and to report to the duke that he treads the path of the Mean he uses a *gui* [jade tablet]" (1994:399). Translated as above, the core idea of the line statement regarding the individual situation of its subject can be explained as follows. The subject at the third position, the leadership position of the subordinate group, is described as one who himself "brings about Increase." This evokes an image of someone who has accumulated wealthy resources for himself and thus has secured a superior position over others. Yet, the line statement also offers the suggestion to the third position holder to share this wealth or resources with others, should such a circumstance arise. Wang Bi interprets the line statement's advice to say, "if he were to use it [his increase] to save a bad situation [famine or other emergencies], he should be without blame" (Lynn, 1994:399). In other words, the subject at the third position is advised to use his resources to help others in emergency situations so that he too can be saved from unfortunate outcomes that may likely happen. The remaining portion of the line statement, "He has sincerity, and to report to the duke that he treads the path of the Mean he uses a *gui* [jade tablet]," is subject to the same interpretation. The subject in the third position is advised to keep a modest profile with all-proper decorum and attitude towards his superiors in the higher echelon so that he can avoid possible anger or punishment from those above.[95] Compared to the above interpretation, Legge's interpretation yields the following translation:

> The third line, divided, shows increase given to its subject by means of what is evil, so that he shall (be led to good), and be without blame. Let him be sincere and pursue the path of the Mean, (so shall he secure the recognition of the ruler, like) an officer who announces himself to his prince by the symbol of his rank. (1963: 150)

According to this translation, the third yin line, inappropriately occupying a yang position, is considered to face some adverse condition, yet he will turn it into a means through which Increase (growth) is attained. The remaining portion is interpreted in the same way as the previous version. We may wonder which of the two translations renders a better, or more sensible, interpretation, Lynn's or Legge's. Yet, judging the adequacy of one interpretation over the other is a moot point because, as previously mentioned, the *I Ching* does not lend itself to such judgments.

In contrast to divergent views adopted in interpreting the line statement of the third yin line, the line statement of the fourth yin line is unanimously interpreted as depicting a dutiful official on whom the ruler at the fifth position relies for important decision making. The line statement itself is straightforward; it reads, "The fourth line, divided, shows its subject pursuing the due course. His advice to his prince is followed. He can with advantage be relied on in such a movement as that of removing the capital" (Legge, 1963:150).[96] The reason for which the subject at the fourth position is viewed to act as duly as expected of anyone who occupies that position would be explained by the fact that a yin line is incumbent appropriately where a yin is expected to be present. This allows for a good match with the fifth yang line that also occupies appropriately a yang place. Moreover, as we will see under this specific situation, the fifth yang line, despite being a strong line at a strong position, figures as a person intent on giving Increase to others. Hence, with the characteristics of the two lines being considered together, the subject at the fourth position is described as a dutiful official "pursuing the due course" and, due to his relationship with the ruler above under the situation, as one whose "advice to the prince (in such important matters as moving the capital) is followed."

The fifth yang line, as Wang Bi explains, "is the ruler of the *Yi* [Increase] hexagram," yet not as a receiver but a benefactor. This means that, as Wang Bi also explains citing a passage taken from *Lunyu* (Analects), the subject at the fifth position is one who "brings benefit to the common folk through things that they find beneficial and so kind to them without bestowing largesse" (Lynn, 1994:401, 403n13). Accordingly, the line statement states, "This one has sincerity and a heart full of kindness, so he should have no doubt that he shall have fundamental good fortune. As he has sincerity, his own virtue will be taken to be kindness" (Lynn, 1994:401). Judging from this line statement, there would be no doubt that under this situation that the top leadership represented by the fifth yang line is fully dedicated to bringing Increase (whether it be material prosperity or growth in another dimension) to the people below. The *I Ching* seems to characterize the essential virtue of this type of leadership intent on giving Increase to the people under his leadership as "kindness," indicative of a moral orientation of the political ideology so typical of Confucian thought.

The discussions on the line statements thus far conjure up an image of a group being more or less integrated around activities centering on bringing Increase to the people in the lower echelon. Generally in the *I Ching*, integrated situations are not perfectly integrated in the sense that there is always a certain member (or members) who is not well integrated into, or excluded from, networks of people involved in the collective unit represented by the hexagram. In this particular situation represented by the hexagram *Yi* (Increase), the top yang line is figured as such an element who stands apart from the rest of the members. For some reason which is not clear, the subject at the top position is described as someone who "brings Increase to no one." Since "There is no consistency in the way he sets his heart and mind," he will not make any positive contribution to the welfare of the other people involved in the situation and "so there are those who strike at him" (Lynn, 1994:401). The *I Ching* or later commentaries, however, offer no clearly stated reason why the subject at the top position is considered an unproductive and unpopular individual against whom others display repulsive reactions.

Hexagrams: Types of Social Situations 283

Summary of theoretical and empirical propositions

1) Although penalty has to be applied whenever necessary, restrictions do not help to bring enlightenment to the minds of the people in need of instruction; both restrictions and a free atmosphere are needed in good education or in socialization.

2) An essential factor for success in teaching people who are subject to education or socialization is kindness and understanding.

3) A successful outcome cannot be expected from teaching people who want education purely for materialistic gains.

4) Although we may have to apply punishment in educating people, it has to be done with appropriate principles, restraining hostile emotions.

5) In general, political offenses committed among the common people will be dealt with less severely than those committed by the people at the upper strata.

6) Under certain situations, intellectuals who are positioned outside the formal hierarchical line of the officialdom will emerge as forces exercising what may be called the spiritual or ideological leadership for a society. If this kind of a situation should come to exist, the informal power exercised by spiritual or ideological leaders will operate as the most powerful factor influencing a political community.

7) People at a lower echelon, even the common folk in the lowest position in society, may try to influence those at the higher echelon to work for their interests, but more often than not fail largely due to factors operating against their wishes. Thus, an exercise of social influence is possible only when one is equipped with a certain measure of formal power or a situationally determined capability to make his influence felt real by others.

8) Although a person possesses a strong influence potential, unless he acts in a firm and dependable manner and thereby wins confidence from others, he will not be followed. In this sense, to succeed in influencing others requires not only such effective resources as formally endowed power but also appropriate moral postures.

9) It is not advantageous for a leader to use his influence over trivial

matters.

10) Hexagrams Representing Social and Political Institutions

In sociology, the term "institution" refers to either established ways of carrying out important functions in any area of organized social life or organizations themselves that are "institutionalized" in the sense stated above. For example, the family as a social institution refers to established human practices through which such important functions as the procreation and rearing of the new generation are carried out. The five hexagrams to be introduced here deal with topics related to some social and political institutions that existed at the time when the *I Ching* was written. Of those, the hexagram *Jiaren* (the Family) depicts an ideal type of family, and each line statement in the hexagram describes each family member at a respective position acting as ideally as expected of the position holder at the position. The hexagram *Sun* (Diminution) features a hierarchically organized tributary system that consists of two groups of people — ones at inferior positions who yield their valuable resources to others above and the others who, seated at the dominant positions, take in the resources yielded. Its line statements, accordingly, involve brief descriptions about the kinds of roles performed by each position holder under the system and offer advice considered appropriate regarding the subjects' positions each involving a specific task. In the hexagram *Jian* (Gradual Advancement), the line positions represent a series of specific situations that people are expected to face at each step or position while they are gradually moving up a hierarchically ordered ladder of social positions. The line statements also involve advice or warnings about what can be called occupational hazards that people may experience at each step or position in the process of upward social mobility. The hexagram *Jing* (Well) tells about various types of wells that are supposed to represent various types of government, some functioning well and others functioning badly. Since each line statement in this hexagram refers to a specific type of government, the line statements taken as a whole can be read as dealing with a typology on various types of government. The hexagram *Guimei* (Marrying Maid) differs from the hexagrams above; its line statements taken as a whole can be read as an essay written to give words of advice to the maid who is sent for marriage or to those who are to send their younger sister for marriage. It may appear obvious from the brief summaries above that what interested the author(s) of the *I Ching* in these five hexagrams was not the structural features of the institutions per se, but rather giving words of wisdom to the actors involved in the mentioned institutions. This will become obvious in fact as we examine each of the hexagrams in the following list.

1) The hexagram *Jiaren* (☴☲, The Family) (Hexagram No. 37)

2) The hexagram *Sun* (☶☱, Diminution) (Hexagram No. 41)

3) The hexagram *Jian* (☴☶, Gradual Advance) (Hexagram No. 42)

4) The hexagram *Jing* (☵☴, Well) (Hexagram No. 48)

5) The hexagram *Guimei* (☳☱, Marrying Maid) (Hexagram No. 54)

The hexagram *Jiaren* (☴☲, The Family)

The hexagram *Jiaren* (The Family) refers to a situation in which the core units of the hexagram, the four lines located in between the bottom and the top lines, are arranged in a formation that symbolizes the ideal family. Yang lines occupy the third and the fifth positions, two leadership (yang) positions, while yin lines occupy the second and the fourth positions, subordinate (yin) positions. This is the formation of a social unit organized according to the principle of the ideal family in which "male and female should keep to their proper places" (Lynn, 1994:137). Here, however, we may be reminded of the fact that there are several other hexagrams in which the middle four lines have the same line structure as this one. Then, why is only this hexagram called *Jiaren* (The Family)? A possible answer may be sought in that the meaning of this hexagram is derived from the unbroken lines at the two boundary positions, the bottom and the top positions, giving a pictorial image of a house wall with a family (represented by the middle four lines) residing inside. Once the hexagram is viewed as representing a situation or a type of organization that shows the characteristic of the ideal family, each line seems to convey a specific meaning associated relevantly with the position it occupies.

Then, let us look at the line statement of the first yang line: "If this one is prevented from acting like the master of the household, then there will be no regret" (Lee, 1997[II]:47, translated by this author).[97] If we accept the interpretation that the first yang line represents growing children in the family, or probably the youngest son as Lee suggests, the intent of the line statement is clear: the failure to put growing children, or neophyte members of a group, under strict disciplines is good for neither themselves nor for the family.

The rest of the lines except the top yang line are divided into two kinds — two yin lines at the second and the fourth positions (the yin positions) and two yang lines at the third and the fifth positions (the yang positions). Each of the two strong lines appropriately occupies a yang position and is "riding on" a yin line that appropriately occupies a yin position; this is interpreted as an ideal human organization composed of position holders who behave appropriately according to their expected roles. Although the two yin lines, each belonging to either the lower trigram or the upper one, differ in social standings, their basic functions under this situation are regarded as the same. The same can be said of the two yang lines. The subjects represented by the two yin lines at the second and the fourth positions are described similarly as females who carry out faithfully house-keeping duties, and both the subjects at the third and the fifth positions as patriarchal figures who exercise leadership or regulative functions. To the eyes of the people in old China and in many Asian societies of today, this hexagram represents the ideal family or, by analogy, of an ideally composed and operating human organization in general. What the *Commentary on the Judgments* says of this hexagram is a clear expression of this:

> Male and female should keep to their proper places; this is the fundamental concept expressed by Heaven and Earth. The family is provided with strict sovereigns, whom we call Father and Mother [Fifth Yang and Second Yin]. When the father behaves as a father, the mother as a mother, the son as son, the elder brother as elder brother, the younger brother as younger brother, the husband as husband, and the wife as wife, then the Dao of the Family will be correctly fulfilled. When the Family is so maintained with rectitude, the entire world will be settled and at peace. (Lynn, 1994:363)

The thought expressed in the above commentary recites what is called Confucius' thought on the Rectification of Names. According to Confucius, if everybody in the society acts as he or she is expected according to his or her role, the society will be kept in harmonious order.[98] Thus, there is little doubt that this hexagram represents an ideal situation or type of social organization as seen from the value system of old Chinese culture.

Now, since the two yin lines, the second and the fourth, are described as playing quite similar roles, we will examine them together.

> *Second Yin*: This one has no matters to set off to and pursue but stays within and prepares food. Such constancy means good fortune.
>
> *Fourth Yin*: This one enriches the Family, so there is great good fortune. (Lynn, 1994:364-5)

There is a common theme in the above two line statements; both subjects at the two positions are described as females dealing with domestic affairs inside the family. If the situation were to be referred to a social organization at a larger level, they would represent administrative workers who carry on assigned roles dutifully and obediently, according to what is expected of their subordinate positions in relation to those in leadership. Also suggested quite clearly in the account given above is the fact that those yang lines at the third and the fifth positions represent strong leaders who rule over the family or a social organization with patriarchal authority. The line statements of the two yang lines states quite clearly the nature of the leaderships as such:

> *Third Yang*: If the Family is run with ruthless severity, one may regret the degree of it, yet there will be good fortune. But if wife and child overindulge in frivolous laughter, in the end it will result in basement.
>
> *Fifth Yang*: Only when a true king arrives will there be a real Family, so let him be without worry, for he shall have good fortune. (Lynn, 1994:365-6)

There seems to be little ambiguity that both the above two line statements tell about patriarchal leaders. However, we can notice some important differences between the two. The subject at the third position, the leader of the subordinate unit, is described as one who exercises direct control over lowly ranked group members such as "wife and child," referring to both the first yang and the second yin lines. A warning that "if wife and child overindulge in frivolous laughter, in the end it will result in basement" reflects a long held belief that the elites in old China had toward women, children and, by analogy, the illiterate common folk — if not dealt with by strict regulations, they are likely to overindulge in undisciplined, pleasure seeking behaviors. Because of this, the subject at this position is advised that "the family should be run with ruthless severity," although he may have regretful feelings for exercising such strict discipline on his own kinfolk. Compared to the third yang line, the fifth yang line is described as a "king," not a disciplinarian like the subject at the third position; it represents a higher and more general type of leadership, the central figure around which the family is integrated. This becomes clearer as the *Commentary on the Images* supplements the line statement with an explanation, "This one maintains the Family with the perfection of a true king, so each attends to the other with love" (Lynn, 1994:366). While the role of the leader in the third position is to make people under his rule tread on the right track, the role of the fifth yang line is described to be largely for integrating the entire group's members.

Now, in this situation characterized as being held together like one big family under paternalistic leadership, what would be the role played by the subject at the sixth position? Let us read its line statement, first: "This one inspires trust and is awesome, so in the end there is good fortune" (Lynn, 1994:366). The *Commentary on the Images* adds a very interesting comment on this line statement: "That good fortune follows upon the inspiration of awe means that one has to reflect upon what awe means to himself" (Lynn, 1994:367). The above commentary suggests that the trust and awe that the subject at the sixth position may inspire among the others involved in the situation depend largely on how he manages himself. Since he has no formal position, his ability to inspire "trust and awe" in others will not be derived from the power associated with his formal position; it has to be rooted in informal authority of moral or spiritual kind. In the family situation, the authority of this kind may remind us of that of a grandfather who does not involve himself in the daily affairs of the family yet whose presence and moral standards have significant influence over all the family members. But, to enjoy the "great fortune" as such, the commentary suggests, will require its subject to reflect upon himself to see whether he in fact is worthy of being placed in such a position.

The hexagram *Sun* (☶☱, Diminution)

The next hexagram, *Sun* (Diminution), refers to a situation in which those represented by the lower trigram diminish while there is increase for those above. To what specific thing or property the diminution or increase occurs is not clearly explained. Legge points out that "every diminution and repression of what we have in excess to bring it into accordance with right and reason is comprehended under Sun" (1963:148). But, the making of one's gain out of others' loss could happen only to such limited resources as power, wealth, or labor force. As a matter of fact, in my opinion, the most sensible interpretations of the line statements of this hexagram can only be made with a view that power, wealth, or labor force is what is diminished or increased. Interpreted in this way, the situation that this hexagram represents can be figured as that in which scarce resources are transferred from the people in the lower echelon to those at the higher. As we proceed with the line statements, the main theme of this hexagram will emerge more clearly.

The line statement of the first yang line states, "Once one's duties are finished, he should quickly set forth, for then he shall be without blame, but he should take careful measure of how much diminishment takes place" (Lynn, 1994:389). The above line statement involves advice for the subject at the first position: as soon as he finishes his own work, he has to go quickly to serve those in the upper echelon (specifically, the subject at the fourth position as interpreted by most commentators). It would help us understand the above line statement if we note that the common folk in old China could be called into compulsory labor service by the state when judged necessary. But, there is a question regarding to whom the line stating, "he should take careful measure of how much diminishment takes place," is addressed. Regardless of what "diminishment" specifically refers, the statement itself seems to make sense: one should take careful measure of how much diminishment the common folk represented by the bottom line can afford. However, the assessment of diminishment may not be a matter for the common folk to decide. With this consideration, Wilhelm interprets it as being addressed to "the one above who claims the services of the one below." That is, according to Wilhelm, when "self-decrease" is made "on the part of the one below for the benefit of the one above . . . . It is his duty (i.e., of the one above) to weigh in his mind how much he may require without injuring the one below" (1967:592). With this interpretation, the situational meaning of the hexagram becomes clearer: it represents a situation in which power, wealth, or labor service of the common folk is decreased (or levied) for the benefit of those in the upper echelon. Modern conflict theorists may put this phenomenon in a simpler word, "exploitation." Parsons may think otherwise and say that "mediums of exchange" are transferred from one functional subsystem to another (1967:264-296; 1970:13-72).

The line statement of the second yang line describes its subject as one who "can give increase (to his correlate) without taking from himself" (Legge, 1963:147).[99] "His correlate" is interpreted as the subject at the fifth position. Then, why is he described as being in a position that "can give increase" to the ruler without incurring loss on himself? Most commentators give a moralistic interpretation which is predicated on the preceding passage that reads, "The second line, undivided, shows that it will be advantageous for its subject to maintain a firm correctness, and that action on his part will be evil" (Legge, 1963:147). Thus, the subject at the second position can prevent his own loss while also giving increase to the one above because his position and the condition associated with the situation help him "maintain a firm correctness" and, therefore, cope with the situation with no loss on his own part. But, I doubt if the above explanation would convey any sensible idea. A simpler and more meaningful interpretation would be that officials in the second position act as intermediary agencies between the common people and the state in collecting taxes or levying labor services. Therefore, their role would be simply to transfer what was collected from the common folk to the state, yet with no loss on their own part. These are not the people who have to undergo "diminution" themselves.

The line statement of the third yin line poses a difficult case to interpret in that it seems to bear little relevance to the main theme of the hexagram. It states, "If three people travel together, one person will be lost, but when one person travels, he will find his companion" (Lynn, 1994:390). Taken in itself, however, the line statement may be understood to set forth an interesting proposition: it will be hard to form a harmoniously cooperating unit out of three parties or persons and easier when people seek the formation of an alliance on a one-to-one basis. This interpretation finds support in Cheng Yi's writings. Commenting upon this line statement, he holds that "Everything in the world is dual. The interdependence of one and two is the basis of continuing creation. Three is excess, and should be reduced" (1988:134-5). Kim also adopts this interpretation and translates the line statement as follows: "When three people work together, one of them may set himself against the other two and break away with them. When one works alone bearing all responsibility by himself, it will be easier to obtain a partner to work with" (1997:320, translated by this author). The line statement of the third line interpreted as above involves an interesting sociological hypothesis: the dyadic relationship is much more stable than the triadic one. However, what does this line statement have to do with the main theme of the hexagram? Cheng Yi relates this line statement to the idea of increase or diminution in the sense that since "three is excess" and, therefore, there is a need for reduction by one. Yet, it is unclear how the line statement is related to the attributes of the third line as interpreted from its position, line characteristic, and the positioning of other lines. Of course, commentators make attempt at some explanations to resolve this difficulty. However, of the rationality of such explanations, I am fully in agreement with Legge who says, "I cannot lay hold of any thread of reason in this" (1963:149).

The line statement of the fourth yin line states, "One here may diminish his anxiety, for if he were to act quickly, he should have cause for joy and so be without blame" (Lynn, 1994:391). "Anxiety (*ji*)" is interpreted differently and thereby translated variously as "sickness," "fault," "not good," or "shortcomings" (Lynn, 1994:390n13). If we insert "shortcomings" in the place of "anxiety," the beginning line of the line statement would read, "One here may diminish his shortcomings." As power, wealth, or labor service is transferred from those at the lower echelon to those at the upper echelon, the subject at the fourth position will be a beneficiary in the receiving party. So says the line statement, "if he were to act quickly, he should have cause for joy and so be without blame."

In the receiving party, the subject at the fifth position may be expected to occupy the most favorable position for "increase", rather than diminishment. The line statement in fact confirms this expectation: "The fifth line, divided, shows parties adding to (the stores of) its subject ten pairs of tortoise shells, and accepting no refusal. There will be great good fortune" (Legge, 1963:147).[100] According to Zhu Xi' interpretation, "ten pairs of tortoise shells" means "a great treasure, something of tremendous value" (Lynn, 1994:395n18). Thus, the line statement fits well with the main theme of the hexagram — what is taken from the common folk will go into the hands of the state whose power and authority the subject at the fifth position represents.

The only yang line in the upper hexagram represents the subject at the sixth position. Despite the weakness associated with its "informal" position, the subject possesses a strong influence potential over others under the situation. Having this in mind, let us read its line statement:

"This one suffers no Diminution but enjoys increase without blame. The practice of constancy means good fortune, and it would be fitting if he were set out to do something. It acquires subordinates and ministers, and private interests cease" (Lynn, 1994:392). As might be expected, the judgment on the subject's situation is favorable, although the situation requires him to keep a correct and firm posture in conduct. The line statement describes its subject as the pillar of integration around which people are united into one. However, why the subject is described as someone who, "With this acquisition of subordinates and ministers," makes "the whole world .... become(s) one" (Wang Bi, in Lynn, 1994:392-3) is not clearly explained in the text or in later commentaries. Perhaps the line statement views the probable effect of "Increase" (whether it refers to power, wealth, or labor force) achieved by the ruling class as one of the primary conditions for them to organize the government and therewith to rule a country. That is, with the acquisition of such resources, the government attracts loyal followers, and a country will operate as a well-integrated unit. In light of this interpretation where the governing elites are facilitated with necessary resources, the line stating, "it would be fitting if he were set out to do something," would have a clearer meaning.

The hexagram *Jian* (☴☶ , Gradual Advance)

According to the *Commentary on the Images*, the meaning of the hexagram *Jian* (Gradual Advance) was taken from its line composition that consists of the lower trigram *Gen* (mountain) and the upper trigram *Sun* (wood), thus conveying the image of "the Tree above the Mountain" (Lynn, 1994:472). Trees grow on mountains slowly and take a long time to reach any significant size; hence, the hexagram represents a situation in which "gradual progress" takes place. In the line statements, respective subjects are described as geese that "gradually proceed" to various places. According to Cheng Yi, "The lines use geese for a symbol because geese form orderly flocks at specific times" (1988:180). Judging from Cheng Yi's commentary above, it may be understood that the hexagram is descriptive of "orderly flocks of geese at specific times" through which things or affairs that develop in orderly and gradual fashions are represented in symbolism. Perhaps to the author(s) of the *I Ching*, the orderly pattern of the seasonal migration of geese and the gradually ordered processes in which they descend to their destination, settle down, mate, have a new generation of geese, raise them, and depart for their original location might have been thought to symbolize a situation where the orderly and gradual development of human affairs such as marriage takes place. It would be with this view that the *Commentary on the Judgments* tells about marriage and advancement in social positions; both, as understood by the author(s) of the *I Ching*, would have to be done in orderly and gradual fashions. From the line statements we will notice that there is some good sense for the hexagram being called "Gradual advance": each of the line statements describes geese that advance to a certain place, and as the line statements move from the bottom to the top, there is a gradual elevation of the heights to which the geese advance. Geese advance to the shore at first, then to the rocks at the water, to the high land next, to the tree, to the hill, and finally to the sky. All the accounts are clearly indicative of the fact that the various places signify social positions organized in a hierarchical order along the ascending steps of which individuals are expected to move. In other words, the line statements of the hexagram as a whole can be regarded as describing a chain of social positions along the track where social mobility (that takes place in a gradual and orderly way) occurs. Interestingly, the line statements contain ideas, if somewhat vaguely expressed, about the specific risk that each position involves. For example, the line statement of the first position, that is supposedly addressed to young people who yet hold no official position, warns that if they get too impatient to land cautiously in wanted positions, they may get into difficult situations. I think this, in view of our image of ambitious and impatient young people in general, is not wholly an implausible idea. The same may be said for the other line statements; they say things that sound more or less plausible regarding the potential risks that respective positions may involve. Aside from this aspect of the line statements, I have an impression that this hexagram was written with the pedagogic purpose of showing people an ideal example of "gradual advance," of which the social success of an ideal person achieved in orderly and gradual fashion would be one example. Now, let us look at the line statements and see how the process of gradual advance is figured specifically in this hexagram.

The first line statement reads, "Geese gradually approach the shore. Young ones who hurry up may be in danger. But, if they are given talks of warning and slow down, there will be no blame" (Kim, 1997:407, translated from the Korean text by this author).[101] In things that require a cautious and gradual approach, inexperienced young people may commit mistakes by making movements in haste, so they have to be given warnings not to act as such; they then would not make mistakes for which they might be blamed. Interpreted in this way, the line statement contains sensible advice to impatient young people who rush into things seeking for quick outcomes. Now, if the hexagram represents a social occasion or process such as marriage or status acquisition that requires well ordered steps, each line has to feature a specific situation that individuals face at each stage of the gradual progress. The line statement of the first line seems to support this interpretation; it contains advice for people just starting out on the first step in a series of gradually developing phases leading to the completion of a task. The interpretation of the first line statement compels us to interpret the line statements of other positions likewise as representing the specific situations of an event at certain phases of its development. We will see, however, that this perspective with which the line statements are interpreted as representing temporary development phases of an event will face difficulty in accounting for all the line statements. This may mean that as far as this particular hexagram is concerned, it is not possible to identify a unitary perspective that will apply coherently throughout all the line statements. With this recognition, we will move on to the next line statements and see how the mentioned difficulty arises with some of them.

The second line statement, interpreted as describing the stage of "settling-down" of the geese after landing on the shore, seems to pose no particularly difficult problem in interpretation. It reads, "The second line, divided, shows the geese gradually approaching the large rocks (at water), where they eat and drink joyfully and at ease. There will be good fortune" (Legge, 1963:179).[102] It is not immediately clear from the text or any later commentary what kind of a specific social situation the line statement is to represent. It may be said to convey the idea that the image of the geese settling down in safe places and nourishing themselves to prepare for the coming mating season symbolizes someone who has stepped properly into the second stage of development and is preparing for the next.

The line statement of the third yang line features geese that advance to a higher place than "the rocks at water," signifying the subject's promotion to a higher position. However, at the same time, it tells about difficulties that the geese have to experience at the place where the conditions supposedly differ entirely from their natural habitat described in the second line statement. The line statement reads, "The wild goose gradually advances to the high land. The husband sets forth but does not return, and the wife gets with child but does not raise it, which means misfortune. It is fitting here to guard against harassment" (Lynn, 1994:475). The line statement, if taken at face value, tells about geese that go to the high land, leaving their natural habitat, and therefore are exposed to predatory animals from whose attacks they have to "guard" themselves. Commentators such as Wang Bi (Lynn, 1994:475) and Cheng Yi (1988:181) have attempted to explain what the line statement supposedly indicates in terms of a human situation, but I am not able to make any clear sense out of them. The line statement may suggest that as the geese in the high land would face difficult situations, the middle leader in the third position must defend himself from the many hazards innate in his position. Interpreted in this way, the line statement of the third yang line certainly seems to make sense: the middle leadership position ranks higher than the second position, but, as compared to the relatively comfortable and safer situation that the subjects at the lower administrative positions can enjoy, the one at the middle leadership can easily suffer under political cross-fires from both above and below and therefore would be in a tougher situation to fight off "harassment."

The line statement of the fourth yin line describes its subject as advancing to a higher level position than the third one. Accordingly, it reads, "The wild goose gradually advances to the tree. Perhaps it obtains a proper perch for itself, and, if so, there would be no blame" (Lynn, 1994:476). A tree does not offer comfortable and safe places for geese whose body and feet shape have adapted to swimming in water. According to Cheng Yi, "Geese have webbed feet and cannot grip a tree branch, so they do not roost in trees." Thus, trees for geese are interpreted to indicate in metaphor that "the position of the fourth is basically dangerous" (1988:182). The line statement, however, involves at the same time a suggestion that trees have flat branches that would provide safe footings for geese's flat feet. This is interpreted to mean that amidst the danger associated with the fourth position, the subject can find ways to maintain a certain measure of well-being, and, if so, he will come out well with no serious damage to his reputation or welfare. Of course, it is not clearly explained why the fourth position is viewed to involve such occupational hazards and what would be specific ways through which the subject at the position could survive the potential hazards inherent in the position.

The line statement of the fifth position describes its subject as advancing further to a still higher place. It reads, "The wild goose gradually advances to the hill. The wife for three years does not bear a child. But, in the end none shall triumph over this one, and there shall be good fortune" (Lynn, 1994:476). The subject to whom the above line statement is addressed has finally reached the hill, the leadership position. But, why is this one viewed to take three years in order to "bear a child"? And, what does "to bear a child" mean? On this, Wang Bi's explanation sounds plausible: "If this one advances in order to rectify the state, in three years he shall have success, and with that success the Dao will be saved. Thus it will not take more than three years" (Lynn, 1994:476). It is not easy to produce great achievements within a short period of time after one assumes power, yet he is able to do it gradually under the situation of "gradual advancement" as indicated by the hexagram. A conflict in interpretation, however, arises due to some commentators' explanations that the reason for which there is the delay in bringing about successful achievements on the part of the subject at the fifth position lies in the fact that the subjects at the third and the fourth positions block the union between the subjects at the second and the fifth positions (Cheng Yi, 1988:182; Wang Bi, in Lynn, 1994:476). In this explanation, the idea that the lines in the hexagram represent temporal stages of an event in gradual development is discarded and replaced with one in which they represent unequally ranked people interacting with one another in a hierarchical organization. As I see it, this kind of shift in referred dimensions of reality is also found in some other hexagrams. And, on such occasions, explanations provided by commentaries seem to be more confusing than helpful in making sense out of what is said in the text. Thus, a more straightforward and clearer interpretation that coheres better with the interpretations of the previous lines will be obtained if we accept the previous interpretation that says the task of the leadership takes time to yield results, yet wanted outcomes will come about gradually following the overall trend of the time.

The line statement of the sixth line describes its subject as geese that have reached the final stage of gradual development at which they are ready for flying up into the sky. Of what is implied by the symbolism involved in this line statement, Cheng Yi explains; "In human terms, this represents those who transcend ordinary affairs. When progress reaches this point without becoming disorderly, this is a high attainment of the wise. Therefore, it can be used as a standard, and is auspicious" (1988:182). In support of Cheng Yi's interpretation, Wilhelm also explains, "This suggest flight through the clouds. The line is strong and already outside the affairs of the world. It is regarded by the others solely as an example and thus exerts a beneficent influence. It no longer enters into the confusion of mundane affairs" (1967:662). After everything has been done, like geese flying up into the sky for another round of migration, the subject at the sixth position retires and becomes a model figure showing how a man should lead and end his life. As I see, the line statement is a rather poetic expression of a model individual who has gone through an entire ladder of social positions, doing his best in each step, and is about to live out his remaining years gracefully in retirement.

The hexagram *Jing* (☵☴ ,Well)

In the hexagram *Jing* (Well), few will miss a pictorial resemblance between the graphic shape of its line structure (☵☴) and the Chinese character for the name of the hexagram *Jing*, 井. Of course, the hexagram is not actually concerned about topics related to the well itself, but something else that it as an emblem represents. In ancient China, the fields given to eight households would be divided into nine pieces in a manner figured by the character 井. Each household settles on and cultivates each parcel of the field except the one in the middle, which belonged to the government. The parcel in the middle was cultivated jointly by all the eight households and the yield went to the government as tax. A well was located in this portion of the field. In this communal tradition, the well was a common resource shared and used by all villagers, and, therefore, in symbolism represents the public function of the government (Legge, 1963:166; Wilhelm, 1967:631). It is with this symbolism that the hexagram is interpreted to concern topics that have to do with the operation of the government rather than the well itself.

Meanwhile, compared to most other hexagrams, the hexagram *Jing* may be considered unique in that its line statements describe different kinds of wells which supposedly refer to various types of government, good and bad. Accordingly, Legge suggests that this hexagram "might be styled 'Moralisings on a well,' or 'Lessons to be learned from a well for the good order and government of a country'" (1963:166). A unique feature of this hexagram, as hinted above, is that no relational pattern based on hierarchical distinctions and situationally determined tendencies among the component lines was taken into consideration for this specific hexagram. Every line statement in this hexagram instead presents respectively a certain kind of well, and this refers in metaphor to a certain kind of government or type of functionaries which has a distinct trait whether it be a positive or negative one.

The line statement of the first yin line describes the line as representing a well which "is fouled with mud," as a well of which "one should not partake," and as an old well at which "there are no birds" (Lynn, 1994:439). Thus, in its metaphoric representation, it refers to a "bad" government or functionary that gives benefits to no one. The line statement of the second position, a yang line, reads, "Here the Well shoots like valleylike for the little fishes, as if a water jar so worn out that it leaks" (Lynn, 1994:440). As referring to an operation of government, the line statement describes a defective government that does not function properly so that it only offers benefits to a limited number of people leading parasitic lives off the malfunctioning of the government. The context in which the next line statement for the third yang line is addressed differs from the other lines; it tells specifically about an official, rather than a government, who can be compared to a "cleansed well," thus one who contributes to an effective functioning of the government. The interpretive rule of the *I Ching* is applied to this line; since a yang line is located at a yang position, the subject at the third position represents someone who acts properly in accord with his formal capacity determined by the position he occupies. However, the line structure of the hexagram is read in such a way that the third yang line is isolated from the others and, therefore, is compared to a well that no one uses, due to which its subject would "feel pain in his heart."[103] The line statement ends with a consoling remark, "If there be a bright sovereign, then this one shall receive all his blessings" (Lynn, 1994:440-1). The line statement of the fourth yin line is described as a well that is "relined with bricks," thus, representing a government which is kept in good order or a functionary who "takes (good) care of himself" (Legge, 1963:167). However, again, the subject is interpreted as someone who "does nothing for others" (Legge, 1967:167) or who can "correct and amend his own errors, but nothing more than that" (Lynn, 1994:441). Accordingly, although "there would be no blame," no great deal of contributions for others would be made by the subject at this position. The above interpretations rendered by Legge and Wang Bi give a picture of a government or functionary with limited capability far short of producing any real benefits for the people involved in a given situation — one who "repair(s) the faults in the Well (government)" (Lynn, 1994:441) but fails to get drinking water (to achieve goals to bring out benefits for the people) out of it. Compared to the type of government engaging in meticulous housekeeping but lacking in productive capacity as the line statement of the fourth line depicts in metaphor, the line statement of the fifth yang line describes its subject as an ideal figure, namely a well which "is icy clear, being from a cold spring" (Lynn, 1994:441). According to Legge, the line statement "suggests the well, full of clear water, which is drawn up, and performs its useful function." Thus, in terms of its metaphoric representation, it conveys an idea of "the good Head of government to his people" (1963:167). The line statement of the top yin line also outlines the various attributes of good government. It reads, "The topmost line, divided, shows (the water from) the well brought up to the top, which is not allowed to be covered. This suggests the idea of sincerity. There will be great good fortune" (Legge, 1963:166).[104] Here in Legge's translation, "sincerity" is interpreted as a moral virtue that an uncovered well metaphorically represents. An uncovered well also conveys the idea that the water drawn up from the well is freely available to everyone who is in need of it, hence, the idea of an effectively functioning good government.

I would like to add a brief note concerning the interpretation of this hexagram. The above interpretation, which I adopted, is largely based on Legge's perspective where this hexagram is viewed as a brief essay on various types of government or functionaries written in the metaphor of the well. Interpreted this way, each line statement gives a description of one particular type of government or functionary, which is described largely in terms of its capacity to serve the people. Another way to interpret this hexagram is to view each line statement as describing a specific situation or situationally determined trait of the position holder at each position. However, as I see it, if we notice the fact that the line statements in the hexagram render progressively more and more favorable judgments as they move up from the bottom line to the top one, the latter interpretation certainly fails to account for why the line statements vary in such an ordered fashion.

The hexagram *Guimei* (☳☱, Marrying Maid)

The title name of the hexagram *Guimei* (Marrying Maid) is interpreted to mean "the maid who is sent to marry." An impression that I have come to have after reviewing all the text accounts is that the hexagram does not describe a pattern of collective situations, but is rather intended as an essay of a pedagogic kind written mainly to give lessons for either maids who are about to be sent for marriage or those who are to send their younger sisters (*mei* means younger sisters) for marriage. The *Commentary on the Judgments* explains about this hexagram: "Marrying Maiden expresses the great meaning of Heaven and Earth. If Heaven and Earth did not interact, the myriad things would not flourish, so Marrying Maiden is an expression of humankind from beginning to end" (Lynn, 1994:480). There seems to be no doubt from the above commentary that the meaning of the hexagram has to do with the institution of marriage. However, the *Judgment* at the same time suggests that the hexagram features a type of marriage that is far less than ideal as it says, "The Marrying Maiden is such that to set forth would mean misfortune. There is nothing at all fitting here" (Lynn, 1994:480). The two accounts presented above connect this marriage to misfortune. This is because the Marrying Maiden here refers to one who is given in marriage as a second wife, not the first wife.[105] In the marriage custom of the later period of the Shang kingdom up to the early Zhou period, "a feudal prince" married, in addition to the one who would become his first wife, several women at the same time, one of whom would be "a half sister (of the first wife), a daughter of her father by another mother of inferior rank" (Legge, 1963:183), or a younger sister of the older sister (who would be the first wife) (Kim, 1997:415). Thus, the marrying maiden represented by this hexagram refers to the woman who was given and therefore had to bear an inferior status as a second wife by the marriage custom of the time. It seems that the line statements of this hexagram can be understood best as a collection of instructions for women who were subjected to marriages of such unfortunate kind.

The line statement of the first yang line reads, "The Marrying Maiden marries as a younger secondary wife. If this one as a lame person can still keep on treading, to set forth here mean good fortune" (Lynn, 1994:481). In the above line statement, a younger secondary wife is described as a lame person, which is understandable considering her inferior status as compared to the first wife. But, what the last line, "to set forth here means good fortune," intends to mean is not clear. Cheng Yi, interested in whatever moral lessons might be there to be found in the text, gives a moralistic interpretation with which a second wife would be viewed as "the lame walking" if she is of great service to her husband by being "wise and upright" (1988:184). Legge also renders a similar interpretation explaining that "The mean condition and its duties are to be deplored, and give the auspice of lameness; but notwithstanding, the secondary wife will in a measure discharge her service" (1963:184).[106]

The subject at the second position is rendered a judgment that, in essence, does not differ much from the one at the first position. The line statement reads, "As a one-eyed person who can keep on seeing, how fitting is the constancy of this secluded one" (Lynn, 1994:482). The expression, "a one-eyed person who can keep on seeing," is thought as involving a meaning similar to "a lame person (who) can still keep on treading" in the previous line statement; she has disadvantages as a second wife, but if she maintains a correct posture, she still can play a beneficial role for her husband. This is the way Legge reads, if partially, the line statement. He explains that ". . . . the able lady in 2 cannot do much in the discharge of her proper work. But if she thinks only of her husband like the widow who will die rather than marry again, such devotion will have its effect and its reward" (1963:184).[107] Interpreted as above, the line statement also contains advice for a marrying maiden concerning how she, as a second wife, has to behave under the disadvantageous situation associated with her low status.

The line statement of the third yin line is interpreted and translated in so many various ways that no agreement is come to on what it really intends to say. Most English translations do not seem to convey any meaningful ideas.[108] As I view it, the simplest and clearest version of translation is rendered by Lee who translates the line statement as "If one insists on giving his younger sister in marriage to be the first wife, he will have to marry her off instead as a concubine." In support of this interpretation, Lee also translates the *Commentary on the Images* as saying, "It is not appropriate to give one's younger sister in marriage as the first wife" (Lee, 1997[II]:211-2, translated from the Korean text by this author). Translated in this way, the line statement is interpreted as containing advice that fit the marriage custom of the day: one's younger sister had to be given as a second wife, not the first one; if one insisted on marrying her as the first wife (in violation of the prevailing norm of the society), no marriage would take place as wished so that she might have had to be given away as concubine in the end. Kim offers another interesting interpretation in which the line statement is translated as "The marrying Maiden is accompanied by a maidservant when she is given in marriage (as a second wife). But, the maidservant stays while the Marrying Maiden is turned back home with her elder sister" (1997:414, translated from the Korean text by this author). "The Marrying Maiden is turned back home with her elder sister" because a yin line is present inappropriately at the third position, a yang place; thus, the line represents a marrying maiden who acts contrarily to what is expected of her position as a second wife. As her misbehavior may disturb the peace in her husband's family, she will be sent back home with the first wife who is her elder sister. According to Kim, the line statement, when interpreted as above, contains a warning that if the marrying maiden does not act in the way of a second wife, she will get a worse treatment than even her maidservant. The two translations rendered respectively by Lee and Kim, although each may sound plausible in its respective context, share no common idea concerning what the line statement actually intends to say.

A yang line that inappropriately occupies a yin position represents the subject at the fourth position, thus symbolizing a marrying maid who has not found an appropriate partner and therefore has to put off her marriage. The line statement points to the obvious fact: "The Marrying Maiden exceeds the allotted time and marries late, for that is the time for it" (Lynn, 1994:482). Accordingly, most commentaries on this line statement only paraphrase what is already stated in the line statement: she must wait until the right partner is found, and this will be a virtue found generally among wise people who know how to wait until the right time comes.

The fifth line entails a longer line statement:

> The fifth line, divided, reminds us of the marrying of the younger sister of (king) Ti-yi, when the sleeves of her the princess were not equal to those of the (still) younger sister who accompanied her in an inferior capacity. (The case suggests the thought of) the moon almost full. There will be good fortune. (Legge, 1963:182)[109]

The lesson involved in the above line statement seems clear: doubtlessly, it emphasizes that modesty is an essential virtue especially for a marrying maiden with a family background higher than her husband's. The following commentary by Cheng Yi will provide good background material with which we can understand the point that the line statement makes:

> Royal princesses have married down since ancient times, but after a certain emperor it becomes a proper rite of marriage, to symbolize the status of man and woman — even if the woman is of the highest social status, she must not lose flexibility and willingness to cooperate. There are those in high positions who become haughty, so in the *I Ching* where the yin is noble and yet humbly descends it says the emperor marries off his younger sister, here and in the *Tranquility* hexagram (*Tai*, Peace). When a woman of high status marries, only mannerly humility is worthy of her nobility. She does not strive to decorate herself outwardly to please others. (1988:185)

The line statement of the sixth position reads, "The woman might present a basket, but it would contain no fruit; the man might have a sheep cut up, but there would be no blood. There is nothing at all fitting" (Lynn, 1994:484). In the above line statement, its subject is described as a woman who should present a basket of fruits, but has no fruit to fill the basket, or as a man who should "have a sheep cut up" to take blood, but finds no blood in it. According to Kim, in the old

Chinese custom, it was the duty of a wife to prepare a basket of fruits for the sacrificial rite of a family whereas it was the man's duty to kill a sheep to take blood for a sacrificial offering (1997:417). Understood in this context, the line statement is interpreted as describing a marrying maiden who has failed to fulfill her family obligation. It is not clear why the subject at the sixth position is interpreted as representing an unfortunate maiden who fails in fulfilling the traditionally given role of a wife. Of this commentators such as Cheng Yi (1988:186), Legge (1963:184), and Wang Bi (Lynn, 1994:484) explain that the subject's situation is indicated by the line structure of the hexagram that shows no one with whom the subject can have a complementary or corresponding relationship. In view of all line statements including this one, however, the explanation as above does not seem to make sense. Why should the marrying maiden represented by the sixth yin line be in need of, thus seek for, a union with any other marrying maiden? The explanation would require us to interpret the hexagram as representing a family organization that is made up of a number of wives and concubines placed in situations as characterized by the respective line statements. But, the line statements are not amenable to such an interpretation. As I view it, therefore, the line statement of the sixth yin line should be understood simply as representing a marrying maid who has failed for some reasons to fulfill successfully her role in her husband's family. Or, it might have been written as a warning to any marrying maiden of the possibility that her marriage could end in failure for whatever reasons that may interfere with the fulfillment of her role in the family.

Summary of theoretical and empirical propositions

1) Failure to properly discipline growing children in the family, or neophyte members of a group, would do no good to either the children themselves or to the family.

2) Strict discipline of dependent family members such as children, women, and, by analogy, the common folk, may bring about undesirable outcomes for which one may have feelings of regret, but strict discipline is better than no discipline at all.

3) A main function of the middle leadership, the subject at the third position, lies in a disciplinarian role exercised over people who are subject to his authority. In contrast, that of the top leadership at the fifth position is focused upon the emotive-oriented task of

bringing unity to the entire group.

4) A dualistic relationship will be much more stable than a tripartite one. It is because the tripartite one can split more easily as two of the parties hold together against the other or one against the other two.

5) It is only with the facilitation of wealth and labor force that a state can operate effectively as an integrated unit. The basic function of such valuable resources levied from the governed subjects is that they provide the ruling class with necessary means to carry out the government functions.

6) The middle leadership position ranks higher than the second position — the position of lower administrative workers. But, compared to the relatively comfortable and safer situation that the subjects at the lower administrative positions enjoy, the one at the middle leadership can easily fall under political cross-fires from both above and below and therefore would be in a tougher situation to fight off "harassment."

7) The tasks for the top leadership involve long-term goals that require time to yield an outcome. It is because of this that it is not easy to produce great achievements within a short period of time after a leader takes power.

11) Hexagrams Representing Patterns of Power Relations

The three hexagrams examined here can be classified into two kinds. As we will see, in both the hexagram *Daxu* and the hexagram *Dazhuang*, the subordinate units are represented by the trigram *Qian* (☰) while yin lines appear equally at the fifth position, the position of the top leadership. This means that for each of the situations represented by the two hexagrams, there is a strong subordinate group under a weak leadership. The hexagram *Cui* differs from the above two hexagrams in that the subordinate unit is represented by the trigram *Kun* (☷) which is symbolic of conformity and docility and that the two positions at the higher echelon, the fourth and the fifth positions, are represented by yang lines. Thus, it may be said that the hexagram *Cui* has a power structure inverse to the above two hexagrams, one in which the dominant group has a strong power potential to rule the

Hexagrams: Types of Social Situations   305

conforming subordinate group. The contrasting patterns of power structure represented by these hexagrams again will remind us of the fact that the *I Ching* views the relational patterns of position holders in the social stratification system as phenomena that are subject to a wide range of situational variations.

1) The hexagram *Daxu*(☰☰, Great Domestication, The Taming Power of the Great[110]) (Hexagram No. 26)

2) The hexagram *Dazhuang* (☰☰, Great Strength) (Hexagram No. 34)

3) The hexagram *Cui* (☰☰, Gathering) (Hexagram No. 45)

The hexagram *Daxu*(☰☰, Great Domestication, The Taming Power of the Great)

Before readers are introduced to the hexagram *Daxu* (the Taming Power of the Great), I would like to advise them to go back to the hexagram *Xiaoxu* (the Taming Power of the Small) (p. 138) and take a look at its structural feature and the situational meanings attributed to it. The only difference in the line structures of the two hexagrams is found in that a yin line instead of a yang line is present at the fifth position, the top leadership position, in the hexagram *Daxu*. By comparing the line structures of the two hexagrams and the text accounts of the *I Ching* appended to them, we will have a chance to analyze more sharply the logic of the *I Ching* with which the meanings of hexagrams are interpreted (or, we may say, constructed) in reference to their respective line structures.

The "Taming Power" refers to the controlling power exercised by the fourth and the fifth yin lines over the strong subordinate group represented by the lower trigram *Qian*. "The Great" seems to be used to emphasize simply the fact that the taming power is exercised doubly by the two yin lines at the fourth and the fifth positions, unlike the case for the hexagram *Xiaoxu* (the Taming Power of the Small) in which power is exercised by a single yin line at the fourth position. However, the two hexagrams share a common underlying theme referring to the "taming (controlling) power" of a weak leadership over a strong subordinate group. This is evident in the following line statements of the fourth and the fifth yin lines:

> *Fourth Yin*: Here is a horn cover for the young ox, so there is fundamental good fortune.
>
> *Fifth Yin*: Here one removes the boar's tusks, so there is good fortune.
> (Lynn, 1994:302)

Although the expressions are different from each other, the above line statements are interpreted as conveying nearly the same meaning. Of the line statement of the fourth line, Wang Bi explains that "Fourth Yin checks the hard and the strong one (i.e., the second yang line) with its compliancy and yielding." A similar interpretation is also given to that of the fifth yin line. Wang Bi in his commentary explains that "Second Yang advances with its hardness and strength, but Fifth Yin is able to remove its tusks, so the yielding and compliant manages to control the strong, nullifying its viciousness and preventing the growth of its power" (Lynn, 1994:302). From Wang Bi's commentaries, however, it is not clear what political control method he describes as "[checking] the hard and the strong one with (its) compliancy and yielding." Perhaps he describes the way in which political control is achieved through accommodation or negotiation. The only available clue is provided by Cheng Yi who, as a moralistically oriented philosopher, answers the question with a view biased toward a strong ethical flavor. His view is expressed with an example that he uses to illustrate the essential nature of the type of political control mentioned above:

> Let us take stopping thievery as an example. When people have desires, they will act upon seeing the possibility of gain. If the leadership does not know how to educate them, and oppress them with hunger and cold, even executions carried out daily cannot overcome the desire of the masses to get what will benefit them. Sages know the way to stop this is not to threaten and punish them, but to improve the government and teach the people how to work for their livelihood and have a sense of conscious. Then they will not steal even if they are rewarded for it.
> (1988:81)

The above passage seems to contain useful teachings for the people in leadership position. However, it still seems difficult to see a clear logical connection between what Cheng Yi has to say about the line statements and what can be inferred about the weak controlling power of those at the fourth and the fifth positions from the line statements of the hexagram.

As was the case with the hexagram *Xiaoxu*, the first and second yang lines are described as being in positions having a certain measure of strong power potential, yet not enough to hold off the "taming power" of those at the higher echelon. The line statements of the two positions are expressed in different words, but are not much different in their implied meanings. The line statement of the first yang line states, "Here there is danger, so it is fitting to desist" (Lynn, 1994:300). Wang Bi explains that "there is danger" for the subject at the bottom position because, if he "were to advance," there is "Fourth Yin that exerts domestic control over First Yang." (Lynn, 1994:300). For the second yang line, the line statement reads, "The carriage body would be separated from its axle housing." Wang Bi's commentary given to this line statement is not much different from that for the first yang line: "Fifth Yin is located where domestication (the taming power) is at its strongest, so at Second Yang one cannot yet act in defiance. To advance here under such circumstances would result, as the text says, in 'the carriage body' getting 'separated from its axle housing'" (Lynn, 1994:300). The only important difference between Wang Bi's two commentaries for the first and the second yang lines is that while the first yang line, who is likely to act "in defiance" against the line of authority laid down by the hierarchical system, is said to be held off by the one at the fourth position, the fifth yin line is controlling the one at the second position instead. Of course, it would not be a strange idea at all to think that there could be a functional division in the performance of roles regarding who is assigned to exercise control over whom. But, as pointed out before, we still do not know why the *I Ching*, as a general rule, views specific corresponding relationships between the first and the fourth positions and between the second and the fifth positions.

An essential difference between the hexagram *Daxu* and the hexagram *Xiaoxu* is found in the conditional statuses of the subjects at the third positions. For the hexagram *Xiaoxu*, the condition of the subject at the third position is described similarly to the second position's condition under the situation represented by the hexagram *Daxu*. Meanwhile, according to the line statement of the third yang line, the third position in the hexagram *Daxu* enjoys a freer and more advantageous position compared to that in the hexagram *Xiaoxu*. Let us read its line statement: "With fine horses to drive fast in pursuit, it is fitting to practice constancy in the face of difficulties. Even though it be said that there will be attempts to check one's carriage, he will defend himself, so it is fitting to set out to do something" (Lynn, 1994:301). A careful reading of Wang Bi's and also Cheng Yi's commentaries on this line statement reveals two reasons why the condition of the subject at the third position is thought to be favorable. One is that there are two weak (yin) lines above it, interpreted as possessing less effective power to "tame" the position holder at the third position. Here we have to take into account the fact that the third yang line is at the leadership position of the subgroup characterized by the *Qian* trigram, which symbolizes a strongly integrated group with dynamic strength. Thus, although "there will be attempts to check (his) carriage (by the superiors above him), he will (be able to) defend (his autonomy and interests)." And, consequently, he can "set out to do something" on his own initiative. The other reason is related to the presence of the sixth yang line. According to Wang Bi, the freedom that the third yang line is said to enjoy has to do with the fact that "Third Yang shares the same goals as Top Yang" (Lynn, 19p4:301). Here, again, the subject at the third position is viewed as forming an alliance with the one at the top position. Although there is no absolute reason for the two position holders not to have a specific affinity to form a friendly relationship exclusively with each other, we can also think of no absolute reason for which anyone other than these two position holders should be excluded from forming an alliance.

Now, we are left with the line statement for the sixth position, which reads, "What is the Highway of Heaven but prevalence!" (Lynn, 1994:303). "The Highway of Heaven" by implication must have no fixed direction. As Cheng Yi points out, it is the road that "is going through freely," or that "is open and unobstructed" (1988:82). Why is the subject at the sixth position able to enjoy such unlimited freedom under this situation? By reading the line structure of the hexagram Wilhelm (1967:518) identifies two reasons. One is that "the top line is honored as a sage by the six (i.e., yin line) in the fifth place" because the sixth yang line is on top of the two weak lines below. The other reason is that, as pointed out already, it "stands in the relationship of congruity (correspondence or alliance) to the nine (yang line) in the third place" who is considered to be another most powerful figure in the hexagram. Viewed from this perspective, the most distinctive characteristic of the situation represented by the hexagram *Daxu* can be seen in the fact that there are two strong actors in alliance with each other, thus jointly enjoying privileged positions under the situation.

The hexagram *Dazhuang* (☰☰, Great Strength)

Regarding the name of the hexagram *Dazhuang* (Great Strength), Wang Bi explains that "the great" refers to the yang lines" (Lynn, 1994:345). Wilhelm echoes this opinion, saying, "the four yang lines are the basis of power of the hexagram, with the fourth at their head" (1967:555). Meanwhile, notice that the two top-notch positions are occupied by yin lines, indicating a weakness in power of those who are at the highest positions. Thus, we may say, the hexagram *Dazhuang* as a whole represents a situation in which strong power is in the hands of those in subordinate positions. But, amongst the strong lines, the primary figure who stands out among all the others in the hexagram is found in the fourth yang line. The line statement of the fourth yang line describes the subject of this line as "an axle housing of a great carriage" (Lynn, 1994:348). As Cheng Yi (1988:108) puts it, it is "the hub (which) is the central point of the wheel." In other words, the fourth yang line is the central figure in the front who leads the activities of the group with great strength. Thus, the line statement of the fourth yang line states, "The hedge is sundered and does not sap one's strength." To this, Wang Bi adds the comment: "Fourth Yang obtains its strength, and the yin lines above do not hem it in and deny its path" (Lynn, 1994:348). To put it simply, the subject represented by the fourth yang line is dominant over the lines above him and the latter are not in a position to interfere with what the former is doing. Of course, the *I Ching* does not forget to offer a moral teaching. It advises, "Constancy (or, a careful adherence to normatively correct behavioral norms) means good fortune, so regrets vanish" (Lynn, 1994:348). The advice calling for a careful observance of moral standards, especially important when applied to a person in an advantageous or powerful position, is one of the moral commands frequently voiced throughout the *I Ching*.

The line statements given to the three yang lines in the lower group are similar to that of the fourth yang line, but there are some variations that can be understood in relation to the positional characteristics of the respective lines. The heading of the first line statement, "Here strength resides in the toes" (Lynn, 1994:346), explains that the subject at the lowest position has some measure of, but not adequate, strength to exercise power over others. The line statement continues with a passage that contains advice for the one at the position. It says, "so to go forth and act would mean misfortune, in this one should be confident" (Lynn, 1994:346). This statement again reflects the value perspective typical of old Chinese culture that power residing in the hands of lower class people is not viewed as desirable. Therefore, the *I Ching* advises that they should not play with power by trying to gain something from it. With this interpretation, we may have to take into consideration that although the first yang line is in possession of a certain amount of power, his power as such has to be tempered by the presence of three strong lines above him. This seems to be why the line statement contains a warning about the definite possibility of ill fortune that will result from poking into places where low status people are not permitted.

Compared to the line statement of the first yang line, that of the second yang line states only briefly that "Constancy here means good fortune" (Lynn, 1994:347). As we can see, a strong (yang) line is present at the second, middle position that is regarded as advantageous and stable.

It is common for the *I Ching* to give advice containing words of warning against possible abuses of their advantageous position to position holders who come to enjoy especially favorable or powerful positions under a given situation. It is again in line with this sort of a morally tempered perspective that sterner words warning of a possible peril involved in the misuse of an advantageous position are uttered to the subject at the third position. The line statement of the third yang line says, "The petty man considers this an opportunity for his strength, but the noble man considers it a trap, for even with constancy there would be danger, as when a ram butts a hedge and finds its horns deprived of power" (Lynn, 1994:347). As Wang Bi points out in his commentary, "as a yang line that occupies a yang position, it (the third yang line) represents one who would employ his strength" (Lynn, 1994:347). Yet, notice that a strong (yang) line, the fourth yang line, is positioned immediately above and, as was already pointed out, the subject at the fourth position represents the most powerful figure leading the entire group. Thus, the warning, "even with constancy there would be danger, as when a ram (the strong third line) butts a hedge (the fourth yang line above him) and finds its horns deprived of power," is issued.

Judging from the overall structure of the hexagram, the situational condition that characterizes the fifth yin line is that while a weak subject occupies the position of the top leadership, strong subordinates are present at each of the four positions under the formal authority of the fifth line. It is in view of this condition that the line statement of the fifth yin line, "Losing the rams at ease, one has no regret" (Cheng Yi, 1988:109),[111] is considered sensible advice for this subject. Of this line statement, Cheng Yi, explains:

> As the four yangs are growing and advancing together, the fifth occupies a superior position with flexibility. If one in this position tried to control by strength, it would be difficult or impossible to prevail, and there would be regret. Only if one treats peacefully and easily will the yangs have no use for their strength. So this is losing in peace and ease, whereby it is possible to have no regret. (1988:109)

To paraphrase, the line statement advises that having rather weak power, the subject in the leadership position should not try to stand up to hard willed, strong subordinates equally with strength. And, it goes on to say, there would be no regret if he "treats (them) peacefully and easily." Or, interpreted differently by Kim (1997, 269, 270), Lee (1997:24) and Zhu Xi (Lynn, 1994:350n6), the situation confronted by the one at the fifth position is compared to one who raises rams in a border territory surrounded by rough people that occasionally steal away with the rams. But, the implications of the latter interpretation differ little from the former: the subject at the fifth position will gain no benefit if he tries to deal with the situation with forceful measures.

The line statement of the top yin line states, "This ram butts the hedge and finds that it can neither retreat nor advance. There is nothing at all fitting here, but if one can endure difficulties, he will have good fortune" (Lynn, 1994:349). Of the "difficult" situation of the top yin line which is symbolically expressed in the above line statement, Wang Bi explains:

> Top Yin is in resonance with Third Yang [where another ram butts the hedge], so it is unable to retreat; it is afraid of the growing power of the hard and the strong, so it is unable to advance. Beset by doubt and paralyzed with hesitation, the will is utterly undirected, so if one were to decide matters under such circumstances, nothing would ever come of it. (Lynn, 1994:349)

Compare Wang Bi's above interpretation with the following one by Cheng Yi:

> People like this are basically weak in capacity, so they cannot overcome themselves in the interests of duty and justice. This is inability to withdraw. Negative, weak people may be extremely desirous of using power, but they cannot sustain that power to a conclusion; when thwarted, they will shrink back. This is inability to go ahead. If your way of life is like this, it will not help to go anywhere;

there is nowhere you can go to gain anything. (1988:109)

We here can see interesting contrasts in interpreting the same line statement and also in the context with reference to which the line statement is interpreted. In the case of Wang Bi, the frame of reference is of a more or less sociological kind. Wang Bi sees the source of the top yin line's difficulty in the top yin line's alignment with the third yang line, the one described as a ram butting hard at the hedge. In spite of this alignment, the top yin line finds it hard to go along with the third yang line due to his own weak position under the situation. It may be said that he is wedged between conflicting situations, one in which he has to go along with the third yang line and the other in which he is in too weak a position to go against one (referring to the one at the fourth position) who presses with strong will. Wang Bi's interpretation can be characterized as sociological in the sense that it attempts to explain the situation of the subject at the top position mainly in terms of the relational pattern formed among the position holders. Compared to Wang Bi, Cheng Yi (1988:109) in his interpretation sees in the top yin line a person who falls into a dilemma due to his ambivalent personal trait. The top yin line is described as a "negative, weak people" who are "extremely desirous of using power." These are people who are unable to hold back from the place where power is played because they are by nature "extremely desirous of using power." Yet, at the same time, since they are "basically weak in capacity," "they cannot sustain that power to a conclusion." What Cheng Yi presents is a portrait of a person who has incompatible desire and ability, thus falls into an impossible situation to take action. Taken by itself, this way of describing a personal situation in terms of counteracting psychological factors may remind us of Kurt Lewin's field theory perspective. In this sense, Cheng Yi's interpretation can be characterized as social psychological as compared to Wang Bi's sociological one. Of course, many people including myself may raise the doubt that Cheng Yi might have tried to insert too much of his own social-psychologically oriented moralistic teaching wherever, just as shown in this case, he deals with ambiguous line statements.

Finally, in relation to the above mentioned difference in interpretation, it is interesting to note that the second verse of the line statement is rendered different interpretations depending upon how the previous verse is interpreted. In Lynn's version of the text that relies mainly on Wang Bi's commentary, the second verse of the line statement is translated as "if one can endure difficulties, he will have good fortune." This translation is supported in view of Wang Bi's commentary, which reads, "If one secures the position allotted to him here, keeps his will steadfastly on Third Yang, and in this way maintains his own place, disaster will vanish" (Lynn, 1994:349). By taking into account Wang Bi's interpretation, the statement, "if one can endure difficulties, he will have good fortune," is understood to mean that if he holds fast to an alliance with Third Yang despite difficulties in doing so, he will have a fortunate result in the end. Meanwhile, if we take Cheng Yi's psychologically oriented interpretation, the same passage will be interpreted to involve a quite different sort of advice: "Using power is not beneficial; knowing the difficulty, live as the weak, and you will be fortunate" (1988:109).

The hexagram *Cui* (☱ ☷, Gathering)

With the hexagram *Daxu*, we may be reminded of the fact that the power structure shows, figuratively speaking, a pattern that is hollow at the center where the two central figures occupying the fourth and the fifth positions are located. As a matter of fact, the real power resides in the hands of the position holders at the third and the sixth positions, subjects positioned outside the central region of formal power. In contrast to this, in the hexagram *Cui*, "the rulers of the hexagram are the nine (yang line) in the fifth place and, secondarily, the nine (yang line) in the fourth." "Only these two yang lines are in high places" (Wilhelm, 1967:614). Thus, it may be said that the power is concentrated, in contrast to the hexagram *Daxu*, in the central region of the formal power structure. The hexagram name *Cui* (Gathering), as Wilhelm (1967:614) also points out, is used to indicate a situation where all the yin lines in the hexagram are gathered around the two powerful figures represented by the two yang lines located at the fourth and the fifth positions. In addition to this, the *Judgment* on the hexagram carries a passage that may arouse our interest for its sociological implication. It states, "Only when a true king arrives, will there be an ancestral temple" (Lynn, 1994:417). To assess the sociological implications of the briefly stated passage above, let us assume that it has been given as an answer to the following questions: Why is there an ancestral temple?; what is the social function of an ancestral temple? In light of the question above, the *I Ching*'s brief statement suggests a great deal. It sets forth an interesting hypothesis that only when a powerful political leadership is established, is it able to "gather" people around an ancestral temple through the worship of which a political community achieves a normative integration. This may sound familiar if one is familiar with the functionalist tradition in sociology as most clearly manifested in Durkeim's theory and also as espoused by Parsons.

Then, let us examine first the line statements of the fourth and the fifth positions, the ones described as the two dominant figures over the others in the hexagram. The line statement of the fourth line describes its subject simply as being placed in an enjoyable condition. The *Commentary on the Images* supplies a reason for why such an auspicious judgment is given to the position holder at this position: "'Great good fortune. No blame,' for the place demands nothing."[112] Under this situation of gathering, the subject at the fourth position who "occupies the place of the minister" performs a primary role in "bringing about the gathering together on behalf of his prince, the nine (yang line) in the fifth place" (Wilhelm, 1967:618). In doing this, there would be no great difficulty. To understand why it is interpreted as such, notice simply that the subordinate group is represented by the trigram *Kun*, which indicates the presence of a weak subordinate group who is ready to act in compliance with the one at the fourth position. But, for some reason which cannot be understood from either the text itself or any other commentary, the subject of the fourth position is said to remain free of seeking his own share of glory for his actions. Wilhelm's interpretation presented above, as far as the role of the subject of the fourth position in relation to other position holders is concerned, also agrees with what Cheng Yi explains about the role performed by the fourth yang line under this situation. It reads:

> The fourth line near the fifth yang leadership in a time of gathering indicates that leadership and administration have managed to get together. Its nearness to the group of yins in the trigram below indicates that it has gotten the lower echelons together. To get those above and below all together can be called good indeed. (1988:151)

Compared to the interpretation offered by Wilhelm, however, Cheng Yi inserts a little different interpretation, including one aspect that seems quite perplexing to me. For the reason that a yang line is present at the fourth position regarded as a yin place, Cheng Yi (1988:151) sees the fourth position as occupied by someone who is not doing things "in the right way," or is doing things "in unprincipled and immoral ways." Of course, Cheng Yi concedes, "there are certainly cases (as indicated by this hexagram) in which the gathering of those above and below is accomplished without doing it in the right way." Yet, due to the inappropriate ways in which things are administered, the line statement is interpreted as issuing a warning — the subject at the fourth position will be able to escape blame only when there is quite a deal of good fortune. But, to me, this seems to insert too much of one's own imagination into the brief line statement.

The fifth position carries a bit longer statement. It states, "Gathering is such that this one has his position. There is one without blame, but that is not because of his sincerity. Fundamentally and constantly does this one practice constancy, so this regret disappears" (Lynn, 1994:421). Although the line statement does not seem to permit an easy understanding at the first glance, commentators do not differ much from one another over its meaning. The line statement emphasizes two things. One is simply the fact that the subject at the fifth position holds the central position around which the group represented by the hexagram is gathered. The other thing is that since his position as such is owing largely to the specific condition of the situation, not necessarily to his personal worth, the unity of the group under this situation may be achieved through a reluctant gathering of people who do not have trust in him. Therefore, the *I Ching* advises, to bring the union of the group to a "perpetual stability" the one at the fifth position has to "cultivate virtues to bring people to it (leadership)" (Cheng Yi, 1988:152). Wilhelm explains this more aptly: "To the influence of the position must be added the influence of personality" (1967:618).

Now, let us look at how the line statements for other positions make assessments on their respective situations. The line statement of the first yin line carries a message that looks a bit long considering the shorter, average length of other line statements:

> If this one has sincerity but does not let it run its course, there would be confusion one moment then Gathering the next. But if one declares that it would be for a handclasp and were to make smiles, he should feel no grief, for setting forth would incur no blame. (Lynn, 1994:419)

Wang Bi (1994:419) and Wilhelm (1967:616-617) differ in explaining why the subject at the first position is described as displaying an unstable behavior holding back in "confusion one moment" and then coming forth for "gathering the next." According to Wilhem and Cheng Yi (1988:149) who holds a view similar to Wilhelm concerning the above passage, the subject at the first position would be in a conflicting situation having his loyalties divided between the fourth yang line and his own group made up of the three yin lines below. The fourth yang line is viewed as one who is the most likely to form an alliance with the first yin line under the situation. And, the subordinate group that consists of members having similar characteristics is viewed as a cohesive one. So, viewed from the position of the first yin line, the situation poses a dilemma in choosing the "right" relationship to which he has to give his commitment. This explains Wilhelm's comment, "the weak line at the beginning is not yet stabilized" (1967:616). When one is attracted equally to his own group and someone outside the in-group, he would experience a dilemma in choosing either one or the other between two favored alternatives. This interpretation seems to be based upon commonsense psychology that everyone would have acquired through everyday experience. On the other hand, Wang Bi interprets this differently (Lynn, 1994:419) and thinks that the difficulty of the first yin line has to do with the fact that the third yin line stands in between the first and the fourth lines. This positioning therefore poses a barrier to a corresponding relationship (union) to form between the two parties as sought by the first yin line. This latter interpretation offered by Wang Bi also is based on commonsense knowledge in human psychology rather familiar to anyone. Human individuals by nature seek unions with others who are favored for certain reasons and would feel distressed or alienated when they see their favored partners form a relationship with someone else. Despite the soundness of the psychological proposition involved in either interpretation, however, we see here again a crucial problem with the *I Ching*: the opaque symbolism of the line statement has left itself open to a number of different readings. The remaining portion of the line statement, "But if one declares that it would be for a handclasp and were to make smiles, he should feel no grief, for setting forth would incur no blame," again sounds vague and irrelevant, yet is interpreted to contain advice for the dilemma described above. It advises, "If one at First Yin were content to be submissive, to withdraw, and to take care of himself in all modesty, then 'he should feel no grief, for setting forth would incur no blame'." (Lynn, 1994:419). To put it briefly, the one at the first position is advised to keep up a low profile when he seeks for a union with the one at the fourth position.

The line statement for the second yin line is shorter and seems easier to understand: "This one is summoned, so he has good fortune and is without blame. If one is sincere, it would be fitting to perform a *yue* sacrifice here" (Lynn, 1994:419). At the time of Gathering, the one at the second position displays an action orientation represented by a yin line, which is interpreted to abide by the "summon" issued by the fifth one at the leadership. A *yue* sacrifice refers to a simple sacrifice or ceremony. According to Cheng Yi, "a simple ceremony is used only as a metaphor for offering sincerity" (1988:150). Then, "to perform a *yue* sacrifice" would mean that the one at the second position has to join the Gathering with all sincerity.

With this hexagram, the third and the sixth yin lines are interpreted to form a special relationship due to their common fate under this situation. Commentators share the same opinion that the overall pattern of social relations among position holders alienates the third and top positions from the rest of the group. The unhappy situation of the third position with no stable partnership is read from its line statement that says, "Now Gathering, now sighing, there is nothing at all fitting here, but one can set forth without blame, for it involves but a little baseness" (Lynn, 1994:420). Of this line statement, Wilhelm (1967:617) explains: "This line has no relationship of correspondence, hence sighs, the forlornness and helplessness." His situation of isolation causes him to seek a relationship with one at the sixth position who is also described by Wang Bi as "(standing) alone, with no one near or far to give him aid" (Lynn, 421). Thus, according to interpretations rendered by most commentators (Cheng Yi, 1988:151; Legge, 1963:159; Wang Bi, in Lynn, 1994:420) the two at the third and the sixth positions could manage to overcome their alienation by forming some sort of alliance although the relationship may "involve(s) . . . . a little baseness." Why does the *I Ching* think that it involves a little baseness? Wang Bi answers this question with the explanation that it is because for "two yins to unite is not as good as the resonate relationship between a yin and a yang." However, concerning this seemingly contrived explanation, let us read a critical comment that Legge (1963:159) has to make: "But that an ordinary rule for interpreting the lineal indications may be thus overruled by extraordinary considerations shows how much of fancy there is in the symbolism or in the commentaries on it." However, to assert that alienated people tend to form relationships among themselves and that, even if they are successful in forming them, such marginal relationships would not be evaluated by anyone as fully satisfactory does not seem to be a wholly unreasonable ("fanciful") idea at all.

Summary of theoretical and empirical propositions

1) The patterns of power distribution among people holding positions in hierarchical systems represented by hexagrams vary from situation to situation. Accordingly, the manners in which

power is exercised by the ruling elites will, and should, vary from one situation to another, for differences in power potential would require different ways of dealing with people under their political control.

2) A good government and education provide much more effective means than such strong measures as threat and punishment in dealing with people whose characteristics or conditions under specific situations may lead them to act against the authority of the government.

3) If a person at the leadership position is of weak power, no benefit will be gained by an effort to stand up to powerful subordinates who are equal in strength. Accommodation or negotiation would be the best possible strategy to deal with them under the situation.

4) Only when a powerful political leadership is established, it is able to "gather" people around an ancestral temple through the worship of which a political community achieves a normative integration. The *I Ching* therewith suggests that the religious function is closely linked with the political function.

5) The stability of a leadership is assured by not only "the influence of the position" but also by "the influence of personality," which means that the effectiveness of the leadership is derived from two factors — the formal power endowed with the position of the leadership and the appropriate personal quality of a person incumbent at the position.

6) Individuals by nature seek union with others who are favored for certain reasons and would feel distressed or alienated when they see their favored parties form relationships with someone else. Concerning a party with whom two competitors seek an alliance, if he is attracted equally to his own group and someone outside the in-group, he would experience a dilemma in choosing between the two favored alternatives.

7) People who are excluded from a network of social relationships within a group tend to seek an alliance among themselves, and, even if they are successful in forming them, such marginal relationships would not likely be experienced by anyone as fully satisfactory.

12) Hexagrams Representing Organizations with Ill-Balanced Structures

As suggested by the title above, the two hexagrams to be dealt here can be viewed as sharing a common feature in that the both represent organizations with ill-balanced structures. In the hexagram *Daguo*, all middle four positions that represent the formal power structure are occupied by "strong" (yang) lines while "weak" (yin) lines represent the two boundary positions at the bottom and the top positions. On the other hand, the hexagram *Xiaoguo* consists of two yang lines at the two middle positions and four yin lines that lie outside, enclosing the yang lines between them. *Da* of *Daguo* and *Xiao* of *Xiaguo* mean "the great" and "the small" or "the strong" and "the weak," respectively, and *guo* means "excess." Thus, organizational structures in which either strong or weak components are predominant, or in excess, over those with opposite characteristics are indicated by both the hexagrams. Of course, the idea of excess is not only an excess of yang or yin lines in terms of numeric majority, for there are many other hexagrams with an imbalance of yang and yin lines. As I figure, and as we will see, it has to do more with the graphic patterns in which strong and weak lines are aggregated: they give images of natural objects with ill-balanced structures. This kind of imagery is interpreted as conveying the idea of defective social organizations with ill-balanced structures. It is perhaps due to this dubious analogy that the meanings of these two hexagrams, when they are interpreted as representing types of social situations or organizations, seem ambiguous at most.

1) The hexagram *Daguo* (☱☴, Major Superiority, Preponderance of the Great[113]) (Hexagram No. 28)

2) The hexagram *Xiaoguo*(☳☶, Minor Superiority; Preponderance of the Small[114]) (Hexagram No. 62)

The hexagram *Daguo* (☱☴, Major Superiority, Preponderance of the Great)

Since all the strong elements are congregated at the four centrally located formal positions and the two end lines at the bottom and the top positions are weak, the hexagram *Daguo* features a "ridgepole that sags." All heavy duties are borne upon the shoulders of the position holders at the middle four positions. The subject at the third position is thought to bear the heaviest and hazardous burden like the high-hanging ridgepole that has to bear more weight than any other part of a house because it occupies the highest position in the lower subgroup (represented by a lower trigram).[115]

Provided that the social organization represented by the hexagram *Daguo* is symbolized by a bending ridgepole with its middle parts bearing much heavier weight than the two ending portions, this analogy groups the lines of the hexagram into three different categories as follows. The first category is, of course, the two yin lines, weak components in the hexagram, located in the bottom and the top positions. The second category includes the second and the fourth yang lines. These two yang lines under an ordinary situation would have been considered "inappropriately positioned" ones because they are occupying places that perform "yin" (supportive) functions. However, the situation represented by the hexagram is regarded as possessing such an extraordinary characteristic that each of the two yang lines contributes rather positively to remedy problems associated with the ill-balanced structure indicated by the hexagram. The third category consists of the remaining two yang lines, the third and the fifth yang lines occupying the leadership positions (i.e., having "yang" functions) for the lower and the higher groups respectively. Under ordinary situations, these two yang lines should have been considered "appropriately positioned" because yang lines are appropriately occupying "yang" positions. However, as is the case with the two yang lines positioned right below them, an opposite principle is also applied to these lines: the yang lines at the third and the fifth positions are considered too firm or rigid under this situation where some degree of flexibility is required to protect its ill balanced structure from possible collapse. Of course, as some readers may have noticed already, all these interpretations concerning the line statements of this hexagram are done by utilizing a dubious analogy with which meanings associated with an object symbol, a ridgepole overweighing at the middle part, are introduced into descriptions on certain properties of position holders acting under the defined situation. A problem arising from using this kind of analogy which is not supported by a convincing argument for the existence of certain common properties between things is just as this hexagram shows itself as an example: when the hexagram compares a social situation to, say, a sagging ridgepole, it would not be easy to understand what sorts of relevant and meaningful information either the hexagram as whole or its line statements respectively convey in terms of either patterns of social relationships or specific conditions associated with social positions of individuals. This problem will come to be understood more clearly as our discussion continues.

Let us examine the line statements, pair by pair, as we have classified them. The two yin lines at the bottom and the top positions are weak in their situational characteristics and occupy positions with no formal power. Both lie outside the official hierarchical system. Moreover, all the middle four components that fill in the formal power structure are strong (yang) lines. Thus, we can visualize a situation in which the subjects, due to both their situationally and positionally determined attributes, have little power potential and find themselves in utterly powerless situations before the powerful position holders who are in formal offices. Indeed, such a reading squares quite well with the line statements and with Wang Bi's commentaries on them. Let us look at the line statement of the first yin line: "Use white rushes for a mat, and one will be without blame." On this line statement, Wang Bi comments:

> This bottom position is occupied by the soft and yielding. Can anything other than cautious and prudent behavior serve to keep one free of blame here at this time of superiority? (Lynn, 1994:313)

Cheng Yi takes the same perspective and explains that "using reeds ("white rushes" in Lynn's translation) is excessively deferential" (1988:87). There seems to be little ambiguity concerning this line statement: considering the existing power structure under the type of situation represented by the hexagram, the only survival technique available to the subject at the first position is "cautious and prudent behavior."

Compared to this, the line statement of the top yin line involves a judgment that sounds far less favorable. There is a plausible reason for this unfavorable judgment. After all, anyone who is in such a high position as the sixth would not experience this situation as a happy one, for he enjoys no influence potential whatsoever under the situation in which all the power resides in the hands of those in formal office. Thus, the line statement reads, "If one tries to ford across here, he will submerge his head, and there will be misfortune, but there will be no blame" (Lynn, 1994:315). The last verse, "there will be no blame," implies that if the subject at this position sets out to do something about the situation, his effort as such has justifiable cause considering that this is a problematic situation. That is, as Wang Bi explains, "as this one's ambition is fixed on saving the times, there cannot be any blame attached to him" (Lynn, 1994:315). However, as the line statement renders a clearly stated judgment on the possible outcome of his action as such, the *I Ching* predicts no chance of success for his endeavor to bring about improvement to the situation.

Two others who are equally unfortunate under the situation are the subjects at the third and the fifth positions. Judging strictly from the text accounts of the *I Ching* and related commentaries, the situations of these two position holders seem to be connected with a mode of thought that presumes an analogous relationship between certain perceived properties of natural objects and social relations. For example, the line statement compares the condition of the subject at the third position to a sagging ridgepole. Why is the position holder viewed as overburdened with unbearably weighty responsibilities like a bending ridgepole with a heavy structure borne upon its center? From the commentaries appended to this line statement, two reasons may be developed. One is that being located right at the center of the hexagram, the image of the third position is that of a person who has to perform an unbearably heavy duty. The second reason is found in that the difficult situation of the third yang line is made even worse by the fact that, as the social relational patterns among position holders or their behavioral orientations are interpreted by commentators, there is no one to form an alliance with the subject at the third position. As we have pointed out time and again in previous discussions, as far as the *I Ching* is concerned, isolation is one of the worst conditions a man as a social being can face during his social life. The subject at the third position is interpreted as having fallen into the helpless situation of isolation. But, why is he viewed as being isolated from other people? Wilhelm notes that a yang line is occupying a yang place and "this gives too much firmness for an exceptional time" (1967:528). In other words, the situation in which the officialdom at the center is filled with actors with active action orientations requires some degree of flexibility from the actors involved. Considering the nature of such a situation, the strong subject at the strong, third position is considered as being "too adamant and strong" (Cheng Yi, 1988:88), "confident in his own strength" (Legge, 1963:118), or as one, "through obstinacy," who "cuts oneself off from the possibility of support" (Wilhelm, 1967:528). Behaving as such and thus unable to secure help from others, the subject at the third position alone has to bear all the burdens imposed upon him under the situation; hence the image of "a ridgepole that sags."

As for the fifth yang line that is compared to the third, this line also is not given an auspicious judgment but a somewhat tempered one. The line statement of the fifth yang line states, "A withered popular puts forth blossoms. An old woman gets a young husband for herself. There is no blame, but there is no praise either" (Lynn, 1994:315). The above line statement describes the subject at the fifth position as a young husband getting an old woman, an affair viewed as a scandalous one but with no serious implication involving moral degradation. "A withered popular" with flowers on it involves a similar meaning: flowers will not bring new life to a withered popular or they would not last long on a withered tree. Commentators seem to be unanimous in viewing that "blossoms on a withered popular" and "a young husband getting an old woman" signify a union between the subjects represented respectively by the fifth yang line and the sixth yin line. This union is made possible because the two subjects, a yang and a yin having complementary characteristics to each other, are located in close proximity. This is why the line statement for the fifth yang line renders a much less ominous judgment on its subject's situation. Notice, however, that the line statement says in effect that the union with the sixth yin line under the situation is not a productive one. Regarding the situation the sixth line faces, recall that he himself is quite helpless, thus in less of a position to render any amount of meaningful assistance to others. But, again, why is the situation of the subject at the fifth position symbolized with such a negative image as a withered tree? No detailed explanation of this as was addressed for the third yang line is found either in the *I Ching* or in later commentaries. My own guess is that the explanation applied to the third yang line may be applied here again: the fifth yang line, a yang line occupying a yang position, is interpreted as maintaining too rigid a posture for an exceptional time (of the hexagram *Daguo*) that requires a certain measure of flexibility; hence the image of a withered tree. Along with this interpretation, remember that there is no yin line in the middle four lines meaning there is no willing subordinate who is submissive to the fifth one's high-handed-style leadership suggested in symbolism by a rigid withered tree. Implied here is a situation in which the top leadership has lost a full control over his administration.

In contrast to the third and fifth lines, the other two yang lines, the second and fourth ones, located right below them in their respective trigrams are given quite favorable judgments. Here also the logic of "an exceptional time" is viewed to be at work. That is, the "great strength" in the two yang lines' behavioral orientations is viewed to be somewhat tempered by the nature of duties assigned to the second and the fourth positions which require subordination towards those in a leadership position. Thus, these yang lines occupying yin places are interpreted as factors contributing rather positively to bring some desirable balance to the situation of *Daguo* that could otherwise involve the possibility of collapse. Then, first, let us read the line statement of the second yang line: "A withered popular puts forth new shoots. An old man gets a young wife for himself. Nothing done here fails to be fitting" (Lynn, 1994:313). It may not be immediately apparent that the line statement above says anything related to the positive function that the subject at the second position performs to "save the ridgepole from sinking" (Lynn, 1994:313). Although the line statement as it stands may not be read as saying such things, Wang Bi came up with the interpretation that the second yang line is viewed as carrying out an invaluable public function to "save the ridgepole from sinking." Despite doubt that can be raised regarding the source of his interpretation, what is obvious from the line statement of the second yang line is that it depicts a happy union with which the subject at the second position meets an opportunity for an active new life. By relying on the logic of the *I Ching* with which we should have now become well familiar, it is not difficult to understand with whom the second yin line achieves the happy union (described as an old man getting a young wife). The second yang line is located in the only place contiguous to the bottom position where a yin line who is described to exhibit an "excessively deferential" behavior is located; therefore, there is no doubt that the "young wife" in the line statement refers to the first yin line. According to the *Commentary on the Images*, this union results in such a desirable outcome as if "An old man and a young wife take what is too much on each side and share it" (Lynn, 1994:314). The passage in the *Commentary on the Images* says that the subjects at the bottom and the second positions possess some extreme opposing characteristics and that the union between the two makes those characteristics blended into more or less harmoniously balanced ones. This seems to explain why Cheng Yi interprets the second yang line as representing "people who are surpassing in strength but who can control themselves by balance, using softness and flexibility to complement firmness and strength" (1988:88). Probably, Wang Bi's interpretation with which the subject at the second position is viewed to be in a position to make a positive contribution to "save the ridgepole from sinking" is also related to the idea of complementary relationships between the two actors.

The line statement of the fourth yang line also depicts its subject as a ridgepole that "is kept high" or one who can "save the ridgepole from sinking and being bent down by the line below" (Lynn, 1994:314).

This auspicious judgment is explained with the same logic as that for the second yang line: under this extraordinary situation, "having strength in a weak position is considered appropriate" (Cheng Yi, 1988:89), or "the firmness of the fourth place is modified by the yieldingness of its position" (Wilhelm, 1967:528). In other words, the hard pressing action orientation indicated by a yang line at the fourth position is viewed as somehow being moderated by the attribute of the position itself that requires submissiveness. However, the line statement at the same time alludes to a possibility that the subject at the forth position may set out to expand his influence by winning the first yin line over to his side. It is because, as viewed from the unique perspective of the *I Ching*, the first and the fourth positions may have inclinations to form a corresponding relationship due to their positions having a specific affinity and complementary action orientations (yin-yang combination). Nevertheless, the line statement gives a warning to the subject at the fourth position about a negative consequence resulting from such a union. Although the line statement itself does not explain why any attempt to form a union between the two actors results in rather undesirable consequences, commentators offer some explanations, yet their explanations do not seem very illuminating. For example, Cheng Yi explains that since "strength and weakness are already in balance" in the fourth yang line, a "further involvement with yin (i.e., the first yin line)" causes some "strain" on his posture (1988:89). In other words, the subject at the fourth position has achieved a harmonious balance in action orientation by combining a hard driving energy with a certain degree of flexibility, and, therefore, if a willing subordinate such as the one at the first position is brought into his sphere of influence, he will have no advantage but an additional strain that may work against his balanced posture.

The hexagram *Xiaoguo*(☱ ☶ , Minor Superiority; Preponderance of the Small)

The main theme of the situation represented by the hexagram *Xiaoguo* (Preponderance of the Small) seems to be derived from two sources. One is its composition of lines where two strong lines are hemmed between four yin lines; this gives an idea of a preponderance of the small (yin lines). The other is the pictorial shape of the hexagram; the two yang lines may be seen as the body of a bird, and with the pairs of two yin lines above and below looked at as wings spread open, the shape of the hexagram gives a pictorial image of a flying bird. Then, with the above two ideas being combined, the hexagram is read to represent a situation that is characterized in metaphor as a flying bird lacking high soaring power. It is exactly along this line that the *Judgment* describes the situation represented by the hexagram, ". . . . Small matters may be undertaken. The flying bird is losing its voice, for it should not go up but should go down, because then there would be great good fortune" (Lynn, 1994:530). Yet, what does the condition represented metaphorically, a flying bird in a weakly state, mean specifically in terms of a social situation? When we read the line statements of this hexagram, we find a common theme underlying most of them: it is a message that people involved in the situation should not try to fly high, meaning they should not aim at lofty goals or attempt great things. However, the text provides no clue to answer the question of what specific sort of unfavorable conditions operate in this situation to frustrate individuals who pursue lofty goals. This question will remain until we finish our discussion on this hexagram.[116]

Then, let us look at the line statements. The line statement of the first yin line states briefly: "To be a flying bird here would mean misfortune" (Lynn, 1994:531). Its message is in line with the main theme of the hexagram: the subject at the position is advised to stay put where he is now; the time offers little advantage for him to derive good results from attempts at great things.

The line statement of the second yin line involves complex symbolism that has caused difficulty for some commentators in grasping its meaning. Thus, as I have done in similar instances involving much ambiguity, I made my own choice, of which Kim's following translation seems to be the most reasonable: "(If one finds it difficult to talk directly to the grandfather,) he will pass by the grandfather, and meet with his grandmother (through whom what he wants to say will be relayed to the grandfather). Likewise, the subject here does not go directly to his prince, but meets with the official. Then, there will be no blame" (1997:470, translated from the Korean text by this author).[117] Interpreted and translated as above, the line statement of the second yin line again depicts its subject as one who refrains from high flying; he avoids direct contact with the one at the top leadership bypassing the normal chain of authority, but meeting his immediate superior "with whom he is united through the relationship of holding together" (Wilhelm, 1967:707). This line statement implicitly issues a warning against an overreaching ambition or conduct that goes over a moderate limit. Thus, the message is again clear here. This is not a situation that favors the promotion of ambitious projects.

The line statement of the third yang line may be viewed as deviating somewhat from the main theme of the flying bird. Judging from the line statement, the subject at the third position can be understood as one who faces a risky situation. However, the line statement itself is translated differently as it is interpreted differently. So, before the line statement of the third line is introduced, we first must have some idea about the situational context in which the subject at the third position is said to invite hostile actions from others. Presumably, the reason for which he draws hostility from others is that the subject at the third position is in a more advantageous position than any other under the situation: a yang line appears appropriately at a yang position and is the only strong line whose situational attribute fits well with its positional function. Thus, according to Legge, "The subject of line 3 is too confident in his own strength, and too defiant of the weak and small enemies that seek his hurt" (1963:204). With this interpretation he translates the line statement; "The third line, undivided, shows its subject taking no extraordinary precautions against danger; and some in consequence finding opportunity to assail and injure him. There will be evil" (1963:203). Rendered as above, we can see a warning against excessive or overreaching behavior (as symbolized by a high-flying bird), the main theme of this line statement. What is troubling, however, is that an opposite interpretation is derived from the very same line statement. For instance, Lynn's version of translation based on Wang Bi's interpretation reads as follows: "If this one does not exert his superiority and ward them off but instead follows along, they are likely to kill him, which means misfortune" (1994:532). According to this latter interpretation, the subjects represented by the first and the second yin lines are viewed to have the inclination for overreaching behavior. Therefore, unless put under proper control by the third position, undesirable consequences to their superior are likely to occur. Obviously, this difference in interpretations again represents the vulnerability of the tersely phrased symbolic narration of the *I Ching* that oftentimes leave large gaps in meaning for readers to fill in. I am inclined to side with Legge's interpretation for the sake of consistency; Legge's appears more consistent with the main theme of the hexagram that we have set down earlier.

The line statement of the fourth yang line seems clearer than that of the third yang line; it reads, "That this one is without blame is because he deals with circumstances in such a way that he does not exert his superiority. If he were to set forth, there would be danger, so he must take warning. One must not use this one where perpetual constancy is required" (Lynn, 1994:533). The subject at the fourth position is expected to refrain from exerting his superiority because his assertive action orientation, indicated by a yang line, is moderated by the fact that his position is related to supportive, rather than leadership, functions (Cheng Yi, 1988:208; Wilhelm, 1967:708).[118] The advice that follows involves a warning against an activist orientation that the "strong" subject may feel tempted to take. The last verse reading, "One must not use this one where perpetual constancy is required," is difficult to understand. The text itself can be translated literally as "do not use perpetual firmness here," (or, as Lynn translates it with Cheng Yi's interpretation of it, "He must not hang on tenaciously to constant principles") (1994537n9), which is much easier to interpret; it emphasizes the virtue of moderation under the situation.

The line statement of the fifth line states, "The fifth line, divided, (suggests the idea) of dense clouds, but no rain, coming from our borders in the west. It also (shows) the prince shooting his arrow, and taking the bird in a cave"[119] (Legge, 1963:203). The described situation as a whole seems to be a strenuous one in which the subject is not likely to find himself in a happy or expansive mood. Rain means a resolution of one's problems, and to shoot the bird in a cave with an arrow would not be a kind of hunting that produces good yields or gives pleasure. Thus, the line statement as a whole describes the situation of the subject at the leadership position as quite constraining. Commentators' explanations on why the one at the ruler's seat is in a strained situation show little divergence from one another. A weak subject represented by a yin line is incumbent at the fifth position, a yang (leadership) position, and the overall formation of the lines is read to suggest that its subject does not have a strong alliance to support his power. Thus, the subject in the leadership position is understood as having a weak power potential as explained by Cheng Yi; "the fifth line has a yin weakness in the honored position; even though one like this want to excel, it is impossible to effectively achieve excellence" (1988:209).

The meaning of the last line statement is clear and simple; the subject at the sixth position is described as one who flies so high that he meets with unfortunate consequences. It reads, "The sixth line, divided, shows its subject not meeting (the exigency of his situation), and exceeding (his proper course). (It suggests the idea of) a bird flying far aloft. There will be evil. The case is what is called one of calamity and self-produced injury" (1963:203). The above line statement can be read in two different ways. One is that it contains a warning that is generally given to anyone involved in this type of situation. It warns against the pursuit of high-flying (ambitious) goals that go beyond a moderate limit. The other reading of this line statement is that the subject at the sixth position in fact falls into such a position so that he will meet unfortunate consequences. With the latter interpretation, we will have to explain why the subject is viewed to behave in such an excessive manner that he brings injury upon himself. A key idea that underlies this interpretation seems to have to do with the image of a flying bird that symbolizes the situation represented by the hexagram. Represented in metaphor by a flying bird, the subject at the topmost position may be figured as a bird that flies too high and shows no willingness to descend to the ground. Hence, the line statement depicts the subject as someone who refuses to come to terms with the exigencies of the time.

Summary of theoretical and empirical propositions

1) Depending upon the distribution patterns of strong or weak elements, organizations may have unbalanced compositions that cause operational malfunctions. For this kind of case, we may say that the source of problem lies in the organizational make-up in which actors with specific action orientations are positioned along the hierarchical line of the system represented by a given hexagram.

2) Under extraordinary situations, normal rules of behavior that are considered appropriate under ordinary circumstances may not apply any longer. This implies that, as far as the *I Ching* is concerned, given norms or rules can be judged as either appropriate or not in the context of a given situation.

13) Hexagrams Representing Military Situations

The meanings of four hexagrams to be dealt with here are interpreted to represent military situations, as clearly suggested by their titles. The hexagram *Xu* (Waiting) represents a situation in which troops stationed at various locations are waiting before the launch of an operation to advance into enemy territory. The hexagram *Dun* (Withdrawal) features a line-up of a retreating army whose members, depending upon their positions or modes of behavior, are subject to various types or levels of risk. The next two hexagrams, the hexagram *Weiji* (Ferrying Incomplete) and the hexagram *Jiji* (Ferrying Complete), feature situations before and after "a crossing of the river," implying a military operation of grave importance that concerns the fate of a nation. Besides these four hexagrams, there are may other hexagrams in the *I Ching* that contain accounts related to military conflicts between neighboring states. This seems to suggest that militaristic situations were an important reality for the time in which the author(s) of the *I Ching* lived.

1) The hexagram *Xu* (☵/☰, Waiting) (Hexagram No. 5)

2) The hexagram *Dun* (☰/☶, Withdrawal) (Hexagram No. 33)

3) The hexagram *Weiji* (☲/☵, Ferrying Incomplete) (Hexagram No. 64)

4) The hexagram *Jiji* (☵/☲, Ferrying Complete) (Hexagram No.63)

The hexagram *Xu* (☵/☰, Waiting)

Regarding the hexagram *Xu*, the *Commentary on the Judgments* explains, "*Xu* means 'waiting,' as danger lies in front" (Lynn, 1994:165). The meaning of the situation as explained above is derived from the two trigrams, the upper trigram *Kan* and the lower trigram *Qian*, that constitute the hexagram. Since the trigram *Qian* symbolizes "strength and dynamism" and the trigram *Kan* "pitfall (danger)," the hexagram as a whole is understood to give the image of a situation in which a force moving forward is suspended, if temporarily, by danger that lies in front. From the line statements we can conjure up a scene in which the advancing armed force is at one side of a river "waiting" to cross the river while the source of danger, perhaps enemies trying to stop it, lie somewhere across the river.[120] Accordingly, the respective lines, except the fifth one, do not involve meanings related to hierarchically differentiated social positions, but instead physical locations where waiting troops are stationed and thereby exposed to varying degrees of danger. Then, let us read individual line statements.

The line statement of the first yang line states, "When waiting in the countryside, it is fitting to practice perseverance, for then there will be no blame." The *Commentary on the Images* explains that the subject at this position "does not risk engaging himself in difficult matters" (Lynn, 1994:166). The reason behind describing the subject as waiting in a relatively safe place as in the countryside is not clearly explained anywhere in the text. Nevertheless, the line statements of this hexagram involve a peculiar sequence that applies only to this hexagram: starting from the bottom line moving up to the fourth, each of the line statements contains a description of a location where the subject at the respective position waits to embark on a dangerous enterprise. We can see the variations in the levels of danger involved with the locations increase by degrees from the first position to the fourth. As the source of danger lies in or across the river, if one moves closer to the river, he will get closer to more dangerous places. From this perspective, the line statement of the first yang line is interpreted to say that the first position is waiting in a relatively safe place; the countryside, a place away from the river, is thus a less dangerous place.

The subject at the second position is described to wait "on the sand" — a place, as Wang Bi explains, "close but not so close that he is oppressed by danger and far but not so far that he will be too late for the moment when it happens" (Lynn, 1994:167). Let us read the line statement first: "When waiting on the sand, it might slightly involve rebuke, but in the end, good fortune will result" (Lynn, 1994:167). Legge points out that he does not find any clue to explain why the subject suffers from "the strife of tongues (rebuke)" (1963:68). Of this, however, Wilhelm explains that "minor discords" between the subjects at this position and the fifth position are indicated by the fact that they are supposed to be in a corresponding relationship but do not possess complementary characteristics (both are yang lines) (1967:413). Compared to Wilhelm's explanation, Wang Bi's explanation, as already hinted at in the passage presented a short while ago, notes the fact that although the sand is a safer place from possible enemy attacks, at the same time it is not the appropriate place from which to launch an operation to attack the source of danger. Therefore, the subject at this position may be rebuked for not coming at the very moment when the operation begins. The feasibility of the above explanations cannot be read directly from the text itself, and thus must be viewed as having been produced from a commentator's imagination or point of view. Despite such differences in interpretation, however, the core of what the line statement says comes within the purview of the main idea of the hexagram where the relative fortunes of people vary according to locations and not their social status.

The line statement of the third yang line indicates that the subject at this position is waiting at a location much closer to the source of danger, the river. It reads, "When waiting on the mud, it attracts robbers to him" (Lynn, 1994:167). Cheng Yi's commentary on this line statement simply paraphrases this statement, but conveys a more clearly stated account regarding the situation that the subject at the third position faces under the situation:

> Mud is near to water, which represents danger; so this is a situation very near to danger, which brings on the difficulties of opposition. The third yang is strong but not balanced, and is also at the top of the trigram representing power; there is the image of forward movement, and this "brings on opposition." If they are not careful, people in this position will bring on destructive defeat. (Cheng Yi, 1988:11)

The place where the people are located is said to be "very near danger" that may "bring on opposition."

In the line statement of the fourth yin line, no reference is made about a specific location, but, judging from what the line statement says, its subject should be understood as being located at the foremost front line where skirmishes with enemies take place. The line statement thus reads, "When waiting in blood, one has to come out of the pit" (1994:167). What the passage, "one has to come out of the pit," means is not clear. Wang Bi's commentary suggests that some sort of conflict occurs between the subject at the third position who "advances hard" and the one at the fourth position who "cannot ward it off" and therefore "has to fall back" (Lynn, 1994:168). Thus, "one has to come out of the pit" is interpreted as referring to a disadvantageous situation encountered by its subject that requires him "to fall back." Wilhelm's interpretation differs from Wang Bi's in viewing that the dangerous situation of the fourth yin line is indicated by the fact that it is a weak line "hemmed in between two strong lines" at the third and the fifth positions. But, both interpretations presented above seem to pose difficulties in two respects. One is that it does not seem clear how the line statement interpreted as such is related to what is stated for the third or the fifth lines. The other is that it also does not seem clear how the line statement interpreted as such is related to the main theme of the hexagram, "waiting." In my opinion, the easiest and most logical interpretation is as follows: the danger suggested by the line statement is related to the physical location where the subject is waiting to cross the river, i.e., the launch of a crucially important military operation. Then, the passage, "one has to come out of the pit," may have to be translated rather differently as "this one gets out of the pit (to meet the dangerous situation)." This interpretation seems to be supported also by the *Commentary on the Images*: it states, " 'Waiting in blood': as he is compliant, he obeys" (Lynn, 1994:168). To interpret, on orders from his superior (probably the ruler at the fifth position) he will wait obediently in such a dangerous place.

The subject at the fifth position, also waiting, is described to be in a quite comfortable situation. The line statement states, "The fifth line, undivided, shows its subject waiting amidst the appliances of a feast. Through his firmness and correctness there will be good fortune" (Legge, 1963:67).[121] Implicitly suggested in the above line statement is an optimism held by the subject at the fifth position; he is described as having a seemingly sufficient reason to "wait amidst the appliances of a feast." The favorable judgment given to the subject at the fifth position is based on the typical logic of interpreting the *I Ching* as exemplified by Cheng Yi's explanation on this line statement:

> The fifth line has positive strength correctly balanced, placed in the position of leadership; this represents those who have done all that they have to do. Now they can wait on this basis, and since what they are waiting for will surely be attained they can eat, drink, and make merry as they await it. Since they have attained true correctness, what they need and await will surely arrive; this certainly can be called auspicious. (1988:12)

Cheng Yi's above commentary seems to contain a persuasive moral lecture. However, we certainly can raise doubt about its truth with respect to what is likely to take place in a real situation as a consequence of the moral posture that the subject takes in waiting. It seems true that to Confucian scholars like Cheng Yi the significance of the *I Ching* lies, more than anything else, in moral teachings it can offer for governing elites on whose conduct the welfare of a nation depends. Thus, it would be understandable that Cheng Yi's commentary focuses upon moral lessons that he could draw from every line statement.

The line statement of the sixth yin line states, "When entering the pit, one finds that three uninvited guests have arrived. If one treat them with respect, in the end, there will be good fortune" (Lynn, 1994:168). The beginning line, "when entering the pit," contains a phrase that is directly opposite of the fourth line statement, "to come out of the pit." Thus, if we interpret it to carry a meaning opposite of that conveyed by the fourth line statement, the subject at the sixth position will be understood to be in a relatively safer position. Commentators converge on the view with which "three uninvited guests" are interpreted to refer to those represented by the three yang lines in the lower trigram. Given this interpretation, "three uninvited guests" is better translated in Cleary's text as "(three) guests not in haste" (Cheng Yi, 1988:12). Then, the line statement as a whole can be understood from a perspective quite different from Lynn's translation. The line statements of the three lines in the lower trigram describe the respective subjects as waiting at various points exposed to varying levels of danger. Thus, the line statement of the sixth line can be interpreted to suggest that after waiting (felt as "long") the troops begin to push forward into the dangerous territory probably as the proper moment draws closer. Thus, the line statement of the sixth line sounds more like an epilogue, a statement of the final outcome of the situation. That is, it is interpreted to say that as the waiting troops represented by the lower trigram come forward after waiting, the final resolution to the confrontation with the enemy will result provided that the troops are well managed with "respect." Of course, interpreting the line statement in this way, to whom is the line statement addressed? As we have observed in some hexagrams, the line statements of the sixth line often involve narration that may be characterized as "a concluding remark," "epilogue," or "final outcome." Generally in such cases, there seem to be two possible answers concerning the question of to whom the line statement is addressed. One is that it is addressed to no specific individual, but to everyone involved in the situation. The other is that it is addressed to the key individual who plays the most decisive or dominant role in managing the affairs of the time. In the case of this hexagram, my guess is that it is addressed to the subject at the fifth position, who is designated by Wilhelm (1967:410) as the ruler of the hexagram who bears the chief responsibility for bringing the aimed project to fruition through "patient waiting."

The hexagram *Dun*(☰ ☶, Withdrawal)

According to Wang Bi's sub-commentary on the *Commentary on the Judgments*, the concept underlying Withdrawal is that "only by withdrawing will one [eventually] prevail" (Lynn, 1994:340). Since "one" is interpreted as referring to the subject at the fifth position and the situational condition that forces him to withdraw is said to be the forces of yin lines growing in strength below, this situation may be characterized in terms of an interplay between the yin and yang forces, one advancing and the other in retreat. On the other hand, the reading of the line statements features a situation entirely different from that which is explained above in the *Commentary on the Judgments*. And, again, depending upon how we construct the meaning of the overall situation from the individual line statements, the hexagram may yield still different ideas of the situation. From one perspective, the hexagram can represent an army in retreat, a formation of a retreating army with soldiers at the rear represented by a yin line at the bottom position. If viewed as such, the individual line statements are interpreted as describing situations that the subjects at various positions are likely to encounter while a retreat is underway. To take another perspective, the hexagram can be viewed as featuring a situation in which there are some adverse conditions forcing people in office to retire from their positions. If viewed in this way, the line statements can be understood as describing the way subjects at various positions retire or things that they, when pressed with a forced retirement, have to consider. Although this hexagram can be interpreted either way, I would like to point out two reasons in favor of the former one. First, we can hardly imagine a real social situation that forces all office holders to retire from their positions. Second, the line statements involve warnings of possible danger and the urgency of danger is related to the location of the positions that the lines occupy: the degree of danger lessens as one's position moves away from the bottom position through the middle up to the top. And, in the line statement of the first line, the bottom position is described as the tail of Withdrawal, the immediate point of attack from a pursuing enemy. This makes the sixth line represent the subject at the head of the retreating army moving away from the enemy attack. His location, far from the tail of the retreating army, ensures him a safe position; thus, as Wang Bi comments on this line statement, "No disaster can entangle him as no harpoon arrow can reach him" (Lynn, 1994:344). Also for other lines, one's distance from the tail measures his exposure to the source of danger. Now, let us look at the line statements.

The line statement of the first yin line reads, "There is danger at the tail of Withdrawal, so do not use this opportunity to go forth." Here the subject at the first position is described as soldiers in retreat moving at the rearmost point, thus exposed to attacks from a pursuing enemy. Accordingly, the line statement involves advice for the subject to avoid using this opportunity to carry out important things, which is reasonable in view of the perilous situation he is facing.

The line statement of the second yin line is interpreted differently from one commentator to another and its translations differ accordingly. I here take Legge's version, which states: "The second line, divided, shows its subject holding (his purpose) fast as if by a (thong made from the) hide of a yellow ox, which cannot be broken" (1963:128). According to Legge, "his purpose" in the line statement means "the purpose to withdraw" that he shares with the subject at the fifth position with whom he is collaborating (C.f., Cheng Yi, 1988:105). Thus, the subject at the second position is described as officials or field officers who carry out the operation of Withdrawal "correctly" as ordered by the leader at the fifth position.

The third yang line represents the leader of the subgroup denoted by the lower trigram. In its line statement, according to Wang Bi's interpretation, this one is described as one who "ought to withdraw but . . . . remains attached to the place where he is located." The underlying idea is regarding the type of people who refuse to withdraw because of their attachment to what is dear to them (things, persons, or places), thus putting themselves into dangerous situations. Why the subject at this particular position is described as one who displays such unwise behavior is not clear. Wang Bi explains that this is indicated by the composition of lines in which the third yang line is right next to the yin line at the second position; since "a yang line adheres to a yin line; it ought to withdraw but is attached" (Lynn, 1994:342). But, this interpretation is clearly in conflict with the interpretation given to the second line by other commentators. As I see it, in some hexagrams, the line statements seem to have little relevance to the attributes of the hierarchical statuses of the respective positions, but contain only accounts on types of personalities, patterns of behavior, or sub-types of a situation, etc. Generally in such cases, the line statements are meaningful only if they are interpreted as presenting a typology coupled with moral lessons given to individuals characterized as behaving in certain typical ways. This case seems to be of this category. The line statement of the third line must be accepted as describing only a certain type of people and the expected outcome of their behavior under the given situation. Meanwhile, the *I Ching* adds an interesting remark at the end of the line statement: "but, a kept servant will have good fortune." Wang Bi explains this as a remark expressing what he regards to be a plain truth: "To be so attached to where one finds himself is quite acceptable for a kept servant" (Lynn, 1994:342-3). In other words, it is the rightful duty for a kept servant to stay put where his master stays, although doing so may endanger his life.

The line statement of the fourth yang line, if we adopt Wang Bi's interpretation, seems to repeat the same idea as that of the third line. It reads, "Here one should withdraw from that of which he is fond, so the noble man will have good fortune, but the petty man will be obstructed." According to Wang Bi, a noble man refers to someone who "would withdraw from that of which he is fond," whereas a small man "remains attached to what he loves and so is obstructed" (Lynn, 1994:343). What this line statement intends to say is obvious: once one finds it necessary to carry out Withdrawal, he should do it despite his lingering affections for things that may tempt him to stay on.

The line statement of the fifth yang line is brief and seems difficult to understand. It states briefly, "Here is praiseworthy Withdrawal, in which constancy brings good fortune." In the context of the overall situation represented by the hexagram, Wang Bi's commentary seems to provide a sensible explanation. He explains, "Fifth Yang withdraws in such a way that it achieves rectitude, and it practices control back upon the inner trigram (the lower trigram), where the petty man [Second Yang with which it is in resonance] . . . . obeys orders and rectifies his will completely" (Lynn, 1994:343). Thus, here, the subject at the fifth position is described as the leader who "practices control back upon" the retreating army, especially the one at the second position who "obeys orders" and does not "break away" from the column of the army in procession with a firm sense of duty. Of course, there is one thing of which we always have to remind ourselves regarding how we interpret the line statements of a given hexagram. In this particular line statement, for instance, "praiseworthy Withdrawal" can be interpreted as meaning either "an existing state of affairs where Withdrawal is underway" or "the way in which one at a given position with a certain situationally determined trait ought to act when Withdrawal is underway." Then, interpretations will depend upon how we conceptualize the overall context of the situation from all the related accounts on the hexagram. Regarding this issue, I have an impression that native commentators were not willing to give up either interpretation and, thereby, took up a rather ambivalent view permitting different ways of looking at the line statements. In a sense, this ambiguity has been a blessing for students of the *I Ching*. They could learn facts about the world from this book and also moral teachings about how they ought to conduct themselves living with fellow human beings.

The line statement of the sixth yang line is also very brief and, therefore, difficult to understand. It states, "This is flying Withdrawal, so nothing fails to be fitting." But, as was the case with the line statement of the fifth line, Wang Bi's commentary (Lynn, 1994:344) seems to provide a sensible explanation. First, he notes that the line formation of the hexagram indicates that the subject at the sixth position "is not in resonance with any other line," or, in other words, he has no close attachment to hold him from Withdrawal. Thus, "this is (described as) flying Withdrawal." The second thing that Wang Bi notes is associated with the location of the sixth position and its comparison to a column of the retreating army. Since the first line is described as the tail of it, the sixth line represents the head, the farthest point from the tail of the retreating army. His comment, "No disaster can entangle him as no harpoon arrow can reach him," can be clearly understood in the context of the situation as interpreted above; he is in a safe position that cannot be reached by enemy attack.

The hexagram *Weiji* (☲☵, Ferrying Incomplete)

The line composition of the hexagram *Weiji* shows that all yang lines are incumbent at yin positions and all the yin lines are at yang places. Thus, it may be thought that this hexagram represents a disorderly or unstable situation. Judging from the accounts in the text, however, it seems more appropriate to say that the hexagram *Weiji* represents a type of organizational structure or a situationally determined structure of an organization in a reverse order to carry out "Ferrying," i.e., an emergency task of grave importance. In other words, as a political community faces a dangerous or difficult situation, a social organization in its ordinary form may be unfit to deal with the extraordinary situation, and, then, it is radically transformed into a type, as the hexagram *Weiji* represents, to meet an emergency situation. As we can see, there are two yang lines at the second and the fourth positions each with a yin line above it, the arrangement of which may be viewed as detrimental to the maintenance of a harmoniously working, hierarchical order. In their line statements, however, the subjects at the two positions are described as primary actors who carry out the task implied by the hexagram. Then, let us look at the line statements of these two lines, first:

Second Yang: This one drags his wheels. Such constancy means good fortune.

Fourth Yang: Constancy results in good fortune, thus regret vanishes. As a burst of thunder, this one attacks the Demon Territory, for which after three days he is rewarded with a large state. (Lynn, 1994:547-8)

The nature of the situation represented by the hexagram and the active roles that the two actors play are clearly suggested by Wang Bi's commentary: "This attack on the Demon Territory is a campaign that determines whether the realm rises or falls. Thus each time the realm reaches such a life or death crisis, such a one should choose this course as the right thing to do" (Lynn, 1994:548). The subject at the second position is also described as one who will "rescue the times from danger and difficulty, (as) someone who can put things in order and make them go smoothly again" (Wang Bi, in Lynn, 1994:547). Thus, both actors are described as powerful figures who both bear chief responsibilities in carrying out the emergency task implied by the hexagram. Notice that there are yin lines respectively at the third and the fifth positions, which means that they are weak leaders whose powers are transferred to those in subordinate positions to meet the emergency situation. However, since strong lines are at weaker (subordinate) positions, their line statements involve cautionary remarks for the subjects at the positions, as the *I Ching* usually does whenever a subject's situation is judged to involve a danger of excessive behavior: they must behave prudently and correctly to have good outcomes.

The line statements of the third and the fifth yin lines accord well with what can be expected from the line statements of the second and the fourth yang lines. They read:

Third Yin: Ferrying Incomplete is such that to set out to do something here would mean misfortune, but it is fitting to cross the great river.

Fifth Yin: Constancy results in good fortune, and thus this one avoids regret. The glory of the noble man is due to the sincerity he has, which brings good fortune. (Lynn, 1994:547, 549)

In the line statement of the third yin line, its subject is advised that under the circumstance it would not be favorable for him to try to put himself into a leader's role in the process of overcoming the difficult situation implied by the hexagram. According to Legge, a negative might have been omitted from the ending line, "it is fitting to cross the great river" (1963:209); if so, it has to be read as, "it is not fitting to cross the great river." Then, the line statement as a whole is made consistent in that it contains advice against its subject's taking an active leadership role under the emergency situation. The subject at the fifth position is also described as the leader who has transferred his power to his subordinates at the second and the fourth positions who engage in field operations to complete "Ferrying."[122] Accordingly, the line statement contains advice requesting correct and prudent behavior on the part of its subject so that he can "avoid regret" under the situation.

Now, let us examine the remaining two lines. These two lines are related, but not in the same manner as the other four lines. The line statements of these two lines seem to be descriptive of contrasting personality types or behavioral orientations when dealing with a crisis situation. Both of them entail negative connotations, and, therefore, can be understood as aiming at practical teachings regarding what people should or should not do when dealing with a crisis situation. Let us read the line statements first:

> *First Yin*: This one gets his tail wet, which means misfortune.
>
> *Sixth Yang*: This one has confidence and so engages in drinking wine, about which there is no blame, but he might get his head wet, for this one with his confidence could do violence to what is right. (Lynn, 1994:546, 550)

The line statement of the first yin line may be understood in connection with a verse in the *Judgments* that says, "The young fox uses dry conditions to ferry itself across, but it still gets its tail wet" (Lynn, 1994:543). According to Legge, "The symbolism of the young fox suggests a want of caution on the part of those, in the time and condition denoted by the hexagram, who try to remedy prevailing disorders" (1963:209). That is, whereas the emergency situation denoted by the hexagram requires a very cautious approach and well thought-out preparations, the subject at the first position is figured as someone who plunges hastily into the water without due caution and preparations. This interpretation is also echoed by other commentators such as Wang Bi (Lynn, 1994:546) and Wilhelm (1967:716). However, why is the subject at the first position interpreted as someone who may commit errors by acting hastily? No reasonable answer to this question seems to be offered by either the text or any later commentary. Considering that the line statement of this particular line is related to the overall judgment on the entire situation, a reasonable explanation seems to be that the line statement is a maxim applied generally to people under the situation suggested by the hexagram. It intends to teach individuals involved in the situation that overcoming the difficulty at hand requires a very cautious approach.

The line statement of the sixth yang line can be understood in the same context, and, accordingly, is interpreted as containing the advice that confidence and carefree diversion to a certain extent would not be harmful in dealing with the situation, but an overindulgence (till he gets his head wet) "could do violence to what is right."

The hexagram *Jiji* (䷾ **, Ferrying Complete)**

The hexagram *Jiji* (Ferrying Complete) has a line structure inverse to that of the previous hexagram *Weiji*; thus, every line under the situation is in its rightful position, yang lines in yang positions and yin lines in yin positions. It is due to this line composition that the *Hexagrams in Irregular Order* notes that "*Jiji* (Ferrying Complete) signifies stability" (Lynn, 1994:539). This signifies a stable situation that has returned to normalcy after the emergency situation represented by the hexagram *Weiji*. However, the *Judgment* issues a warning, "It is fitting to practice constancy, for although in the beginning good fortune prevails, things might end in chaos." Of this Wang Bi comments, "If one were to misconstrue Ferrying Complete to mean perfect security, its Dao would come to an end, and no progress would occur, so that in the end only chaos would ensue" (Lynn, 1994:539). It is not clear why this situation of Ferrying Complete is believed to involve within itself a danger of losing its stability. Wilhelm reasons that a possible collapse of order is indicated by the composition of its component trigrams (1967:711); it consists of the upper trigram *Kan* (water) and the lower trigram *Li* (fire) and a union of these two components with mutually counteractive tendencies signals instability. According to the hexagram statement, a social situation, however stable, always contains a seed of instability that could lead to disorder, therefore, we must keep ourselves aware of things operating to bring about disorder.

Then, let us look at the line statements of this hexagram and examine how individual subjects at varying strata fare respectively under this situation. The line statement of the first yang line states, "This one drags his wheels and wets his tail, so there is no blame" (Lynn, 1994:539). This line statement is interpreted differently by commentators. However, if we take into consideration both the meaning of the overall situation of this hexagram and the relationship of this hexagram with the previous one, I think, Legge's explanation seems to adhere most closely with the above considerations. He explains:

> Line 1, the first of the hexagram, represents the time immediately after the successful achievement of the enterprise it denotes; — the time for resting and being quiet. For a season, at least, all movement should be hushed. Hence we have the symbolism of a driver trying to stop his

carriage, and a fox who has wet his tail, and will not tempt the stream again. (1963:206)

Interpreted as above, the subject at the first position is advised to refrain from making active movements; it is a time for resting and staying away from activism. But, what places this one into such a fragile position that he must keep a cautious posture ducking his head low on the ground? There is a yin line right above him and another yin line at the fourth position whose subject supposedly has a specific affinity with the subject at the first position. Under ordinary situations, a stable pattern of yin-yang combinations such as this marks a favorable situation for the first yang line. All indications show that he has an activist action orientation and the circumstances are in line for him to go forward with his action orientation indicated as such. Why then is the subject at the first position discouraged from staging active movements with a progressive spirit? An answer to this question seems to lie in the nature of this situation. The *I Ching* seems to have conceived the situation represented by this hexagram as being in a very delicate equilibrium, an integrated but fragile situation. Perhaps this is why there is no line statement in this hexagram that tells about "good fortune" for its subject. All the line statements involve words referring to difficulty, caution, prudence, and patience instead of security, happiness, or stability. The text offers little hint to explain the specific characteristics that make this state of equilibrium so precarious that it may break down any time unless the people involved take all necessary precautions to avoid possible inherent dangers. The text only offers the idea that this hexagram represents a situation which is stable yet, at the same time, involves forces conducive to instability; thus all the position holders are advised against unnecessary or unwise actions that may disturb the precariously balanced situation. The line statement of the first yang line will be understood properly in this light.

The line statement of the second yin line can be understood in the same context as explained above. It states, "This wife loses her headdress, but she should not pursue it, for in seven days she will obtain it" (Lynn, 1994:540). The subject at the second position is described as a wife because, as a yielding line, it is in corresponding relationship with the governing ruler at the fifth position. Commentators interpret the line, "this wife loses her headdress," as symbolizing a situation in which the subject at the second position is hemmed between two strong lines and therefore exposed to possible intimidation from them. Nevertheless, the advice offered in the line statement keeps the same tone of voice as that attributed to the first yang line; it is not the time to creat commotion in pursuit of the lost headdress, it is better to be patient and wait until the situation changes. Although the line statement touches upon the idea of internal conflicts between the subject at the second position and the two subjects above and below him, there is no passage indicating such a conflict in the line statement of either the first yang line or the third yang line. Despite such an inconsistency, however, this line statement contains in essence the same message as the first yang line: this is not the time to take action and it is sufficient to calmly watch how things move.

The line statement of the third yang line contains a remark that cautions the subject of the difficulty of the task at hand. The nature of the task is not clear, but from the line statement we can understand at least that it would be an enormously difficult one; it reads, "When Exalted Ancestor attacked the Demon Territory, it took him three years to conquer it. The petty man must not be used here" (Lynn, 1994:540). Cheng Yi interprets this passage as referring to difficulties involved in the task of ruling people with "threat or military force" (1988:211). This interpretation corresponds with the strong possibility that the situation represented by the hexagram *Jiji* (Ferrying Complete) is related to the completion of a military operation that might have started in the face of an emergency event endangering a country. Implied here is the prediction that there will be a great deal more difficult tasks lying ahead once the military operation comes to completion. It is the subject at the third position, the leader of the lower group at field operation level, who will bear the heaviest responsibility.

The subject at the fourth position is also described as someone who "should take warnings," although "there are rags .... to stop leaks in a boat" (Lynn, 1994:541). The nature of this situation, a state of a precarious equilibrium, continues to loom here as the subject at the fourth position is bound to a situation in which he "should take warnings." He is interpreted as being equipped with means ("rags") to deal with an emergency situation ("leaks"). Although the nature of the emergency situation is not elaborated, the subject at the fourth position is portrayed as bearing the responsibility of taking care of the situation.

Judging from the line formation, there seems to be no doubt that the subject at the fifth line is both the constituting (*de jure*) and governing (*de facto*) leader, although there is no explicit mention of this in its line statement. The line statement, however, has this to say about the conduct of the government under this delicate situation: "The neighbor in the east slaughters an ox, but this falls short of the *yue* sacrifice of the neighbor in the west, which really provides that one with blessings"[123] (Lynn, 1994:541). The *yue* sacrifice refers to a simple ritual that becomes truly potent with the sincerity and virtue of the person who conducts it. The sincere and simple spirit symbolized by the *yue* sacrifice is recommended here as a wiser or more timely way to deal with the situation. Thus, the *Commentary on the Images* emphasizes again the need for a sincere and modest posture on the part of the top leader by saying, "The neighbor to the east who slaughters an ox is not as timely as the neighbor to the west" (Lynn, 1994:542).

Meanwhile, the line statement of the sixth line involves a judgment that is quite unfavorable. The reason for the unfavorable judgment is not explained clearly in either the text or any later commentary. According to Wang Bi, the subject represents someone who "does not stop but advances too far" (Lynn, 1994:542; c.f., Cheng Yi, 1988:212). But, why the subject is viewed as someone who acts as such is not explained clearly. Regardless, the dominant theme of the hexagram is repeated here again: this situation calls for a cautious approach in taking care of things left unsettled after Ferrying (most likely a military operation) is complete.

Summary of theoretical and empirical propositions

1) A certain measure of confidence and carefree diversion does little harm in dealing with an emergency situation, but too much confidence or overindulgence in diversion may frustrate one's effort to successfully deal with the situation.

2) A social situation, however stable or orderly, always involves counteracting forces conducive to instability.

14) Hexagrams Representing Specific Political and Social Occasions

Of the five hexagrams to be examined here, the hexagram *Xikan* (the Constant Sink Hole) features a society that has fallen into an extremely difficult situation. It is indicated that this dangerous situation is connected with the recurrent historical experience of floods in China that swept through the basin areas of the two great rivers, the Yangze River and the Yellow River. The hexagram *Guan* figures a specific political moment in which the ruling elites and the governed subjects are viewing or trying to measure up one another as the former group is newly instituted into the leadership. The situation represented by the hexagram *Li* (Cohesion) features a vigilant society as it encounters external threats at a specific moment of a social cycle that agrarian China experienced. The hexagram *Jian* (Adversity) is about a specific political crisis situation that had been experienced by the author(s) of the *I Ching* while his kingdom was contending with his neighboring state over the hegemony of the entire Chinese Empire. Lastly, the line statements of the hexagram *Lü* (the Wanderer) give accounts of various situations that people in political exile in a foreign country may find themselves. Of the above five hexagrams, therefore, we may note that the situations represented by them may be related to unique historical experiences of the people in ancient China or the personal experience of the author of the *I Ching* as a seasoned politician. It is with this consideration that they are grouped together here as representing specific political and social occasions that are understood with specific reference to the historical or cultural background of the *I Ching*.

1) The hexagram *Xikan*(☵ ,The Constant Sink Hole) (Hexagram No. 6)

2) The hexagram *Guan* (☴ , Viewing) (Hexagram No. 20)

3) The hexagram *Li* (☲ Cohesion) (Hexagram No. 30)

4) The hexagram *Jian* (☵ , Adversity) (Hexagram No. 39)

5) The hexagram *Lü* (☲ , The Wanderer) (Hexagram No. 56)

The hexagram *Xikan* (☵ , The Constant Sink Hole)

To this author, the situational meaning of the hexagram *Xikan* is derived purely from its pictorial image: the hexagram can be seen as flooding water (yin lines that represent torrential water) flowing over low grounds (where yin lines are located) with patches of high ground still remaining intact from the danger of the flood (as shown by two yang lines).[124] Accordingly, all the subjects in the hexagram are exposed to more or less degrees of danger and the hexagram is thought to represent a crisis situation in which the collectivity as a whole experiences danger arising from an outside source. We find no account in the *I Ching* that explains the nature of the outside source. The only available clue is provided by one feature of the line statements' descriptions of their subjects' situations. In this hexagram, regardless of whether there is a yang or yin line at any specific position, position holders in the three positions, the first, the third, and the sixth positions, are described as facing more serious situations than the other positions, the second, the fourth, and the fifth positions. It is interesting to note that the subjects who are rendered far less favorable judgments under this situation are those who, due to the characteristics of their positions, are said to enjoy less advantages or "fortunes" even under most ordinary situations. The first position ranks at the bottom of the hierarchical order and the sixth position ranks high in prestige but occupies no official position, thus has no real power. The third position is regarded as a transitional or ambivalent, thus unstable position that lies at the boundary between the subordinate and the dominant groups. Generally in the *I Ching*, even when the subjects at the aforementioned three positions enjoy advantages permitted by favorable conditions of any given situation, their advantages seem to appear somewhat tempered by the basic limitations associated with their positions. Thus, compared to the other three positions, their line statements are less likely to involve favorable judgments. It follows that if a collectivity as a whole falls into a perilous situation as indicated by this hexagram, the subjects at the mentioned three positions might be the most vulnerable ones who would suffer the most. And, the specific vulnerability of those positions also seems to be enforced by the pictorial image of this hexagram; as we can see, all three positions are represented by yin lines which, in this hexagram, offer the image of flooded lowlands.

As was pointed out, the situations of individual position holders are described mainly in terms of the various levels of risk that each of them faces under the overall situation represented by the hexagram. Consequently, as far as this hexagram is concerned, the patterns of internal relationships among the position holders are not crucial factors in accounting for how well or badly they fare respectively in this dangerous time. We may say, the individual situation of a subject is mainly determined by his position or, more specifically, each subject will go through this situation with a certain advantage or handicap arising from the position he occupies in his collectivity. Then, let us look at the line statements of the three positions mentioned.

First Yin: Here in the Constant Sink Hole one falls into the drain hole at the bottom, and this means misfortune.

Third Yin: Whether one comes and goes, there is a Sink Hole before him. In danger and stuck here too, it would not do to fall down the Sink Hole drain.[125]

Top Yin: Here it is as if for bonds two- and three-ply cords were used or as if one were put inside a bramble wall stockade. Such a one is not successful for three years, which means misfortune. (Lynn, 1994:319-20, 321)

The actual contents of the above line statements do not differ much from one another. All the subjects are described to have fallen into helpless situations. Neither the *I Ching* nor any later commentary tries at a rationally constructed explanation as to why they fall into such predicaments. Nevertheless, it is not difficult to construct one from what is already suggested by the line statements. If the situation is figured as one in which people are deluged by torrents of water flooding over their fields and houses, the subject at the first position represents the common folk who live in the lowest land and, accordingly, are affected most directly and seriously by the flood. Hence, the line statement describes its subject as "falling into the drain hole at the bottom." In assessing this metaphor, we should keep in mind the historical background of ancient China. Of course, compared to "falling into the drain hole," common people in ancient China had gotten into worse situations during floods. However, if the situation represents something more than a flood situation, the metaphor with which the subject at the first position is compared to someone who is unfortunate enough to reside near "the drain hole of the bottom" may become a quite problematic one.

The subject at the third position is located at the boundary of the two *Kan* trigrams, therefore he is interpreted as confronting dangers at both sides, below and above. Hence, the line statement says, "Whether one comes and goes, there is a Sink Hole before him"; he is left no room for movement. Accordingly, the *I Ching* offers the advice that "there should be no action (in such a case)." The line statement of the sixth line does not differ much from that of the third line. In both line statements, the subjects are described as having fallen into an utterly helpless situation where inactivity would be the best possible option available to them.

The subject at the second is also described to be in a dangerous situation, but a somewhat moderate level of danger is suggested. The line statement reads, "Here in the Sink Hole, where there is danger, one may only strive for small attainments" (Lynn, 1994:320). The subject at the second position is located "where there is danger," but the line statement also suggests that he, considering that he is at least in a position to "strive for small attainments," is in a better situation than the others discussed above. One aspect that may bother us with this judgment is that a yang line is present at the second position which is regarded as a yin place. The ordinary logic of the *I Ching* may consider this a case of an "inappropriately occupied position," in which its subject is expected to meet with ill fortune. The rendered judgment can be considered as deviating from such expectation. Why is the subject at the second position judged to be in a less distressful situation than the other three positions that were explained above? As I see, two things can be taken into consideration. One is that the line statement is related to the pictorial image of the hexagram in which the second yang line is viewed as a patch of safe space in the middle of the flooding water. The other is that the second position under normal circumstances is generally regarded of itself as a secure position.

A similar reasoning applies equally to the fifth position: the fifth yang line is in the middle of two yin lines and its position is regarded as the most stable one among all the six positions. Hence, its line statement reads, "The Sink Hole is not filled up, but here only when one is level with top will there be no blame" (Lynn, 1994:321). "The Sink Hole is not filled up" is interpreted by most commentators including Wang Bi to mean that the subject at the fifth position, under this situation, does not have sufficient capability "to fill up the Sink Hole," or to bring deliverance from danger to the group under his leadership. Why does he have such limited capabilities? To this question, commentators offer similar answers. Cheng Yi's following explanation is a model one:

> The fifth yang has strong and balanced capacities in the position of honor and should be able to get through danger, but it has no help from below. The second yang has fallen into danger and cannot yet get out, while the others are yin and weak, without the capacities to help out in danger. Even if a ruler is talented, how can one person alone save a whole country from danger? To be in the position of leadership yet be unable to bring the whole group out of danger is to be blameworthy. Only after leveling can one become blameless. (1988:92-3)

Here the subject at the fifth position is described as a leader with a limited capacity to help his country in danger. This incapacity in his leadership is attributed to the fact that there is "no help from below." This is understandable because, as we have seen, everybody below has fallen into danger and, accordingly, should be busy fighting for his own life. Especially, the latter portion of the line statement, "only when one is level with top will there be no blame," involves an interesting view: it warns the subject at the leadership position that if the country falls into such a dangerous situation, he "never manages to avoid blame" (Wang Bi, in Lynn, 1994:321) until the situation returns to normal.

The remaining one, the fourth yin line, occupies appropriately a yin position, and, accordingly, its subject is described as a faithful minister who serves the ruler at the fifth position "with an unostentatious sincerity" (Legge, 1967:120). A modest and cautious approach that the subject takes in rendering his advisory service to his superior is only suggested in metaphor, yet the line statement seems to involve little ambiguity in that no other interpretation seems plausible. The line statement states, "For a cup of wine and food bowls two, use plain earthenware. Provide this frugal fare through the window, and in the end there will be no blame" (Lynn, 1994:321). Words such as "a cup of wine," "food bowls two," "plain earthenware," and "Provide this frugal fare through the window" all indicate a plain and modest posture taken by the subject and a roundabout way of offering words of advice to his superior at the fifth position. Thus, as Wang Bi points out in his commentary, "there is no question of mutually incompatible positions" between the subjects at the fourth and the fifth positions (Lynn, 1994:321). Interpreted in this way, the pair constitutes a unit that operates in harmony. However, how is this interpretation related to what has already been rendered to the fifth yang line? It is possible that because the fifth yang line occupies appropriately a yang place and rides over a yin line occupying also appropriately a yin place, the subject at the fifth position represents a strong and effective leadership having enough potential to handle the crisis situation. Perhaps with this alternative interpretation in mind Legge points out that this "subject is not one who can avert the danger threatening himself and others" (1963:120). Thus, if we follow Legge's interpretation, the subject at the fourth position will be able to avoid to mistakes by behaving as described in the line statement, yet he is hardly in a position to avail himself of helping himself and others out of the troubled situation.

Before we finish with this hexagram, I would like to add a brief note. It is possible for a society or collective unit to face a crisis situation of such grand magnitude that even the upper strata find themselves in utterly helpless situations to tackle it, but can only watch and wait until it passes away. This seems to be the essential nature of the situation that this hexagram intends to convey. Judging from the related text accounts, all indications points to the strong possibility that the meaning of this hexagram originated from the historical experience of the Chinese people with floods. The flood was the most dangerous natural disaster that could happen to agrarian China that developed along the basin areas of the two great rivers, the Yangtze River and the Yellow River. Nevertheless, it is not clear at all whether the dangerous situation represented in metaphor of the flood intends to refer to human or social events of a more general kind. Scholars assume that the hexagram refers to a crisis situation of a more general kind, not just confined to the emergency situation associated specifically with the natural disaster in China.

The hexagram *Guan* (☴ ☷, Viewing)

First, let us look at the line structure of the hexagram *Guan* (Viewing). Four yin lines fill the bottom position up to the fourth and the two yang lines are present at the fifth and the top positions. Probably, the situational meaning of this hexagram is associated with the pictorial image brought to mind by the line formation of the hexagram; two yang lines at high places are looking down at four yin lines while the latter, when viewed from their own perspective, are looking up at those standing high over them. In addition, it will be helpful to imagine a political situation in which a powerful leadership emerges newly into the scene and those who are subject to the new authority are watching to see what will come out of the new leadership. The *Commentary on the Judgments* says, "the great subject of Viewing resides above" (Lynn, 19260). The subject who resides above refers to the yang line at the fifth position, the one designated as the ruler of the hexagram by Wang Bi (Lynn, 1994:263). Thus, the subject occupying the leadership position is recognized as the primary figure who does "Viewing." The *Commentary on the Images* elaborates on whom the primary figure watches and why: "The former kings made tours of inspection everywhere and established their teachings in conformity with their Viewing of the people" (Lynn, 1994:261). The commentary cited above suggests that the hexagram *Guan* (Viewing) represents a situation in which the newly instituted power holder is making inspections over the governed subjects under his rule. However, commentaries and the line statements also suggest that the "Viewing" is done mutually. In other words, while the leaders at the top echelon are making inspections of those below, they are at the same time also observed by the latter who are supposedly also curious about their newly instituted leaders. Thus, as we read through the line statements of this hexagram, we notice that the hexagram as a whole sketches out a scene taken out of a political event in traditional Asian society. The scene here highlights a sovereign on inspection tours parading in front of onlookers who are watching the parade at proper distances relative to their respective social standings. Of course, the meaning of the situation represented by the hexagram contains more than the scenery itself as being reflected by the line statements. *Guan* (Viewing) does not simply refer to a specific occasion like a political ritual where the mutual viewing between the ruling and the ruled subjects is exchanged in a purely physical sense of looking at each other eye to eye. More accurately, "Viewing" as meant by the hexagram *Guan* refers to an effort made by not only those at the leadership but also the governed subjects to size each other up to determine the most appropriate ways to cope with the newly emerging situation. Exactly in this context, the passage in the *Commentary on the Images*, "the former kings made tours of inspection everywhere and established their teachings in conformity with their Viewing of the people," renders a meaningful interpretation. That is, it was through "Viewing" the people that policies of the government were decided. The hexagram *Guan* represents a situation or a transitional period in which "Viewing" as such is in progress, probably after the establishment of a new leadership.

Regarding this hexagram, examining the four line statements from the bottom yin line up to the fourth one collectively adds more meaning and context.

First Yin: This is the Viewing of the youth. If it be a petty man, he would suffer no blame, but if it be a noble man, it would be base.

Second Yin: This is Viewing as through the crack of a door, so it is fitting that a woman practice constancy here.

Third Yin: Here one's Viewing is of his own activity: should it involve advance or retreat?

Fourth Yin: Here one's Viewing extends to the glory of the state, so it is fitting therefore that this one be guest to the king. (Lynn, 1994:261-263)

Regarding the subject at the first, bottom position, the line statements states, "This is the Viewing of the youth." The line statement compares the common people at the bottom position to the youth. The subject at this position is looking at things and affairs occurring before his eyes, but like a young child does not realize the meaning of the events. Then, a somewhat degrading remark is added, "if it be a petty man, he would suffer no blame." In effect, this says that although this subject sees things like a young child, he is not considered particularly worse off, for ignorance as implied here is properly expected of "petty people." Only "if it be a noble man (the *I Ching* adds a provision here), it would be base." Wang Bi explains this passage by saying, "but if a noble man were to find himself at a time of *Guan* [Viewing] and were limited as one is here by the 'Viewing of the youth,' would that not be despicable?" (Lynn, 1994:261).

Compared to the subject at the bottom position, the one at the second position is more closely positioned to the "great (ruling) subject" and, therefore, has a better "Viewing" position. However, the *I Ching* hints that the second position in the subordinate group does not provide its occupant a full view of what is occurring in the upper stratum. Thus, the line statement of the second yin line reads, "This is Viewing through the crack of a door," which means that the subject at the second position only receives limited knowledge of events occurring in the sphere of the top elite. So, the *I Ching* gives advice to the second position holder that the most fitting option in behavioral policies for him under this situation will be that he, like a woman,[126] keep on doing only what is considered proper in view of his weak position.

The *I Ching* seems to think that the third position, the leadership position of the subordinate group, offers a somewhat higher ground from which to watch things in progress. According to Wang Bi, "it (the subject at the third position) is at a place to do Viewing of which way the wind blows" (Lynn, 1994:262). Thus, knowing which way the wind is blowing and being in a position most immediately affected by the wind from the power center, the subject at the third position should find himself in a position to observe his own situation. "Should it involve advance or retreat?" indicates that depending upon what he observed about his own situation, he must decide whether he will "advance or retreat." "Advance or retreat" as used here can be replaced with (whether one has to) "resign or continue" (from or in his office).

Lastly, regarding the fourth position, let us imagine a scene showing a sovereign on inspection tours with entourages consisted mostly of ministers. The line statement of the fourth yin line portrays a snapshot picture of this scene focusing on the subject at the fourth position, interpreted to represent ministers or ones with equivalent status in the social hierarchy of the Chinese Empire. Thus, from the eyes of these people, the glory of the kingdom is witnessed while participating in such "state ceremonies" in "close proximity" to the "noble one (fifth yang)" (Lynn, 1994:20). And, as Wang Bi explains in his commentary, it is also in this context that the *I Ching* says of the fourth yin line, "it is fitting that this one be guest to the king."

The status of the fifth yang line under the situation is anticipated from the line statements that we have examined so far. He is both the constituting ruler and the governing one, the most powerful figure under the situation. One crucial difference from other situations in which the dominant power is held by the fifth position can be found in that the subject of this position is being watched by those at subordinate positions trying to measure up how or where he will lead the country. The line statement addressed to the fifth yang line thus involves a moral lesson for its subject: "Here one's Viewing is of his own activity: if it be a noble man, he shall be without blame" (Lynn, 1994:263). The line statement stated above contains what may be considered the sternest lesson given to the ruler of a country. It emphasizes that what the leader of an organization observes in his country is nothing other than the product of his own activity. Thus, let us read what Cheng Yi comments about this line statement:

> The fifth yang is the position of leadership. The order or disorder of the times, the good or bad morals of the people, are connected to the leadership. If the leaders observe the morals of the people, and see that the people are all worthy individuals capable of leadership, then their government is good and there is no blame. If, on the other hand, the morals of the people do not conform to the way of enlightened people, then the government as carried out by the leadership is not yet good, and cannot avoid blame. (1988:62)

Meanwhile, the line statement of the top position is interpreted and thus translated in a number of different ways. If we follow Lynn's version translated in line with Wang Bi's interpretation, the line statement means that "one (the subject at the top position) is Viewed by the people" (1994:264). Under the hexagram *Guan* (Viewing), the one in high status becomes the object of observation from the people below. Wilhelm who renders the following commentary offers a more interesting interpretation:

> Here one ruler of the hexagram looks from the vantage of the greatest height upon the nine (yang line) in the fifth place. He has not yet forgotten the world and is therefore still concerned with its affairs.(1967:489)

In the above passage, the subject at the top place is referred to as "one ruler of the hexagram" which means that he also possesses the potential to exercise influence over the situation. Then, we can think of many different possible relations, perhaps including one in which friction arises between the two rulers, the one represented by the fifth yang and the other by the sixth yang line. Thus, their relations seem to involve much more than merely observations on events occurring in another actor's field of activities.

The hexagram *Li* (☰☰, Cohesion)

The hexagram *Li* (Cohesion, or Clinging) may be viewed as one of the rarer cases among the hexagrams in that most commentators seem to have failed to identify the core theme of it. The name of the hexagram *Li* is derived from its line structure that is obtained by doubling the trigram *Li* that symbolizes Fire or Cohesion. *Li* (Cohesion or Clinging) denotes the observed property of fire that burns ("attaches to") wood to produce heat and light. The most difficult problem that commentators would have encountered in interpreting this hexagram is that its line statements do not easily fit into the overall theme implied by the name of the hexagram. There is, however, one interpretation that has taken a radically different perspective in capturing the main theme of the hexagram and thereby seems to succeed in closing up the logical disjunction between the overall theme of the hexagram and the respective line statements. Before I introduce this interpretation, I invite readers to look at the line structure of the hexagram and imagine it as a symbolic figure that represents an agrarian society at a certain stage. During the harvest season, new crops are harvested and kept in storage and people burn fire at night to guard against probable invaders; this hexagram thus symbolizes a vigilant society (the state of vigilance being symbolized by fire). Kim (1997) has adopted this perspective and thereby rendered translations for the line statements of this hexagram *Li* in accordance with this view.

Then, let us look at the first line statement: "There are awry footmarks. Be cautious and watch out for thieves, then there will be no blame" (1997:244, translated by this author from Korean). An interesting thing to note from this hexagram is that only subjects represented by yang lines are described as people who stand on guard against thieves or chase away outsiders who attempt raids. Included here is the subject at the first position. From this perspective, the line structure of the hexagram is seen as four yang lines standing on guard to protect the middle portions of the two *Li* trigrams, represented respectively by the two yin lines at the second and the fifth positions. In the light of this perspective, the line statement of the second yin line is interpreted and translated as, "The earth shines brightly with yellow light, and there will be fundamental good fortune."[127] According to Kim's explanation, this symbolizes "a scene that shows farmers harvesting crops grown abundantly in rich lands" (1997:244-5, translated by this author from Korean).

The line statement of the third yang line essentially expresses the same idea as the first yang line in that it calls for vigilance against possible attempts by outsiders to pillage the second yin line's location. It reads, "In the light of the setting sun, unless people beat the earthenware pot and sing, the old aged folk will lament over their misfortune" (Kim, 1997:244, translated by this author from Korean). According to Kim, people in the old days beat earthenware pots and sang at sunset to sound warnings against potential pillagers and wild animals approaching their village, and if an unfortunate event in fact took place, the elderly would suffer the most seriously.

The line statement of the fourth yang line repeats the same theme. It reads, "If one neglects getting himself prepared, with a sudden arrival of thieves he will see houses in blaze, people dying and properties thrown away" (Kim, 1997:244, translated by this author from Korean). The line statement of the fifth yin line also involves the same kind of message. The only distinguishable aspect is that the subject at the fifth position is described as someone having deep anxiety and concern about the present state. The line statement of the fifth yin line states, "Tears in floods, sighing and lamenting. Good fortune" (Wilhelm, 1967:538). Kim explains that the "good fortune" of the subject at the fifth position is the product of his shedding "tears in flood, sighing and lamenting." In other words, his deep anxiety and concern will bring out a fortunate result, for only the leader who is really anxious and concerned about defending his country will succeed in it.

The line statement of the top position contains advice addressed to someone who sets out for a military expedition to take punitive actions against bands of looters. What is said in the line statement seems clear enough as to require no further comment: "It is right for the king to launch a punitive expedition with this one. It is praiseworthy to remove the head, and to take prisoners those who are not of the same ugly sort will spare one from blame" (Lynn, 1994:327).[128] In this hexagram, as was already pointed out, only the yang lines are described standing guard against probable invaders. Since the subject at the fifth, leadership position is represented by a yin line and therefore interpreted as figuring a weak and dependent leader, the line statement states that "it is right (under the situation) for the (weak) king to launch a punitive expedition with (the help of) this one."

The hexagram *Jian* (☵☶, Adversity)

The hexagram *Jian* consists of the trigram *Kan* (Water) above and the trigram *Gen* (Mountain) below. Thus, it gives an image of water flowing through the steep and rocky terrain of a mountainous region, from which the idea of adversity is derived. In contrast to the meaning of the hexagram as a difficult situation, however, a notable feature of its line composition is found in that it shows a well ordered structure; all the lines at the four middle positions in the formal power structure show their appropriate situational characteristics as expected of their respective positions. As we can see, two yang lines are incumbent at yang positions, and two yin lines at yin positions. The composition of the lines itself therefore may lead us to the interpretation that the hexagram represents a well-integrated group. As a matter of fact, the conclusion that we draw from the line statements is not very different from the nature of this hexagram as we judge it on the basis of its line composition: adversity of any sort is not indicated by the pattern of internal relationships among the members of a group represented by the hexagram. It may be said rather that the pattern of internal relationships as indicated by the line composition of the hexagram exists as a given condition to deal with a certain sort of difficulty suggested by the hexagram name. Of course, neither the *I Ching* nor any later commentary contains specific accounts that explain to what kind of adversity the situation refers. A small yet seemingly useful clue is found in a passage in the *Judgment*; it says, "Adversity is such that it is fitting to travel southwest but not fitting to travel northeast." According to Wang Bi, "the southwest consists of level ground . . . . (and) the northeast consists of mountains." Interpreted in this way, the passage suggests a way to overcome the difficulty: it is easier for water to flow down toward flat land than to go toward the mountains (Lynn, 1994:373). Judging from the way that Wang Bi interprets subsequent passages and line statements, the metaphor of going toward either flat land or mountains should be interpreted as a choice that one can make in the face of the difficult situation suggested by this hexagram. Of the two available options, it is obvious that the *I Ching* considers movement toward flat land to be more natural and a morally justifiable way of conducting oneself under this specific situation. Then, what does "going toward flat land" specifically mean? Wang Bi interprets it as it is stated. That is, when people go through a difficult situation as denoted by the hexagram, it will be too risky for them to venture into "mountains" (i.e., adventurous enterprises), and, accordingly, it will be much wiser for them to turn back home and engage in safer business.

In comparison to Wang Bi's above interpretation, Legge introduces another interpretation. According to a view held by the Khang-shi editors on which Legge relies, the two regions in the southwest and the northeast refer to the territories that were under the influence of the Zhou family and the Shang, respectively. The central portion of the region was under the control of King Wen of the Zhou, known as one of the authors of the *I Ching*, and lay in the southwest side of the Shang territory, while the latter was located in the northeast side of the former (Cheng Yi, 1963:143; c.f. Kim, 1997:305). If interpreted in this way, the mentioned two regions, as Legge points out, involve "less symbolism," and the passage, "Adversity is such that it is fitting to travel southwest but not fitting to travel northeast," will be understood to carry a political message that under this situation people would be better off if they decide to remain with the Zhou kingdom. When the line statements are analyzed as a whole, this latter interpretation seems to fit well with the way in which the line statements are arranged in the overall framework of the hexagram.

A cursory examination of the line statements would show that the line statements at the four positions — the first, the third, the fourth, and the sixth positions — carry the same message in essence. Let us look at them all together:

First Yin: If one sets forth here, he shall have Adversity, but if he comes back, he shall have praise.

Third Yang: To set forth here would result in Adversity, so this one comes back.

Fourth Yin: To set forth here would result in Adversity, and to come back would mean involvement.

Top Yin: To set forth here will result in Adversity, but to come back means great success and so good fortune. It is fitting to see the great man. (Lynn, 1994:376-8)

In the above line statements, all the subjects at the respective positions are described as facing similar situations in which they have to choose between either setting forth toward the northeast or coming back to the southwest, this being interpreted as a choice between the two contending kingdoms. The line statements suggest that, given the situation, the people would be far better off returning to, or remaining in, the southwest region, thereby staying with the Zhou kingdom. In reference to the historical background, we can guess from the text that a difficult political situation developed in the kingdom of Zhou and the people reached a point at which they had to decide to which side they would go. Understood in this context, it seems obvious that the line statements contain a political message to appeal to the people to make a wise choice at this critical political juncture.

The subjects at the second and the fifth positions are described to be in a corresponding relationship. The one at the top leadership is the fifth yang line and its subject can be interpreted as representing the ruling figure of the Zhou kingdom. Then, first, let us look at what its line statement has to say about the subject at the fifth position: "To one in great Adversity friends will come" (Lynn, 1994:378). The message of the above line statement is already implied by the other line statements. That is, if the people represented by the four lines make the correct choice and thereby "come back to" this one, in the eyes of this subject at the fifth position, "friends" will come to help him. It is uncertain what underlying logic or perspective this line statement was based on. It could be that the line composition of the hexagram offers a prediction, "friends will come," for the subject at the fifth position concerning a future affair he is expected to have. Or, it may be more realistic to think that the line statement was written with hindsight on actual historical occurrences witnessed by the author of the *I Ching*. Whichever perspective we take, the subject at the fifth position is described as the central figure who plays the key role for fending off the difficult situation by gathering people at his side. On the other hand, the line statement of the second line shows that the leader is not alone in his mission: the second position is described as enthusiastic supporters who devote their utmost with no selfish motive despite the difficult condition suggested by the hexagram. The critical role that the subject at the second position plays under the situation is suggested by the line statement, "This minister of the king suffers Adversity upon Adversity, but it is not on his own account" (Lynn, 1994:376). It seems that to the author of the *I Ching*, there is no suspicion about this subject's loyalty toward the sovereign. The unconditional faith that is expressed in this particular subject can be contrasted to the other subjects whose alliance is still pending. Thus, in this situation represented by the hexagram *Jian* the strong alliance that exists between the subjects at the second and the fifth positions operates as the main axis of integration that induces other members to join.

The hexagram Lü (☲☶, **The Wanderer**)

The line statements of the hexagram *Lü* (The Wanderer), as its name suggests, involve topics about travelers. To be more specific, they present a series of possible situations in which travelers, especially people in political exile, may find themselves while making journeys away from their home country. Of course, practical lessons believed to be appropriate under respective situations are also offered with the typology of the situations, if only implicitly in some line statements.

The line statement of the first yin line describes its subject as a traveler who is likely to be "occupied by trivial matters . . . . (and) by doing so . . . . (may) bring disaster upon himself" (Lynn, 1994:495). According to Wang Bi, the subject at this position represents a traveler who does not obtain the means to secure himself and "(therefore) . . . . would be beset with menial tasks (to secure his livelihood)" (Lynn, 1994:495). Thus, as also explained by the *Commentary on the Images*, the disaster mentioned in the line statement refers to the probable consequence of its subject's "becoming exhausted" (1994:496) from his efforts to survive. It is not difficult to understand why the subject at the first position is described as one who has to engage in such hard or demeaning labor to eke out living. The first line is a yin line occupying the lowest position, and, therefore, he represents a traveler who is at the bottom level or in the most unfortunate situation.

The line statement of the second yin line describes its subject as a traveler who is in a far better situation than the one at the first position. This is indicated with no ambiguity in the line statement that reads, "The second line, divided, shows the stranger, occupying his lodging-house, carrying with him his means of livelihood, and provided with good and trusty servants" (Legge, 1963:188).[129] The contrast between the subject at this position and the one at the first position is obvious; the former is described as capable of staying at a lodging-house and carrying with him sufficient means to afford such comfort. But, why is this subject in a far more fortunate situation than the one at the bottom position? The most probable reason is the fact that a yin line appropriately occupies the second position, a yin position. However, if explained in this way, we may notice that the positions of the hexagram become divested of positional meanings related to social hierarchy. This is why I interpret the line statements of this hexagram as presenting a typology of various situations of travelers.

The line statement of the third yang line reads, "The third line, undivided, shows the stranger, burning his lodging-house, and having lost his servants. However firm and correct he (tries to) be, he will be in peril" (Legge, 1963:188).[130] According to Cheng Yi, the subject at the third position represents someone whose arrogance and self aggrandizement causes his lodging-house to be burnt and "the faithfulness of attendants" lost (1988:192). Cheng Yi's commentary offers two reasons why the third yang line represents a person who is "exceedingly adamant and self-important," whereas his status (probably as a political refuge) calls for "adaptability and humility." One is that the third position, a yang position, is occupied by a yang line, this giving the image of a person with a strong personality that is judged incompatible with what is required of his objective situation. The other is that the third yang line occupies the top place of the trigram *Gen* (signifying Mountain). This symbolizes "self-aggrandizement." The interpretation of the line statement offered by Cheng Yi seems to present a view that sounds quite plausible enough: "On a journey (especially in political exile), to be exceedingly adamant and self-important is to bring on trouble" (Cheng Yi, 1988:192). Understood in this context, the line statement seems be both informative and prescriptive. In the former, the line statement informs us of a type of traveler among various types of travelers — one who would not give up his pride and overbearing attitude although he in exile possesses practically no means to maintain his previous status. In the latter, the line statement involves a warning that if one behaves in the fashion described in the line statement, he will be deprived of the shelter and services provided by the host country.

The line statement of the fourth line describes yet another situation in which a traveler feels discomfort or insecurity. The translations of the line statement differ depending upon how commentators interpret the meaning associated with the word "axe *(fu)*" in the line statement. According to Wang Bi, upon whom Lynn's interpretation relies, "An axe is what one uses to chop away brambles and thorns, something to make one's stopping place secure." Based on this interpretation, Lynn's translation reads, "The Wanderer takes refuge where he can find it and so obtains a place where he has to use his axe, so this one's heart is not happy" (Lynn, 1994:497). Meanwhile, in Legge's translation and the commentary appended to it, the axe is a weapon to be used for defensive purposes. Thus, the line statement is interpreted to describe a situation in which the subject is provided with shelter and money but threatened with insecurity that may cause him to use the axe for self-defense (1963:188-9). With this latter interpretation, the line statement is translated: "The fourth line, undivided, shows the traveler in a resting-place, having (also) the means of livelihood and the axe, (but still saying), 'I am not at ease in my mind'." In general, the insecure or uncomfortable situation that the subject is described as experiencing seems to be a highly probable situation that anyone in exile in a foreign country might encounter.

The subject at the fifth position is pictured as being in the most fortunate of all situations of travelers described so far. The line statement reads, "The fifth line, divided, shows its subject shooting a pheasant. He will lose his arrow, but in the end he will obtain praise and a (high) charge" (Legge, 1963:188).[131] According to Legge (1963:190), the pheasant symbolizes a gift that the subject at the fifth position offers to introduce himself to the feudal court of his host country. In symbolism, to shoot a peasant with an arrow indicates both his ability and loyalty to gain acceptance in the host country. The last passage of the line statement explains the result of his actions saying "in the end he will obtain praise (from people in the country that he seeks asylum) and a (high) charge." There is an additional comment made by Legge regarding the meaning of the positions of this hexagram that may interest us. He seems to hit upon a crucial issue when he points out that "It will be seen how the idea of the fifth line being the ruler's seat is dropt here as being alien from the idea of the hexagram, so arbitrary is the interpretation of the symbolism" (1963:190). However, as we also have seen in some other hexagrams, this hexagram would not be an exceptional case in this respect. As a matter of fact, the line statements of some hexagrams including this one do not make much sense if we try to understand their meanings in reference to the hierarchical order of ordinary hexagrams. We will find this to be the case whenever the line statements of a hexagram make sense only as they are interpreted as a typology of a certain specific category of situations or personal characteristics.

The line statement of the sixth yang line conveys an idea somewhat similar to that at the third position, an arrogant traveler whose house is burnt. Let us read it first; "The bird gets his nest burnt. The Wanderer first laughs and then later howls and wails. He loses his ox in a time of ease, which means misfortune" (Lynn, 1994:498). According to Wang Bi's interpretation, the subject at the sixth position makes his residence "at a lofty and dangerous place" and, therefore, his residence as such "is called a 'nest'" (Lynn, 1994:498). With this symbolism, the subject is described as someone who place himself in a highly visible position so that he may become "the object of envy" by people in his host country. Legge gives a similar interpretation in translating "ox" in the line statement as "ox-like docility," thus describing the subject as someone who behaves in a way opposite of "what a traveler should be" (1963:190). Understood in this way, the passage, "The Wanderer first laughs and then howls and wails," yields an easy interpretation. First, the subject will feel elated about his high standing in his host country, but later as he becomes the object of envy, he will be deprived of all the privileges he has earned in his host country. Although this is practical advice, dubious metaphoric reasoning enters into the explanation of why the subject at the sixth position is viewed as one who is likely to display such an undesirable trait. "The Wanderer occupies the uppermost position that he is envied alike by all" (Wang Bi, in Lynn, 1994:498). The sixth yang line is located at the highest place of the hexagram and this spatial location of the subject gives rise to an image of a person who rises high to a lofty and highly visible place in social standing, attracts envy and thus loses support from his host country.

Summary of theoretical and empirical propositions

1) If a country falls into a difficult situation of grave magnitude and no one bears responsibility, the leader cannot avoid blame until the situation returns to normal.

2) The closer one's position gets to the top leadership, the more knowledge he is likely to have about the incumbent leadership. For example, the middle leadership position (the third position) allows its subject to gather enough information to decide whether he should stay in or resign from his position.

3) Observation of a country by its leader reflects nothing more than the product of his own activity. In other words, he has to bear full responsibility for everything that he sees from the country under his rule.

4) Only a leader who is deeply anxious and concerned about the successful management of his country will actually succeed in it.

5) A person who is exceedingly adamant and self-important while in political exile in a foreign land will be deprived of the privileged status he desires from his host country.

6) The best strategy to gain acceptance from a host country is to serve the host country with the best of what one has whether done with ability or with a show of loyalty.

Chapter 5

Conclusion: Theoretical Implications of the *I Ching* in Modern Social Sciences

1) The *I Ching* as a Field Theory

I would like to begin this conclusion with a question that is quite appropriate and important to me in this final stage: as a theory (if regarded as a theory), what is the most distinctive feature of the *I Ching*? Let me answer first, and then explain the essential features of the *I Ching* in the context of the answer which, I will argue, provides quite adequate characterizations of the *I Ching*.

Overall, the *I Ching* can be characterized as a field theory. The term "field theory" referred to here is borrowed from the concept proposed by Kurt Lewin in psychology. But, it is important to note that the *I Ching* does not share any theoretical propositions with Lewin's field theory on the subject matter in which each of them is interested. As Lewin points out, his theory involves for the most part what should be more properly called a "method" rather than a "theory" proper (1997a:201). Whereas a theory refers to a system of knowledge constituted by a set of propositions that state lawful relations between things or properties of things, a methodology denotes a set of general orientations towards reality, on the basis of which specific modes of analysis or approach are applied to the study of subject matters for a research area. Then, by calling Lewin's "field theory" a theory, in effect we use the term "theory" to mean what can more properly be called "methodology." When comparing the essential feature of the *I Ching* to the field theory of Lewin, I am referring to the methodological substrate of Lewin's so called theory, not to a "theory" in its true and proper sense. In other words, if the *I Ching* and Lewin's field theory are viewed to share certain similarities in some essential aspects, it is mostly in their methodologies with which the realities to be analyzed, the objects of knowledge, are subject to specific approaches for meaningful understanding. Before I continue, therefore, let me offer a brief explanation of Lewin's field theory or, more properly speaking, his "method."

One of the essential features that characterizes Lewin's field theory is found in its employment of what Lewin calls "the principle of contemporaneity." It states: "Any behavior or any other change in a psychological field depends only upon the psychological field *at that time*" (1997a:201). On a more formal level, Lewin recapitulates; "The field-theoretical principle of contemporaneity in psychology . . . . means that the behavior *b* at the time *t* is a function of the situation S at the time *t* only (S is meant to include both the person and his psychological environment)" (1997a:203). The "field" is a concept or construct that refers to the totality of factors that, arranged in a specific way at the time *t*, constitutes the situation S at the time *t*. Thus, for example, if a person is extremely hungry and sees a loaf of bread on a table in his own house, yet he at the same time has a strong desire to maintain fitness in his body weight by refraining from taking extra food, we may say that whether or not he will eat the bread (behavior *b*) will be a function of the situation (S) that is constituted of the three factors — the bread that is present before his eyes, how hungry he is, and the strength of his will to maintain bodily fitness. As we can see, it is an important consideration in the principle of contemporaneity that a field where a behavior takes place be constituted only of factors that exist contemporaneously at the time when the behavior is about to take place. But, why is behavior viewed to be explainable by taking into account only contemporaneously existing factors that are observed when the behavior takes place? Of this, Lewin remarks:

> It has been accepted by most psychologists that the teleological derivation of behavior from the future is not permissible. Field theory insists that the derivation of behavior from the past is not less metaphysical, because past events do not exist now and therefore cannot have effect now. The effect of the past on behavior can be only an indirect one: the past psychological field is one of the "origins" of the present field and this in turn affects behavior. (1997b:214-5)

For the reason stated above, a psychological field constituted of all the effective factors affecting behavior or changes in behavior must be constituted only of the factors existing at the time when the behavior is about to take place. To recapitulate, then, "behavior or any other change of behavior in a psychological field depends only upon the psychological field *at that time*."

The other important feature of the field theory is found in its emphasis upon the holistic approach: the analysis in the field theory "starts from the characterization of the situation as a whole" and proceeds to a more specific and detailed analysis on various aspects and parts of that situation (Lewin, 1997b:214). Underlying this holistic approach is the perspective that the meaning of a part depends upon the position, or function, that it occupies, or plays, in the whole to which it belongs. This perspective also involves a further implication: for this perspective to have validity or any measure of utility, the whole, once certain elements combined are constituted into that whole, should acquire unique patterns or properties of its own on which the meanings of its parts, in turn, depend. On the meaning of the entire situation of a field as a whole, or the "properties of the field as a whole," Lewin holds:

> Of course, such a method presupposes that there exists something like properties of the field as a whole, and that even macroscopic situations, covering hours or years, can be seen under certain circumstances as a unit. Some of these general properties — for instance, the amount of "space of free movement" or the "atmosphere of friendliness" — are characterized by terms which might sound very unscientific to the ear of a person accustomed to think in terms of physics. However, if that person will consider for a moment the fundamental importance which the field of gravity, or the amount of pressure has for physical events, he will find it less surprising to discover a similar importance in the problems of atmosphere in psychology. In fact, it is possible to determine and to measure psychological atmospheres quite accurately. (1997:214)[1]

Now, one of the basic propositions of the field theory which is expressed as

$$b^t = f(S^t) \quad \text{(Lewin, 1997:204)} \quad [1]$$

can be understood more specifically as meaning that the behavior *b* at the time *t* is a function of the properties of the situation that are determined by the constitution of the entire field that gives rise to the situation. Of course, this should not be interpreted as a one-sided affair where any event that takes place in the situation S at the time of t is *determined* by that situation S. To more accurately understand the nature of the functional relationship between the two, b^t and S^t, we have to know that the person who produces the behavior also is a part of that situation. In other words, as Lewin points out, "S is meant to include both the person and his psychological environment" (1997a:203). Since it would be a truism to say that without the parts each having a determinate property there will exist no whole, we have to say that there will be no S unless there exist the psychological conditions of the person and his psychological environment, which affect the ways the person produces the behavior. This would suggest that the functional relationship between the whole and its components, unlike the one-directional causal relationship in which changes in a factor end with changes in another factor, is of mutual interdependence or recursive relationship. The holistic approach including Lewin's field theory is characterized rather by its emphasis on the mutual interdependence between the whole and its parts.

There is another important characteristic of the field theory that has specific relevance to our task. Lewin (1997b:212-3) points out that one of the essential features of his field theory is found in the use of the "constructive method." To explain what the constructive method is, I should first explain what Lewin calls the "classificatory method," the opposite of the former, because we, the social scientists of today, are far more accustomed to and familiar with the use of the latter. According to Lewin, we will use the classificatory method when we are interested in "generalization" by "abstracting individual differences." For example, "Such a generalization leads from individual children to children of a certain age or certain economic level and from there children of all ages and economic levels" (1997b:212). To take another example in sociology, the general phenomenon of "social stratification" can be abstracted from numerous concrete individual cases that show innumerably varying patterns or degrees of differences among individuals in wealth, power, life styles, or whatever dimensions of social value. This method, however, has one crucial drawback: "there is no logical way back from the (general) concept 'child' or 'abnormal person' to the individual case" (Lewin, 1997b:212). To illustrate with the concept of "social stratification," the concept, once constructed by generalization, cannot explain anything more specific about the unique features of a specific case in a stratified situation other than the general features of social stratification the concept itself represents in abstraction. Consequently, all the individual differences among individual cases or specific aspects in which the individual differences arise are eliminated from the theory or concept and only the general characteristics or aspects that are abstracted into a theory or concept are represented. Lewin's constructive method is distinguished from this in that it aims at "the representation of an individual case with the help of a few "elements" of construction" (1997b:212). This may sound very much like an "individualizing" method which, as used in writing biographies, is geared toward pure descriptions of an individual situation. However, judging from his explanation, it seems obvious that his constructive method is not oriented toward the "ideographic (case-specific)" description of an individual case subject to analysis for understanding its entire individuality in terms of not only the ordinary features shared with others but also its specific and unique characteristics. Lewin offers an explanation on the aim of his constructive method:

> The essence of the constructive method is the representation of an individual case with the help of a few "elements" of construction. In psychology, one can use psychological "positions," psychological "forces," and similar concepts as elements. The general laws of psychology are statements of the empirical relations between these constructive elements or certain properties of them. It is possible to construct an infinite number of constellations in line with those laws; each of those constellations corresponds to an individual case at a given time. In this way, the gap between generalities and specificities, between laws and individual differences, can be bridged. (1977b:212-3)

In the passage quoted above, Lewin in effect points out that although psychological fields vary from situation to situation, we can determine "a few (basic) elements" through which we can develop a good understanding of the critical properties of individual behavioral situations despite an infinite variety of differences among them. The individual differences among situations, then, will be understood as related to the ways or patterns in which those elements are arranged to give rise to individually specific situations. Now, of course, a field is viewed to consist of a "few elements," yet the properties of it would be more than just the "few elements." It is because, as emphasized already, the whole is more than just the arithmetic sum of its individual parts; the whole, once constituted, will acquire a unique meaning of its own on which the meanings of its individual parts in turn depend. The constructive method, as Lewin intends it, therefore, starts from formulating ideas about the "few elements" that compose the individual situations, seeks to determine "empirical relations between theses elements or certain properties of them," and then proceeds to an analysis of the individual case to get an explanation of the events that take place in the specific situational context of that case.

Some of the essential features of the field theory as characterized by Lewin have been summarized above. Now, I will go back to and examine the claim that I put forward at the outset of this chapter, that as a theory the *I Ching* can be characterized as a field theory. Since the field theory has been characterized by 1) the principle of contemporaneity, 2) the holistic approach, and 3) the constructive method, the *I Ching*, if the claim has validity, also should involve the same essential features of the field theory as described by Lewin. Then, first, let us examine how the system of knowledge presented by the *I Ching* features the principle of contemporaneity.

A hexagram, the symbolic representation of a social situation, consists of six lines. Since the lines symbolize individuals with certain behavioral dispositions, it is interpreted that in the *I Ching* a social situation is defined as a function of activities of individuals who are involved in the situation represented by a hexagram. Here, we may say in principle that among the individuals represented by the lines of a hexagram, there is *no time differential*. They all belong to the situation that exists at the time t. The idea that a hexagram consists of elements that coexist at the time t can be expressed graphically as <Figure 3> (p. 369).

<Figure 3>, as its title suggests, illustrates a hexagram as a representation of a social field, or situation, constituted of elements (individuals) that exist contemporarily at a certain point in the temporal dimension, on the space cut along the spatial dimension at the time t.

Now, as applied to the *I Ching*, the principle of contemporaneity can be expressed as follows:

$$L_{ijk} = f(H_k) \qquad [2]$$

where L_{ijk} refers to a specific situation of an individual actor (or group of actors) at the ith position (one of the six positions in a hexagram), with the jth type of action orientation (expressed as either a yin or yang line), under the kth type of a situation represented by the kth hexagram (H_k) (among the 64 hexagrams).

Conclusion 369

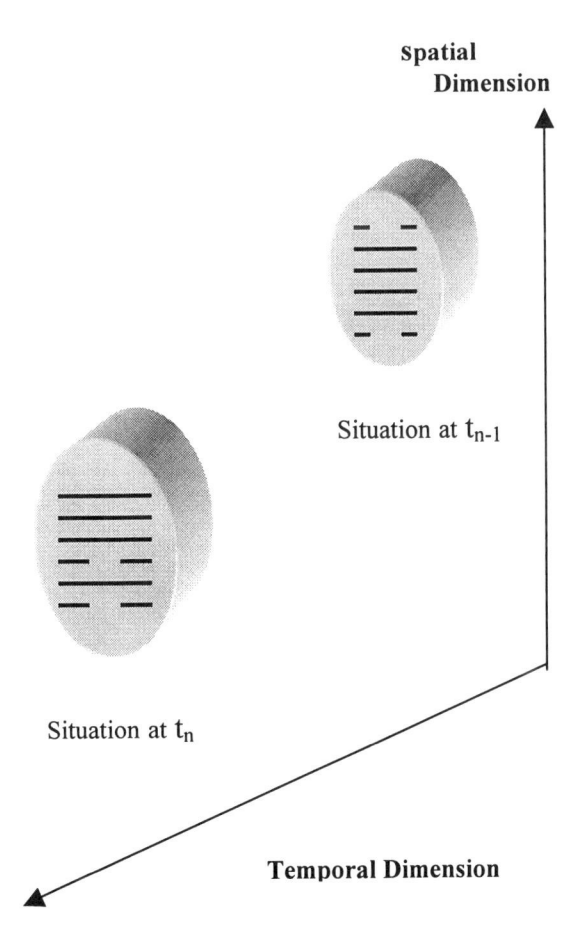

Spatial Dimension

Situation at t_{n-1}

Situation at t_n

Temporal Dimension

<Figure 3> A Graphic Representation of the Contemporaneity of a Hexagram

Verbally expressed, the above formulation says that a specific situation of an individual actor (or group of actors) at a specific position is a function of the situation (as represented by a hexagram) in which the actor is situated. And, since a hexagram represents a situation that exists at the time t, the above stated proposition can be rephrased as: "the specific situation of an individual position holder at the time t is a function of the situation S at the time t only (as represented by Hk^i)."

This is a restatement of what Lewin defines as the principle of contemporaneity. As a matter of fact, as we have observed throughout this treatise, in the *I Ching* the specific situation of an individual position holder is interpreted only in relation to those factors that exist concomitantly with the line that represents the subject. These factors could be the properties of an overall situation represented by a hexagram as a whole or the properties of the other component lines comprising the same hexagram. As far as this characterization of human situations by the *I Ching* is concerned, there seems to be no ambiguity about the core idea the *I Ching* is based upon. Jung, the German psychologist who noticed the significance of the *I Ching* especially with respect to this principle of contemporaneity ("synchronicity" as he calls it), observed:

> This assumption involves a certain curious principle that I have termed synchronicity, a concept that formulates a point of view diametrically opposed to that of causality. Since the latter is a merely statistical truth and not absolute, it is a sort of working hypothesis of how events evolve one out of another, whereas synchronicity takes the coincidence of events in space and time as meaning something more than mere chance, namely, a peculiar interdependence of objective events among themselves as well as with the subjective (psychic) states of the observer or observers. (1967:*xxiv*)[2]

From the discussions so far, readers may have noticed already that the principle of contemporaneity is closely connected with the second important feature of the field theory, the holistic approach. As a matter of fact, the formulation L*ijk* = f (H*k*) can be regarded as stating not only the principle of contemporaneity but also the holistic approach. With respect to the holistic approach, the formulation states that a specific situation of an individual actor (or group of actors) is a function of the total situation (as represented by a hexagram) in which the actor is situated. But, as I pointed out already, the relationship between the whole and its parts should be of mutual interdependence. Thus, we will have to add another formulation to the one given above to fully express the interdependence between the parts and the whole, roughly expressed as follows:

$$H k = f (L1jk, L2jk, L3jk, L4jk, L5jk, L6jk) \quad [3]$$

Combined with the previous formulation L*ijk* = f (H*k*), the above formulation expresses a very complex relationship of interdependence that exists between the overall social situation represented by a hexagram as a whole and the specific situations of individuals represented respectively by its component lines. A change of a line will change the structural make-up of a hexagram, and, as the formulation [3] indicates, the hexagram will change into another, meaning that one type of situation has changed into another. This is because the overall situation represented by a hexagram depends on the state of each of its component lines. To put it in terms of social reality, the overall situation of a given social unit is determined by the specific ways in which each of its members behaves in relation to one another. Yet, an individual's behavior toward others is not a matter of independent chance variation. As is indicated by the formulation Lijk = f (Hk), the specific situation of an individual actor (or group of actors) is a function of the total situation (as represented by a hexagram) in which the actor is situated. Thus, to get a meaningful understanding of what is stated by the hexagram statement or its line statements, the interdependent relationship between them must be taken into consideration. The logical relationship between the hexagram statement and the line statements may be described as circular, suggested by formulas [2] and [3]. Their meanings refer back to each other, and, therefore, an interpretation must be made by moving back and forth between the hexagram as a whole and the individual lines. Hence, the interdependent relationship that exists between the overall situation, the specific situations represented by the hexagram as a whole, and its component lines renders evidence to the fact that the holistic approach is one of the basic orientations of the *I Ching* in understanding social reality.

Another important feature of the field theory, the use of the constructive method, also seems quite evident from the *I Ching*. The constructive method carries specific significance in the *I Ching* in that its use is indicative of its interest in building up a body of knowledge that is specific enough for, and thus "useful" to, individuals acting under real social situations. Lewin points out that the constructive method differs from generalization in that it aims at "the representation of the individual case." Yet, the representation of the individual case must begin with the abstraction of some basic elements of which individual cases are constituted. Things will be experienced only as an endless, passing flow of appearances in infinite variety until we are able to reduce their specific features into some basic elements. In Lewin's psychological field, concepts such as "positions," "forces," and "positive or negative valences" refer to some of such basic elements, or properties of them, which are abstracted from all the specific variations among individual situations (Lewin, 1997b). The unique situation of a psychological field then would be represented by mapping the ways or the "dynamic" patterns in which "positions," "forces," or "valences" of certain psychologically determined factors are distributed or operative in that specific field. With respect to the use of the constructive method, the *I Ching* does not seem to differ much from the field theoretical orientation described above. There are two basic assumptions underlying the *I Ching*. One is that social situations undergo change, and, therefore, there will be widely varying types of social situations, each characterized by a unique feature with specific kinds of objective conditions imposing different life chances upon involved individuals. The other assumption is that despite the differences among situations there are "constant" elements, the basic ingredients of the situations, which will not change while all the changes take place. In the *I Ching*, the basic ingredients of the situations are reduced to two elements, the social positions of individuals and their action orientations. Every individual case among all the specific situations is constructed from, thus analyzable in terms, of these two basic elements. Therefore, regarding the use of the constructive method, we will not miss an obvious similarity that exists between Lewin's field theory and the *I Ching*.

The preceding discussion render sufficient evidence in support of my initial assertion that the *I Ching* shares enough essential features with Lewin's field theory to be considered a field theory unto itself. At the same time, however, there is an important difference between them. Evidently, Lewin's field theory concerns the psychologically determined field; as he himself points out, his task as a psychologist "is to find scientific constructs which permit adequate representation of psychological constellations in such a way that the behavior of the individual can be derived" (1997b:213). The field, as he defines it, therefore, would be a theoretically formulated construct that aims at the representation of "constellations" of psychological factors. In contrast to this "psychological approach" employed by Lewin' field theory, the hexagrams in the *I Ching* aim to represent varying situations in what may be called "the social field" whose component elements are undoubtedly of sociological nature. Thus, in the following, we will examine in more detail the essential features of the social field as put forward by the *I Ching* in its constitution of the social world, whose essential features are seized systematically through the hexagrams.

2) The *I Ching* as a Field theory on the Constitution of the Social World

Unlike Lewin's psychological field that is represented by theoretically formulated concepts or "constructs," the social field as represented by the hexagrams (or more specifically the hexagram lines) consists of acting individuals. In this sense, the hexagrams intend to portray the social world as it exists in reality. Of course, there is virtually no way to mirror or reproduce all the existing realities of the social world as they are. The task of describing all the characteristics of individuals in every minute detail would be not only impossible and but also unnecessary. Then, the question boils down to the selection of the characteristics that are regarded as the most fundamental in determining the essential conditions of the social world that significantly affect the welfare, fortunes and misfortunes, of individuals. Regarding this question, the *I Ching* marks two factors as most important: the social position that an individual occupies in his social stratification system and the type of actual action orientation or real power potential that is exercised by and characteristic of each individual or a group of individuals under a specific situation. Thus, the hexagram, the symbolic device representing the social world, accordingly, contains the two pieces of basic information about the individuals (or groups of individuals) who constitute a social field. This aspect of the hexagrams has been observed throughout the preceding discussions.

The general view stated above may sound familiar and reasonable to us in that, even in modern days, we would not disagree about the idea that one's rank in the hierarchical order of the society and how he acts in relation to others are critically important factors in determining his life chances, whether fortunate or unfortunate. The most distinctive feature of the *I Ching*, however, as its title (the Book of Changes) indicates, is found in its thesis on change. The main premise of the *I Ching* on social change is that although there is a fixed structural order in society, changes occur in the ways in which it actually operates, in the patterns of the relations among individuals or groups, and, accordingly, in the fortune or misfortune of each of them. Of course, there is no doubt that one of the primary factors that determines the patterns of the interpersonal or inter-group relations is the positions that individuals or groups occupy in the formal hierarchical structure of a society. The structure of this formal order was explained in details and illustrated in <Figure 1> (p.27). The most characteristic feature of this formal order is found in that it forms a rigid stratification system that differentiates people into unequally ranked positions entailing different rights and duties. The *I Ching*, therefore, counts this as a crucial factor in determining the patterns of interpersonal or inter-group relations expected to take place under any given situation. Yet, the positional structure of the hexagram does not change throughout the 64 hexagrams, and, therefore, the formal social order represented by it is viewed to maintain the fixed feature. This symbolizes the constant social order, or the infrastructure of society, which is not subject to situational changes. And, accordingly, the positional structure itself should not be the factor that accounts for the situational variation in the patterns of the relations among individuals.

As we know well by now, in the *I Ching*, the primary factors that account for the situational variation in the ways the formal social order actually operates are represented by yin and yang lines. To restate, yin and yang lines are viewed as representing properties of acting individuals which are responsible for the situational variation in social conditions, and these have been, so far, *roughly* characterized as "types of actual action orientations" or "real power potentials." Why is it characterized only as "roughly" rather than more precisely? Since the properties of individuals that a yin or yang line symbolizes constitute one of the two principal elements constituting the social field represented by the hexagram, the essential features of the social field as figured by the *I Ching* would not be clarified sufficiently until the meanings that the yin-yang duality has in the specific context of the hexagram become clear. Hence, we will take a more thorough look at the meanings that this critical element has in the social world as captured by the *I Ching*.

I will start with the question that I have already raised; why it is so difficult to *precisely* define what the yin or the yang line signifies *in general*? A simple, yet definite answer will be found in the fact that a line is a component of a specific hexagram and, therefore, its meaning would be *hexagram-specific*. The meaning of a part depends upon the overall meaning of the whole to which the part belongs, thus the meaning of a yang or a yin line will only be understood clearly in reference to the specific hexagram to which it belongs. This explains why the meanings of yin and yang lines vary from one hexagram to the next and also why they have such a wide range of meanings that cannot be compressed into a few narrowly defined concepts. Yet, we should remind ourselves that the holistic approach emphasizes interdependence between the whole and its parts, not the one-sided dependence of the parts on the whole. This leads us to the conclusion that while the meanings of the yin and the yang lines cannot be analyzed in isolation from the overall context of their specific hexagram, the meanings of a hexagram also cannot stand apart from the meanings of its constituent elements, yin and yang lines. Thus, if we look carefully at the ways in which the lines have been interpreted throughout the hexagrams, it is not difficult to delineate the basic ideas that the author(s) of the *I Ching* had in mind when he used the yin and the yang lines to represent certain critical properties of individuals (or group of individuals).

We can start from the obvious. The dual concepts of yin and yang refer to the ways in which individuals are disposed to act in relation to others. Viewed in this way, a given combination of yin or yang lines, as represented by a hexagram or a trigram, is descriptive of certain characteristic patterns of relations that have developed among individuals at a certain phase of changing social processes. Here, remember that the positions of the hexagrams arranged hierarchically are referred to as either *yang or yin positions*. This implies that the patterns of relations among position holders in a social unit are to a certain extent determined or regulated by rights or duties attached to each of the positions. Thus, the positions themselves, as I have emphasized several times, operate as critical factors affecting the patterns of relations among position holders. But, each position is occupied by an individual or group of individuals, whose characteristic is expressed with either a yin or yang line; this certainly brings in a variable of another dimension which is distinguished from that of formal social structural kind. What, then, are the factors that the lines represent? But, before I answer this question, I would like to draw up a list of several possibilities.

One possible factor is the moral orientations of individuals. It could be reasonable to think that there are differences among individuals in moral orientations and they do affect a person's action orientations toward others, yet an association cannot be assumed between the social position of a person and his personal moral orientation. Thus, I include the moral orientations of individuals, in addition to their social positions, as an additional factor affecting the patterns of the relations among individuals.

The second category of factors that I would like to include in the list is personal dispositions that are classified with sets of such contrasting concepts as "active" or "passive," "progressive" or "conservative," "leading" or "following," "domineering" or "submissive," "creative" or "receptive," "independent" or "dependent," "extroverted" or "introverted," "rigid and strong" or "docile and pliable," and so on. These terms are descriptive of different modes of action orientations with which people relate to one another. How these dispositions affect the patterns of the relations among individuals is merely a matter of tautology: the above personal dispositions refer to the different modes of action orientations with which individuals are disposed to relate to each other, and, therefore, they are in effect defined already as factors affecting the patterns of the relations among people. The issue then comes down to a different question: how critical are such action orientations in bringing about some crucial differences in the conditions of group living for individuals? Here let me point out that the *I Ching* considers them to be very critical.

The third important factor that I would like to point out is what may be considered as "situationally determined power potentials" of position holders. A once-powerful leader may see his power being depleted and his subordinates becoming harder to control. The common folks, once loyal subjects appearing docile in the eyes of people in power, may grow increasingly bold and demanding and turn into active campaigners to bring about changes in the government. A position holder who is in a position to exercise control over others may in fact find himself being controlled by others. Situational circumstances may force the one at the formal leadership position to yield to the demands of people in subordinate positions. There are many situational circumstances that can bring about differences in real power potentials among position holders as seen in the above instances. Thus, differences in situationally determined real power potentials could affect the patterns of the relations among people.

Now, of the three categories of the factors that I have listed above, which one matches most closely with how yin and yang lines are actually interpreted with respect to the situations represented by individual hexagrams? Those who have been faithfully following the preceding discussions on all the hexagrams may come forward with a ready answer: the meanings of yin and yang lines are interpreted differently from hexagram to hexagram or even from line to line, and, therefore, we may have to say, they range over all three of them. In some hexagrams, yin and yang lines are interpreted as denoting certain kinds of moral orientations of individuals. And for other hexagrams, the yin-yang dualism is interpreted as indicating a wide variety of contrasting or complementary action orientations as "active" or "passive," "progressive" or "conservative," "leading" or "following," "domineering" or "submissive," "creative" or "receptive," "independent" or "dependent," "extroverted" or "introverted," "rigid and strong" or "docile and pliable," and so on. And, of course, on some other occasions, yin and yang lines are interpreted as denoting differences in real power potentials. Then, how can we make coherent sense of the yin-yang dualism if it is accompanied by such a confusing array of various meanings as these? Regarding this question, Wang Bi's following opinion that I quoted before seems to point to a way out of this problem:

> Images (i.e., trigrams and hexagrams)[3] are the means to express ideas. Words [i.e., the texts] are the means to explain the images. To yield ideas completely, there is nothing better than the images, and to yield up the meaning of the images, there is nothing better than words. The words are generated by the images, thus one can ponder the words and so observe what the ideas are. The ideas are yielded up completely by the images, and the images are made explicit by the words. Thus, since the words are the means to explain the images, once one gets the images, he forgets the words, and, since, the images are to allow us to concentrate on the ideas, once one gets the ideas, he forgets the images.(Lynn, 1994:31)

Following Wang Bi's advice offered in the passage above, let us forget about yin or yang lines themselves, and pick up *ideas* that they symbolize or are interpreted to symbolize. Then, we are left with the plausible thesis that the patterns of the relations among individuals are affected by such various factors as their moral orientations, various modes of action orientations towards one another, and situationally determined real power potentials.

Of course, there are other issues that still may bother us. One is that on many occasions commentators differ in their interpretations concerning the specific ideas that are supposedly meant by specific lines and attached statements in particular hexagrams. Thus, for instance, regarding the yin line at the fourth position of the hexagram *Mengyi* (36th hexagram), Cheng Yi interprets it as "dishonest petty people in high positions following the leadership obediently, being weak and devious" (1988:115), whereas Wang Bi reads the same line more straightforwardly as indicating that the subject represented by the line "takes compliance as his course of action" (1994:360). Unlike the former, the latter entails no moralistic implication. Such disagreements among commentators concerning the interpretations of the individual lines of the hexagrams, after all, can be attributed to the fact that the line statements, often narrated in ambiguous symbolism, are not amenable to easy and clear understanding.[4]

Thus far, we have identified two broadly defined categories of factors that affect the patterns of the relations among people, positions that they occupy in the formal hierarchical order of society and their actual action orientations or situationally determined real power potentials. Let us call these the "essential elements" which compose the social world of the *I Ching*.

Now, let us turn to the overall characteristics of the social field that each hexagram depicts as a whole. Obviously, any given situation that is formed by individuals or groups of individuals would be a function of how the essential elements characterizing each of those individuals are composed as a whole. This is as is expressed through the formulation [III] $Hk = f(L1jk, L2jk, L3jk, L4jk, L5jk, L6jk)$: the characteristic situation, or the overall pattern of the relations among individuals involved in a given situation, represented by the kth hexagram will be the function of moral orientations, behavioral dispositions or power potentials that are characteristic of the individuals or groups of individuals located at their respective positions. But, since the properties of each individual (or group of individuals) represented by a given line is determined in the context of the entire situation, as the formulation [II] $Lijk = f(Hk)$ expresses, to define the properties of each position holder requires some prior understanding about the meaning of the situation as a whole. In the *I Ching*, as we have come to know quite well by now, a rough idea about the meaning of a situation as a whole is outlined by the hexagram name and the hexagram statement. And, since, as was pointed out already, the hexagram statements together with the names of the hexagrams were written prior to the individual line statements, the former should have provided a conceptual foothold on the basis of which the specific situations of individual position holders were interpreted and the line statements were written accordingly.[5] This renders evidence to the fact that, as far as the *I Ching* is concerned, the meanings of the social situations conceived overall took precedence over the understanding of the specific situations of individual position holders. Notwithstanding the evidence that hexagram statements had been in existence before the line statements were composed, however, it would be more accurate to say that the meanings of the hexagrams had remained largely ambiguous until the former was supplemented by the latter. This is understandable because no explanation of the whole will be complete without explaining its parts. In this sense, the hexagram statement together with the hexagram name gives at best only a very rough idea about the condition or conditions of the situation which any given hexagram represents. As comparable to the case of the relationship between a sentence and words composing it, a general idea about the overall condition of a social field and the properties of acting individuals in unequally ranked social positions and with specific action orientations had to be considered together to render a meaningfully specific and clear idea about the characteristic condition of a given social field. At any rate, given both the hexagram and the line statements, the hexagrams came to feature respectively a certain type of critical condition or conditions characterizing the entire social field composed of individuals interacting with one another in situationally determined, specific forms of mutual relationships. Now, having completed the review of every individual hexagram, we can draw an obvious conclusion that the characteristic features of the social world that we have observed through examining the varying situations represented by the 64 hexagrams reveal a unique mode of thought, or paradigmatic perspective, with which the *I Ching* take cognizance of the essential realities of the human collectives. Then, what would be most characteristic of the mode of thought as it is reflected in the meanings that the *I Ching* has about the social situations? Or, to put it in other words, what would be most characteristic of the mode of thought as we can judge it from the hexagrams with which the *I Ching* intends to mirror in essence the critical conditions of the social world?

One of the most distinctive aspects of the *I Ching* is suggested by its title, the Book of Changes: situations of society change, and these changes bring about different opportunities for acting individuals whose power and life chances depend on the objective conditions of the society in which they live. Under a certain situation, an individual or group of individuals in a certain stratum may find their situation becoming difficult, feel powerless or threatened by being surrounded by hostile environments, having no one to whom he can stretch out his hands for help. Under another situation, harmonious and peaceful relations among people prevail, and, therefore, few people under such a harmonious situation of unity will find themselves alienated or acted against. And, in still another situation, political power is concentrated solely in the hands of the leader at the top, and the rest of the people may have no choice but to march straight along the tight paths set by the ruling figure. This kind of strong unity may eventually break up and turn into a situation in which, as history often shows, people are divided into contending camps, fight each other, and sometimes even become drawn into armed conflicts. Under some situations, a society may undergo radical changes as a certain situational condition motivates people to engage in activities that bring about radical changes. Or, a society may rather move backward, retrogressing rather than progressing. According to the *I Ching*, all these *changing* facets of the social world are the *unchanging* truth about social reality. And, in this sense, one of the essential features of the social world as depicted by the *I Ching* is found in that the critical conditions affecting the life chances of individuals change from situation to situation, or, to put it differently, from one social field to another. To recapitulate, society undergoes changes and the changing situations affect the life chances of individuals differently depending upon the existing conditions at each phase of the ever-changing situation. Each of the 64 hexagrams then is descriptive of the typical conditions affecting the fates of people involved in a given situation or a social field.

Of course, a change of an overall situation into another means that changes have occurred in the total sum of the relations including all possible dyadic and triadic relations formed within a social unit represented by a hexagram. Then, how does this change from one situation to another come about? According to the *I Ching*, "As the firm (yang) and the yielding (yin) lines displace one another, change and transformation arise" (Wilhelm, 1967:287-9). As far as the hexagrams and the trigrams are concerned, it is obvious that the displacement of a yin or yang line (or lines) into its opposite will change a given hexagram into another. And, this also will bring alterations in the patterns of relationships between all the possible triadic and dyadic pairs within the hexagram. But, a given composition of the lines in a hexagram simply shows the result of some prior change that had taken place before the situation indicated by the hexagram came to existence. Thus, all we can say about the change of a given situation is only two things as follows. One is that the change of the situation will be brought about by changes in the properties of individuals or groups who constitute a given social field. The other is that some prior change had occurred to bring about the present situation and some future change will alter the present situation into a different one. The question concerning the specific causal mechanism of the change still is left unanswered. The *I Ching* explains, "As the firm (yang) and the yielding (yin) lines displace one another, change and transformation arise." Yet, how or why does the displacement of the lines take place so that "change and transformation arise"? We find some accounts in the *I Ching* that may be considered as offering an answer to this question, but they do not seem very enlightening. For instance, such passages as "The firm (yang) and yielding (yin) are images of day and night" (Wilhelm, 1967:289), or "That which lets now the dark, now the light appear is *tao*" (Wilhelm, 1967:297) supposedly explain, if in metaphor, why or how the alteration in the properties of yin and yang lines occur. But, "images of day and night" and like do not seem to be appropriate analogies when used to signify changes in phenomena related to patterns of human relations. It simply puts forward an idea, vague at best, that revolving cycles of changes moving back and forth between the two states operate as the underlying mechanism to bring about changes in social situations. What brings about, or to put it more strongly, *causes* the cyclical changes, however, is not clearly explained anywhere in the text.

The use of the dubious analogy with which the *I Ching* explains, only in metaphor at best, what supposedly brings about the cyclical changes in social situations may be thought to be one of the serious problems that the *I Ching* has as a knowledge system. Yet, when assessing the problem of the *I Ching* addressed above, we must return to the logic of the *I Ching* and grant it to speak for itself with its own frame of reference. Perhaps, as far as the *I Ching* is concerned, what causes a yang state to turn into a yin state, and vice versa, may not be a critically important issue after all. What is important is not whether an individual has a defined characteristic represented by either a yang or a yin line itself, but rather what kinds of relationships he, having the characteristic as such, forms with others in the overall context of his situation. As the principle of comtemporaneity states, a specific situation of an individual actor (or group of actors) at a specific position would be a function of the situation (as represented by a hexagram) in which the actor is situated. To understand one's behavior and its probable consequences requires the knowledge of his relative position in the network of relations in which he is involved. This is like a word having a broad range of possible meanings so that only in the context of a specific sentence it can assume a specifically definable meaning. The same may be said of human dispositions or potentials that should have been formed through causal processes that had taken place in the past. For instance, a person with a conforming personality is seen as a *coward* if he is made to conform by a bully, whereas he will make a *good team player* if he conforms to the norms of a well integrated group. Whether he becomes a coward or a good team player is determined by the nature of social relations in which he is situated. Hence, w*here he is* determines *what he is*, not vice versa. This seems to explain why the *I Ching* showed little interest in acquiring *causal* knowledge on the specific mechanism by which changes in society takes place. Its main concern rather focuses upon mapping out all the probable types of social situations, each of which has certain characteristic features either allowing specific opportunities or imposing limitations in the life chances of individuals. It is why, in interpreting the meaning of a yang or yin line, all possible patterns of relations formed in an entire social field are taken into consideration. And, it seems to be why understanding the essential features of the social field that is constituted of individuals or groups of individuals existing contemporaneously at a critical moment of social phases is given priority over the understanding of causal mechanisms supposedly operating behind the changes of it.

3) Theoretical Implications and Relevance of the *I Ching* for Some Issues in Modern Social Sciences

At the end of each section dealing with the individual hexagrams, I presented a summary of theoretical and empirical propositions that were implicit in the interpreted meanings of each hexagram and individual line. Those accounts reflect the specific aim of this book: to extract the propositions relevant to the concerns of modern sociology. In the preceding sections of the conclusion, I analyzed the characteristic features of the *I Ching* as a theory on society. Now in this section, I will examine theoretical, or to put it more properly, methodological implications that the *I Ching* has in relation to two very important issues in sociology or, more generally, in social sciences. There would be little disagreement among sociologists that the dichotomy between integration and conflict models of society and that between social structure and human agency have been critically important issues concerning the basic assumptions on the essential nature of man and society. These have been issues that arouse heated controversies in sociology. Thus, how these issues are approached by the *I Ching* in its view on the nature of the social world will draw some interest from sociologists. And, analyses focusing on these issues will highlight the implications and relevance that the *I Ching* has for modern social sciences.

One of the main concerns of sociology and of social sciences in general is to develop systematic understandings about the basic realities of society, from the perspective of which individuals grasp the critical conditions of the world that shape their lives. Some sociologists hold that society can be viewed as a system devoted to carrying out various tasks, or solving various functional problems, related to the collective goals and needs that arise by people who, being social animals, are bound to live together. Since *integration* is included as one of the required conditions for any human collectivity to maintain itself as an effectively functioning unit, society as a system is believed to have developed certain institutional devices or mechanisms to maintain an adequate level of integration for proper functioning. Generally, if society manages to survive, it is regarded as evidence of the fact that it is succeeding in integrating itself, or at least preventing itself from falling apart. This perspective is often called the integration model of society. As we can see, the image of society cast through this model imparts an idealized image of society; it depicts society as a well-integrated entity in which internal mechanisms are operating to maintain "unity and consensus" among its members. It is assumed that these internal mechanisms as a rule are working successfully and, therefore, serious frictions and disunities are kept under control most of the time. Conflicts, therefore, are not a matter of important concern when the essential features of the society are cast into the theoretical mold of the integration model, and this is why Dahrendorf (1958; 1969), who believes that conflicts are rather "ubiquitous," calls this model of society a "utopia."

On the other hand, there is an opposing view to the integration model. Some sociologists maintain that conflicts are an ever-present reality of society because unequal distributions of valuable resources among members of a society occur universally in every existing society and, accordingly, there are always conflicting interests among people who have more and those who have lass. These conditions have led those in advantageous positions to develop institutional means to ensure the security of the existing system and thereby to protect their interests by suppressing or regulating possible challenges to their system of inequalities. And, it is due to such institutional means of control that possible conflicts, rooted in the incompatible interests of people in different positions, do not always break out. Yet, conflicts do occur whenever conditions develop into such a way that colliding interests no longer remain "latent" (Dahrendorf, 1969:220).

The polemic between the integration and the conflict models summarized briefly above is one of the hottest issues that has been preoccupying sociologists. The core issue is whether or not social inequalities, as we see them, have justifiable grounds for the common welfare of the members of society as a whole. Understandably, the issue has raised a great deal of interest and tempers among scholars, and, consequently, has produced staunch contestants arguing for each side. Yet, there seems to be one curious aspect in this polemic: if we ask individual scholars where they stand on this issue, most reply that they prefer a synthesis between the two positions rather than taking a stand on any of the two extremes. This inclination toward the in-between position is obviously related to the belief that, as van den Berghe (1967:202) points out, functionalism (the integration model) and the Hegelian-Marxian dialectic (the conflict model) each stress one of the two essential aspects of social reality." Even, Dahrendorf, the ardent advocate of the conflict perspective, admits:

I do not intend to fall victim to the mistake of many structural-functional theories and advance for the conflict model a claim to comprehensive and exclusive applicability . . . . It may well be that in a philosophical sense, society has two faces of equal quality: one of stability, harmony, and consensus and one of change, conflict, and constraint. (1958:127)

There are also many sociologists (Coser, 1967; Lenski, 1966; Ossowski, 1963) who echo the same conviction: society has two faces and, therefore, neither perspective is wholly entitled to lay claim to exclusive validity. But, although there is widespread agreement among sociologists on the need for a synthesis between the two contending camps, why has an actual synthesis not emerged? What are the difficulties involved in working out a synthesis between the seemingly incompatible views? I will examine this question briefly, first, and then turn to a theoretical implication that the *I Ching* has in relation to these questions.

To begin with, what is the source of difficulty in synthesizing the two contradictory perspectives? Some may say that it will be only a matter of time for someone to come up with a beautiful solution; the crux of the matter is only that, at this moment, there is no person to achieve this feat. Now, given that we eventually will find such a person, what kind of knowledge do we expect him offer? Considering the long aspiration that modern Western sociology in general has been pursuing, it seems obvious that what we would be presented with is a theory on the structured order of the society underlying all complex realities which may look confusing, disorderly, or even contradictory to our naïve everyday experiences. But, again, what specific kind of *order* will it address? This question leads us to a cherished methodological tradition of Western sociology in which order is conceived as that of logical non-contradiction. Our perception of order is inseparably connected with the logically ordered structure of knowledge through which the world can be explained as ordered phenomena. Our sense of order in the world is based on our belief that it can be described and explained with systematically ordered knowledge involving no logical contradiction. Accordingly, as Husserl (1969:65) points out, only logically non-contradictory knowledge is regarded as revealing the "true" order of things. This does not necessarily mean that the notion of order as such will discourage us from dealing with such contradictory forces as Marx's classes. The contradictory relation between opposing forces in Marxist theory, of course, represents a social order. The point is that social reality is viewed as being constituted of "harmoniously combinable experiences" of conflict: it is an order in which no social phenomenon betrays the sense of being in "conflict" and of being exclusively and coherently related to the theme of conflict. This is also a non-contradictory order in the sense that the conflict perspective and the social world it depicts are thematically coherent and uniform against possible "functional" implications or dubiousness. In other words, when the "true" order of society is revealed for conflict theorists, it is also an order built against any possible counter-sense: social phenomena, conceived as "conflicting," are constituted coherently and exclusively of "conflicting" realities. Of course, no theory is perfect, and, therefore, we will find that the logical structures of conflict theories in actuality are not ideally organized in a perfect order as described above.

The line of the reasoning presented above suggests why, despite the widespread recognition that actual realities are "mixed" or "in-between types," it is so hard to develop a synthesis that accommodates logically incompatible theories into one coherent body of knowledge. The logic, by nature, tends to exclude "middles" or "mixed" phenomena, and, for the same reason, it tends to exclude theories that involve logically incompatible ideas and concepts. In this respect, theory building may be viewed as a conscious effort to impose a logically coherent order upon realities which in fact have far more complexities and diversities than any theory can handle within the purview of its logic. And, it is perhaps for this reason that although most scholars tend to agree on the need for a more inclusive theory that can handle both "integration" and "conflict," they find it so hard to develop a viable synthesis.

The overarching point is that the principle of non-contradiction and excluded middle in logical reasoning is the core of the problem with theories that have been criticized for their one-sided emphasis on certain partial aspects of social reality. This also explains why it has been so difficult to derive a synthetic theory from theories involving logically incompatible perspectives. Then, how can this kind of logic be compared to that of the *I Ching*?

Of the *Ten Commentaries*, there are two commentaries that are devoted to explaining the nature and basic functions of the *I Ching*, the *Commentary on the Appended Phrases* (*Xici zhuan*) and the *Great Commentary* (*Dazhuan*). These commentaries contain some fragmentary clues from which we can partially reconstruct the mode of thinking applied by the *I Ching* in its effort to acquire a meaningful understanding of social reality. This thinking should have originated from what is easily observable from past historical records of Chinese society. The society has numerously variable facets. During a certain period of time people work together in harmony and peace prevails; yet, as time goes by, the unity of the society weakens, conflicts among people spread out, and disorder prevails. Under a certain situation, society undergoes rapid and radical changes; yet, as the situation changes, everything revolves around routine processes and rules, and the stagnating stability gnaws away little by little at the vitality of society. Should all these changing historical phases of society be viewed as operating on a set of principles, these principles, if expressed into a set of logically interrelated propositions, constitute what we call a theory. Viewed from a little different angle, theory builders in modern social sciences, say, "dig into" or "go behind" all those varying phenomenal realities to find out an *essential* order underlying them. The resulting set of logically interrelated statements that describes this underlying order will constitute a theory.

In contrast to this approach, the *I Ching* "flies over" all those varying phenomenal realities and takes a bird's-eye view over them. Then the *I Ching* can be viewed as a book that has recorded characteristic features of the social world that have been observed from a survey over changing phenomena occurring in it. The *I Ching* by observing the varying types of situations in human collectivities has yielded knowledge that may be classified into four categories as follows:

1) a typology of the 64 possible social situations each with a title name to characterize the specific condition(s) of the situation as a whole;

2) the uniform feature in the forms of human association, found generally throughout the 64 situations despite their situational variations;

3) varying aspects in which situations differ from one another;

4) how the specific condition(s) of each situation affects the life chances of acting individuals under that situation.

For some readers, the methodological orientation that has produced the outcomes above may not be unfamiliar: it reminds us in its essential aspect of Simmel's *formal* sociology (1950). But, the point I am trying to emphasize here is not the fact that the *I Ching* and Simmel, a modern scholar, happened to have taken similar approaches in their intellectual pursuits for a meaningful understanding of social reality. In spite of some obvious similarities that the *I Ching* shares with Simmel in its methodological orientation, the ideas that the former has about the changing situations of society seems to be couched upon a very unique perspective on the essential nature of the social world. This has no counterpart in the intellectual traditions of the West. In the West, the search for the *essential reality* lying behind or under the phenomenal appearances of things or events has long been a cherished intellectual tradition, and this tends to make theoreticians see most appearing realities as mere "epiphenomena" of certain underlying realities which are regarded as more fundamental and essential. Moreover, observed realities will be pushed aside as something of little significance, irrelevance, exception, or even unreal if they cannot be accounted for by an accepted theory. It may be said that they are out of the range of what a paradigm can handle, thus are regarded as "*mere* facts, unrelated and unrelatable" (Khun, 1970:35) to the *true* nature of the reality under investigation. Undoubtedly, the tendency for such selective cognition of reality is related, if only partially, with the logical coherence required in the formulation of a theory. Theoreticians tend to shun facts as trivial, irrelevant, or exceptional if an explanation of those facts cannot be deduced logically from the theory they favor.

The logic of the *I Ching* seems to operate in a way that is distinguished clearly from that described above. As I see it, the underlying logic of the *I Ching*, in essence, is much closer to that of commonsense reasoning in the sense that average people take cognizance of the nature of realities they experience mainly in terms of *types* or *patterns* rather than in theory. When a person is anticipating an important meeting, he will imagine himself to be placed in one of various situations: either interesting or dull, either relaxed or tense, either friendly or hostile, either profitable or unprofitable, and so on. Every individual should have a repertory of imaginable situations considered significant in relation to his own specific interests and concerns. Yet, if a typology of possible situations is to be meaningful, each type of situation he can think of should have an important bearing on his life in some critical aspects. Of course, it is not an easy task to develop such a meaningful typology. The *I Ching* seems to have been born in response to pragmatic concerns of individuals who should have felt a need for such a useful typological scheme with which they could locate what type of life situation they were in at critical moments of their life. In the case of the *I Ching*, as we have seen so far, its main concern for the type-building task focuses upon situations in the social world, the most important environment on which the life chances of individuals depend.

Then, what are the implications of the *I Ching's* typological scheme on issues related to the difficulty of achieving a synthesis between the integration and conflict models? First of all, the fact that the *I Ching* presents various types of integrated, conflict, and mixed situations means that each of the situations is viewed as having specific features which are distinguished by unique and significant ways they affect the welfare of individuals involved in it. In this sense, each situation, whether it be an integrated situation or conflicting one, is as real as any other situation for the individuals involved. This means that not only various types of integrated situations but also situations cluttered with conflicts have important bearings on the lives of individuals in some significant way that is characteristic of each situation.

Then, can the inclusion of various types of integrative and conflict situations in the typological scheme of the *I Ching* be considered an adequate solution to the difficulty associated with one-sided accentuation of either integration or conflict? Perhaps not, for there still remains the issue of which aspect explains more or pertains more to the *essential* nature of society. Concerning the essential nature of the social world, or the world in general, however, the *I Ching* reiterates the heart of its worldview: *change* is the unchanging truth about the world and change is the *essence* of the world. Thus, for the *I Ching*, there are no essential or more fundamental realities from which all observed variations can be explained with the use of deductive logic. As far as the *I Ching* is concerned, every situation has a special kind of factuality, affects individuals in specific ways that differ from other situations, and has a unique organizational order. If any situation is as significant as any other situation to the welfare of individuals and there is no other essential reality than those experienced by the individuals in their everyday lives, any effort to reduce the essential nature of society to any one aspect will put us into a difficult position. This in fact has been what we witness from each of the two contending camps, integration and conflict theorists. Each accuses the other of neglecting other essential realities of society. An essential feature of the *I Ching* as a system of knowledge therefore lies in its unique approach towards the problem that may arise from an one-sided accentuation of an aspect of society. It seriously considers each of the varying situations as constituting an essential aspect of social realities, and this implies that the essential nature of the social world lies in its subjection to varying types of situations that undergo changes over time. Now, we will understand clearly why the *I Ching* was given the title the Book of Changes. Thus, for instance, from the *I Ching*, we will find no answer for such questions as "which aspect, integration or conflict, captures more pointedly the essential nature of the society?" Perhaps the *I Ching* would answer that the various situations characterized as integrated, disintegrated, or conflict-ridden are all represented in the *I Ching* and any situation represented by any particular hexagram, whether it be integrated or in conflict, cannot be singled out as representing the essential nature of social reality. Each of the varying situations constitutes only, if as real and essential as any other situation, a partial feature of social reality. As far as the *I Ching* is concerned, therefore, the essential nature of society should be found rather in its conditional variability that changes from one situation to another.

It seems quite appropriate here to quote a comment made by a sociologist, which, I think, shows a welcome sign of taking cognizance of the dynamic nature of the social reality as being subject to such varying conditions as depicted by the *I Ching*. Proposing his own conception of social change alternative to that of the "conventional approach," Sztompka remarks:

> The image of the object undergoing change is modified accordingly. Society (group, organization etc.) is no longer viewed as a rigid, 'hard' system, but rather as a 'soft' field of relationships. Social reality is inter-individual (inter-personal) reality, which exists between or among human individuals, a network of ties, bonds, dependencies, exchanges, loyalties. In other words, it is a specific social tissue or social fabric binding people together. Such an inter-individual field is constantly in motion; it expands and contracts (e.g., when individuals join or leave), strengthen or weakens (when the quality of their relationships change, e.g., from acquaintance to friendship), coalesces and disintegrates (e.g., when leadership appears and dissolves), intermeshes or separates itself from other segments of the field (e.g., when coalitions or federations appear or secessions occur). (1993:10)

On the basis the perspective stated as above, Sztompka offers a typology of different patterns of social change as progressing, retrogressing or stagnating. This typology looks too simplistic when compared to the enormously complex typological scheme of the *I Ching*. Nevertheless, the general idea espoused by him is in tune with the perspective with which the old classic grasps the essential reality of the social world; both view that the social field undergoes changes and in the process is subject to varying types of situations.

Here, it seems instructive to go back to the question; why is the word *I* of the *I Ching* interpreted to mean "the change," yet, at the same time, "the easy"? This is because the main function of the *I Ching* is to assist individuals with an easy method to make diagnoses on the conditions they face at critical moments of their life so that they can lead more conscious, thus rationally managed lives in the welter of changing situations.

Compared to the complex typology on the varying situations of society, however, it may be thought that the structural order of the social world is represented in a scheme that appears too simplistic to social scientists of today. But, as I see it, ideas implicated in its graphic scheme of six yin or yang lines are no less complex than any ideas found in modern social theories. One important idea concerns the well-known issue related to the dichotomy between social structure and human agency. Social structure refers generally to forms of interpersonal or intergroup relationships that have been institutionalized through norms and values shared among members of a society. This has been treated as one of the primary variables of sociology by many sociologists who believe that social structure defined as such explains people's conformity to socially shared expectations or tendency to act in certain characteristic ways generally observed within the boundary of a society, culture, or group to which they belong. Meanwhile, human agency refers to operations that are carried out by individuals, or "the events that an actor perpetrates" (Turner, 1986:468). Obviously, social relations would be nothing more than "the events" that unfold through actions carried out by human actors. "Human actors" as referred to here carries a specific image which other animals or inanimate things lack. They can make reflections on themselves and the world around them, explore alternative courses of action, make a choice out of them and, therefore, on some occasions decide to take action that they have never ventured before. In view of the active potential with which human agents produce, reproduce, or bring in changes to, their lives, the "constraining" or "determining" power that social structure allegedly has on individuals is viewed as a misconceived idea. Rather, there exists no concrete external reality to label as social structure apart from ways in which individuals themselves act creating the very conditions of the society that exerts constraints upon them. Thus, the deterministic notion that the social lives of individuals are governed and explained by the objective conditions of social structure in which they are situated is antithetical to the image of man acting as the active agent who produces and reproduces his own world.

Of course, just as in the case of the issue over integration vs. conflict regarding the essential nature of society, this issue over determinism vs. voluntarism regarding the essential nature of man in society poses a dilemma: to choose either of the two positions forces one to take a stand against the other position that may involve an equally reasonable view that cannot be rejected outright. Or, in other words, we may say that either of the two positions does not seem entirely false in view of actual experiences that we ourselves have about our lives. But, why do most of us take a stand anyway despite a sure feeling that by sticking to either one of the two positions they will betray facts of life they know by experience? I think that there is a clear reason in this: they are more afraid of betraying the logic by upholding at the same time the two positions that are logically inconsistent with each other.

Giddens' so-called structuration theory (1984) is known to represent an effort to get us out of this dilemma. The key formula in his solution lies in conceptualizing the nature of social structure in a way that can embrace what he regards as its dualistic aspects. As he defines it, social structure refers to "rules and resources" that individuals draw "in the diversity of action contexts," and it has dualistic properties in the sense that "it is not to be equated with constraint but is always both constraining and enabling" (1984:25). It may be compared to linguistic rules and resources: linguistic rules and resources enable users of a given language to participate in the very process of producing and reproducing the language, yet, at the same time, they operate as constraints on individuals' usage of that language. They enable people to say what they want to say, yet, on the other hand, they put constraint on what and how people communicate. Conceived in this way, social structure, if put to use effectively, may furnish individuals with "the capacity to achieve desired and intended outcomes" (1984:15). Yet, as people often experience under many circumstances, it may not enable them to accomplish anything desirable or creative, but may exist only as debilitating facts of life which may be felt as oppressive, overpowering, or like being trapped in a revolving door with no way out. Conceived in this way, the dual aspects of social structure may be considered as opening a way to solve the logical dilemma of blinding ourselves to only one side of social reality by choosing the alternative, in this case determinism or voluntarism. With the dualistic conception of social structure, Giddens' aim seems clear: he now can have both, determinism and voluntarism, in a single basket, in his "structuration theory." But, can we also conclude that he at last has succeeded in patching up the long held division between social structure and human agency?

Giddens has at least succeeded in patching up two *concepts* that have long been considered at odds with each other: properly viewed, he suggests, they are only two sides of one coin. However, redesign for the creation of a usable theory in the empirical sciences must be done on another, perhaps more important, level. Theoretical concepts should be hooked to reality, if only with some parts of it here and there. Now, since social structure as defined by Giddens is said to have duality, it should have double links connected respectively with different moments or phases of reality. The inclusion of contrasting dual notions into a single concept can impose heavier burdens than blessings on us. By introducing a concept as having dualistic aspects, we now must address the thorny issue of "which (aspect) is likely to prevail under what conditions and circumstances" (Archer, 1990:77). Commenting on problems in the conceptual maneuverings done by Giddens to dissolve the long held division between social structure and human agency, Archer focuses on a shortcoming that Giddens' dualistic conception of social structure has in relation to the issue mentioned above:

> Although the 'duality of structure' spans both images, it provides no analytical grip on which is likely to prevail under what conditions or circumstances. The theory of structration remains fundamentally non-propositional. In other words, the central notion of the structuration approach fails to specify when there will be more voluntarism or more determinism . . . . Rather than transcending the voluntarism /determinism dichotomy, the two sides of the 'duality of structure' embody them respectively. They are simply clamped together in a conceptual vice. This oscillation between contradictory images derives from Giddens not answering 'when' questions: when can actors be transformative (which involves specification of degrees of freedom), and when are they trapped into replication (which involves specification of the stringency or constraints)? These answers in turn require analysis of the potential for change, which is rooted in systemic stability/instability, and the conditions under which actors do/do not capitalize on it. (1990:76-78)

Giddens appears to have come close to recognizing the variable conditions of society either restricting or laying open the capacities of individuals to exercise autonomy in actions when he says that "The nature of constraint is historically variable, as are the enabling qualities generated by the contextualities of human action" (1984:179). Yet it is important to note that his comment on "the nature of constraint" as above is immediately followed by an argument against interpreting it as "structural constraint," i.e., interpreting it "law-governed conditions that put limits on the bounds of free action." Undoubtedly, Giddens' abhorrence towards "structural constraint" is connected with his basic position that in human affairs no external social reality other than human agents themselves can be offered the ontologically privileged status of producing or reproducing man's actions. Notwithstanding the soundness of his ontological position as such, however, Giddens' theory as a whole offers us little help in grasping the variable conditions of social reality, as Archer is critical about the theory's utility particularly in this respect. Regarding the limitation of Giddens' theory in dealing with the variable conditions of society Thompson also raises an objection that in essence is similar to that by Archer:

> The differential distribution of options and needs implies that certain individuals or groups of individuals have greater scope for action and choice rather than other individuals or groups of individuals: freedom, one could say, is enjoyed by different people in differing degrees. To explore the space between the differential distribution of options, on the one hand, and the wants and needs of different kinds and of different categories of individuals, on the other, is to examine the degrees of freedom and constraint which are entailed by social structure. Such an analysis would show that, while structure and agency are not antinomies, nevertheless they are not as complementary and mutually supporting as Giddens would like us to believe. (1997:327)

By now some readers may be beginning to wonder what the *I Ching* has to do with the critique of Giddens' solution to the problem of dichotomy between social structure and human agency. In my opinion, however, the issue of social structure and human agency, or determinism and voluntarism, indeed has a great deal of relevance to a core feature of the *I Ching*. Of course, the perspective of the *I Ching* may be said to be *deterministic* in the sense that the situations presented by the *I Ching* depict the objective conditions in which the fortunes and misfortunes of individuals are determinable. Yet, the determinism of the *I Ching*, if characterized as such after all, will have to be understood in a paradoxical way that it at the same time involves a view on the voluntaristic nature of human action. How much freedom one can exercise in relation to others or how constraining the external forces will be on him will be *determined* by the conditions that vary from situation to situation. It is with this particular mode of determinism that the *I Ching* addresses itself to the question, "when can actors be transformative (which involves specification of degrees of freedom), and when are they trapped into replication (which involves specification of the stringency or constraints)?" (Archer, 1990:78). The answer is that it depends on situations. Accordingly, individuals, depending upon the conditions of their situations, will have different opportunities for free or creative actions or will be subject to different degrees or types of constraining forces operating upon them. As a matter of fact, a situation represented by a hexagram in the *I Ching* depicts a set of specific conditions which determine how well or badly individuals or groups of individuals will fare largely in terms of whether one can exercise autonomy or power over others, or in terms of the extent to which his life chance will be constrained or conditioned by others who act more freely on their own initiative. Thus, for instance, the hexagram *Qian* and the hexagram *Kun* feature diametrically contrasting situations. The former represents a situation in which all the individuals or groups of individuals are charged with creative spirits so that the main feature of the situation is marked by activism to bring about changes. The latter represents a situation in which the lives of the people in it revolve around a fixed order in which static harmony prevails. Of course, the *I Ching* includes many other mixed types of situations with reference to the varying conditions that answer the question of "when there will be more voluntarism or more determinism (for individuals)."

It should be obvious to readers of this book that, as far as the *I Ching* is concerned, the question of how free or constrained individuals are cannot be answered without considering specific conditions of their social field or their patterns of social relations under given situations. In other words, regarding the latitude of freedom that individuals can exercise in relation to others or potentials that individuals have for bringing changes into existing reality, there is no uniform principle that applies generally throughout all human situations. Opportunities for realizing the wills and desires of individuals will vary depending upon the situation. The typology of the *I Ching* would have been developed with a keen recognition of this fact: people sometimes are the makers of their own lives, yet there are also times in which their lives fall prey to the wills of others or social forces of an impersonal kind. Thus, we may say figuratively, the social situation "opens" or "closes" life chances of individuals. When it opens, the creative potential of individuals is allowed to hold sway over whatever is there for them. And, when it closes, individuals will remain in a state of "dependent determination:" they will be guided, controlled, and regulated by external forces. In the *I Ching*, then, the issue of determinism and voluntarism, or social structure and human agency, may not be considered an issue at all. It may merely reflect the prevailing bias of our thought, not the fact of life itself, with which we believe that human phenomena operate on a set of principles that obey the rules of conventional logic.

4) Issues and Problems

Here it would be unnecessary to recapitulate in detail all the problems in deriving sociologically relevant interpretations from the *I Ching*. The *I Ching* is a classic that has been known for its peculiar symbolism for which there exists no clearly set rule to interpret its intended meanings. This has been a book for which personal interests and perspectives of interpreters play large roles in bringing to light whatever knowledge or wisdom they find to be interpreted out of it. Thus, personal preferences reflected in the choice of the meanings remains as a salient problem to any version of the interpretations of the *I Ching*. Of course, since the schematic representation of the social situations by the *I Ching* has a systematic feature in terms of both the uniformity and variability among the situations represented by the 64 hexagrams, one's interpretation of any hexagram or line statement cannot be made purely "subjectively or arbitrarily" ignoring the systematic perspective(s) that the *I Ching* has about the structured features of the social world. Still, as we have seen throughout this book, the latitude of exercising one's discretion in the choice of the meanings is open considerably wide so as to give rise to many different versions of interpretations. With a recognition of this problem an exaggerated claim for being the truly authentic interpretation of the *I Ching* also will not have to be made for this study: I will only put forward a modest claim for this study to be one of many possible interpretations of the old classic.

There is also another critical problem with the *I Ching*. How can we relate any given social reality to a specific hexagram? In other words, how can the typological scheme of the *I Ching* be utilized in making judgments about what kind of specific situations we actually experience? Without an adequate procedure or method to match the situational types represented by the *I Ching* to real life situations in which individuals are situated, the *I Ching* would be nothing more than a collection of symbolic maps drawn on paper having questionable utility at best. Of course, there is a method that the *I Ching* recommends — an oracle procedure that "consists in a manipulation of yarrow stalks (or coins) which yields certain numbers and group of numbers" (Wilhelm, 1960:98). These numbers yielded by the prescribed procedure are transformed into yin and yang lines to determine a hexagram. This procedure relies purely on chance in which a heap of yarrow stalks are divided step by step in random-like manners until all the steps of the defined procedure are exhausted. This has been the standard practice for people who consult the *I Ching* to get divination messages. However, as far as our interest in the *I Ching* here focuses on the acquisition of rational knowledge about social conditions, few social scientists including myself will see any rationality in using the divinatory practice. Thus, for those who share no propensity to take part in the mystic culture of the divination practice, the *I Ching* provides no rational or specific guideline for its actual application. Instead of using the oracle method, we may make careful observations on the essential conditions of a given social reality, examine each of the 64 hexagrams, and then make comparisons between the observed features of the reality in question and the situational features described by each hexagram. In the process, we may be able to hit upon a specific hexagram that features in most meaningful ways the essential conditions of the reality we have observed. This seems to be the only reasonable alternative to the oracle method. Yet, unless there is a set of appropriate rules, methods, or "operational definitions" to relate the *I Ching* to existing realities, anyone's intuitive, subjective attempt to pair a reality with one of the situations listed in the *I Ching* may never go beyond a mere guess or claim having dubious validity. Regrettably, as I hinted already, the lack of a clearly defined methodological procedure to apply the typological scheme of the *I Ching* to existing conditions of the social world is one of the most serious problems of the *I Ching* as a system of knowledge.

Now, I would like to raise an important issue that I have postponed until this point. It concerns the question of how the *I Ching* can be utilized to deal with the conditions of modern societies. How seriously do I consider the possibility that the *I Ching* involves theoretical perspectives and ideas that can cope pertinently with essential features of modern societies? The book was written in ancient China where there existed no other social institution of noticeable significance except the two primary ones, the political and family institutions. This situation of low social differentiation changed little in China and other Asian societies until they began to go through "modernization" processes modeled after Western industrial societies. This is apparent in the stratification system depicted by the hierarchical ordering of the lines in the *I Ching*; it mainly represents a political community constituted of the hierarchically arranged layers of the governing elites and the governed. Understanding the general conditions of their society in terms of the varying situations occurring in the political arena should have made ample sense to succeeding generations of Chinese intellectuals. But, the society has undergone enormous changes in both quantity and quality. Business elites, office and factory workers, cultural elites of various sorts, and others in innumerably varying occupations who did not exist in pre-modern societies or remained only at obscure edges of society have emerged as influential forces in modern social scenes and are playing critical roles that are no less significant than those performed by political elites. Then, question may be raised; is the conceptual scheme that assumes a neatly defined formal hierarchy embodied in the vertical arrangement of the six positions of the hexagram really applicable to a complex modern society such as, for instance, American society? Modern society now has become highly differentiated into various institutional sectors and divested of the one-dimensional hierarchical structure depicted by the hexagrams. Does this make the *I Ching* such an outdated a system of knowledge that it has little utility for understanding the conditions of complex modern society? How can we assess its field theoretical approach towards the representation of social reality? What about the implications of its theoretical perspective regarding the variability of the social situations has had on such important issues as the dichotomy between integration and conflict models of society and that between social structure and human agency? My own assessment is that the theoretical ideas underlying the *I Ching* laid bare through this study are worth serious examination for their possible applicability in modern social sciences. Of course, they must be elaborated, modified where judged necessary, and thus made more relevant in accordance with conditions of the modern society.

Now we have reached the point at which to end this thesis. So, by way of closing this rather long discourse, I would like to add a brief "epilogue" which can be meaningful in view of the present state of my own profession. At the outset of writing this treatise, I pointed out that modern sociology, and more generally social sciences at large, seem to be experiencing a crisis situation running out of creative ideas. In efforts to overcome the crisis situation, theoreticians have been working mostly on diagnosing problems in existing theories so that they can salvage the valuable portions from each of the theories and assemble or "synthesize" them into a better theory. I do not think, however, that such a patch-up job or eclectic approach will be a good remedy for the problems of existing social theories. A far better solution will be found in replacing old ones with a "bravely" new one, or introducing a new paradigm by a total switch of the world-view. But, how? All I can think of is that we just make every possible effort to search out whatever sources of knowledge we can and examine them carefully to see if they contain perspectives or ideas with the help of which we can embark in a new round of productive intellectual business. As far as the analyses done on the theoretical implications and relevance that the *I Ching* has in relation to current issues in modern social sciences are concerned, I regard my study reported in this book as a small effort, made in that direction to explore new and useful ideas, that, I hope, will stimulate some interest among fellow scholars in concerned areas.

Notes

Chapter 1: Introduction

[1] In ancient China, diviners read divination signs by interpreting cracks created by burning a tortoiseshell.

[2] To show an example, let's take the hexagram *Khwei*, as translated and in the format presented by Legge (1963:139):

Khwei indicates that, notwithstanding the condition of things it denotes, in small matters there will be good success.

1. The first line, undivided, shows that (to its subject) the occasion for repentance will disappear. He has lost his horses, but let him not seek for them; — they will return of themselves. Should he meet with bad men, he will not err.
2. The second line, undivided, shows its subject happening to meet with his lord in a bye-passage. There will be no error.

(The statement attached to each line figure continues in this way up to the sixth line.)

[3] In support of this view, one of the Commentaries (*Ta Chuan*) explains that every important human invention was initiated by a person who modeled his invention after an image suggested by a hexagram. The following passage presents an example typical of such explanation: "He split a piece

of wood for a plowshare and bent a piece of wood for the plow handle, and taught the world the advantage of laying open the earth with a plow. He probably took this from the hexagram of *Increase(I)*" (translation as rendered by Wilhelm, 1967:330).

Chapter 2: Structural Components of the Hexagram

1. With a simple calculation, we can easily figure out how the 64 hexagrams of the *I Ching* had been derived. Since there are six different positions and each position would be expressed as being either in a yang or yin state, 2 x 2 x 2 x 2 x 2 x 2 will result in the 64 unique combinations of the lines.

2. In actual practice, the six-line composite figure of the hexagram is given much broader applicability and characterizes situations of any entity or organization that is regarded as hierarchical. For instance, if a family situation is represented, the positions of the hexagram may be interpreted respectively, from the bottom position moving up the top one, as "youngest child," "older child," "oldest child," "mother," "father," and "grandparents" (Choi, 1992:23; Lee, 1997:43-46). This "world view," that various human collectives are in essence entities organized with the same hierarchical ordering, extends to natural phenomena. Thus, the six line composite of the hexagram is said to indicate the structure of a human body, with the positions of lines respectively corresponding to important parts of a human body such as legs, abdomen, head, etc. (Choi, 1992:23)

3. Cheng Yi (1033-1107), a famed Confucian philosopher during the Sung period, warned against a limited interpretation applied only to a certain specific phenomenon, saying, "If you cling to one thing, then the three hundred and eighty-four lines of the *I Ching* can only apply to three hundred and eighty-four things" (quoted in Cleary, 1995:xvii).

4. This is not an expression merely to avoid a commitment to a risky overgeneralization. That is, "under ordinary situations" means literally that the *I Ching* in fact involves some hexagrams representing "extraordinary" situations in which the bottom or top position does not remain in its position as characterized here. In other words, there are some situations in which persons who occupy the bottom or top position have a certain measure of influence over other positions in formal office.

5. The quoted statement is not originally made by Wang Bi. As Wang Bi himself names its source, this statement appears in the *Commentary on the Words of the Text* (one of the *Ten Commentaries*) for the hexagram *Qian* (Lynn, 1994:33).

6. The terms "regulating unit," "governing unit" and "operative unit" used

in this discussion are taken from Spencer (1974:15, 32-47). The meanings of these words and the overall context in which these words are used in Spencer's writing do not seem very different from what Wang Bi with his native cultural background would have in mind with his own terminology of "nobility" or "servility." If we take the meanings of the terms together with those implied in actual applications of the hexagram, Wang Bi's terminology, "servility" and "nobility," can be compared also with Spencer's polar concepts expressed with the terms "dominant centers " and "subordinate centers." For similarly comparable notions, also refer to Eisenstadt's "groups in the center" and "peripheral groups" (1971).

[7] Yang and yin are opposite concepts in the sense that they represent mutually opposite qualities in things, social positions, or individuals. However, there is a crucial difference in the world views of this Oriental dualism and any concepts in the West, such as Dahrendorf's "Up and Down" or "They and Us." The logical relation between any two contradictory concepts is mutual exclusion. Thus, in the case of Dahrendorf, the relationship between "dominant group" and "subordinated group" is characterized as one of "(mutually) opposite interests," of being in conflict with each other (1969). In contrast, the dualism of yang and yin does not imply a contradiction. They are a pair of opposite qualities that requires the other as an indispensable partner, such as the case in husband and wife. Thus, a pairing of yang and yin means a union, not a conflict or contradiction, in which the two elements play complementary roles according to their own particular capacities.

[8] The five basic human relations include the relations between ruler and ruled, father and son, wife and husband, young and old, and between friends. A question may be raised about why public relations such as those among citizens, contractual relations between employer and employee in the labor market, or commercial ones are not included here. This is because China had been a society composed mainly of rural communities where such relations had developed little.

[9] Nevertheless, Wilhelm does not seem to maintain this "temporal" perspective consistently when he presents more detailed illustrations regarding the interpretations of the positions of the hexagram. For example, refer to the following illustration: "Some lines stand in a particularly close relation to one another. Thus the first and third, the second and fourth, the third and fifth correspond, particularly when the lines in question differ in character. The correspondence is notably strong between the two central lines and is favorable as a rule where a strong official corresponds to a yielding ruler. The opposite case is nothing like as favorable. Naturally, the relation between ruler and minister, the fifth and fourth lines, is also close. The relation is usually favorable when a strong ruler has an obedient and adaptable minister; a strong minister all too easily involves a yielding ruler in difficulties. Other neighboring lines

can also have relationships, as for instance the two top lines, which then symbolizing a ruler who yields to the counsel of a sage" (1960:47).

[10] The inserted commentary within the brackets [ ] is Wang Bi's.

Chapter 3: Patterns of Relationships among the Structural Components of the Hexagram

[1] Another indication is offered through an examination of his index. It is easy to see how large a relative proportion these terms take up in the index of his book (1950) in comparison with other terms.

[2] For example, compare the integrative situation represented by the hexagram *Bi* with the idea of superordination as described by Simmel (1950:190): "The subordination of a group under a single person results, above all, in a very decisive unification of the group. This unification is almost equally evident in both of two characteristic forms of this subordination. First, the group forms an actual, inner unit together with its head; the ruler leads the group forces in their own direction, promoting and fusing them; super-ordination, therefore, here really means only that the will of the group has found a unitary expression or body...."

[3] "*Carrying*" and "*riding*" are adopted from Lynn's translation. Wilhelm translates them as "*receiving*" and "*resting upon,*" respectively.

[4] "*Carrying* and *riding* provide images of congruity or incongruity" (Lynn, 1994:29). The term, congruity or incongruity, is used obviously to refer to whether the actual role one plays in a given situation is congruous or incongruous with what is required of the position he occupies in the formal hierarchy of a social organization.

[5] I would like to note that we sociologists trained in the Western tradition may feel more at home with the first type of dyadic relations presented above (—— —— : the yang above, the yin below), the pattern of congruity. This "congruous" situation may seem to be more in accordance with what is thought to be "typical." Being so, the dyadic situation presented here (═══ : the yin above, the yang below) puts forward an unusual type of social relation. But, is it truly unusual? This is an interesting empirical question, but not a critical issue as far as the *I Ching* itself is concerned; the *I Ching* will simply regard it as a possible situation among many.

[6] A more detailed explanation by Wilhelm (1967:361) reads as follows: "As a rule, firm lines correspond (應 *ying*, translated as "resonation" by Lynn) with yielding lines only, and vice versa. The following lines, provided that they differ in kind, correspond: the first and the fourth, the

second and the fifth, the third and the top line. Of course, the most important are the two central lines in the second and the fifth place, which stand in the relationship of official to ruler, son to father, wife to husband. A strong official may be in the relation of correspondence (resonance) to a yielding ruler, or a yielding official may be similarly related to a strong ruler."

7   The inserted comment inside the parentheses (   ) is Wang Bi's.

8   Words inside the parentheses (   ) are by this author.

9   This is from Wilhelm's translation instead of Lynn's. It seems to me that, as far as this portion is concerned, the essential characteristic of this trigram is caught much more sharply in the former's translation than in the latter's.

10 Concerning the aspect of the *I Ching* related to this, a commentary (*Commentary on the Appended Phrases, Part Two*) explains: " The rise of the *Changes* (i.e., *I Ching*), was it not just the end of the Yin [Shang] era when the virtue of the Zhou had begun to flourish, just at the time when the incident between King Wen and King Zhou (the author's note: Wilhelm (1967:353) explains that this incident refers to the historical event that "King Wen the founder of the Chou dynasty, was held captive by the last ruler of the Yin dynasty, the tyrant Chou Hsin.") was taking place? This is why King Wen's phrases [i.e., the *Judgments* (hexagram statements)] are concerned with danger. Being conscious of danger allows one to find peace and security, but to be easy brings about downfall. The Dao involved here is so great that its sustenance of everything never fails. It instills a sense of fearful caution about things from beginning to end, and its essential purpose is to permit people to be 'without blame'" (Lynn, 1994:93).

Chapter 4: Hexagrams: Representations of Various Types of Social Situations

1   Simply by "(taking) the broken line for a zero, the unbroken for a 1," as Leibniz did, we can obtain "the numerical sequence of the binary system" that "would look as follows: 1, 10, 11, 100, 101, 110, 111, 1000, etc." (Wilhelm, 1960:90-91).

1   According to Parsons, a "moving equilibrium" refers to a state of a system in which "an orderly process of change of the system" is taking place while maintaining integration. Parson contrasts this situation to a "static equilibrium" which refers to an unchanging state engaged only in a self-maintaining process, with no occurrence of change in the basic structure of the system.

[2] [Footnoted by Lynn] I.e., the third line is on top of two yang lines.

[3] Compare different interpretations offered respectively by such commentators as Cheng Yi (1995:2), Lee (1997[I]:76-78), Legge (1963:60), Wang Bi (1994:139-140) and Wilhelm (1967:10)

[4] Of these types of residues, Pareto explains: "after the group has been constituted, an instinct very often comes into play that tends with varying energy to prevent the things so combined from being disjointed, and which, if disintegration cannot be avoided, strives to dissemble it by preserving the outer physiognomy of the aggregate. This instinct may be compared roughly to mechanical inertia: it tends to resist the movement imparted by other instincts. To the fact the tremendous social importance of Class II residues is to be ascribed" (1935:598). Coser (1971:396) sums up this tendency or instinct to preserve an existing social order with the phrase "conservative forces of 'social inertia'."

[5] The characteristic quality (or virtue) of the hexagram *Kun* is often compared to that of Earth. Refer to following commentaries: "Here is the basic disposition of Earth: this constitutes the image of *Kun*" (from the *Commentary on the Images*); "As Heaven is high and noble and Earth is low and humble, so it is that *Qian* [Pure Yang, the hexagram 1] and *Kun* [Pure Yin, the hexagram 2] are defined" (from the *Commentary on the Appended Phrases*) (Lynn, 1994:144).

[6] Considering all the advice that the *I Ching* gives to actors involved in given situations, the *I Ching* seems to make allowances for the fact that, even if the action orientations and outcomes of human actions are determined in the context of objective conditions, there is a latitude of actions in which a person can exercise free choice.

[7] Each hexagram is given a serial number following the sequential ordering in which the hexagrams are arranged in the text.

[8] Compare this translation with other ones as follows; "Good return is auspicious" (Cleary's translation, Cheng Yi, 1988:73); ". . . . shows the admirable return (of the subject). There will be good fortune" (Legge, 1963:108); "This one returns with delightful goodness, so there is good fortune" (Lynn, 1994:288); "Quiet return. Good fortune" (Wilhelm, 1967:507).

[9] For example, Wang Bi in his commentary says of this yin line, "Here Second Yin is located on top of First Yang, but it obeys First Yang as its adherent, and this is what is meant by saying that it 'subordinates itself to benevolence.' Once Second Yin has located itself in this central position, it has benevolence for its close companion and delights in the goodness of its neighbor. And this is what accounts for the 'delightful goodness' of its Return" (Lynn, 1994:288).

10   In Cleary's (Cheng Yi, 1988:74), Wilhelm's (1967:507) and Legge's (1963:108) translations, this line statement is translated as "repeated return." It is because the word 頻 (*pin*) can be translated as either "repeat" or "urgency." In Lee's Korean translation, the whole statement of this third yin line is translated "if one (a person at this position) hurries return, he may encounter some hardship; but, he will end up with no blame" (1997[I]:301). I here will take Lee's and Lynn's translation as shown above for the simple reason that it seems to fit better with the overall situational context.

11   According to Lee's explanation, a "forceful man" as used here means a man with practical skills, strong body and will power, but not the type of person who is talented in abstract thinking or in theoretical reasoning (1997[I]:140).

12   Also refer to Lynn's endnote (7) on this line statement: " 'Use carriages to transport corpses' translates *yu shi*. Zhu Xi's interpretation follows that of Wang Bi, but Cheng Yi explains *yu shi* differently, as 'many leaders,' which involves possible, secondary meanings for the two characters respectively. Cheng's reading of the passage would read something like: 'if perhaps the Army has many leaders [i.e., no unified command], it would result in misfortune' " (1994:183).

13   Legge also seems to have the same opinion. His translation of the line statement of the third yin line reads, "the third line, divided, show how the host may, possibly, have many inefficient leaders. There will be evil." And, he explains his translation as follows; "the meaning I have now given is more legitimate, taken character by character, and more in harmony with the scope of the hexagram. The subject of line 2 is the one proper leader of the host. But, line 3 is divided and weak, and occupies the place of a strong line, as if its subject had perversely jumped over two, and perched himself above it to take command. This interpretation also suits better in the 5th paragraph (the line statement of the fifth yin line)" (1963:72-73).

14   Compare the following translations; "the Army camps; no blame" (Cheng Yi, 1988:18); "the fourth line, divided, shows the host in retreat. There is no error" (Legge, 1963:72); "if the Army pitches camp to the left, there will be no blame" (Lynn, 1994:180); "the Army retreats. No blame" (Wilhelm, 1967:423).

15   I can only make a guess as to the reason for this. Understandably, it would be very hard to imagine what kind of a situation the top position holder is likely to be under in any given situation. This is probably because he is described as a man of high honor and prestige yet playing no officially assigned role. He is in a very ambiguous position indeed. Therefore, perhaps, the author(s) of the *I Ching* might have thought that for many hexagrams it would not be crucially important to take into account the

role the top position holder plays. Because it may be close to the reality to believe that the role of "retired former leaders" or "sages (intellectuals)" contributes little to the determination of a given situation, the author(s) of the old classic might have decided to have the top line represent the final stage of that situation.

[16] A "happy community" seems to fit well with the state which all the involved actors are able to achieve as the result from exercising their modesty; refer also to the passage in the *Commentary on the Judgments* (Lynn, 1994:229-300).

[17] As used here, this refers to a moral instruction of the Orient that also involves an empirical proposition. It instructs people to comply with a certain normative principle, yet, at the same time, involves a prediction for a probable outcome to be expected from behaving according to the moral principle.

[18] I quote here Cleary's translation instead of Lynn's because the former seems to convey a clearer meaning and to be more consistent with the line structure of the hexagram and also with the interpretations rendered to other lines.

[19] I here adopt Wilhelm's translation instead of Lynn's "contentment" for the hexagram name *Yu* because "enthusiasm" seems to convey the meaning of the hexagram somewhat better than "contentment."

[20] The varying translations of the line statement are as follows: "Ignorant delight has taken place; if there is a change, there will be no fault" (Cheng Yi, 1988:50); "The topmost line, divided, shows its subject with darkened mind devoted to the pleasure and satisfaction (of the time); if he changes his course even when (it may be considered as) completed, there will be no error" (Legge, 1963:92); "The top yin line represents one who meets the situation of enthusiasm with an apathetic attitude. Thus if after completion one changes, there will be no blame" (English translation by this author; Lee, 1997[I]:228); "Here the benighted pursuit of Contentment is complete, but if one changes course, there will be no blame" (Lynn, 1994:239); "Deluded enthusiasm. But if after completion one changes, There will be no blame" (Wilhelm, 1967:71).

[21] The latter translation "Holding Together [Union]" is Wilhelm's.

[22] Wilhelm's translation instead of Lynn's is cited here because the latter seems to involve some misinterpretation. And, the following explanation supplied by Wilhelm will also aid us with some background information to understand this line statement: "In the royal hunts of ancient China it was customary to drive up the game from three sides, but on the fourth the animals had a chance to run off. If they failed to do this they had to pass through a gate behind which the king stood ready to shoot. Only animals that entered here were shot; those that ran off in front were

permitted to escape. This custom accorded with a kingly attitude; the royal hunter did not wish to turn the chase into a slaughter, but held that the kill should consist only of those animals which had so to speak voluntarily exposed themselves" (Wilhelm, 1967:38-39).

23 The latter translation of the hexagram name "Splitting Apart" is Wilhelm's.

24 The words inside the parentheses ( ) are inserted by this author to facilitate understanding.

25 This situation described for the first yin line in some essential aspect may be compared to what Simmel (1950:232) calls "relative subordination." Refer to the following passage in Simmel's writing: "In regard to the existing quantum of freedom on the part of the subordinates, the situation usually introduces a process of growth which sometimes reaches the point of dissolving the subordination itself. An essential difference between the medieval bondsman and the medieval vassal consisted in the fact that the former had, and could have, only one master, whereas the latter could take land from several lords and make the feudal vow to each of them. Through this possibility of entering several feudal service relations, the vassal gained solidarity and independence in regard to the single feudal lord, and, thus, was compensated very considerably for the basic subordination of his position." Meanwhile, Simmel suggests another variable situation in which a subordinate "under a heterogeneous plurality" may fall: This situation characterized as "total subordination" in contrast to the previous one, "relative subordination," denotes a "conflicting" situation in which "the situation appears as a 'conflict of duties' to a subordinate under a plurality of strong superordinates" (1950:230).

26 An interesting question may be raised here: Why is it likened to a "weak pig" rather than to a "strong pig (boar)"? Presumably, a ready answer may be given that it is because the yin line is located in the lowest position. In other words, although he may able to "romp around" as he wills, his range of potential ability to do harm to the organization to which he belongs will be limited to the very extent that an influence accruing from his lowest position would have a limited potential under many powerful superiors.

27 The line statement produced many versions of translation that differ from this one as shown as follows: "2 yang: Fish in the bag, there is no fault. It is not beneficial for a guest" (Cheng Yi, 1988:145); "Nine in the second place: even if a fish is kept in the kitchen, there will be no blame. But, it is not beneficial to invite guests" (Lee, 1997[II]:116, translated from Korean by this author). "The second line, undivided, shows its subject with a wallet of fish. There will be no error. But it will not be well to let (the subject of the first line) go forward to the guests" (Legge, 1963:155); "Nine in the second place means: There is a fish in the tank. No blame.

Does not further guests" (Wilhelm, 1967:172). But, as we can see, there seems little variation among commentators (and translators) in the ways in which they read the essential message conveyed by this line statement.

28 "Wrapping a melon in willows, embody beauty, and there will be a descent from heaven" (Cheng Yi, 1988:147); "a medlar tree overspreading the gourd (beneath it). If he keeps his brilliant qualities concealed, (a good issue) will descend (as) from Heaven" (Legge, 1963:155); "With his basket willow and bottle gourd, this one harbors beauty within, so if there is destruction, it will only come from Heaven (Lynn, 1994:413); "A melon covered with willow leaves. Hidden lines. Then it drops down to one from heaven" (Wilhelm, 1967:173).

29 For example, Wang Bi explains the reason the subject represented by the fourth yang "should be fearfully cautious, so that in the end he will have good fortune": ". . . . since this is a yang line occupying a yin position, it takes modesty as its basic principle, so although it is located in a dangerous and fearful place, in the end it will achieve its goal" (Lynn, 1994:203). But the contrary could also be the case. That is, if a yang line occupies a yin place, this "inappropriately occupied" line may be interpreted as acting aggressively rather than modestly so that it would cause some trouble in relating itself to other neighboring lines. These kinds of arbitrary interpretations, couched upon different principles varying from one case to another, are found in numerous instances throughout a number of commentaries.

30 As Wilhelm points out from the text accounts on this hexagram, "one can note such a difference between the judgment pertaining to the hexagram as a whole, and that pertaining to an individual line" (1967:439).

31 The latter translation, "the Taming Power of the Small," is Wilhelm's. This translation seems to fit more squarely with the meaning of the hexagram.

32 The characteristics of the upper trigram *Sun* (≡) are represented by many different symbols, one of which is the Eldest Daughter (Lynn, 1994:124).

33 This line statement has yielded various interpretations and is thereby translated in many different ways. But taken as whole, the statement makes far better sense with Lee's interpretation. Compare Lee's above translation with other ones as follows: "The trust is mutual. Sternness bodes well" (Cheng Yi, 1988:43); "The fifth line, divided, shows the sincerity of its subject reciprocated by that of all the others (represented in the hexagram). Let him display a proper majesty, and there will be good fortune" (Legge, 1963:88). "Trust in him makes him attractive, makes him awesome, and this means good fortune" (Lynn, 1994:226). "He whose truth is accessible, yet dignified, Has good fortune" (Wilhelm,

1967:460).

34 Only Lynn translates this line somewhat differently from others, including Wilhelm's translation as above. According to Lynn's translation, the line statement reads, "Although one never encounters calamity here, to remain blameless he should bear up under difficulties, for only then will there be no blame" (1994:224).

35 This translation by Lynn is based on Wang Bi's interpretation. But other commentators such as Legge (1963:88), Wilhelm (1967:459), and Kim (1997:135) interpret this line differently, thus rendering different versions of translation. For example, Wilhelm's translation reads, "A prince offers to the Son of Heaven. A petty man cannot to do this." This difference is related to differences in opinion on how to interpret the Chinese word *heng* (亨) in the line statement (Lynn, 1994:228n6). However, to this author, the second part of the line statement, "a petty man cannot to do this," seems to fit more meaningfully with the first portion of the line statement as interpreted by Wang Bi.

36 At least in content, Lynn's translation is not much different from Legge's quoted here. However, as far as the hexagram statement of this hexagram *Kuai* is concerned, Legge's translation seems to allow a much easier reading and somewhat clearer understanding.

37 According to Wang Bi, "The *xianlu* [pokeweed] is a weak and fragile plant, so it is easiest thing possible to deal with decisively" (Lynn, 1994:408).

38 Lynn's translation, "This one put his strength into his advancing toes, went forth but was not victorious, and so incurs blame" (1994:406), by using past tenses, interprets this line statement with a somewhat different perspective. But, as I pointed out repeatedly, since there is no objective criteria to guide the choice for interpretation, I here will take Wilhelm's translation as a more suitable one for our analysis at hand.

39 Regarding whom this "ram" or "sheep" actually refers to, other commentators do not agree with Wang Bi's interpretation introduced here. Refer to the following note added to Wang Bi's commentary by Lynn (1994:410): "Zhu Xi interprets the *yang* (ram) as something in front of Fourth Yang, which Fourth yang should follow to be able to advance, but Cheng Yi thinks the *yang* (sheep) refers to Fourth Yang itself — one here should allow himself to be led like a sheep (get himself under control) and advance together with the other yang lines upward; thus his "regret would disappear." But, as Fourth Yang is in a yin position — soft, weak, but recalcitrant — one here will not listen and so comes to grief...."

40 "Stability" is this author's own translation for *Heng* (恒). As I understand it, the term "stability" fits better with the overall meaning of the hexagram and what individual line statements describe about relationships among

component lines or situational conditions of them.

41 Wilhelm's translation is quoted here because it seems more concise and clearer than Lynn's. Written with italics inside the parentheses ( ) is the *Commentary on the Images* attached respectively to the related parts of the line statement.

42 For instance, the fourth line statement of the hexagram *Shihe* reads, "Bites in dried grisly meat. Receives metal arrows. It furthers one to be mindful of difficulties / And to be persevering. Good fortune." Commenting on this line statement, Wilhelm explains; ". . . . This is dried by the sun (Li, in which this is the beginning line). The nuclear trigram K'an means arrows . . . ." (1967:493). In comparison, notice that Legge is trying to make a more rational interpretation based on documented historical facts. For this, refer to Legge's following commentary: "Of old, in a civil case, both parties, before they were heard, brought to the court an arrow (or a bundle of arrows), in testimony of their rectitude, after which they were heard; in a criminal case, they in the same way deposited each thirty pounds of gold, or some other metal" (1963: 103).

43 Legge's translation, instead of Lynn's (1994:245-6), is chosen here because, as I see it, the former's interpretation on the line statement of the sixth yin line and the resulting translation seems to fit more squarely with what is said in that for the fifth yang line. Legge's interpretation seems to be made in accordance with Cheng Yi's and Zhi Xi's interpretations, as Lynn also notes in his *Notes* (1994:247n12).

44 Of this difference in interpretation, refer to Lynn (1994:258n1).

45 Legge's translation instead of Lynn's is adopted here because the former seems simpler, clearer and therefore amenable to an easier interpretation.

46 In Lynn's translation, "the grandmother (*wangmu*)" is translated as "his departed mother." As translated by Legge, "the grandmother" is interpreted to refer to the subject at the fifth position (1963:133; Cheng Yi, 1988:111), in which case the line statement is subjected to an easier interpretation as we will see above. If "the grandmother" is translated as the departed mother," she may refer to a deceased woman who actually gave birth to the subject at this position (Kim, 1997:276; Legge, 1963:133). And, this will put the line statement and the entire situation represented by the hexagram into a context entirely different from what we have interpreted so far.

47 Wilhelm's translation, instead of Lynn's, is adopted here because the line statement in the way it is translated by Wilhelm seems to fit better with the overall context of the situation as we have interpreted so far.

48 With whom contention will occur is not clear from the line statement. Wilhelm (1967:418) suggests that there would be "a brief altercation with the neighboring nine (the subject at the second position)," whereas Wang

Bi (1994:172) suggests that it has to do with the subject at the fourth position.

49 Regarding the interpretation of this verse as rendered above, I owe a debt to Legge's commentary on this line statement; " 'He keeps in the old place assigned for his support' is, literally, 'He eats his old virtue;' meaning that he lives in and on the appendage assigned to him for his services" (1963:71).

50 Legge's translation, instead of Lynn's, again is adopted here because it is simpler and easier to interpret. Compare the above version of the translation and the interpretation that goes with it with that of Lynn based on Wang Bi's commentary (Lynn, 1994:174).

51 This term is used here exactly in the context used in Parsons' four functional requisites. As has been well known, the term "patterns" refers to "beliefs and values" shared by the members of a society, and, therefore, it may be said that the cultural basis of a society consists mainly of "patterns," i.e., shared beliefs and values. Then, the function of "pattern maintenance" should have to do with cultural activities related to the maintenance of beliefs and values shared by the members of a society, "that concerned with the maintenance of the highest "governing" or controlling patterns of the system" (Parsons, 1966:7). We may say that the function of pattern maintenance has to do with the function related to intellectual activities focused upon the "governing" or "controlling" principles of a society.

52 Cheng Yi: ". . . . This represents the state of the most petty sort of people. What they hold within is craft and deviousness, which knows no limits; this is shameful" (1988:36); Legge: "The third line is weak. Its place is odd, and therefore for it incorrect. Its subject would vent his evil purpose, has not strength to do so. He is left therefore to the shame which he ought to feel without a word of warning" (1963:85); Wang Bi: "Both the petty man and the great man here utilize the lesser Dao in taking orders from the ruler, yet because this position is not appropriate for the great man, he has to bear his shame" (Lynn, 1994:213); Wilhelm: "The third line is weak in the strong place of transition. This is an incorrect place for it, hence the idea of humiliation" (1967:449).

53 Legge's translation, instead of Lynn's, is quoted here because the one rendered by Legge seems to be much clearer in meaning.

54 According to Wang Bi, "although at first Third Yin suffer difficulties," "things will end well" for him since "in the end it acquires the assistance of the hard and the strong [Top Yang]" (Lynn, 1994:371; c.f., Wilhelm, 1967:577). This interpretation is based on the perspective that the third and the sixth positions have a specific affinity. A complementary pair of yin and yang lines occupies these two positions under the situation, and, therefore, they are in a corresponding relationship to each other. Of

course, the patterns of alliances among groups or classes of people would be an extremely important factor in explaining how an individual or a group of individuals fare through a difficult situation. In this sense, I think, there is nothing strange about the perspective that a corresponding relationship, once formed, would render help to people when such help is needed. However, what bothers me concerning this explanation is that neither *the I Ching* nor any later commentary provides a rationally constructed explanation about why such alliance is formed only between, for instance, the subjects at the third and the fourth positions. This is why I prefer taking the interpretation presented above to the "alliance theory" proposed by Wang Bi and other commentators.

55   Cleary's translation, instead of Lynn's, is presented here because the line statement translated as such seems to yield an interpretation that is more closely related to the main theme of this hexagram.

56   Compare this translation with other versions as followings: "Regret disappears. The partner bites the skin. What is wrong with going?" (Cheng Yi, 1988:123); "The fifth line, divided, shows that (to its subject) occasion for repentance will disappear. With his relative (and minister he unites closely and readily) as if he were biting through a piece of skin. When he goes forward (with his help), what error can there be?" (Legge, 1963:140); "Regret disappears. His clansman bites through skin, so if one were to set forth here, what blame would there be?" (Lynn, 1994:372); "Remorse disappears. The companion bites his way through the wrappings. If one goes to him, How could it be a mistake?" (Wilhelm, 1967:578).

57   Cleary's translation, instead of Lynn's, is presented here simply because it seems to be more accurately worded and thus seemingly more effective in conveying the intended message of the line statement.

58   According to Legge, the meaning of the hexagram is twofold; ". . . . their masses (of mountains that symbolize the hexagram) rest on it in quiet and solemn majesty; and they serve also to arrest the onward progress of the traveller. Hence the attribute ascribed to *Kan* (*Gen*) is twofold; it is both active and passive — resting and arresting" (1963:177). Viewed in this way, "Restraint" (Lynn's translation) and "Keeping Still" (Wilhelm's translation) focus respectively on one aspect of the twofold meanings of the hexagram.

59   According to Kong Yingda, " 'The great vessel [*daqi*]' refers to the relationship between the state and the person of [the ruler]" (Requoted from Lynn, 1994:472n8). But, the word itself refers to such magnificent entities, tools, or phenomenon as nature, society, the human body, or the heroic person, not the relationships among them. As I see it, the great vessel as referred to here would make better sense if it were interpreted to refer to the society.

[60] According to Cheng Yi, the main source causing problems to some position holders including the subject at the second position is found in that the subject at the fifth position is a weak leader with "insufficient capacities to be a help to the second." Interpreted this way, however, the meaning of the line statement of the fifth yin line has to be entirely recast, to which the line statement is translated as follows: "Bring forth the excellent, and there is joy and praise. This is auspicious." To interpret, if the leader at the fifth position "can bring forth excellent people from the lower ranks and employ them, then there will be the joy of good fortune, and they will be praised, which is auspicious" (1988:189). Cheng Yi's interpretation is in line with the general rule with which a yin line at the yang position is interpreted to represent a subject who has insufficient capacities to fulfill the task assigned to that position. With this interpretation, however, the main theme of the hexagram may have to be understood from an entirely different perspective.

[61] This hexagram, as we will see, represents a situation in which no stable pattern of dominance and subordination in power relationships has emerged. Since the powerful figure that plays the central role of bringing about political integration has not yet emerged in the field, this situation is the disorderly and difficult time that exists right before a new order emerges onto the scene. In this sense, this hexagram may also be included in "disintegrated" situations. The name of the hexagram, *Zhun* (Birth Throes), however, seems to reflect the intention of the author(s) of the *I Ching* who seems to have viewed this situation as a condition that should exist prior to the birth of a new order for a political community. It is with this consideration that this particular hexagram is included here as one of the situations in which "order is established for a newly emerging state."

[62] Regarding this particular portion of the line statement there is no standard interpretation agreed upon among commentators. According to Wilhelm (1967:401), "this line is (interpreted as) the efficient helper needed to overcome obstacles in times of difficulty at the beginning." Legge's interpretation also seems to accord with Wilhem's view as above. Interpreted in this way, the line statement may have to be translated rather as "it is fitting to make this one a chief (or feudal lord)." On the other hand, Wang Bi's reading of this hexagram suggests an unsettling situation arising due to a rivalry for leadership between the two subjects represented by the first yang and the fifth yang lines who are "pulling (those who seek for leadership under the situation) at odds." Then, the line statement should be interpreted as it is stated, "it is fitting to establish a chief"; that is, it should be beneficial for the subject at the first position to establish a chief. Cheng Yi's interpretation does not seem to differ much from Wang Bi's in essence, yet still introduces subtle changes in meaning to this troublesome line statement. Refer to his commentary on this line statement (1988:6).

414   *The I Ching on Man and Society*

63   Interpreted in this way, it may be more appropriate to interpret the "chief" or the "helper" of the first yang's line statement as referring to the subject at this position. However, this interpretation for the first yang line does not seem to square well with the overall meaning of the hexagram.

64   Other versions of translation, with the exception of Lynn's, are not much different from Legge's translation presented above. Legge's one is presented here simply because, as far I am concerned, it yields an easier interpretation.

65   This has been well recognized by most commentators. For instance, refer to Cheng Yi's following commentary: "There are two ways of construing the image. In terms of the whole body, the bottom is the legs, the solid middle is the belly of the cauldron, the solidity in the middle is the image of the cauldron containing something. The separated fifth line above is the knobs, and the solid top line is the handle. This is the image of a cauldron. / In terms of the upper and lower trigrams, there is an open center above, while there are legs below to bear it. This too is an image of a cauldron." (1988:168).

66   Occasionally in the *I Ching*, rainfall is described as a turning point where a tense situation is resolved with an upward movement towards a better situation.

67   For instance, in this hexagram, notice that there is a yang line at the second position and also at the fifth position. This means that although these two positions have a specific affinity to each other, the two position holders do not show action orientations complementary to each other under this situation and, therefore, are not likely to form mutually helping relationships. The same can be said of the first yin and the fourth yin lines.

68   For this particular hexagram, I would like to rely mainly on Wilhelm's translation, for his translation seems simpler, clearer, and, most of all, easier to interpret than Lynn's.

69   Refer to the *Explaining the Trigrams*: ". . . . It is the trigram of the blood, of the color red . . . ." (Lynn, 1994:124).

70   Refer to Wilhelm's following commentary: "K'an is blood. Wind dissolves. Occasion for bloodshed is removed. Not only does the line itself surmount the peril, but it also helps the six (yin) in the third place, to which it is related" (1967:963).

71   For this line statement at the fifth position, Legge's translation, instead of Lynn's, is presented here for the simple reason that the former seems to be somewhat easier to understand the way it is phrased.

72   Compare the above translation by Legge with Lynn's which reads as follows: "One straightens out Ills to Be Cured caused by the father. If there is such a son, a deceased father will be without blame . . . ."

(1994:250). In my opinion, Lynn's translation presented above, if understood literally as it stands, makes little sense. To carry meaningful information, the phrase "One straightens out Ills to Be Cured caused by the father," should come after and not before the conditional "if" clause (perhaps like "if there is a son who is able to deal with the task suggested by the hexagram *Gu*"). However, Wang Bi's following commentary, appended to Lynn's translation of the line statement, seems to fit more closely with Legge's translation: ".... one is here is in danger, but if he is equal to dealing with that problem, 'in the end, there will be good fortune' " (Lynn, 1994:250).

73   The *I Ching* comments on this ambivalence associated with the third position as follows: "Third lines usually concern misfortune, while fifth lines usually concern achievement, this because of the different levels involved, the one lofty and noble and the other lowly and servile" (Lynn, 1994:92).

74   Wilhelm's translation is adopted here because, as I see it, it seems to be only with his translation that the first and the second verses of the line statement are put into a meaningfully related sequence. Compare the translation presented above with Lynn's, "Here one deals with leniently with Ills to Be Cured caused by the father, but if he were to set out he would experience hard going" (1994:251).

75   This hexagram can be interpreted from an entirely different perspective. Refer to Kim (1997:373-80). As interpreted by Kim, the hexagram can be understood as an essay on revolution that involves a series of practical advice for people who are about to stage a revolution. In this interpretation, for instance, the line statement of the first yin line, translated as saying, "To bind himself tight, this one uses the hide of a brown cow," is understood to involve advice that "one should not act (prematurely) before the right time comes." Compare this interpretation with Wang Bi's that I use.

76   Probably in line with Wang Bi's interpretation, Lynn's translation reads as: "When Quake comes, this one trembles, but if he acts in this quake-affected way, he should stay free of disaster" (1994:462). But, translations rendered by other versions of the text (Cheng Yi, 1988:174; Lee, 1997[2]:183; Wilhelm, 1967:650) give readings similar to Legge's translation presented here. If we adopt Lynn's translation and Wang Bi's interpretation, the line statement is interpreted as emphasizing "a careful action."

77   I chose Legge's translation here, for it seems to allow a more coherent and meaningful interpretation that fits better with the interpretations having been presented so far in relation to all the other lines.

78   The idea of this hexagram name presented above is taken from Legge's suggestion. Refer to Legge's following commentary: "Confucius once

said (Analects 12. 19): — 'The relation between superiors and inferiors is like the wind blows upon it.' In accordance with this, the subject of the hexagram must be understood as the influence and orders of government designed to remedy what is wrong in the people" (1963:191).

79 For example, compare the following translations and see how they differ from one another: "The fourth line, divided, shows one looking as if adorned, but only in white. As if (mounted on) a white horse, and furnished with wings, (he seeks union with the subject of the first line), while (the intervening third pursues), not as a robber, but intent on a matrimonial alliance" (Legge, 1963:104); "Is it to be consummate Elegance or perfect simplicity? She keeps her horse white and, lingering there fresh and spotless, goes to marry only when the robber is no more" (Lynn, 1994:276); "Grace or simplicity? A white horse comes as if on wings. He is not a robber, /He will woo at the right time" (Wilhelm, 1967:498).

80 Wilhelm translates this line statement precisely as he interprets it, as stated as above. The following is his translation: "Use no medicine in an illness / Incurred through no fault of your own / It will pass of itself."

81 Lynn's translation of the line statement reads as follows: "If one here does not do the plowing but tends only to the reaping and does not develop new land but deals only with mature fields, it would be fitting for him to set out to do something" (1994:295). The literal content of the line statement is understood differently by other commentators including Cheng Yi, Zhu Xi, and others (Cheng Yi, 1988:76; Legge, 1963:110; Lynn, 1994:298n7; Wilhelm, 1967:512). However, there is a common theme in their interpreted meanings; the line statement depicts the subject at the second position as one who performs his assigned role with no selfish motive and utmost modesty.

82 In the *I Ching* or any later commentary, it is not entirely clear what sort of activities "Climbing" specifically refers to, although it definitely seems to refer to men's activities to bring about either advancement in their social standings or achievements in collective enterprises.

83 I take this translation by Cleary purely for the reason that it makes more sense than any other version. The original text can be interpreted and translated in various ways (Legge, 1963:160; Wang Bi, in Lynn, 1994:426; Wilhelm, 1967:622).

84 Commentators have different opinions concerning whether the historical episode at Mount Qi is related to King Wen or King Tai, the grandfather of King Wen (Lynn, 1994:428n7).

85 Refer to the passage that reads, "Kun [Impasse] is such that the hard and strong are hindered." Of this Wang Bi comments, "The hard and the strong suffer hindrance at the hands of the soft and weak" (Lynn,

1994:429).

[86] Legge's translation, instead of Lynn's, is presented here because the line statement translated as such seems to yield a meaning that is more closely related to the interpretation of the previous line statements.

[87] "Reciprocity" is Lynn's translation for *Xian*, whereas it is rendered as "Influence" by both Wilhelm and Legge. Although both translations can be used interchangeably, I prefer the latter version for the reason that we will understand when our discussion deals with the line statements.

[88] Lynn's translation reads, ". . . . she sees a man strong as metal . . . ." (1994:161). As Lynn notes, Cheng Yi and Zhi Xi translate "a man strong as metal (*Jinfu*)" as a "wealthy man" (1944: 164n6). Obviously, Legge's translation presented above is based on the two commentators' interpretation as above. Here, I take Legge's version simply because it seems to yield a simpler and clearer interpretation.

[89] Legge's translation instead of Lynn's is presented here mainly because the former presents his version of translation with good reference materials drawn from an old book with which the line statement can be understood more clearly and meaningfully. Refer to his commentary as follows: "Of old, in a civil case, both parties, before they were heard, brought to the court an arrow (or a bundle of arrows), in testimony of their rectitude, after which they were heard; in a criminal case, they in the same way deposited each thirty pounds of gold, or some other metal" (1963:103).

[90] Lynn's translation is considered a unique one in the sense that it is distinguished from most other versions which converge on more or less similar ideas. Wilhelm's rendering of this line reads, "Awareness of danger brings good fortune" (1967:524), and other translations differ little from this one. The meaning of the line statement, in line with this translation, is explained by Wilhelm as follows: "The danger comes from the responsibility of the position at the top of the hexagram and from the fact that, in addition, the line receives authority and honor from the yielding ruler in the fifth place" (1967:524).

[91] Refer to Kong Yingda's commentary quoted by Lynn in his note to the *Commentary on the Images*: "The nature of the lake is such that it lets flow down from it, so it can provide nourishing moisture to what is below. The substance of the Mountain is such that it accepts things from above, so it can receive this nourishing moisture" (Lynn, 1994:333n3)

[92] Since my interpretation relies largely on Legge, his translation will adopted for all the line statements in discussing this hexagram.

[93] The ideas of corresponding, carrying, or riding relationships would allow us to examine social relationships between or among classes or strata of people in terms of the patterns of alliance, dominance, or compliance that exist in varying forms depending upon situations. As I see it, in most

stratification theories in Western sociology, the patterns of relationships among classes or strata of people are defined on the basis of fixed models set down by respective theories. In other words, the theories, in general, involve proposals claiming that some fixed patterns of relationships among classes of people have come to exist due to certain determining factors such as functional needs or materialistically determined conflicting interests. In contrast, the ideas of corresponding, carrying, or riding relationships in the *I Ching* lead us to view patterns of alliance, dominance, or compliance among classes of people as involving aspects that can vary from situation to situation.

94   Refer also to the following comment by Wilhelm: "The nine (yang line) in the fourth place is in the place of the heart. The heart holds mastery in influence, hence the fourth line is here a ruler of the hexagram" (1967:540).

95   Cheng Yi's interpretation differs a little from this. According to his interpretation and accompanying translation, envies and penalties of the superiors in the higher echelon are interpreted as possible outcomes that may result from the fact that the subject at the third position uses "what is beneficial in unfortunate situations." In other words, he, by using his own resources to help people in distress on his own initiative, thereby demonstrating his goodness to bring benefit to the people, may arouse some suspicion from his superiors above him. In the context of this interpretation, the line statement dictating a modest posture on the part of the subject at the third position is viewed as sensible by Cheng Yi (1988:138).

96   Legge's translation instead of Lynn's is presented here simply because the former seems to yield a simpler reading than the latter.

97   This line statement is interpreted and translated differently from one commentator to another. Lee's translation is adopted here because it yields an interpretation more consistent with the perspective that has been applied throughout all the hexagrams dealt with so far.

98   Refer to the following account in *Lunyu* (Confucian Analects) 12:11: "The duke Ching, of Ch'i, asked Confucius about government. / Confucius replied, 'There is government, when the prince is prince, and the minister is minister; when the father is father, and the son is son.' " (Legge, 1971:256).

99   This portion is, presumably by mistake, missing from Lynn's translation.

100   Legge's translation, instead of Lynn's, is presented here because it is more in line with the main idea of the hexagram as we have understood it in our discussion here.

101   Kim's translation is adopted here because it is the only translation in which the line statement makes coherent sense. Compare Kim's above

translation with other translations; for example, Lynn's translation which reads, "The wild goose gradually advances to the shore. The youngest son is in the danger, for he has words, but there will be no blame" (1994:474). Translated in this manner, I cannot see any sensible connection existing between what is said in the beginning line and the following lines.

102 In Lynn's translation based on Wang Bi's commentary, *pan* (磐, translated by Legge as "the large rocks") is translated as "the crag," which is supplemented with Wang Bi's explanation that it means "a safe place on mountainous rocks" (Lynn, 1994:475). But, it does not seem to make any sense to say that the geese "eat and drink with delight" on "mountainous rocks." Thus, it would be with this problem in mind that Kim translates it as "rocks at water," yielding a translation of the line statement that reads, "the geese (water fowls) gradually approaching the rocks (at water), where they eat and drink joyfully and at ease. There will be good fortune" (1997:407).

103 Concerning an interpretation of this portion of the line statement which sees the subject at this position isolated from others, Legge's following comment would provide interesting reference material: "I do not find anything in the figure that can be connected with this fact. The author was wise beyond his lines" (1963:167).

104 Compare Legge's above translation with Lynn's following translation; "The Well gives its bounty here. Do not cover it, for if one has sincerity, he will have fundamental good fortune" (1994:442). Notice the difference between the two translations.

105 That this hexagram represents the marriage of a woman given as second wife would be related to the fact that the lower trigram *Dui* symbolizes the Youngest Daughter.

106 Legge views that this lesson applies more generally to the relationship between a superior and his subordinates. Accordingly, he adds to the above explanation a passage that is to point out a more general lesson supposedly intended by the line statement, which reads, "Notwithstanding apparent disadvantages, an able officer may do his ruler good service" (1963:184).

107 However, Legge's interpretation is premised on an explanation that does not seem sensible at all to me. According to Legge, the disadvantage of the subject at the second position is explained by the fact that the one at the fifth position, with whom she has in a corresponding relationship, "is weak, and in a place of a strong line." It is due to "such correlate, the able lady in 2 cannot do much in the discharge of her proper work" (1963:184). Why should one's weakness be explained by a defect in her counterpart? It may be viewed otherwise that the mismatch between the subjects at the second and the fifth positions works rather in favor of the former over the latter. Cheng Yi's explanation (1988:184) differs somewhat from Legge's,

420   The I Ching on Man and Society

but seems to involve the same difficulty. In my opinion, the simplest and clearest interpretation may be obtained if we interpret that "a one-eyed person who can keep on seeing" is an expression to denote the handicapped situation of a second wife.

[108] Refer to various versions of translation as follows: "A young woman marrying with anticipation turns back from marriage to be a junior wife" (translated by Cleary, in Cheng Yi, 1988:184); "The third line, divided, shows the younger sister who was to be married off in a mean position. She returns and accepts an ancillary position" (Legge, 1963:182); "The Marrying Maiden should take a waiting approach to marriage, that is, return and then marry as a young secondary wife" (Lynn, 1994:482); "The marrying maiden as a slave. She marries as a concubine" (Wilhelm, 1967:667).

[109] Legge's translation, instead of Lynn's, is presented here, for the former seems to be subjected to an easier interpretation than the latter. Compare Legge's translation presented above with Lynn's that reads as follows: "When Sovereign Yi gave his younger sister in marriage, the sovereign's sleeves were not as fine as the sleeves of the younger, secondary wife. When the moon is almost full, it means good fortune" (1994:483).

[110] The latter translation, "the Taming Power of the Great," is Wilhelm's, which, I think, seems to fit more squarely with the meaning of the hexagram.

[111] The line statement for the fifth yin line is interpreted and translated variously according to the perspectives of individual commentators (Cheng Yi, 1988:109; Lee, 1997[II]:24; Legge, 1963:131; Lynn, 1994: 348 on Wang Bi's interpretation and see 350n7; Wilhelm, 1967:558-559). Cheng Yi's version is chosen here, for it is simple and clear, and, at the same time, supplemented by a commentary stated clearly with few ambiguous words.

[112] Lynn translates this as " 'Only if this one were to have great good fortune would he be without blame,' for his position is not correct" (1994:421), which translates literally the original text. Wilhelm's translation, done by "following suggestions of the Chinese commentators," is presented here because it seems easier to interpret in relation to the meaning of the hexagram as a whole and also in view of what are stated in other line statements.

[113] Lynn's translation of the title name, "Major Superiority," does not seem to be appropriate in view of the meaning of the hexagram as a whole. "Preponderance of the Great" is Wilhelm's translation, which, I think, comes somewhat closer to the meaning of the hexagram. But, my choice would be, "Overbalance of Strength." This will be explained later when the hexagram *Daguo* is discussed.

114 "Preponderance of the Small" is Wilhelm's translation for *Xiaoguo*. As I am going to explain, this seems to be a better choice than Lynn's "Minor Superiority." The reason for which I think Wilhelm's is preferable will be explained in the succeeding discussion.

115 Personally, I have some reservation about this analogy comparing the highest, leadership position of the subordinate group to a ridgepole, thus equating the difficulties both have to bear. It seems undeniably obvious that the *I Ching* oftentimes juggles such a dubious analogy with no supporting argument to substantiate a resemblance between things or events.

116 It may be because of this ambiguity that Legge comments on this hexagram as follows: "The symbolism of the bird is rather obscure. The whole of it is intended to teach humility" (1963:204).

117 Compare this translation with other versions of it as follows: "Going past the grandfather, one meets the grandmother. Not reaching the ruler, one meets the minister, blameless" (Cheng Yi, 1988:207); "The second line, divided, shows its subject passing by his grandfather, and meeting with his grandmother; not attempting anything against his ruler, but meeting him as his minister. There will be no error" (Legge, 1963:202-3); "This one is superior to his ancestor and meets his ancestress. He does not go as far as his sovereign but does meet his minister, so there is no blame" (Lynn, 1994:532); "She passes by her ancestor / And meets her ancestress. He does not reach his prince / And meets the official. No blame" (Wilhelm, 1967:706-7).

118 When a yang line occupies a yin position as in this case, either one of two different rules is applied in reading the situation of its subject. One is that since the position is occupied inappropriately by an unfitting line, such incongruity denotes an unfavorable situation for the subject. The other rule is that the strong quality of the subject is interpreted as being moderated by the weak function of the position he occupies, therefore enabling the subject to practice moderation that brings a favorable outcome. As we can see, these two rules of interpretation contradict each other, one rendering a favorable judgment and the other an unfavorable one. As far as I can see, the application of these two rules is largely *ad hoc* depending upon the personal viewpoint of a commentator.

119 For the line statements of the fifth and the sixth lines, Legge's translations, instead of Lynn's, are presented here for the simple reason that the former seem to read somewhat better in their phrasing.

120 Legge's following commentary will give a clearer picture of a situation represented by this hexagram: " 'Going through a great stream,' an expression frequent in the Yi, may mean undertaking hazardous enterprises, or encountering great difficulties, without any special

reference; but more natural is it to understand by 'the great stream' the Yellow river, which the lords of Kau must cross in a revolutionary movement against the dynasty of Yin and its tyrant. The passage of it by King Wu, the son of Wan in b.c. 1122, was certainly one of the greatest deeds in the history of China. It was preceded also by long 'waiting,' till the time of assured success came" (1963:68).

[121] Legge's translation, instead of Lynn's version based on Wang Bi's interpretation, is presented here because I find it hard to put Lynn's translation into the context of the situation as we have interpreted it so far. Compare Legge's translation presented above with Lynn's as follows: "When waiting for wine and food, it means the good fortune that derives from constancy" (1994:168).

[122] Of this, Wang Bi explains, "this one occupies the exalted position in such a way that he entrusts responsibility to the capable and does not attempt to take charge of everything himself" (Lynn, 1994:549). Although this interpretation leaves little ambiguity in its meaning, it certainly involves some ambiguity as an *explanation* of the subject's situation. Wang Bi's above account, as translated by Lynn, explains that the personal quality of the subject at the fifth position is one crucial factor that gives rise to the situation of *Weiji* (Ferrying Incomplete). However, the line statement of the fifth yin line seems to suggest rather that the present situation is that to avoid regret he has to behave in line with what is required by the situation. Viewed from this perspective, the subject's action orientation would be explained as a factor adjusted to the situation.

[123] According to Kim, King Wen of the Chou Dynasty, known as one of the authors of the *I Ching*, developed a divination method that used yarrow stalks instead of cow bones or tortoiseshells. In an agrarian country like the Chou, the use of bones, normally obtained by sacrificing oxen that were used in farming, may have been unaffordably costly, and therefore was replaced with the yarrow stalk method. To the author of the *I Ching*, King Wen of the Chou here referred to as "the neighbor in the west," the *yue* sacrifice conducted with the use of the more simpler and cheaper divination method symbolized a more civilized and enlightened way of managing the government (1997:478). Also refer to Wang Bi's following comment: "An ox is the most splendid of sacrifices, and the *yue* is the most meager [consisting as it does of lowly wild vegetation] .... No greater form of sacrifice exists than the cultivation of virtue. That is why even pond grasses and such vegetation as duckweed and mugort can be offered [by the virtuous] to gods and spirits ...." (Lynn, 1994:541-2).

[124] The trigram *Kan* symbolizes danger (Sink Hole). Notice that this hexagram consists of two *Kan* trigrams one on top of the other. This is why the *Commentary on the Judgments* says, "The Constant Sink Hole (the hexagram *Xikan*) signifies multiple dangers" (Lynn, 1994:318). The meaning of the hexagram, *Xikan* (the Constant Sink Hole), must have

been originally derived from the idea that the structure of the hexagram conveys, "multiple dangers (coming on one upon the other)," or as the *Commentary on the Images* explains, "Water keeps coming on" (Lynn, 1994:318). However, the line statements seem to have been written from a somewhat different perspective: the varying levels of danger to which each position is exposed seems to be best understood from the perspective in which the hexagram is based on a pictorial image as said above.

125 Legge's translation of this line statement, which, I think, is clearer in meaning, reads as follows: "The third line, divided, shows its subject, whether he comes or goes (=descends or ascends), confronted by a defile. All is peril to him and unrest. (His endeavors) will lead him into the cavern of the pit. There should be no action (in such a case)" (1963:119).

126 Regarding the proper role of women in light of what is considered to be their inborn nature, refer to Cheng Yi's following commentary appended to this line statement: "To be unable to see very clearly, yet still be able to follow along, is the Way of woman. Given that people in this position cannot clearly see the Way of the fifth yang, if they can be docile as woman, then they will not lose balance and rectitude; this is beneficial" (1988:60).

127 Compare this translation to the following ones: "The second line, divided, shows its subject in his place in yellow. There will be great good fortune" (Legge, 1963:121); "It is to yellow that one coheres here, which means fundamental good fortune" (Lynn, 1994:325); "Yellow light. Supreme good fortune" (Wilhelm, 1967:537); "Yellow fire is very auspicious" (Cleary, in Cheng Yi, 1988:94).

128 Kim (1997:244) translates this line statement differently; his translation reads, "The king moves his army to the battle field. It is praiseworthy to kill the chief of the enemy, and to take prisoners of others who are not in the leadership will spare one from blame." Once the line statement is translated as above, we will certainly have to interpret the line statement of the fifth yin line in a different context from that which we have interpreted already. Moreover, Kim's translation does not seem to cohere even with his own interpretation of the fifth yin line.

129 Legge's translation, instead of Lynn's translation, is adopted here because Legge's is simpler and easier to interpret. Compare it with Lynn's translation that reads, "Here the Wanderer arrives at lodgings where he is so attracted by the wealth involved that he becomes capable of the constancy of a young servant" (1994:496).

130 Legge's translation, instead of Lynn's, is presented here for the same reason as for the line statement of the second yin line.

131 Legge's translation, instead of Lynn's, is presented here for the same reason as for the line statements of the second and the third lines.

Chapter 5: Conclusion

[1] Sources of reference noted by Lewin in his text are omitted by this author.

[2] Also refer to Jung's article (1970) dealing with the same topic.

[3] Words inside the parentheses ( ) are by this author.

[4] When one faces perplexing ambiguities like this and tries to delineate sensible ideas from them, he will do one of two things or both as follows. One is that he will look for an interpretation that is *internally* consistent with other interpretations rendered to other parts of the same text. But, as I pointed out at the outset of this treatise, it might have been extremely difficult to formulate a single frame of reference with which interpretations are made consistent throughout all the 64 hexagrams. Then, there is another approach: the meanings that can be related most meaningfully to whatever the interpreter personally believes to be the most essential realities of the human society are projected upon the lines and the hexagrams. This method of interpreting the text, where one's prior ideas or ideals about the social realities are projected upon the symbolic figures and narrations of the *I Ching*, seems to be the case of most later interpretations including that of Wang Bi.

[5] Of course, the overall meaning of a situation described in brief summary by a hexagram statement does not always cohere with what its line statements tell about the situation of each component individual. This seems to imply a possibility that the author of the *I Ching* who wrote the line statements might have thought, for some reason, that the meaning of the hexagram had to be interpreted differently from that rendered by the one who wrote the hexagram statement.

Bibliography

Archer, Margaret. 1990. Human Agency and Social Structure: A Critique of Giddens. In *Anthony Giddens: Consensus and Controversy*, edited by Jon Clark, Celia Modgil, and Sohan Modgil. London: The Falmer Press.

Bodde, Derk. 1953. Harmony and Conflict in Chinese Philosophy. In *Studies in Chinese Thought*, edited by Arthur F. Wright. Chicago: University of Chicago Press.

Bodde, Derk. 1957. *Chinas's Culural Tradition: What and Wither.* Hinsdale(Ill.): Dryden Press.

Choi, Wan-Sik (trans. with an introduction). 1992. *The I Ching* (in Korean). Seoul: Heawon Publications.

Cheng Yi. 1995. *The Tao of Organization: The I Ching for Group Dynamics*, a translation of *Yichuan Yizhuan* (Cheng Yi's Commentary on the *I Ching*) by Thomas Cleary. Boston: Shambhala.

Cleary, Thomas. 1995. Translator's Introduction to *The Tao of Organization: The I Ching for Group Dynamics*, a translation of *Yichuan Yizhuan* (Cheng Yi's Commentary on the *I Ching*) by Thomas Cleary. Boston: Shambhala.

Coser, Lewis A. 1956. *The Functions of Social Conflict.* London: Free Press.

Coser, Lewis A. 1967. *Continuities in the Study of Social Conflict.* New York: Free Press.

Coser, Lewis A. 1971. *Masters of Sociological Thought: Ideas in Historical and Social Context.* New York: Harcourt Brace & Jovanovich, Inc.

Dahrendorf, Ralf. 1958. Out of Utopia: Toward a Reorientation of Sociological Analysis. *American Journal of Sociology* 64 (Sept.), 115-27.

Dahrendorf, Ralf. 1969. Toward a Theory of Social Conflict. In *Sociological Theory*, edited by Walter L. Wallace. Chicago: Aldine Publishing Co. First published in *the Journal of Conflict Resolutions* (1958:2), 170-83.

Eisenstadt, S. N. 1971. *Social Differentiation and Stratification.* Glenville (Ill.): Scott, Foresmand and Co.

Giddens, Anthony. 1984. *The Constitution of Society: Outline of the Theory of Structuration.* Oxford: Polity Press.

Gao, Hui-Min. 1995. *An understanding of the Philosophy of the I Ching* (in Korean), translated by Byong-Suk Chung. Seoul: Munye Publications. Originally published under the title of *The Philosophy of the Great I* (in Chinese) (Taipei: Chengwen Publications, 1978).

Homans, George C. 1969. The Sociological Relevance of Behaviorism. In *Behavioral Sociology*, edited by Robert L. Burgess and Don Bushell, Jr. New York: Columbia University Press.

Homans, George C. 1967. *The Nature of Social Science.* New York: Harcourt, Brace & World.

Husserl, Edmond. 1969. *Formal and Transcendental Logic*, translated by Dorian Cairns. The Hague: Martinus Nijhoff.

Jung, C. G. 1970. Synchronicity: An Acausal Connecting Principle. In *The Structure and Dynamics of the Psche*, 2nd ed., Vol.8 of the Collective Works of C. G. Jung, translated by R. F. C. Hull. Princeton: Princeton University Press.

Jung, C. G. 1967. Forward to *The I Ching* (trans. with an introduction and exegetical notes by Richard Wilhelm), translated into English by Carry F. Baynes. Princeton: Princeton University Press.

Kim, In-Whan (trans. with Translator's foreword and exegetical notes). 1997. *The I Ching* (in Korean). Seoul: Nanam.

Kim, Kyong-Tak (trans. an introduction). 1992. *The I Ching: A New Translation* (in Korean). Seoul: Myongmundang.

Kuhn, Thomas S. 1970. *The Structure of Scientific Revolutions*, 2nd ed. Chicago: University of Chicago Press.

Lee, Ki-Dong (trans. with a general treatise on the *I Ching* and exegetical notes). 1997. *Lectures on the I-Ching*, 2 vols. (in Korean). Seoul: Sung Kyun Kwan University Press.

Legge, James (trans. with an introduction and exegetical notes). 1971. *Confucius: Confucian Analects, The Great Lerning & The Doctrine of the Mean*. New York: Dover.

Legge, James (trans. with an introduction and exegetical notes). 1963. *The I Ching: The Book of Changes*. New York: Dover Publications.

Lenski, Gerald E. 1966. *Power and Privilege*. New York: McGraw-Hill.

Lewin, Kurt. 1997a. Defining the "field at a Given Time". In *Resolving Social Conflicts* (edited by Gertrude Weiss Lewin) *and Field Theory in Social Science* (edited by Dorwin Cartwright). Washington, DC: American Psychological Association. First published in *Field Theory in Social Science*: Selected Theoretical Papers (New York: Harper, 1951).

Lewin, Kurt. 1997b. Field Theory and Learning. In *Resolving Social Conflicts* (edited by Gertrude Weiss Lewin) *and Field Theory in Social Science* (edited by Dorwin Cartwright). Washington, DC: American Psychological Association. First published in *Field Theory in Social Science*: Selected Theoretical Papers (New York: Harper, 1951).

Lockwood, David. 1956. "Some Remarks on 'The Social System'." *British Journal of Sociology* 7(June), 134-146.

Lynn, Richard John (trans. with an introduction). 1994. *The Classic of Changes: A New Translation of the I Ching as Interpreted By Wang Bi*. New York: Columbia University Press.

Mills, C. Wright. 1959. *The Sociological Imagination*. New York: Oxford University Press.

Needham, Joseph. 1954. *Science and Civilisation in China*, Vol. 1. New York: Cambridge University Press.

Ossowski, Stanislaw. 1963. *Class Structure in the Social Consciousness*. New York: Free Press.

Pareto, Vilfred. 1935. *The Mind and Society: A Treatise on General Sociology*, Vol. I-II, edited and translated by Andrew Bongiorno and Arthur Livingston. New York: Dover Publications.

Parsons, Talcott. 1964. *The Social System*. New York: Free Press.

Parsons, Talcott. 1966. *Societies*. Englewood Cliffs: Prentice-Hall.

Parsons, Talcott. 1967. Some Reflections on the Place of Force in Social Process. In *Sociological Theory and Modern Society* by Talcott Parsons. New York: Free Press.

Parsons, Talcott. 1970. Equality and Inequality in Modern Society. In *Social Stratification: Research and Theory for the 1970s*, edited by Edward O. Laumann. Indianapolis: Bobbs-Merrill.

Parsons, Talcott & Edward A. Shils. 1951. Values, Motives, and Systems of Action. In *Toward a General Theory of Action*, edited by Talcott Parsons and Edward A. Shils. Cambridge: Harvard University Press.

Shchutskii, Iulian K., 1980. *Researches on the I Ching*, edited and translated by W. L. MacDonald and Tsuyoshi Hasegawa with Hellmut Wilhelm. London: Routledge & Kegan Paul. First published in 1979 by the Princeton University Press/Bollingen Series (LXII:2).

Simmel, George. 1950. *The Sociology of George Simmel*, translated, edited and with an introduction by Kurt H. Wolff. New York: Free Press.

Spencer, Herbert. 1974. *The Evolution of Society*, edited by Robert L. Carneiro. Chicago: Midway Reprint.

Sztompka, Piotr. 1993. *The Sociology of Social Change*. Oxford: Blackwell.

T'ang Yung-T'ung. 1947. Wang Pi's Interpretation of the *I Ching* and *Lun-Yu*, translated with notes by Walter Liebenthal. *Harvard Journal of Asiatic Studies* 10, 124-161.

Thompson, J. B. 1997. "The Theory of Structuration." In *Anthony Giddens: Critical Assessments* (Vol. II), edited by Christopher G. A. Bryant and David Jary. London and New York: Routledge.

Toynbee, Arnold. 1963. *A Study of History*, 7A. New York: Oxford University Press.

Turner, Jonathan H. 1986. *The Structure of Sociological Theory*, 4th ed. Chicago (Ill.):Doesey Press.

Van den Berghe, Pierre L. 1969. Dialectic and Functionalism: Toward a Theoretical Synthesis. In *Sociological Theory*, edited by Walter L. Wallace. Chicago: Aldine Publishing. First published in the *American Sociological Review* (October, 1963), 695-705.

Whyte, William H., Jr. 1956. *The Organization Man*. New York: Simon and Schuster.

Wilhelm, Richard (trans. with exegetical notes). 1967. *The I Ching*, translated into English by Carry F. Baynes. Princeton: Princeton University Press.

Wilhelm, Helmut. 1957. The Concept of Time in the Book of Changes. In *Man and Time*, Bollingen Series XXX.3. New York: Pantheon Books.

Wilhelm, Helmut. 1960. *Change: Eight Lectures on the I Ching*, translated. by Cary F. Barnes. New York: Harper Torchbooks.

Wolf, Kurt H. 1950. Introduction to *The Sociology of George Simmel*, by George Simmel, translated, edited and with an introduction by Kurt H. Wolff. New York: Free Press.

Index

action orientations, types of, 47, 72, 378, *see also* yang lines and yin lines

Archer, Margaret, 392-93

Bodde, Derk, 34-37, 54

carrying and riding relationship, 43-46, 129, 276, 285, 402n3-n4, 417-18n93

character situations, 242-261

changes of situations, 380-81

Cheng Yi, 4, 9, 400n3

classificatory method, 366-67

Cleary, Thomas, 119-120

Commentary on the Appended Phrases [*Xici zhuan*], 23, 30, 35, 385

Commentary on the Images [*Xianzhuan*], 12

Commentary on the Judgments [*Tuanzhuan*], 12

conflict model of society, 383-84

Confucianism, 4, 11-12

Confucius, 4, 11-2, 44, 222, 243, 287

Constructive method, 366-68, 371-72

conflict situations, 176-208

conflict situation, normatively controlled, 190-195, 201-2, *see also* the hexagram *Kui* under the entry hexagrams

contemporaneity, principle of, 364, 368-370

contradiction, the Marxian notion of, 236

corresponding relationship, 45-46, 119, 121, 166, 276, 402-3n6, 411-12n54, 417-18n93

Coser, Lewis A., 233, 384, 404n5

Dahrendorf, Ralf, 20-21, 75, 81, 383, 401n7

determinism, 390-94

Doctrine of the Mean, 153

dominant group, 401n7

double leadership structure, 88, 120

dyadic relationships, 40-41, 43-47, 50, 290-91

essential reality of the society, 387-89

excluded middle, principle of, 385

field theory, 364-375

firm line, *see* yang line

five basic human relations, 28, 401n8

formal sociology, 42-43, 386, *see also* Simmel

formal (*de jure*) inequaity, 36

Fu Hsi, 2

functional requisites, 411n51

Functional importance of positions, 153-54

Gao, Hui-Min, 44-45, 49-50

Giddens, Anthony, 391-93

governing unit, 23-24, 27-28, 182, 400-1n6, *see also* dominant group

Great Commentary (*Dazhuang*), 385

Great Treatise (*Ta Chuan*), 5, 399n3

Groups in the center, *see* governing unit

Hexagrams

Hexagram *Bi,* 39-40,61, 66, 89, 110-14, 142-43, 150

hexagram *Bi*, 65, 243-46

hexagram *Bo*, 65, 114-120

hexagram *Cui*, 66, 304,, 313-17

hexagram *Daguo*, 66, 319-325

hexagram *Dayou*, 65, 142-45

hexagram *Daxu*, 65, 304-8

hexagram *Dazhuang*, 67, 304, 309-313

hexagram *Ding*, 65, 210-15

hexagram *Dui*, 66, 257-261

hexagram *Dun*, 64, 329, 334-38

hexagram *Feng*, 67, 198-202

hexagram *Fu*, 67, 89-97, 121

hexagram *Ge*, 66, 211, 228-232

Index

hexagram *Gen*, 65, 195-98, 202

hexagram *Gou*, 64, 123-28

hexagram *Gu*, 65, 223-28, 240

hexagram *Guan*, 64, 344, 350-54

hexagram *Guimei*, 67, 284, 299-303

hexagram *Heng*, 67, 162-67

hexagram *Huan*, 64, 215-19

hexagram *Jian*, 64, 284, 292-97

hexagram *Jian*, 66, 345, 356-59

hexagram *Jiaren*, 64, 284-88

hexagram *Jie*, 66, 219-222

hexagram *Jiji*, 66, 329, 341-44

hexagram *Jin*, 65, 167-171

hexagram *Jing*, 66, 284, 297-99

hexagram *Kuai*, 66, 145-48

hexagram *Kui*, 65, 190-95, 201

hexagram *Kun*, 46, 67, 80-87

hexagram *Kun*, 66, 242, 253-57

hexagram *Li*, 65, 344, 354-56

hexagram *Lin*, 67, 159-162

hexagram *Lü*, 51, 64, 133-38

hexagram *Lü*, 65, 345, 359-362

hexagram *Meng*, 65, 261, 263-65

hexagram *Mingyi*, 67, 186-190, 201

hexagram *Pi*, 64, 181-86, 201

hexagram *Qian*, 64, 75-81, 86-87

hexagram *Qian*, 67, 101-6

hexagram *Sheng*, 67, 249-252

hexagram *Shi*, 67, 88, 97-101, 121

hexagram *Shihe*, 65, 261, 265-69

hexagram *Song*, 64, 177-181

hexagram *Sui*, 66, 156-59

hexagram *Sun*, 64, 236-240

hexagram *Sun*, 65, 284, 289-292

hexagram *Tai*, 67, 151-56, 175, 181-83

hexagram *Tongren*, 64, 128-132

hexagram *Weiji*, 65, 329, 338-341

hexagram *Wuwang*, 64, 242, 246-49

hexagram *Xian*, 66, 261, 274-78

hexagram *Xiaoguo*, 67, 319, 325-29

hexagram *Xiaoxu*, 48, 64, 138-142, 150, 305-7

434 The I Ching on Man and Society

hexagram *Xie*, 67, 208-210
hexagram *Xikan*, 66, 344-350
hexagram *Xu*, 66, 329-334
hexagram *Yi*, 64, 262, 278-282
hexagram *Yi*, 65, 261, 269-274
hexagram *Yu*, 67, 106-110
hexagram *Zhen*, 67, 223, 231-236, 240-41
hexagram *Zhongfu*, 64, 171-75
hexagram *Zhun*, 66, 204-7
yang-centered hexagrams, 87-121, *see also* rulers of the hexagram
yin-centered hexagrams, 122-150, *see also* rulers of the hexagram

hexagram statements (*tuan*), 10, 12-14, 69, 371, 378
hierarchical conception of order, 31, 44
holistic approach, 365-66, 368, 370-71, 374
holistic relational perspective, 38, 47
Homans, George, 71
human agency, 382, 390-94
Husserl, Edmond, 384
I, meanings of, 1-2
integration theory of society, 75-76, 383-84

Jung, C. G, 370
Khun, Thomas, 387
leadership position, *see also* yang position
leadership style, types of
  yang type, 150
  yin type, 150
Lee, Ki-Dong, 45, 55, 59,60
Legge, James, 68-69
Leibniz, Gottfried Wilhelm von, 403n1
Lenski, Gerald E., 384
Lewin, Kurt, 364-372
line statement (*yaoci*), 10, 12-14, 378
Lynn, Richard John, 9-12, 28-29

Hegeliamn-Marxian dialectic, 383, *see also* conflict theory of society
mediums of exchange, 290
military situations, 329-344
moderation, virtue of, 220, 246, 260, 328, 421n2
moral orientations, 282, 375
moving equilibrium, 52, 75, 86, 403n2
names of hexagrams (*guaming*), 10, 14, 69, 72, 378
Needham, Joseph, 4-7, 9
non-contradiction, principle of, 384-85

operative unit, 23-24, 27-28, 48, 400-1n6

oracle method, 3, 396

order building processes, 203-223

organization man, 83-84, 242

Oriental moral logic, 105, 107-8, 137, 149

Ossowski, Stanislaw, 384

Pareto, Vilfred, 81

Parsons, Talcott, 52, 70-71, 74-76, 81, 290, 314, 403n2, 411n51

pattern maintenance, 180, 411n51

pattern variables, 70

periphery groups, *see* operative unit

positional interpretation (of the hexagram), 30-34

positions of the hexagram, 18-34

yang positions, 19, 23-26, 43, 375

yin positions, 19, 23-26, 43, 375

power potentials, situationally determined, 373-77, *see also* real power potentials

practical (*de facto*) inequality, 36

psychological field, 364-67, 371-77

real power potentials, 45, 373-77

receiving and resting upon, *see* carrying and riding

Rectification of Names, 44, 287

regulating unit, *see* governing unit

relative deprivation, 202

relative subordination, 407n25

residues of group persistence, 82

resonant relationship, *see* corresponding relations

rulers of the hexagram, 23, 25-26, 40, 61-62

constituting ruler, 87-89

governing ruler, 88-89

satisfaction, modes of, 242, 257-261, *see also* the hexagram *Dui* under the entry hexagrams

School of Righteousness and Reason, 8

Simmel, George, 42-43, 47, 149, 386-87, 402n2, 407n25

single leadership structure, 89, 120

situational ethic, 83

social field, 368, 372-382

sources of power, 148-49

Spencer, Herbert, 400n6

static harmony, 53, 394

static equilibrium, 81, 85-86, 403n2

structuration theory, 391

subordinate group, *see* operative unit

subordinate position, *see* yin position

support-dependent power relations, 149

synchronicity, 370

Sztompka, Piotr, 389

Taoism, 4

T'ang Yung-T'ung, 33

Temporal interpretation (of the hexagram), 30-34

Ten Wings (Ten Commentaries), 2, 10-12

Thompson, J. B., 393

total subordination, 407n25

Toynbee, Arnold, 111-12

triadic relationships, 41-42, 47-62, 290-91, *see also* trigrams

Trigrams, 27, 47-62

trigram *Dui*, 58-59, 60

trigram *Gen*, 57-58, 60

trigram *Kan*, 49, 55-56, 60

trigram *Kun*, 52-53, 60

trigram *Li*, 56-57, 60

trigram *Qian*, 52, 59

trigram *Sun*, 54-55, 60

trigram *Zhen*, 53-54, 60

Turner, Jonathan H., 390

van den Berghe, Pierre L., 383

voluntarism, 390-94

Wang Bi, 4, 9-12, 18-25, 29-30, 33, 45, 50-52, 54-55, 61-62

Wilhelm, Helmut, 1-2, 4, 30-31, 33-34, 54, 56

Wilhelm, Richard, 2, 5, 10, 20, 34, 36, 52, 54-55, 57-59

Wolf, Kurt H., 42

Whyte, William H., Jr., 83, 242

yang line, 34-38, 43, 374-77, 380-81

yielding line, *see* yin line

yin line, 34-38, 43, 374-77, 380-81

Zhu Xi, 4, 9